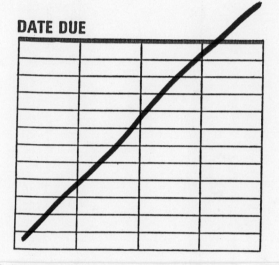

Jesuit Studies

Contributions to the arts and sciences

by members of the Society of Jesus

Jesuit Studies

The Churches and the Schools
FRANCIS X. CURRAN

Deception in Elizabethan Comedy
JOHN V. CURRY

Bishop Lancelot Andrewes
MAURICE F. REIDY

Master Alcuin, Liturgist
GERALD ELLARD

Theodore Dwight Woolsey
GEORGE A. KING

JESUIT STUDIES

The Praise of Wisdom

A Commentary on the Religious
and Moral Problems and Backgrounds
of St. Thomas More's *Utopia*

Edward L. Surtz, s.j.

LOYOLA UNIVERSITY PRESS

Chicago, 1957

IMPRIMI POTEST: William J. Schmidt, S.J.
Provincial of the Chicago Province
November 11, 1955

IMPRIMATUR: ✠ Samuel Cardinal Stritch
Archbishop of Chicago
July 30, 1957

T he author of *The Praise of Wisdom* endeavors to study religion and morality in St. Thomas More's *Utopia:* their meaning and their import in relation to the contemporary scene. It is probably the first work to examine the pertinent sections in the *Utopia* point by point and to determine the relation of each point to fifteenth-century and sixteenth-century formulations of Catholic teaching. Emphasis, of course, is laid upon the doctrine of the Christian humanists, especially Erasmus; but, when necessary and justified, recourse is had to pagan classics, church fathers, and medieval theologians. More's Catholicism cannot be reasonably called into question. Here an attempt is made to define the extent of More's religious conservatism or radicalism, approval or criticism, submission or rebellion, at the time of the composition of *Utopia*, which was published on the eve of the Protestant Reformation.

The procedure for religious problems differs slightly from that for moral problems. In general, the order of the *Utopia* itself is followed in the discussion of religious or theological ideas, although it is not perfectly logical and systematic at times. The method, however, helps to an appreciation of More's own sequence of thought. Thomas More, of course, does not treat the moral or ethical problems connected with religion in one place; consequently they have to be lifted from the sections where they occur.

The basic question in the *Utopia* may be said to be that of poverty and wealth. Other and related factors, however, are constantly intruding themselves into the limelight for the simple reason that life is not departmentalized in Utopia but is all of a piece. For example, Utopian philosophy and education influence and reinforce the economic and social system of communism. In like manner religion is most important if the last place in Hythloday's description is to be viewed as climactic and if worship is to be considered a function of the state, especially the communistic state.

The following pages, it is modestly assumed, produce additional evidence, throw more light, modify present interpretations, and draw new conclusions on intriguing but vexing problems. On his part, the author confesses that he has found many religious and moral sentiments in the *Utopia* perplexing, even irritating. He now feels that he has explained them (although not solved them finally) as satisfactorily as present knowledge and scholarship permit. He hopes that others, too, may reach through this book an increase of understanding of the pertinent sections in the *Utopia*.

A mass of material not ordinarily accessible has been made available, but the results of previous studies have been included wherever necessary to give a complete picture. For the book was written to interest both the professional scholar and the serious reader who likes Thomas More as a person or admires his *Utopia* as a masterpiece.

The style is intended to possess succinctness and clarity rather than copiousness and elegance. This restriction is demanded, not only by limitations of space coupled with abundance of material, but also by the approach, which is that of detailed commentary. Hence the presentation may appear slow and plodding as it keeps leisurely pace with interpretation and elucidation of word, clause, and sentence. But the mode of expression is appropriate to subject and purpose.

After much hesitation and debate the spelling and punctuation of fifteenth-century and sixteenth-century quotations have been modernized. The decision was reached in view of the achievement of greater readability, confirmed by the practice of reputable Morean scholars. In perplexing cases—for example, as to the use of *either* for *other* as a conjunction—the obsolete form was retained if it occurred as a main or subordinate entry in *The Shorter Oxford English Dictionary on Historical Principles* (Oxford, 1944). Even here, complete consistency was almost impossible.

As often as practicable, More has been permitted to speak in his own words (in modernized form).

To avoid unnecessary distraction and annoyance by multitudinous footnote numbers in the text, all citations of sources, as a rule, have been grouped in a single footnote at the end of each paragraph. In view of More's Catholicism, Catholic authorities naturally predominate, since they furnish a clear explanation of ideas and institutions in the Catholic background against which the *Utopia* was written.

The present author has usually made his translations from the Latin as literal as possible but with due respect for English idiom. For aid in the refinements of Latinity he is grateful to the Reverend James J. Mertz, S.J., chairman of the Department of Classical Languages, Loyola University, Chicago, Illinois.

Thanks are due to the John Simon Guggenheim Memorial Foundation for the fellowship which made possible the leisure and the travel necessary for research in American and European libraries and archives.

CONTENTS

xi

CHAPTER I

Interpretations
of *Utopia*

The plethora of books and articles on the *Utopia* of St. Thomas More within recent years testifies to the vitality of the work. Like all masterpieces, literary and otherwise, it has stimulated the thought and won the praise of the discriminating and reflective in every age, but has attained a new significance, a greater importance, and a wider audience in view of its pertinency to the peculiar conditions of special times—such as the hectic present with its manifold crises. Although the expression of concern with the *Utopia* has of late been largely scholarly, nevertheless the interest rests fundamentally upon its value for modern life as a whole. It has become a classic for the theories of socialism and communism and has been a source book for the early defense of capitalism, imperialism, and democracy. Little wonder that students have endeavored to fix the ideas behind the *Utopia* as held by More himself, not as expounded by readers who have found in the book the reflection of their own notions.

Why did More write the *Utopia?* His general purpose is certainly clear: the open-minded adoption by the Christian countries of Europe of the most just and prudent institutions which exist anywhere in the world. To this end he has drawn, through the agency of Hythloday, the pattern of an ideal city. Myron P.

Gilmore has pertinently observed that "although the western world was indeed assured of its possession of Christian revelation, it was never completely convinced that its own institutions were the most perfect embodiment of that revelation." Somewhere far away, somewhere east or west, somewhere in the kingdom of Prester John or the lost isle of St. Brendan, a perfect place, a Christian Utopia, might exist. For a European world conscious of the need for reform and alerted by recent geographical discoveries, the humanist More gives a traveler's description of his ideal but pagan world. The difficulty is that More himself at the end of Hythloday's discourse calls a number of Utopian institutions extremely absurd and designates by name the most important: communism, warfare, and religion. Consequently it is impossible to make a blanket statement about More's approval or disapproval of Utopian institutions. The serious or jesting nature of every topic in the *Utopia* must be weighed and determined singly. Sir James Mackintosh's statement, uttered more than a century ago, is still true: the *Utopia* "intimates a variety of doctrines, and exhibits a multiplicity of projects, which the writer regards with almost every possible degree of approbation and shade of assent; from the frontiers of serious and entire belief, through gradations of descending plausibility, where the lowest are scarcely more than the exercises of ingenuity." Detailed and independent discussion must be afforded each perplexing problem in the *Utopia*.[1]

The purpose of this book is the study of the section on religion (with related moral topics, such as war) which bristles with problems. In fact, one scholar recently has said: "We have no notion what relation Utopian religious policy bore to More's opinion of the correct religious policy of a Christian commonwealth. . . . A reconstruction of More's own opinions . . . has shaky foundations." But these foundations need be little more

---

[1] Notes relating to the various chapters are to be found on pp. 315-46.

shaky than those for the reconstruction of More's social, economic, and political views; for example, his communism, his democracy, or his republicanism. Almost three centuries ago Gilbert Burnet in his *History of the Reformation of the Church of England* declared of More's *Utopia:* "By many hints it is very easy to collect what his thoughts were of religion, of the constitutions of the church and of the clergy of that time." A head-on attack, no matter how foolhardy, must be made on the problem sooner or later. Now the scholarly "world is grown so bad / That wrens make prey where eagles dare not perch" (*Richard III,* I, iii, 70-71). That More himself, either deliberately or unconsciously, may have considered these sections important may be surmised from the fact that he places them at the end of the *Utopia* and advances in seemingly climactic order from slavery and marriage through treaties and war to God and religion.[2]

The more one studies the *Utopia,* the more convinced one becomes that it is essentially a product of the English Renaissance, and not only of the movement in its early stage, but even of a particular moment. It was being excogitated, written, and published when the Fifth Council of the Lateran (1512-1517) was holding sessions on the reform of the Church and was passing decrees, excellent in nature but ineffective in practice because evil custom and self-interest thwarted their application. Even if one were ignorant of the date of publication, the *Utopia* could be labeled definitely as a work of the eve of the Reformation. As a document of reform, it contains the diverse elements which, under free will and strong leadership, could lead either to Martin Luther and the Protestant Revolt or to Ignatius Loyola and the Council of Trent. As a product of humanism, the *Utopia* pays special attention to diction and style. The schoolman had centered his whole mind and effort on the thought or truth and on its appeal to the intellect. His manner of expression, mainly the syllogistic form, had been secondary and only a means to clear and unclouded communication. The humanist, on the other hand, held that the manner essentially influenced the matter. He saw communication as imperfect unless truth was made attractive and appealing to heart and emotions. The means for the creation of interest, force, and beauty were of extreme, though not of supreme, importance. He found his ideal expressed in Horace's formula for the successful writer:

> Omne tulit punctum qui miscuit utile dulci,
> Lectorem delectando pariterque monendo.
>
> He that joyns instructions with delight,
> Profit with pleasure, carries all the Votes.[3]

No work of the Renaissance could receive a higher compliment than praise for the actual achievement of this goal of every true humanist: the union of the profitable and the pleasant. There can be little doubt that More intended to call attention to serious problems in an attractive and clever form. His success has been acknowledged from the commendatory verses of Gerardus Noviomagus in the first edition of *Utopia* to the latest analysis of the masterpiece. The careful student, therefore, must never lose sight of what Michels and Ziegler call the "winsome play against a most serious background."[4]

The all-important question is: how earnest or how playful is this truly golden book ("libellus uere aureus"), as *Utopia* is termed on the title page of the first edition? In view of the statement made above that each passage must be judged in its own light and on its own merits, a definite answer at this stage may seem to prejudice the case. But the determination of the general spirit of the *Utopia* is necessary to the evaluation of particular points. No one, to be sure, is so foolish as to claim that the work is wholly jesting or wholly serious. Scholars and biographers, however, clash violently on the predominance of play or gravity in the *Utopia*. In view of our specialized topics, it would be unwise to enter into great detail or extended treatment of the various views. But a brief summary, the reader may discover, is at once necessary and enlightening.[5]

The first group tends to regard *Utopia* mainly as a witty and clever sally of a child of the Renaissance. Strangely enough, a good number of Catholic critics belong to this school. They label the *Utopia* "a youthful *jeu d'esprit*," or "a felicitous trifle," or "the least serious of his literary efforts." Their intention seems to be the exoneration of More, who, after all, is now a canonized saint, from charges of heterodox views on matters of faith and discipline. This emphasis on the literary virtues of the *Utopia* with consequent minimization of its serious purposes has three weighty arguments marshaled against it: the very bulk of the patently earnest and practical passages; the repeated references, expressed or implicit, to European conditions and attitudes; and the unanimous agreement of contemporary and subsequent humanists on the practical profit to be derived from its reading. One must also resist the kindred temptation to excuse More on the plea of humor or playfulness whenever the Utopians appear embarrassingly unorthodox and to presume his seriousness whenever they advocate measures close to traditional Christian doctrine and morality. Considerable regard must always be had, not only for the context in the *Utopia* itself, but for the context in More's life, writings, and times.[6]

The second group of critics swings to the opposite extreme: it stresses too much the gravity of the *Utopia* and sees in it the dangerous, though cautious, advocacy of hard and practical policies. Karl Kautsky views Thomas More as a wholehearted nineteenth-century socialist too far ahead of his own time, the sixteenth century. Hermann Oncken finds in the *Utopia* a strong vindication of Machiavellian principles and an active tendency to *Realpolitik*, manifest especially in a system of colonization and imperialism. For John Mackie, More's "planned state was a danger to world-peace—it resembled strangely the Germany of Hitler." Russell Ames sees the core of the book as dangerously "republican, bourgeois, and democratic"—a document of class struggle. Wherever these interpretations are faulty, the defects are due to the failure either to recognize the *Utopia* as a product of the Renaissance before the Protestant Revolt or to realize how much More wanted the Christian spirit and principles to inform individuals, classes, and institutions.[7]

In opposition to works which take the *Utopia* either too lightly or too gravely, the present study considers the *Utopia* essentially a document of humanistic reform, distinguished by "that delightful teaching," as Sir Philip Sidney writes, "which must be the right describing note to know a poet by." Whether the particular tone of any passage is earnest or playful, serious or light, a pressing problem or issue of the day stands either in the foreground or in the background. Even the anecdote of the friar and the toady, which one might be inclined to regard as pure diversion, reflects the humanists' attitude toward the contemporary religious and the court parasite. In a word, no paragraph in the *Utopia* is completely otiose.[8]

For the comprehension of this third position a thorough understanding of the differences and relations between philosophy and theology, between reason and revelation, between nature and grace, is absolutely necessary. This distinction is not artificial and superimposed on the *Utopia,* but is found at its very origin. The tetrastich and the hexastich prefixed to the work announce that Utopia is "a philosophical city," intended to rival, even to surpass, the republic of Plato ("ciuitatem philosophicam [quae est] ciuitatis aemula Platonicae, / Fortasse uictrix"). In writing to the future Cardinal Pole in 1524, N. L. Tomeo exclaims: "Indeed the Utopian Republic, in my opinion, should be certainly assigned a place higher than any other similar description made by any ancient writer. . . . Would that in some place or other in the world there might really exist a true republic of philosophers!" Utopia is therefore a city which human reason alone, without the aid of divine revelation, has created—in contradistinction to an ideal state, such as Johann Valentin Andreae's Christianopolis, which relies upon the doctrine and discipline of the Christian religion. A clear statement of the distinction, for example, occurs at the end of Hythloday's account of the Utopian philosophical view on pleasure and virtue: "They believe that by *man's reason* none can be found truer than this, unless any godlier be inspired into man [by a *religion* sent down] from *heaven*" ("sententia, qua nisi sanctius aliquid inspiret homini *caelitus* immissa *religio*, nullam inuestigari credunt *humana ratione* ueriorem" [italics added]). Explicit in this sentence is the opposition between natural reason and supernatural revelation. Only two years after the publication of the *Utopia*, Beatus Rhenanus uses the same distinction in his epistolary preface to More's epigrams. He praises More for giving the Utopians doctrine and institutions which are not found in Plato or Aristotle or Justinian, and then continues: "And, in comparison with these men, he [More] teaches perhaps less in the philosophical vein than in the Christian" ("Et docet minus forsan philosophice, quam illi, sed magis Christiane"). There is no contradiction here between the verses in More's *Utopia* and the statement in Rhenanus' preface. More simply describes a philosophical city in order to bring Christians back to their religious principles. He plans to have Utopian culture represent the stage of civilization capable of being achieved solely by the aid of philosophy or reason, but he intends to have this thought run through every passage: If reason alone can reach such heights of morality and happiness, what shame and confusion should fill the hearts of Christians who, in spite of the countless treasures of the revelation and grace of Christ, fall far below Utopian standards of conduct! In brief, insofar as More directly builds his ideal commonwealth upon reason, he is a philosopher; insofar as he directs his admonitions, implicitly but none the less pointedly, to the reputed followers of Christ, he is a Christian teacher.[9]

As far as the relation between nature and grace is concerned, the great theologian of the Renaissance, Francisco Suárez (d. 1617), labels as "common and true" the Catholic opinion that fallen man, by the effect of original sin alone, has not become more weak and vicious in his natural powers than he would have been in the state of pure nature. Very far from being incapable of thinking or doing anything morally good, fallen man, without supernatural grace, can come to the knowledge, not only of speculative and scientific truths, but also of moral and religious truths, such as the existence and perfections of God, the immortality and spirituality of the soul, the duties of man toward his Creator, and the punishments and rewards of the future life. In addition, fallen man, without the aid of grace, can perform deeds which are good by nature *(actus naturaliter boni)*, such as those of parental affection, patriotic heroism, and religious devotion. Only the supernatural grace of Christ, of course, can make these thoughts and acts supernaturally good and conducive to salvation. Thus, most Utopians, even before the coming of Christianity, had attained to true conceptions of the nature of God, the human soul, and the future life, and had become models of natural virtue and piety—and could serve as such even for European Christians![10]

Reason and revelation bear a relation to each other analogous to that between nature and grace. Without revelation—that is, even before the reception of faith—human reason can come to know certain religious truths about God and the soul, such as those mentioned above. All intellectual certitude does not rest upon faith alone. In fact, reason by itself can conclude to the divine character of the Christian revelation. Before a man embraces the faith his reason can and ought to know for certain the fact of revelation and the motives of credibility. Among the latter are those which appealed to the Utopians: the doctrine and miracles of Christ and the remarkable propagation of the Church. But human reason in matters concerning God is weak

and liable to error—and hence it must not be trusted too far—
and it is not autonomous, but is subject to the uncreated Truth.
There is no chance, however, for reason and revelation to contradict each other. The Fifth Council of the Lateran in 1513,
three years before the publication of *Utopia,* had declared:
"Since truth does not at all contradict truth, we define that every
assertion contrary to the truth of enlightened faith is altogether
false." At the session at which this stand was approved, however, Cardinal Cajetan voiced his fears for the independence of
philosophy and for the confusion of philosophy and theology.
From the very definition of philosophy as the knowledge, derived from reason, of the ultimate causes of beings, reason is
supreme in its own realm, philosophy. Christian philosophers,
however, must employ divine revelation as a negative or extrinsic norm; that is, they must keep always before their eyes
divine revelation as a guiding star which, by its light, will guard
them from intellectual error and shipwreck and prevent them
from expounding philosophical theories more or less opposed
to the infallible truths revealed by God.[11]

Brief explanations of certain terms to be used throughout
this study are necessary. What precisely is meant by *natural?*
by *supernatural?* Those goods are *natural* to man which belong
to human nature either constitutively (for example, body and
soul as pertaining to man's essence), or consecutively (for example, man's faculties of intellect and will as necessarily flowing from his essence), or exigently (for example, man's natural
actions as requiring divine concurrence). Those goods are
supernatural which belong to created nature neither constitutively nor consecutively nor exigently, but surpass the order of
nature and exceed all its exigencies. Thus, grace in its strict
theological sense is a *supernatural* gift gratuitously bestowed by
God on a rational creature with a view to eternal life.

One must consequently distinguish between natural and
supernatural *revelation,* between natural and supernatural *reli-*

gion, as carefully as possible. The distinction is basic, indispensable, and illuminating.

The revelation and the religion which the Utopians possess
are natural, not supernatural. In natural revelation God manifests Himself in a way which requires ratiocination on the part
of man. From the visible world, man's moral consciousness, the
course of history, and so forth, the human intellect can gain
a knowledge of God and His nature and therefrom the human
will can conceive a deep love for Him—and this by unaided
natural powers. "For since the creation of the world his invisible
attributes are clearly seen—his everlasting power also and divinity—being understood through the things that are made"
(Romans 1:20). This revelation of God by Himself through
visible creation is natural; that is, *due* to man. The reasons why
such revelation is proper to man are two: first of all, the knowledge gained does not exceed the natural powers and exigencies
of man, whom God has created with an intellect capable of
knowing religious truths and a will capable of loving and obey-
ing Him; and secondly, it would be repugnant to the wisdom
and goodness of God to create man with certain powers and yet
to be reluctant to manifest Himself in this easy way. Natural
religion is nothing else than the complexus of truths about God,
speculative and practical, known through the natural light of
reason, and the duties which flow from those truths. In supernatural revelation God speaks directly to man and testifies to
the truth of what He says in a supernatural manner; that is, in
a way *beyond* nature and *not due* to man. The order of man
and nature does not require that God speak to man directly as
He actually did through Moses, the prophets, and Christ. He
has, moreover, used revelation to disclose, not only mysteries
strictly so called (for example, the Trinity and the Incarnation),
but also the truths already discovered by the natural light of
reason. The complexus of truths known by the direct revelation
of God to man is called *supernatural* religion. It embraces, of

course, all the duties which are logically consequent upon supernatural revelation.[12]

The Utopians, as has been mentioned, are blessed with only a natural religion. Do they have need of supernatural revelation? On account of the elevation of all mankind to a supernatural end and supernatural order, supernatural revelation is *absolutely* necessary for the Utopians, too. But how necessary to the Utopians is *supernatural* revelation for the knowledge of *natural* religion and the pursuit of *natural* virtue? Against the fideists, who maintain revelation is absolutely necessary in this case, the Catholic Church teaches that revelation is only *morally* necessary in order for men to think correctly about God and His worship and to lead their lives in accordance with the precepts of the natural law. *Moral* necessity means that only with the help of supernatural revelation can mankind know these things with ease, with firm certainty, and with no admixture of error.[13]

This assertion about the moral necessity of supernatural revelation even for natural religion and natural morality holds true especially for the more difficult precepts of the natural law about which men very often live in ignorance, doubt, or error. Even at this early stage in the discussion it is interesting to speculate whether or not More intends those features of Utopian thought and conduct which contemporary and later Catholics would find objectionable to represent the aberrations of reason. Such, of course, might be divorce, euthanasia, and assassination. If the Utopians had been fortunate enough to possess supernatural revelation, their mistakes would have become evident to them. Even in their moral philosophy they could have used supernatural revelation as a negative norm and thus avoided a number of errors. But since the Utopians have no other guide than their intellect, they are justified and blameless in following their conscience even if in some few points it happens to be erroneous. As for the people of Europe who, with the rich heritage of Christian philosophy and theology, reproach the Utopians for their conduct and yet, in spite of their superior knowledge, do not hesitate to commit the same or worse crimes, St. Paul would say to them: "Wherefore, thou art inexcusable, O man, whoever thou art who judgest. For wherein thou judgest another, thou dost condemn thyself. For thou who judgest dost the same things thyself" (Romans 2:1). Some beliefs of the Utopians, therefore, may be wrong, but their sincerity is irreproachable. The content of the faith of Europeans is divinely infallible, but their simulation and their behavior are reprehensible by the standards of that very faith.

The distinction and relation between reason and revelation furnish the basis for the "humanistic" interpretation of the *Utopia*. It is not a new interpretation. In fact, it is as old as the *Utopia*. As has been seen, the preliminary verses in the masterpiece label the Utopian state "a philosophical city" like Plato's republic—a commonwealth, therefore, created by human reason and embodying the high achievements of human intellect. If a few institutions in Utopia are labeled absurd, it is because reason, left to itself, can become logical to the point of absurdity. But in the invention of his philosophical city, More is far from being merely academic or theoretical. He has an important ulterior motive or, better, a momentous end in view. He intends to make the "virtues of Heathen Utopia show up by contrast the vices of Christian Europe." The Utopians have only reason and philosophy; the Christians, in addition to reason and philosophy, have faith and revelation, grace and sacraments. And yet in their personal and family relations and in their political, social, economic, and even religious conditions, the pagans in Utopia excel the Christians of Europe![14]

To be sure, More is far from setting up Utopia, the ideal republic of paganism, as the exemplar for Christian Europe. The Christian commonwealth should surpass the pagan state to the degree that, in St. Paul's epistle, the new man is superior to the old man (Ephesians 4:22-24; Colossians 3:9-12). At this very time Erasmus was advising the future emperor Charles V: "Whenever you think of yourself as a prince, remember you are a *Christian* prince! You should be as different from even the noble pagan princes as a Christian is from a pagan."[15]

In a word, *Utopia* is essentially a humanistic document aimed at the reformation of Christendom. Every paragraph or section is related to the contemporary scene in Europe in some way or other which must be determined in each case.

The aspect of reform is stressed by all those sixteenth-century figures who were closely connected with the publication of the *Utopia* or with the writing of More's early biography. A careful study of pertinent passages in the works of Aegidius (Gilles), Noviomagus (Geldenhauer), Grapheus (Schreiber), Buslidius (Busleyden), Paludanus (Van der Broeck), Budaeus (Budé), Erasmus, Lily, Robinson, and Harpsfield discloses that More's foremost purpose is the exposure and description of the vices which ruin a state and of the virtues which cause it to flourish. As a means to this end More has painted an ideal republic, composed of ideal men who work only for the ideal of the common good according to the light of reason. The implication, of course, is that the institutions of the Christian faithful should far outstrip the practices of mere rational pagans.[16]

A great stumbling block to the acceptance of the humanistic interpretation of the *Utopia* has been the philosophy of pleasure espoused by the Utopians. They "seem almost too much given and inclined to the opinion of them which defend pleasure, wherein they determine other all, or the chiefest part, of man's felicity to rest." In spite of the minor qualification and mild disapproval voiced by Hythloday, could More possibly have wished seriously the Christians of Europe to become Epicureans in philosophy? The whole problem, as is evident, is philosophical rather than religious in nature and falls outside the scope of this book. The following sketchy answer must suffice. In

De voluptate et de vero bono, in the first half of the fifteenth
century, Valla had included an active defense of Epicureanism
but had given the final victory to Christianity. Erasmus in
De contemptu mundi (written *c.* 1490) and *The Epicurean*
(published 1533) proved that the life of a true Christian,
whether monk or layman, was Epicurean in nature. He said
nothing of Epicurus' denial of the providence of the gods, the
immortality of the soul, and future retribution, but instead he
stressed the existence of God as man's greatest good and the
joys of a future life. He then employed the principles of selection used by Epicurus in a thoroughly Christian context. By a
rhetorical *tour de force* he showed that "nobody more deserves
the name of an Epicurean than that adorable Prince of Christian
philosophers"; that is, Christ! Briefly, Epicurus was christian-
ized in a rhetorical vein by Erasmus in the Renaissance just as
Plato and Aristotle had been in a philosophical way by Christian thinkers in earlier centuries.[17]

More, like Valla and Erasmus, removes those features of
the teachings of Epicurus which are objectionable to the theistic
or Christian philosopher. The Utopians lay stress on bodily
pleasure, especially health; but the supreme pleasures are those
of the soul. The criteria for *true* pleasure are such as to insure
the supremacy of mental pleasures. The latter, however, are
viewed moralistically rather than intellectualistically, since the
practice of virtue and the possession of a good conscience seem
to be ranked above the contemplation of truth. In the final analysis Utopian Epicureanism becomes as noble in theory and
fruitful in practice as stoicism or Platonism. Far from being
really corrupting and subversive, it is revealed underneath to
be conservative, beneficial, and moral. Utopian hedonism is the
truest of systems—"unless any godlier be inspired into man
[by a religion sent down] from heaven" ("nisi sanctius aliquid
inspiret homini caelitus immissa religio"). This superiority of
a revealed religion to a purely rational philosophy, as has been

seen, is important for the understanding of the position of the Utopians—and of Thomas More.[18]

A word must be inserted here on another perennial problem: Are there two Mores? Are there the More of the *Utopia* and the More of the *Confutation of Tyndale?* One needs to admit that there would seem to be two Erasmuses: the Erasmus of *The Praise of Folly* and the *Colloquies* and the Erasmus of *The Diatribe on the Free Will* and *Hyperaspistes.* In a higher and more marked sense there are two Mores: the More of the pre-Lutheran period and the More of the Lutheran revolution. When More wrote the *Utopia,* he was speaking in the midst of an ostensibly united Christendom. When he launched his attacks against Luther, Tyndale, and others, a fierce civil war in religion was raging. One's policy cannot remain the same in war and in peace—although one's principles must remain inviolable. "For everything there is an appointed time," More seemed to realize with Ecclesiastes (3:1, 7-8). "A time to keep silence, and a time to speak; a time of love, and a time of hatred; a time of war, and a time of peace." After the rebellion of Luther, More became cautious and prudent. Against Luther, Bugenhagen, Tyndale, Fish, and Frith, More felt that he was protecting the very foundations of hitherto accepted Christian ways of life. So-called reformers were attacking, not merely the abuses of Catholicism, but its very uses. Consequently More admitted the existence of abuses but did not expatiate upon them. His goal was clear: the defense of principles.

When principles were not at stake and the disagreements were within the fold—against Catholic opponents—More outspokenly assailed abuses. When *Letters of Some Learned Men* appeared as late as 1520, More's sharp letter against "the raging reviling of a certain monk, both ignorant and arrogant," defended Erasmus' innovations and exposed the defects of contemporary monasticism. In the very same year (1520), however, he urged Budé to use discretion in publishing his (More's) less cautious and less circumspect written statements "on peace, on war, on morals, on married people, on priests, on the nation, etc."—all of which are topics with which the present study is concerned.[19]

The number of times that More anticipates and answers charges to be leveled against him in future years and centuries is surprising, almost phenomenal. Tyndale seems to have been the first to taunt More with a change from radical reformer to conservative reactionary: More was "then far otherwise minded" than he now writes. More does not admit the charge. If it were true, he would thank God for his amendment. But, as a matter of fact, books written earlier by him and Erasmus—for example, *The Praise of Folly*—merely jested about "the abuses of such things" as images, relics, and so forth. The fundamental change exists, not in him, but in the spirit of the times. He continues: "In these days . . . if any man would now translate *Moria* into English, or some works either that I have myself written ere this, albeit there be none harm therein, folk yet being (as they be) given to take harm of that that is good, I would not only my darling's books, but mine own also, help to burn them both with mine own hands, rather than folk should (though through their own fault) take any harm of them, seeing that I see them likely in these days so to do." Erasmus, too, explained that he would never have written *The Praise of Folly*, actually published in tranquil times, if he had been able to foresee the future storm and violent commotion.[20]

When this book uses More's later works to throw new or greater light upon an obscure passage in the *Utopia*, the presumption is that More is consistent in his principles throughout his life but that he uses prudence and discretion after the significance of Luther's revolt became evident to him. Inconsistency must not be asserted but proved. The student should pay More the favor which the latter rendered to Bugenhagen. More declares that his attitude has always been to interpret all the writings of others, as far as he can, in a better and kinder sense ("omnia in meliorem partem . . . et benigniorem flectere"). The differences between the two Mores are those between a loyal leader's criticisms in time of peace, directed to fellow citizens with whom he has sharp differences of opinion, and his public statements in time of war, aimed at rebels against authority and unity.[21]

An explanation of the constant references to Erasmus' works which occur in the present study may seem hardly necessary. Nevertheless, a twofold reason may well be offered: (1) the position of Erasmus as the center of the intellectual life of the early sixteenth century and (2) the lifelong friendship and agreement between Erasmus and More.

As for the first, the ascendancy of Erasmus in the intellectual world of the second decade of the sixteenth century cannot be disputed. His position as the figure who set the pace for contemporary ideas need not be elaborated here. Historians agree that by the year of the publication of *Utopia* (1516), Erasmus had attained, in the words of Philip Hughes, "that position as an influence in European life which no man of letters before, and none since—not even Voltaire—has ever attained." Edward Lee, future archbishop of York, who engaged in controversy with Erasmus after the appearance of the latter's New Testament, declared that he was entering the ring against a man who was "almost the god of this age." To Gerard Geldenhauer, writing in 1522, he was "the prince of theologians" ("Theologorum princeps"). Approximately at the same time Bishop Fisher asserted that for him the judgment of Erasmus on the spuriousness of the Pauline-Senecan epistles outweighed the opinions of a thousand other scholars. To Lee, Thomas More confessed that his love of Erasmus was due to almost no other reason than to that for which the whole Christian world embraced him: the greatest contribution to sacred and profane science in several centuries.[22]

As for the second point, Erasmus has been rightly labeled and hailed as More's *alter ego*. From Erasmus' first extant letter to More in 1499 to Erasmus' death in 1536, neither ever disavows the ideas or writings of his friend. The mutual defense of each other is constant, strong, and edifying. A well-known example may be cited. Tyndale had complained that More had not attacked his "darling" Erasmus for novel translations of consecrated scriptural terms. More answered in 1532: "I found no such malicious intent with Erasmus, my darling, as I find with Tyndale," and then continued: "I find in Erasmus, my darling, that he detesteth and abhorreth the errors and heresies that Tyndale plainly teacheth and abideth by, and therefore Erasmus, my darling, shall be my darling still." On August 31, 1535, shortly after the reception of the news of More's execution, Erasmus wrote to Peter Tomiczki, bishop of Cracow: "In More I seem to myself to have met my own death, so much was there but one soul, to use Pythagoras' dictum, between the two of us" ("In Moro mihi videor extinctus, adeo μία ψυχὴ iuxta Pythagoram duobus erat"). There is only wishful thinking in Stapleton's statement that "as that Protestant heresy increased, . . . More's love toward him [Erasmus] decreased and grew cool." Professor De Vocht explains their scanty correspondence in later years by showing that the responsible positions of the two friends involved the risk of the interception of letters and therefore necessitated the employment of personal messengers, usually Erasmus' amanuenses. There seems to be no word of adverse criticism of Erasmus' dilatory or cautious policies toward Protestantism in More's letters or writings. But absence of disapproval is not to be identified with positive approbation. The two men disagreed, although never openly, upon the liceity and opportuneness of war against the Turks or upon the practical policy to be adopted against heretics. But they were in complete agreement, for example, upon the reform of the universal Church and upon the need for peace between

Christian rulers, two topics that are especially pertinent to the present study.[23]

Erasmus, busy as scholar and littérateur, influenced his friend far more than his friend, busy as councilor and statesman, influenced Erasmus. It is noteworthy how much Erasmus' ideas on the criticism and reform of church and state remain the same in his earlier works (for example, *The Praise of Folly*) and in his later (for example, the *Colloquies*) in spite of the tremendously important changes wrought by the Reformation. The sum and content of his ideas being on the whole unchanged and consistent before and after the publication of *Utopia* and the Protestant Revolt following closely thereon, his works can be used with sufficient justification for the elucidation of More's thought in his ideal commonwealth. But the coincidence of thought and attitude in the two friends was never greater nor more striking than in the years before the Protestant Revolt when they were writing and publishing *The Praise of Folly* and *Utopia*. If allowances are made for different subject matters and different styles, the modern scholar might well feel like a spectator in a different situation: "he knew not which soul spake,/ Because both meant, both spake the same." In fact, Erasmus told Wolsey in 1519 that individuals who ascribed More's *Utopia* to Erasmus were not lacking.[24]

Nevertheless the effect of the two classics was different. Erasmus had laudably aimed *The Praise of Folly* at the reform of the Christian West: his wit had stirred up a hornet's nest. More's *Utopia*, on the contrary, was greeted, and continued to be hailed, with a chorus of praise. The satiric attack of Folly on abuses was direct; but in spite of the positive ideal implied in the satire its general effect was negative and destructive, so that it could become a veritable arsenal for the enemies of Roman Catholicism. The commonwealth described by Hythloday in Book II sets up a positive ideal for Christian states. The method, however, is indirect, for the reader is obliged to draw his own comparisons between the perfect pagan Utopia and the all-too-imperfect Christian Europe. Renaudet correctly sees the *Utopia* as the prolongation of the social and political criticism (and, one may add, of the moral and religious criticism) of *The Praise of Folly* and the *Adages* and as the development of "a positive, concrete, carefully elaborated program of reform." In a word, the *Utopia* is the complement of *The Praise of Folly*. It is the fulfillment of Dorp's suggestion that Erasmus compose a *Praise of Wisdom (Sapientiae laus)* to counterbalance and offset *The Praise of Folly (Stultitiae laus)*. In his *Utopia*, More thus serves as the representative of Erasmus and all the northern humanist reformers.[25]

To sum up, the *Utopia* is a pre-Reformation humanistic document with an eye to the reform of all phases and departments of the Christian state. If an ideal pagan state like Utopia which is based solely upon nature and philosophy can attain a glorious triumph, what a paradise upon earth could not a Christian nation create which has, beside the finest products of reason and antiquity, the surpassing treasures of revelation and grace to aid and sustain it!

CHAPTER II

God: Reason
and Faith

The Utopians have not been blessed by God with His supernatural revelation; consequently they possess only the light of reason to guide them. They lay stress upon the role of reason in religious matters. This state is quite in accord with what Thomas More asserts in his *Four Last Things:* "There is a God, which thou not only believest by faith, but also knowest by reason." In his *Dialogue Concerning Heresies* also, he writes: "Nature and reason giveth us good knowledge that there is a God." At creation God imposed only two or three commands upon Adam and Eve. "And as for all that was for them to do beside, the reason which He had planted in their souls gave them sufficient warning, whereof the whole sum stood in effect in the honor of God and God's friends, with love of each to the other and to their offspring and lineage." More of course knew that a man with his reason could see and approve the better thing and yet unreasonably do the worse. "Many a man that hath a great wit and a great reason, too, and much learning joined unto them both, doth yet more foolishly and more unreasonably than doth some other whose wit and reason is very far under his and, as for learning, hath utterly none at all." But More's purpose in the *Utopia* is not to reveal the defects of reason, but rather to reveal the power of reason to shake off the shackles of error and to come to the freedom of truth. He has no intention, however, of unduly extolling reason as did Reginald Pecock (1395?-1460?), bishop of St. Asaph, against the Lollards, with the unfortunate result that reason became supreme judge and the arbiter of both nature and revelation, "except few places marked for faith." Pecock was charged with heresy and agreed to recantation.[1]

The schoolmen themselves, since the end of the thirteenth century, had been steadily decreasing the number of religious truths capable of philosophical demonstration as well as of Christian belief. Duns Scotus (1265?-1308) had declared that God's omnipotence, omnipresence, immensity, justice, mercy, and providence are undemonstrable by reason alone: they can be proved only in theology. The author of the *Theoremata*, a work often attributed to Duns Scotus, adds to the list the unicity of God as well as the creation of the world out of nothing and its conservation by God. William Ockham (1300?-1349?) asserts that not even the existence of God as an absolutely supreme being can be proved by the traditional arguments based on natural reason. His existence, together with His attributes, can be established in philosophy only as probable. The same applies to the immateriality and immortality of the human soul. All such truths are capable of belief but incapable of rigid proof, even in theology. It is for such Christian philosophers that More may be picturing his Utopians as coming *by reason* to know the existence and attributes of God, especially His paternal providence.[2]

As far as other important religious truths are concerned, More explicitly states that the Utopians use religious principles to bolster their philosophical reasoning on the immortality of the soul and future retribution, and that reason influences men to believe and acknowledge them. Ten years before the publication of *Utopia*, More had apologized for Lucian's incredulity as to the immortality of the soul. Democritus, Lucretius, Pliny, and many others, he claims, had committed the same error. "What does it matter to me," he continues, "what a pagan thinks about these points which hold a place among the chief mysteries of the Christian faith?" In this respect More is a child of his age. For example, contemporary Aristotelians, both those who interpreted Aristotle according to the mind of Averroes and those who did so according to the mind of Alexander of Aphrodisias, denied personal immortality. Even the redoubtable Thomist, Cardinal Cajetan (1469-1534), had opined that reason could not prove conclusively the soul's immortality. In regard to God, however, More clearly holds that reason can demonstrate His existence. If one were to summarize More's position, one would say that he thinks that reason can demonstrate God's existence and attributes, but that it needs the light and help of revelation to hold firmly the soul's immortality and future reward.[3]

More does not describe the Utopians as yet holding the fundamental religious truths with perfect unanimity. This would be against his purpose of showing contemporary disputatious schoolmen, who freely hurl the charge of heresy against their opponents, that truth comes to light most easily in an atmosphere of peaceful and tolerant discussion. Consequently More allows a variety of religions, not only in Utopia as a whole, but even in each city. Some Utopians worship the sun as God; others, the moon; still others, one of the planets. The Book of Wisdom (Chapter 13) regards such worshipers as partially to be pardoned because they are so overwhelmed by the beauty and power of these creatures as to hail them as gods and as to fail to go beyond them to their all-beautiful and all-powerful author. It is worthy of note that More makes no Utopian the worshiper of idols fashioned from gold, silver, or wood, perhaps because Wisdom (Chapters 13-15) finds idolators inexcusable and unpardonable. The average Utopian is far too reasonable to adore the work of the hands of man. More is discreetly silent also on the explanation given in the Psalms, "Omnes dii Gentium daemonia—All the gods of the Gentiles are devils" (Psalm 95:5), and used by Milton in *Paradise Lost* a century and a half after *Utopia*. (Actually the best translation of the original Hebrew word is "idols" or "nonentities," not "devils.") St. Antoninus (1389-1459), archbishop of Florence, for example, had distinguished three classes of gods adored by the gentiles: demons, speaking through statues or possessed persons; irrational creatures—elements like fire or animals like the cow; and men outstanding for their power or the devotion of their followers, such as Hercules for courage, Jupiter for strong rule, and so forth. Some Utopians honor even as the highest god a man once eminent for virtue or glory. Erasmus had declared in his *Adages* that antiquity considered being a god being useful to mortal men ("antiquitas enim nihil aliud existimabat esse deum, quam prodesse mortalibus"), and hence it regarded as gods the discoverers of fruits, of wine, of laws, and so forth.[4]

More might have read the First Decade, published in 1511, of Peter Martyr d'Anghiera's *New World*. Peter Martyr (d. 1526) writes that a Jeronymite friar, Roman Pane, had reported several times that the savages adored only the stars and the heavens but later discovered that they believed ultimately in a "God, whom they represent as one, eternal, omnipotent, and invisible." This statement was especially significant for the humanists, who looked everywhere for signs of agreement among the various religions of mankind. Certainly the Utopians are far more reasonable than naked savages. Consequently by far the greatest part of them—and, as More hastens to add, by all odds the more sagacious—adore neither sun, nor moon, nor planet, nor hero, but believe in one divine nature. This divinity is unknown, inexplicable, and beyond the reach of human comprehension. More evidently does not intend this assertion in the sense of the "Unknown God" of the Athenians, who feared to neglect any god (Acts 17:23), but rather in the sense that man's knowledge of God is analogous, not proper. All the limitations and imperfections contained in our concepts must be negated when our ideas are referred to God. The unspeakable and indescribable nature of God had been much stressed in the mystical works of Pseudo-Dionysius (*c.* A.D. 500) which had exerted immense influence on medieval thought and which in part had been the subject of treatises by John Colet, the spiritual adviser of Thomas More. Christianity, of course, was to reveal to the Utopians much more about the nature of God.[5]

The important thing to note is that, unlike some late schoolmen, the Utopians with the aid of reason alone have come to know the attributes of God. The "philosopher man," Colet had insisted in his comment on St. Paul's Epistle to the Romans, "could easily, through the things that are made, see God, omnipotent and eternal"—a Creator who is good, beautiful, unchanging, one. Erasmus explains that, just as from an incredibly beautiful painting one concludes to the genius of the artist and from a superb performance on the cithara one gathers the admirable ability of the musician, so the whole universe reveals the power, wisdom, and goodness of God. Not only is the God of the Utopian majority eternal and immense, but He is one. Somehow or other, too, He must be in their whole universe. They wisely do not explain this immanence by pantheism, when pantheistic tendencies were disturbing Christian Europe. God is present, not by His "bulk" ("non mole"), but by His *power*. Here More is undoubtedly referring to divine creation, conservation, concurrence, and providence. Hence the Utopians apply to God the title of parent or father. To this provident parent they ascribe the origin, growth, development, alteration, and end of every creature. To this powerful father alone do they offer divine worship. The emphasis upon the fatherhood of the Creator will find its fulfillment in conversion to Christianity since all Christians not merely have God as their father by creation but by grace are His adopted sons and brothers of

His only natural son, Christ. For the sake of convenience, therefore, we may call the God of the majority of the Utopians God the Father.[6]

A few decades later, Raphael Holinshed in his description of Britain was to draw upon Greek and Latin authors for information on Druiyus, "the original founder" of the Druid religion, which proves to be curiously similar to the faith of the Utopians:

> In the beginning, this Druiyus did preach unto his hearers that the soul of man is immortal, that God is omnipotent, merciful as a father in showing favor unto the godly, and just as an upright judge in punishing the wicked, . . . and that as the world and all that is therein had their beginning of Him at His own will, so shall all things likewise have an end when He shall see His time.[7]

There is not hopeless confusion in Utopian beliefs about God. Those who believe in the sun, the moon, a planet, or a hero hold with the majority who believe in God the Father the truth that there is one supreme being. To this supreme being must be attributed creation of the universe and *providence over it*. All commonly call him Mithras in their native tongue. In view of the similarity of the Utopian language to the Persian speech, this use of the name of the Persian god of light is not unexpected. Strabo reports that the Persians "also worship Helius [the sun], whom they call Mithras." Erasmus refers to Mithras at least three times in his *Adages*. The seven classes of worshipers of Mithras are mentioned in one of the letters of Jerome which Erasmus was editing at this time. In a later work, moreover, Erasmus uses the sun as the image of the Father, the sun's rays to illustrate the generation of the Son, and the sun's warmth to explain the procession of the Holy Spirit.[8]

The Utopians disagree as to *who* this supreme being is. They agree that, *whoever* their supreme being may be, he is absolutely the same nature to whose divinity and majesty the sum of all things is attributed by the consent of all peoples. "For albeit

the Gentiles worshiped among them a thousand false gods,"
More tells the Messenger in his dialogue against Tyndale, "yet
all that proveth that there was and is in all men's heads a secret
consent of nature that God there is, or else they would have
worshiped none at all."[9]

More evidently wants to emphasize the fact that the Utopians
agree that the divine nature which created the universe continues to guide and govern it. The Creator does not stand aloof
from the world and leave its progress to chance. The inhabitants
of Utopia are true philosophers and have reached at least the
highest truths grasped by the thinkers of antiquity. In his
Dialogue Concerning Heresies More was to say:

> All the whole number of the old philosophers . . . found out by
> nature and reason that there was a God, either maker, or governor,
> or both, of all this whole engine of the world, the marvelous beauty
> and constant course whereof sheweth well that it neither was made
> nor governed by chance.[10]

All the Utopians believe in a God that both makes and
governs the world. *Some* still say that this God is the sun, or the
moon, or a planet, or an historical hero, but their number is
gradually decreasing. All are beginning to unite in that one
religion which appears to surpass the others according to the
light of *reason*—the religion which believes in God the Father.
The other sects would have vanished long ago if chance had not
caused some misfortune to befall the man deliberating about a
change in his religion and if fear had not caused him to interpret the misfortune, not as happening by chance, but as sent
from heaven by the abandoned deity in punishment of the
impious resolution directed against him. Thomas More had lectured early in life on St. Augustine's *City of God* and must
have known that the bishop of Hippo had declared in his *Retrac-
tations:* "The first five books are a refutation of their position
who maintain that the worship of many gods, according to the
custom of paganism, is essential to the prosperity of human

society, and that the prohibition of it is the source and origin of calamities such as the fall of Rome." Ambrose, too, had earlier silenced Symmachus for blaming a great famine on injuries done to the old gods. The Utopians who have not changed to the religion of God the Father have suffered themselves, like the pagans of Ambrose's and Augustine's day, to be ruled by superstitious fear, not intrepid reason.[11]

It is because the Utopians are pre-eminently reasonable that they accept Christianity with hearts incredibly sympathetic toward it. Raphael Hythloday assigns three reasons for their conversion: (1) the inexplicable and mysterious inspiration of God, (2) the great similarity of Christianity to the faith dominant among the majority of the Utopians, and (3) the fact that the living of His disciples in common had been pleasing to Christ and was still in use among the most genuinely Christian societies, namely, religious houses. More does not wish, of course, to deny that supernatural grace is necessary for every conversion; he merely asserts that some who could not assign any evident reason had to refer their conversion wholly to the secret workings of divine inspiration. The Utopians, therefore, are predisposed and prepared by their dominant religion and by their communism for the reception of Christianity.[12]

Hythloday and his companions propose two motives of credibility to the Utopians: (1) the teachings, virtues, and miracles of Christ and (2) the admirable constancy of countless martyrs whose blood freely shed drew numerous nations far and wide into the fold. More was later to use the latter argument against heretics to prove the truth of the Catholic Church: "This church that we be of, that take your church for heretics, have had many such martyrs therein, that believed as we do against your opinions." In the *Utopia* he may have in mind the Christianization of the natives in newly discovered lands—a problem discussed a few years later with great acuteness by Francisco de Vitoria in *De Indis*. The conduct of Europeans was hardly conducive to conversion. Christians believed because "the things were worthy of belief either because of the evidence of signs or for some other reason of this kind." The aborigines are not bound to believe, since "I hear," writes Vitoria, "of no miracles or signs or religious patterns of life; nay, on the other hand, I hear of many scandals and cruel crimes and acts of impiety." The Utopians do not have to contend with the bad example of Christians. Besides, they are much more civilized than the peoples of the New World and are equal in intellectual and religious achievements to the thinkers of antiquity. Far from keeping them from Christianity, their philosophy and belief actually lead them to accept it.[13]

Implicit in this section of the *Utopia* is the vexing problem of the relation of pagan philosophy and literature to the Christian religion. The humanists felt that the wisdom of antiquity was not inimical to, nor destructive of, the wisdom of Christ. It is true that the really Christian humanist, of course, could not go as far as Lorenzo Valla, who wrote: "It seems to me that holy religion and true literature dwell together, and that the presence of one precludes the absence of the other, and that because our religion is eternal Latin literature will also be eternal." Erasmus sums up admirably the more sober position of the humanistic Christian in his *Antibarbari*, begun about 1489 but published only in 1520. The task of originating and developing the human sciences could not have been committed to the pagans by chance—an assertion hardly to be tolerated by Christians who believe in divine providence. On the contrary, Christ had wished to be served by all past and future ages and desired *all* things to be drawn to Him, *even though unwilling*, with a view to their perfection. It was Christ who had prepared for His commonwealth all the brave exploits, wise maxims, acute theories, and industrious scholarship of the pagans—not that we might contemn their sweat and toil as useless and fruitless, but that we might adorn and support His most excellent religion with their brilliant sciences. Erasmus in his *Ecclesiastes* agrees with Ficino in his work on Plotinus that God in His wisdom wished to lead mankind to the full revelation of Christianity only by gradual stages, one stage embracing the great lawgivers and religious philosophers of antiquity who relied upon nature and reason. Having attained the level of a pure and noble religion, though general in nature, under their tutelage, men devoted to reason could rather easily be converted to the only true faith. Such has been the happy fate of the Utopians who, having reached by reason the knowledge of God the Father, receive with joy the revelation imparted by His Son.[14]

The ancients, claimed the humanists, had discovered many religious and moral truths which agreed with the teaching of Christ. (The similarity of these beliefs to those held by the Utopians must be noted.) According to various Christian humanists Plato had taught the creation of the world and immortality of the soul; Aristotle, the perpetual bond of love and friendship which should exist between husband and wife; other philosophers, the existence of God as an all-wise and all-good spirit; and so forth. Even Epicurus was not deficient in this respect. Above all, however, it was the philosophy of the Platonists that came closest to Christianity. Ficino often quoted enthusiastically the observation of St. Augustine that, changing only a few things, the Platonists would be Christians.[15]

"What else is the philosophy of Christ which He Himself calls a rebirth," exclaims Erasmus, "than the restoration and renewal of a nature created good?" These daring words need explanation, and Erasmus does explain them. The teaching of Christ is efficacious and complete: all fragmentary truths find their harmonious development and agreement only in Christ. The will of the pagan philosophers was by nature inclined toward good, but was not conducive to salvation, unless *supernatural* grace and faith were present. The fact that pagan philosophers agree with us does not raise the authority of our

dogmas of faith, but merely corroborates them: we do not believe philosophers unless they agree with Scripture. The authority of pagan philosophers would be trifling unless every bit
of their teaching were found in Holy Scripture, although not in
the same words. For example, what the philosophers call *reason,*
St. Paul calls now *spirit,* now *the interior man,* now *the law of
the mind.* What they call *passion,* he terms sometimes *flesh,*
sometimes *body,* sometimes *the exterior man,* sometimes *the
law of one's members.* Consequently the Christian reader must
distinguish in the pagan classics between what is useless, dangerous, and deadly, and what is profitable, salutary, even necessary. He must spurn the former and receive the latter. Never
with pagan literature should he take in pagan morals: lust,
avarice, ambition, or superstition. Classic literature shapes and
nourishes the youthful mind and prepares it for the knowledge
of Holy Scripture. In fact, it is profitable to taste all pagan
literature, provided it is done moderately and cautiously and
selectively in one's mature years and, most important of all,
provided that all things are referred to Christ. The reader
should launch into pagan literature like a bold merchant and
convert the spoils of the Egyptians to the adornment of the
Lord's temple. The aim of all erudition and eloquence is the
knowledge of Christ and the glory of Christ. Thomas More admirably sums up the matter in the same way:

> The Hebrews well despoil the Egyptians, when Christ's learned
> men take out of the pagan writers the riches and learning and wis-
> dom that God gave unto them and employ the same in the service
> of divinity about the profit of God's chosen children of Israel, the
> Church of Christ, which He hath of the hard stony paynims made
> the children of Abraham.[16]

The answer of the humanist, just given by More, was enun-
ciated in the most basic terms when an antihumanist, such as
Blessed Giovanni Dominici (1357-1419), vicar general of the
Dominicans, charged that the scholar seeking truth in the pagan

classics was not walking in the ways of the Lord. Coluccio
Salutati answered that *all* truth is from God, who is truth itself.
Nothing true exists outside God, so that he who seeks for truth
anywhere is most certainly seeking God. The Fifth Council of
the Lateran (1512-1517) proclaims the same principle from a
different point of view. Against those lecturers who teach that
philosophical methods lead one to conclude to the mortality of
the soul, the eternity of the world, and so forth, the papal constitution *Apostolici regiminis* declares that, since truth cannot
contradict truth, every assertion contrary to the truth of enlightened faith is altogether false. A number of years earlier the
orthodox view had been well stated by Pico, who asserted that,
just as grace builds upon nature, so philosophy is the beginning
of religion, nor is it philosophy that severs a man from religion.
Philosophy and religion, reason and faith, are to work together
amicably and harmoniously.[17]

The views of Thomas More on this point are clear and
interesting. Martin Luther, he says, who had at first attempted
to defend his heretical opinions also according to natural reason
but had been refuted on this ground, "began . . . to sing another
song. For then, as for reason, he refused to stand to, saying that
the matters of our faith be things above reason and that reason
hindereth us in our faith and is unto faith an enemy." Tyndale,
like Luther, protests against the pope and clergy that "they
meddle philosophy with the things of God." More's reply is
simple and direct: this is "a thing that may in place be very
well done, sith the wisdom of philosophy, all that we find true
therein, is the wisdom given of God and may well do service to
His other gifts of higher wisdom than that is." His answer, in
other words, is that God is the source of all truth, philosophical
and religious, and that philosophy can be of genuine help to
theology. Consequently he defends Catholic preachers against
Tyndale's charge that they "preach Aristotle, philosophers, and
poets," not Christ, by saying that they use the philosophers only

in the discussion of natural phenomena or moral virtues and that in this respect they follow the example of St. Paul in his letters to the Romans and to Titus.[18]

The relationship of reason to faith is even more exactly defined in the *Dialogue Concerning Heresies*. There the Messenger repeats the belief of the Protestants: "What greater enemy can ye find to faith than reason is, which counterpleadeth faith in every point?" Thomas More, therefore, is to be considered foolish if he wishes to "send them twain forth to school together that can never agree together, but be ready to fight together, and either scratch out other's eyes by the way." Faith, More answers, is better than, and superior, to reason. But the Messenger is introducing a conflict where none should exist. Reason, "but if reason be unreasonable," should have no more difficulty in submitting to the truths of faith than to the mysteries of science, such as magnetism. Reason should obey God her Master and Maker when He tells her *what* but not *how;* for example, *that* He was born of a virgin but not *how* this was achieved. "And so must reason not resist faith but walk with her, and as her handmaid so wait upon her, . . . yet of a truth faith goeth never without her." Now, a handmaid, if allowed complete license or intoxication or haughtiness, will quibble with her master and behave foolishly. In the same way reason, if permitted total liberty and excessive pride, will surely rebel against the faith of her master. "But, on the other side, if she be well brought up and well guided and kept in good temper, she shall never disobey faith, being in her right mind." The cardinal principle is the following: "Let reason be well guided, for surely faith goeth never without her."[19]

The difficulty with the Protestant reformers is precisely that they will not submit their reason to their faith. They cannot accept the *what* because they cannot see the *how*. More's friend, John Colet, had much earlier declared: "The cause of every disease, nay rather every disease itself and discord in the

Church, is the distempered state of reason, and its aberration from living faith and wanton transgression of bounds, and departure from *the measure of faith*" (Romans 12:3). All heretics, he insists, trusted too presumptuously to themselves and their reason. "It is the chastening of our reason, accordingly, and observance of the measure of faith, that preserve the society and unity of the Church." Following in the steps of Colet, Thomas More in his controversy with John Frith tells him that "he should believe the letter [of Scripture] and make his reason obedient unto faith." Apparent repugnance—for example, between man's free will and God's foreknowledge—does not invalidate either truth but merely shows that "the poor blind reason of man cannot see so far as to perceive *how* God's prescience and man's free will can stand and agree together." To Frith's objections to the real presence of Christ in the Blessed Sacrament, More offers the following principle and conclusion: "Therefore ought every man abhor, as a plain pestilence, all such unreasonable reasons made for nature by more than natural fools against the possibility of God's almighty power." Such reasoning is nothing else than the "vain philosophy" (compare Colossians 2:8) denounced by St. Paul. More makes the same sort of plea in his answer to Tyndale's *The Supper of the Lord*. Tyndale should subdue his reason to the obedience of faith in things that "may seem repugnant unto us, which things God seeth *how* to set together well enough." In fact, the inability of the mind to effect reconciliation between two apparently repugnant truths, More tells Bugenhagen, should carry us into a most sweet transport of admiration over the majesty of God. Hence scholastic disputations on such points, far from being temerarious, are not only harmless but even advisable and profitable.[20]

All that has been said so far on the relationship between faith and reason is extremely important in the interpretation of the Utopian's present religion and his subsequent conversion to

Christianity. The Utopian is essentially a philosopher—a lover of wisdom who seeks the ultimate causes of realities according to nature and reason. He is unlike the contemporary schoolman, who according to Erasmus is merely "learned in the ways of dialectic or physics"; he is "one who casts aside the false pseudo-realities and with open mind seeks and follows the truth." The moment that the Christian doctrines and the motives of credibility are sufficiently proposed, he receives Christ as the truth. "To be a philosopher and to be a Christian," as Erasmus exclaims, "is synonymous in fact."[21]

Before the arrival of Hythloday the Utopians know only one of God's two books: the book of creation, which, as Colet explains, is "set open before the philosophers of the Gentiles" by God in His goodness. In the striking image developed at length in the *Natural Theology* of the Spanish theologian, Raymond of Sabunde (d. 1437?), later translated by Montaigne into French, every creature is but a letter written by the finger of God, and from many creatures as from many letters a book is put together. The Utopians read this book well: they recognize God and glorify Him as Creator and governor. But there is another book of God's which they do not know: His written word. It was far greater goodness on God's part, as Colet says, to reveal Himself in words to Moses and the prophets, and "far the greatest of all, to show Himself lastly by His Son." The word of God is far superior to the book of creatures—in seven ways at least, according to Sabunde's *Violet of the Soul*.[22]

The Utopians would not fall under St. Paul's condemnation of certain pagan philosophers: "Although they knew God, they did not glorify him as God or give thanks, but became vain in their reasonings" (Romans 1:21). For example, no mention is made of the possession, much less of the worship, of any "image made like to corruptible man and to birds and four-footed beasts and creeping things" (Romans 1:23). Nevertheless the inhabitants of Utopia are all descendants of Adam, infected

with original sin and plagued with its consequences, and therefore have to be "washed in the holy water of baptism." Not a
few ("haud pauci") undergo this rite of ablution.[23]

Independently of the existence of real mysteries which to be
known must be revealed by God and which can never be proved
demonstratively or understood completely by the human intellect, supernatural revelation is morally necessary even for the
truths of natural religion. Scotus, following Augustine, gives
three reasons: (1) slackness of the community in seeking the
truth, (2) weakness of the human intellect, and (3) errors on
the part of philosophical investigators who mix much falsehood
with their truth and leave simple people in doubt of the demonstration to which they should give assent. Aquinas mentions also
the necessity of providing for one's family, the immense amount
of time requisite for investigation, and so forth. The divine
clemency, therefore, revealed supernaturally even those truths
capable of attainment by reason, so that all—not just a handful—might become sharers of the divine knowledge without
difficulty or hesitation or error. Even the Utopian philosophers,
as has been seen, employ principles borrowed from "religion":
the immortality of the soul, happiness as its final end, and
reward or punishment in the hereafter. In their principal philosophical controversy, that on the object of man's happiness, they
consider human reason by itself *(per se)* defective and feeble,
needing the support which comes from "religion." Since this
"religion" is opposed to "philosophy which uses reasons," it
cannot be a merely natural religion in which all the religious
truths are proved by reason with absolute certainty; consequently it must be a religion which involves some form of faith.
This is a most difficult passage in the *Utopia.* On the one hand,
Hythloday always speaks of the reliance of Utopian religion
upon reason: it is therefore a philosophical or natural religion.
On the other hand, there are certain religious truths—for example, the immortality of the soul—which reason can reach or

hold only with the help of another kind of religion, which, of course, must be a supernatural or revealed religion. Consequently the author of *Utopia* might here be accused of being somewhat inconsistent.[24]

The following solution may be offered to the problem. One must admit that the religion of the Utopians does call for some faith. Faith in turn presupposes revelation. Thomas More gives no inkling as to the source of the Utopians' knowledge of revelation. It could be special illuminations sent by God, such as Roger Bacon postulates for Pythagoras, Socrates, Plato, Aristotle, and others. It could be the survivals of a primitive revelation first made when the young human race was still unscattered, and then handed down from father to son. In treating of purgatory in his *Supplication of Souls*, More mentions the possibility that "of the first light and revelation given of such things to our former fathers there hath alway remained a glimmering that hath gone forth from man to man, from one generation to another, and so continued and kept among all people." If the primitive Utopians had lost this revelation, it could have been restored to them in some form by the teaching of the Romans and Egyptians shipwrecked on the coast of Utopia about the year A.D. 300, although the implication of Hythloday's words later on is clearly that his group were the first to preach Christianity as such in Utopia. Whatever be the source, revelation and faith are used by the Utopians to bolster and support conclusions which have been reached also by reason. In a word, Thomas More is not inconsistent. He keeps the main Utopian religion natural or rational but allows the Utopians to use faith to clinch certain religious truths basically known by human reason alone.[25]

Here Thomas More shows himself definitely a follower of Duns Scotus. Reason can prove a truth in one of two ways: first, demonstratively—that is, with irrefutable arguments, and secondly, suasively—that is, with arguments that beget strong probability but not absolute certitude. Among the truths which can be known with certitude only through faith, not through natural reason, Scotus places the immortality of the soul. The arguments brought forth by other schoolmen to prove it are not cogent. For example, Scotus finds inconclusive the proof based upon the beatitude of man and eternal reward because (1) natural reason need not postulate the existence of one who rules men according to the laws of rewarding and punishing justice, and (2) even if it did, everyone might be said to have a sufficient reward in the good act itself and a sufficient punishment in the sin itself. Neither can a strict proof be found in the *natural desire* of man for beatitude, because man seeks only beatitude in general, not beatitude in particular (the happiness of heaven which consists in the beatific vision of God). The reason is that it is not evident from nature that beatitude in particular consists in the beatific vision, which we expect through faith alone. "From these considerations it is clear," concludes Scotus, "what great thanks ought to be rendered to the mercy of the Creator, who through faith has made us most certain in those things which pertain to our end and everlasting continuance." Like Scotus, the Utopian holds these truths by faith, but, once they have been revealed, it is *reason* that induces him to believe and admit them according to strictly philosophical arguments. In other words, reason does play an extremely important role in the religion of the Utopians.[26]

The problem of the salvation of the pagan Utopians before the coming of Christianity to the island need not delay us here. No pagan, Jew, or Christian is saved, as Erasmus insists, by his own efforts but solely by the mercy of God through Christ and His Church. If God is pleased not to vouchsafe a personal revelation to the good pagan, schoolmen, such as Aquinas, hold for the sufficiency of an *implicit* faith in a divine providence which would furnish suitable means for man's liberation from sin. Scotus too teaches that, just as God enjoined on the Jews circumcision for the destruction of original sin, so He must have provided some efficacious remedy for the gentiles, perhaps sacrifices which were pleasing to Him. Thomas More himself cites with approval those doctors who held "that unto all such Paynims as in any place lived naturally well and kept themselves from idolatry, God sent the faith of Christ to keep them from hell, as not suffering any man to be perpetually damned to the sensible pain of fire without his own actual fault." God did so perhaps by a private revelation, perhaps by an angel, at the moment of death.[27]

The Utopians are heathens, but this is no reason why Christians should taunt them with unbelief. Reproach for infidelity should not be directed against heathens by Christians—"those above all," writes Colet, "whose unlikeness in life to Christ is a witness that their own faith is but scanty." Some men who are Christian in name are "more depraved in life than any heathen": they lead a life full of lust, avarice, revenge, fear of death, and war. "Christianity," exclaims Erasmus, "is nothing else than true and perfect friendship, . . . a certain communion of men among themselves such as of the members of the body among themselves." The Utopians, by reason and nature, have attained a remarkable degree of union in joy and suffering, in good fortune and bad. Christ is now to bring this virtue to perfection. It was, according to Colet, the purpose of Christ, the author of nature, to bring back the order and beauty of man's original nature:

> Thus would there be order and agreement on the part of all, fellow aspirations and common desires, mutual good-will, courtesy and beneficence, compassion and support in changes of fortune, common joy and sorrow, loss and gain; in a word, all things common, and nothing whatever private, whether in blessings or misfortunes.[28]

CHAPTER III

Toleration
and Heresy

One of the most hotly controverted issues in the life and character of Thomas More has been his attitude toward and treatment of heretics. Did he preach liberal tolerance in the *Utopia* as a young humanist and practice severe intolerance as an old statesman? A study of all his written works induces one to concede that More was consistent in his *principles*. It is not the purpose of this discussion to marshal and review in detail all the evidence and all the judgments expressed by scholars. In spite of attacks, the conclusions of men like A. I. Taft and R. W. Chambers still stand in their essentials.[1]

Our first task is, not to judge him in the court of modern liberalism, but, above all, to discover and explain the point of view of Thomas More himself. The problem is not as easy as it seems—or as facile as his admirers have made it to seem. In fact, it is extremely intricate. More himself would not declare simply for tolerance or intolerance. This declaration would be an oversimplification of the problem. More would say, "It depends." Depends upon what? The prevailing situation. Circumstances, after all, do change cases.

It is possible to envisage seven situations:

Situation 1: a state in which there are no truths which the people must believe.

Situation 2: a pagan state before the preaching of Christianity in which some truths are of obligatory belief, but persons who do not believe them live and behave according to the law of the land.

Situation 3: a pagan state before the preaching of Christianity in which some truths are of obligatory belief, but persons who deny them spread their opinions contrary to the law of the land.

Situation 4: a pagan state in which Christianity has begun to be preached.

Situation 5: a state entirely Catholic in which heretics are peaceful and reasonable.

Situation 6: a state entirely Catholic in which heretics are indocile and violent.

Situation 7: a state once entirely Catholic but now divided into Christian denominations.

(A state once entirely Catholic or Christian but now permitting the free existence of all Christian, non-Christian, and atheistic groups would revert to Situation 1. There is no need to give this state special treatment.)

As far as Situation 1 is concerned, More—and Utopus—seems never to have visualized a state which would be absolutely indifferent to the worship of the supreme being and which would permit materialists and atheists to move and speak as freely as the upholders of religion. Such a state, in view of all history and of the evidences for the existence of a God, would be anomalous and incredible to More. On tolerance in a state like this, which would necessarily have to be a complete tolerance, he has nothing to say.

Quite different is the case of Utopia before the arrival of Hythloday. Here is a pagan state before the preaching of Christianity, a state which wishes its citizens to believe certain religious truths. Already restrictions have here been placed upon tolerance. The state consequently behaves differently toward

disbelievers who observe and disbelievers who disobey its laws
in regard to religion (Situations 2 and 3).[2]

The fundamental law promulgated by Utopus is that every
man may licitly follow the religion which pleases him best. He
is permitted, moreover, to make converts to his religion. Proselytism, however, is governed by certain conditions. The prose-
lytizer must build up his own religion by cogent reasonings in
a peaceful and moderate manner. If he cannot persuade his
hearers by gentle argumentation, he must not tear down other
religions in a spirit of bitterness and harshness. He should use
no force and should keep himself from all insult and vitupera-
tion. More must here have had an eye on the violent and un-
compromising philosophical and theological quarrels of the
schoolmen in his day. A favorite method of attack was to reduce
one's opponents—logically, of course—to a position of heresy.
If reasonable pagans could practice tolerance in such an important matter as that of religion, how much more ought Christians
to show mutual charity toward one another in their disagreement over excessively subtle and seemingly useless questions.
The schoolmen, moreover, should show tolerance and forbearance toward the humanists, who, after all, are their fellow
Christians and equally zealous for the cause of Christ and religion, however much they may differ on the methods of reform.

The principal reason for this tolerance in Utopia is the
maintenance of order within the country and of unity in the face
of external enemies. Utopus had perceived that the inhabitants
before his coming had been at one another's throats over the
question of religion and that the division into sects, each fighting alone for the country, had been the occasion for his conquest
of them all. More, too, was aware that religious dissensions
could cause Christian Europe to fall before the Turk—another
reason for maintaining the unity of faith at all costs. Utopus
immediately issued a proclamation of toleration with a view
to the preservation of that peace which he saw completely de-

stroyed by continual strife and implacable hate. But this was
not his only reason. A policy of toleration was in the best interests of religion itself. After all, might not God desire from men
a variety and multiplicity of religions and therefore inspire one
man to offer Him one kind of worship and another man to pay
Him another kind? In this state of doubt Utopus dared to issue
no rash definition as to which religion was the true one. It
seemed to him a policy both arrogant and absurd to use violence
and threats to force others to see as true what one personally
believed to be true. When Quintus Aurelius Symmachus (345-
405) engaged in a last defense of the ancient pagan religion
against Christianity, he argued that there was more than one
way of approaching the deity ("uno itinere non potest perveniri
ad tam grande secretum"), but he met a redoubtable and victorious opponent in St. Ambrose. The thought that a variety of
religions might not be altogether unpleasing to God had found
expression also in Ficino's *Christian Religion*. "Perhaps," he
writes, "a variety of this kind, by the ordination of God, pro-
duces a certain wonderful glory in the universe. It is, indeed, of
greater concern to the King of All to be worshiped than to be
worshiped with these particular gestures or those." Alexander
the Great had approved all ceremonies in his honor, but held
some in higher regard than others. The same concept, as it
were, ought to be applied to God. "He prefers," Ficino concludes, "to be worshiped in any manner whatever, no matter
how foolish, provided only that it is human, rather than not to
be worshiped at all on account of pride."[3]

Agrippa von Nettesheim (1486?-1535) voices the same sentiments. The rites and ceremonies of religion, he observes, differ
according to time and place, but every religion has something
good in it. God approves only the Christian religion, to which
man comes only by His grace, but He does not absolutely
reprove other forms of worship practiced for His sake. As
for deeply irreligious and impious persons, however, He hates

and banishes them as enemies. "No religion, on the testimony of Lactantius, is so full of error that it contains no fragment of wisdom." Nevertheless all worship which by excess or defect fails to measure up to the norm of the Christian religion is superstitious.[4]

Tolerance in Utopia is not absolute and complete. There are certain religious truths which Utopus felt a reasonable man and Utopian should believe. It appears strange that no mention is made of the existence of God. Certainly this fundamental concept is presupposed in all that follows in the *Utopia*. Probably Utopus had to promulgate no special law in this respect because he considered no Utopian so unreasonable as to deny the existence of a supreme being. Be that as it may, Utopus conscientiously and sternly forbade any man to suppose that the world was governed by chance and not by providence. The government of the whole world by God and not by chance, as Ficino and Antoninus of Florence insist, is known and proved by human reason without revelation. Note that Utopus did not forbid public preaching of the doctrine *but even thinking it* ("ut . . . putaret")! The Latin wording of this attitude ("mundum temere ferri sublata prouidentia") seems an echo taken from Erasmus' Latin translation of Lucian's *Icaromenippus* ("mundum nullo domino nulloque duce temere ferri").[5]

The Utopians had seemed to Hythloday to be inclined more than was fitting to the philosophy of the Epicureans, who defend pleasure as the object of human happiness. Here, of course, Utopus denied one of the cardinal tenets of Epicureanism because Epicurus, in order to remove the superstitious fears which are the most bitter enemies of human joy, had pictured his shadowy gods as happy but absolutely indifferent to human affairs. On the other hand, Plato, whose spirit pervades the *Utopia*, had enunciated the doctrine that the universe is not "governed by an irrational and fortuitous power and mere chance," but is "ordered and directed by mind and a marvellous wisdom." Hence, no matter what evils befall the just man, "for him all these things will finally prove good, both in life and in death," for the gods will not neglect the righteous and virtuous man who strives "to be likened unto god so far as that is possible to man."[6]

Ordinary Christians of More's day, according to Erasmus, were far too concerned with pleasure and prosperity and the earthly future, with the result that they had forgotten that providence would provide food, clothing, and shelter from day to day if only they strove to be perfect as their heavenly Father was perfect (Matthew 5:48, 6:25-34). Here in the *Utopia* More might therefore be uttering an indirect rebuke of those nominal Christians who lived as if there were no providence in which to trust.[7]

Thomas More, in spite of his ardent belief in providence, is far from being a philosophical optimist of the stamp of Leibniz. He admits that whatever proceeds from the divine goodness "must needs be good" and has "in itself sufficient and right wonderful perfection." He denies that "it is wrought to the utterest point of sovereign goodness that His Almighty Majesty could have made it of." The reason is simple. God created the world, not by compulsion of any kind, but of His free will— "not naturally but willingly." Consequently He made the universe "with such degrees of goodness as His high pleasure liked to limit." This is not the best possible universe which "cannot be mended," and "therefore God might break up the whole world if He would, and make a better by and by." In this way, by a clear understanding and intelligent following of St. Thomas Aquinas on the doctrine of a free creation, More avoids what Anton Pegis describes as "a God whose goodness compels Him to produce the best of all possible worlds and who cannot be good until and unless He does so."[8]

In addition to the pronouncement on providence, Utopus declared for the immortality of the human soul: "Let no one fall so far from the dignity of human nature as to believe that the soul perishes together with the body" ("Ne quis usque adeo ab humanae naturae dignitate degeneret, ut animas quoque interire cum corpore . . . putaret"). Later, in his *Supplication of Souls,* More was to use almost the same words, this time in English, of "such as have so far fallen from the nature of man into a brutish beastly persuasion as to believe that soul and body die both at once." Such was Epicurus, the founder of that philosophy to which the Utopians seem too much inclined, who, in order to remove the fear of death as an obstacle to man's happiness, denied the immortality of the soul. Other pagan philosophers now and then were pictured as holding only a misty belief in the immortality of the soul and future retribution. Thomas Lupset, who edited the second edition of *Utopia* for the press of Gilles de Gourmont in Paris in 1517, says that "they so believed that much doubtfulness was in their belief, in as much as their reason sufficed not to find out the certainty of God's works." Thus Erasmus points out that Aristotle doubts the immortality of the soul. Plato, too, whose belief in immortality provokes his auditor's amazement, holds it, in Shorey's words, as "a pious hope and an ethical postulate rather than a demonstrable certainty."[9]

But why fasten on pagan philosophers? What a rebuke the law of Utopus is even to Christians of More's day! "Not a few, even Christians," observes a marginal note in the *Utopia,* "hold the immortality of the soul a matter of dispute." As we have seen above, More thinks that religion must come to the support of that reason which can establish the immortality of the soul not absolutely and demonstratively but only probably and suasively. Consequently he cannot be speaking against schoolmen like Scotus or even Cajetan, that redoubtable commentator on Aquinas, who holds a similar view. His target is rather a philosopher like Pietro Pomponazzi (1462-1525). Cuthbert Tunstall, More's friend and companion on the Flemish mission of 1515, had studied at the University of Padua *c.* 1499-1505. Here Pomponazzi, who held the chair of natural philosophy, overtly called in question the immortality of the soul as far as philosophical principles were concerned. Nor was Pomponazzi alone. "How many there are among us," exclaims Erasmus, "who neither believe in the resurrection of the body nor believe that the soul survives the body!" The more learned, of course, took refuge in the notorious "double truth" of the Averroists: the human soul is mortal at least according to philosophy.[10]

In 1513 the Fifth Council of the Lateran attempted to cut the ground from under these philosophers by defining the immortality and individuality of the rational soul. It is interesting to note that the council appeals to the gospel, which promises eternal rewards and eternal punishments according to the earthly life of the individual judged—the very truth which More connects with immortality. Plato does the same in his *Republic.* For him "the prizes, the wages, and the gifts that the just man receives [in life] from gods and men . . . are nothing in number and magnitude compared with those that await both [just and unjust] after death." But More was later to declare about philosophers in his *Dialogue of Comfort against Tribulation* that he "never could yet find that those natural reasons were able to give sufficient strength of themself." The reason is simple: "They leave untouched, for lack of necessary knowledge, that special point which is not only the chief comfort of all, but without which also all other comforts are nothing, that is to wit, . . . that by the patient sufferance of their tribulation they shall attain His favour, and for their pain, receiveth reward at His hand in heaven." Little wonder that Erasmus could write of More to Hutten in 1519: "With his friends he so discourses of life in the next world that you recognize that he is speaking from his soul and not without the best of hope." Nor was the fulfillment of this hope to be deferred. More later protests against the doctrine of Luther that "all souls shall sleep and feel neither good nor bad after this life till doomsday." In fact, even Turks, Saracens, and pagans believe, either through a primitive revelation or through nature and reason, that if souls are not deserving of the fire of hell nor yet worthy and pure enough to enter heaven, they are in purgatory first "punished and purged by pain after the death ere ever they were admitted unto their wealth and rest."[11]

In passing, it is necessary to note that Plato in his *Laws* inflicts such penalties as imprisonment (and even death for recidivism) upon that citizen who believes that the gods do not exist, or who "believes that the gods exist, but have no care for men" (providence), or who "believes that they are easy to win over when bribed by offerings and prayers" (just retribution). This last is least reasonable of all.[12]

The Utopians, since they are as yet pagans unenlightened by revelation, have no idea that the reward for virtue in a future life is going to be the beatific vision, "the fruition of the Godhead." This supernatural end of man cannot be known or attained by nature, but "by a special gift and prerogative of His grace." Consequently the Utopians must have a concept of such a heaven as man would have enjoyed if he had remained in his natural state. More describes this natural beatitude as "a life good, quiet, and restful, with spiritual delight, in such knowledge of God and His wonderful works as reason at the least without revelation might attain unto." Neither is there the slightest indication that the pagan Utopians have reached any belief in the resurrection of the body. This is not surprising in view of the fact that when Paul himself preached the resurrection of the body to the learned Athenians, "some began to sneer, but others said, 'We will hear thee again on this matter' " (Acts 17:32). Scotus notes that Paul's words are merely suasive and that bodily resurrection cannot be demonstrated by human reason. This restriction must be laid upon the traditional argument used by such men as Reginald Pecock and John Fisher that God will not perpetually thwart the natural inclination and desire of the soul for union with the body.[13]

What, then, are the basic truths which, according to the law of Utopus, every reasonable Utopian is to hold? First of all, the existence of God is presupposed and implicitly contained in this enactment. All Utopians agree on the existence of a supreme being, but disagree on His identity. No Utopian is mentioned as being so obtuse and stupid as to deny God's existence. Secondly, the belief that God behaves toward man and the universe with a loving providence to which are attributed "the beginnings, the increasings, the proceedings, the changes, and the ends of all things," is enjoined upon Utopians. Thirdly, the reasonable Utopians must maintain the immortality of the human soul. Fourthly, as an important corollary to faith in providence, future retribution for the immortal soul is necessary of belief. In passing, it is worthy of note that Aeneas Silvius declares that "the princes of philosophers," namely, Socrates and Plato and Aristotle, hold the same truths: they believe the same things as Christians about the government of the world, about the immortality of souls, and about God.[14]

Why does Thomas More—and Utopus—insist upon having the Utopians believe in these truths? The reason is evident: More wants his Utopians to attain salvation! In what truths must a pagan believe in order to be saved? The basis of the answer to this question is traditionally found in the words of St. Paul: "he who comes to God must believe that God exists and is a rewarder to those who seek him" (Hebrews 11:6). For pagans and gentiles who had never heard of Christ, "it was sufficient for their salvation," Thomas More writes in his *Treatise on the Passion*, "to believe those two points only which Saint Paul here rehearseth, that is to wit, that there is one God and that He will reward them that seek Him." In support of his view he cites as his authority Nicholas of Lyra, whose biblical commentary he sometimes caused to be read at table and whose scholarship he defended against Tyndale. Belief in these two truths must be *explicit*. Faith in Christ of whom the pagan has never heard need be only *implicit*, for "it is to be considered that Master Lyra there saith, that in the belief of those two points is implied the belief of Christ which is the mean of our salvation, in that that he which believeth that God will reward them that seek Him hath therein implied that God hath a respect unto man's salvation and provideth a mean thereunto, and so believeth he that there is a mean of man's salvation and reward, though he know not that the mean is Christ." God never denies to any man sufficient grace to believe those two truths which everyone must hold explicitly; therefore "is there no man of discretion among the gentiles and paynims unsaved without his own default." God will not suffer "any man to be perpetually damned to the sensible pain of fire without his own actual fault." The same view, which is the traditional one, is held by the Angelic Doctor, St. Thomas Aquinas, and by the great Jesuit theologian of the Renaissance, Francisco Suárez.[15]

Consequently Utopus has enacted a law which, according to Thomas More, would insure the salvation of the Utopians; namely, they are all to believe that, the existence of God being presupposed, the human soul is immortal and that divine providence is intimately concerned with the order of the universe now and with the reward or punishment of the soul hereafter.

Suppose that an Utopian cannot or will not believe these truths? The Utopian government uses neither violence nor threats. First of all, it does not inflict upon the unbeliever any punishment (*supplicium*, a word used especially for capital punishment), such as exile, slavery, or death. The reason is that Utopians are persuaded that no one has it in his power to feel or think whatever he pleases ("ut quicquid libet sentiat"): there must be arguments, demonstrative or suasive, which lead one to hold a particular view or opinion. (This will be explained later.) Secondly, officials do not force anyone by threats to disguise and dissemble his mind. They cannot tolerate acts of deceit and lying: it is wonderful to see how they hate these acts as being very close to criminal fraud.

But the unbeliever is not given the same honor and freedom as believers. (1) Utopians everywhere look down upon him as possessed of a sluggish and base nature. (2) They do not consider him a member of mankind, since he has reduced the sublime nature of his human soul to the worthlessness of a cheap animal body. (3) Far less do they number him among their citizens, since he would not value at a pinhead all their laws and customs, unless it were out of fear. Who can doubt, they say, that he who is restrained only by the fear of punitive laws and who has no hope of surviving the body will evade by stealth and craft the public laws of his native country, or struggle by force to break them, if only he might satisfy his desires as a private person? The Utopians, it is evident, are far from establishing a divorce between morality and religion. Ultimate sanction for the inviolate observance of their laws can come only from a God who will reward the virtuous and punish the criminal in a future life. Plato, too, in his *Laws* stresses a correct view of the existence, providence, and nature of God as the foundation of morality: "No one who believes, as the laws prescribe, in the existence of the gods has ever yet done an impious deed voluntarily, or uttered a lawless word: he that acts so is in one or other of these three conditions of mind—either he does not believe in what I have said; or, secondly, he believes that the gods exist, but have no care for men; or, thirdly, he believes that they are easy to win over when bribed by offerings and prayers." But Plato does admit the existence of a class "who, though they utterly disbelieve in the existence of the gods, possess by nature a just character, both hate the evil and . . . are incapable of being induced to commit unjust actions." (4) Utopians consequently bestow no honor on the denier of divine providence and human immortality; they entrust no governmental office to him; they put him in charge of no public service. (5) They finally forbid him to defend his opinion in the presence of the public. Nevertheless they not only allow him to support his view in private with priests and learned men but even exhort him to do so. They are confident that his madness will at last yield to reason. Plato has a similar prohibition of public discussion in his *Laws:* "If any old man has any stricture to pass on any of your laws, he must not utter such views in the presence of any young man, but before a magistrate or one of his own age."[16]

It is evident from the foregoing that the concept of toleration in the *Utopia* cannot be stressed too much or stretched too far. There are official religious dogmas to which every reasonable and loyal Utopian is expected to subscribe. If he fails to do so, he is not subjected to threats or to physical punishment, but he is made to feel, as man and as citizen, the full weight of social disapproval, even to the extent that he is rendered ineligible for any public office and honor and incapable of the free public defense of his disbelief. Thus, Epicurus, whose philosophy the Utopians seem to approximate most, would not be honored in Utopia insofar as he denied survival after death.[17]

To return now to a consideration of the various situations and, in particular, of Situations 2 and 3. As long as the unbeliever observes the law of the land on silence in public, he is left free to hold his opinion in private and remains unmolested by threats or bodily coercion. This is Situation 2. In Situation 3 the unbeliever insists upon the public defense of his views. Even if he on his part argues peacefully and calmly, he is breaking the law and consequently is liable to the penalty, which is undoubtedly exile or slavery, and if he is recalcitrant as a slave, death, as in the system used by the Polylerites. Consequently to contrast, as some have done, the use in the Middle Ages of war itself on heretics (on the authority of St. Augustine) with the Utopian policy of *never* using "force to coerce *peaceful* dissenters" does not tell the whole story, since the Utopians do use force if even *peaceful* dissenters insist upon the public defense and propagation of their heterodox views.[18]

Let us now turn to an examination of Situation 4, that is, the case of a pagan state such as Utopia which sees the introduction of Christianity. Dominico Soto, O.P. (1494-1560), enunciates the traditional doctrine. *By the natural law* everyone has the liberty and right to teach others and to advise them concerning their obligations. But all mortals, under penalty of eternal damnation, are obliged to receive the Christian faith and its sacraments. Therefore every Christian can advise all men about these things to the limit of peaceable persuasion. Soto warns against the use of violence, for supernatural verities do not force the intellect; every man, however, can teach and explain them with perfect right. Francisco Suárez, S.J., develops this doctrine in greater detail. He declares that (1) it is intrinsically evil to force nonsubjects to receive the faith, that (2) the Church cannot force its temporal subjects to do so, and that (3) Christian princes can use indirect coercion such as high taxes or severe punishment of civil crimes if they judge these policies will be useful in the conversion of the natives (he hedges this latter method with many cautions and safeguards). Ficino, too, in his treatise *The Christian Religion* claims that, while the Talmud and the Koran order adversaries to be killed, Christianity wants them to be taught by reason or converted by prayer or suffered in patience: the primitive Christians persuaded others by their virtuous lives and numerous miracles.[19]

Erasmus looks upon St. Paul as the ideal missionary, who was always seeking "an opportunity for the word, to announce the mystery of Christ" and who urged the Colossians to do the same: "Walk in wisdom as regards outsiders, making the most of your time. Let your speech, while always attractive, be seasoned with salt, that you may know how you ought to answer each one" (Colossians 4:5-6). In his discourse to the Athenians

Paul did not begin: "You are raving maniacs, O Athenians; you are worshiping accursed demons instead of God." No; instead he uses, as St. Jerome observes, a certain pious cunning. The inscription on the altar really read: "To the Gods of Asia and Europe and Africa—To Unknown and Alien Gods," but Paul changed it to the phrase "To the Unknown God," omitting the rest. (The original Greek of Acts 17:23 leaves out the definite article.) This civility, continues Erasmus, ought to be imitated by persons whose duty it is to lead pagans—or princes corrupted by bad education!—to piety; they should not at once antagonize with reproaches and insults the men whom they wish to heal, but step by step should bring them gradually to a better mind. If one reads the popular medieval lives of the early martyrs, one admits some truth in the statement of Ruskin that "most martyrs have been made away with less for their faith than for their incivility"![20]

Now to apply these observations to the situation in Utopia (Situation 4). The Utopians recognize the right of Hythloday and his companions to preach Christianity. They frighten no one away from its acceptance, nor persecute him after his entrance into the Church. There is one exception. One recently baptized convert, against the advice of his fellows, discoursed in public about the Christian faith with greater zeal than prudence. He grew so hotheaded as not only to set the Christian religion above all others but also to damn them without ceasing. He shouted that other religions were unholy, their devotees impious and sacrilegious and punishable with everlasting fire. After he had proclaimed these opinions publicly for a long time, the Utopians seized him, and after a trial convicted and sentenced him to exile, not for having scorned religion, but for having created a disturbance among the people. The basis for his conviction was one of the most venerable laws of the Utopians, namely, that no one's religion is to be for him the source or occasion of damage or ill-treatment ("ne sua cuiquam religio fraudi sit").

The people apparently objected so strongly to the violent tactics and crude insults of the neophyte that a riot might have ensued with disastrous results.

It is possible that More is here hitting back at those conservative and unsympathetic schoolmen who could perceive no good in the pagan classics. They were unable "to see that it was within God's purpose to withhold His revelation until its appointed time, to understand that the full comprehension of Christianity demanded a comprehension of how far the best of men could get without Christianity."[21]

Utopus did not enact the law of toleration and peaceful discussion only in order to secure internal order and a united front against foreign enemies and only in view of the likelihood that God might be pleased with a variety and multiplicity of religions. Suppose, Utopus asked, that one religion be true far beyond the rest and that all the others be false? He foresaw how easily it would come about, provided only the affair were handled with reason and moderation, that at some time or other the truth by its own inborn power would come to light and stand out conspicuously. If arms and riots, however, were to decide the issue, he readily perceived that, since the worst men are the most active and the least yielding, the best and holiest religion would go down overwhelmed by the most vain superstitions, as good seed is choked by thorns (see Matthew 13:7).

The humanists of the time often talk, as Erasmus does, of "a certain innate and natural strength of truth" ("nativa quaedam et genuina vis veritatis"), for nothing is more powerful than truth. In his explanation of the adage "Time reveals all things," Erasmus quotes with approval Gellius' citation of an old poet who called truth the daughter of time because, although it may lie hidden for a while, nevertheless in the course of time it comes to light. Sophocles, Thales, Pindar, Vergil, Plutarch, and Seneca had sentiments to the same effect. In a controversy with Jacques Lefèvre d'Etaples, Bishop Fisher in 1519 cited

Jerome's remark against Pelagius that "the truth can be in peril but cannot meet defeat" and then concluded: "How can the truth which is consistent with itself and squares with itself in every way not be all-powerful?" The humanists applied this adage to religion. For example, Ficino, although he might view a natural or common religion as a genus embracing all positive religions (including Christianity) as species, saw Christianity as notably superior to all others. In this respect he is following the Christian tradition. The medieval figure Reginald Pecock felt that, if Jews and Saracens would only hear and understand the arguments to be marshaled by the Christian clergy, they would be compelled by the force of truth to believe in Christ and be converted, whether "they wolden or nolden." Just as the eye at its own pleasure cannot judge and declare whether a white thing be white or not, so the reason at its own pleasure cannot decide and assert that a true thing is true or not true, but must pass judgment according to the evidence set before it.[22]

Thomas More possesses the same confidence in the pre-eminence of Christian truth. In 1506 he had written to Ruthall that the truth by itself, in its naked splendor, is self-sufficient: it has no need to be supported among the faithful by superstitious lies, even of well-intentioned Christians. Two decades later, when the Messenger in the *Dialogue Concerning Heresies* declares his fond wish that "all the world were all agreed to take all violence and compulsion away upon all sides, Christian and heathen, and that no man were constrained to believe but as he could be by grace, wisdom, and good works, induced," More answers without hesitation or doubt "that the good seed, being sown among the people, should as well come up and be as strong to save itself as the cockle, and God should always be stronger than the devil." This would most certainly obtain in Utopia, where every man may follow the religion of his choice and strive to bring others to his creed in a peaceful and reasonable manner. More goes even further. Christianity would win out even if other faiths could be taught in Christendom. "In case the Turks, Saracens, and paynims would suffer the faith of Christ to be peaceably preached among them, and that we Christian men should therefore suffer in like wise all their sects to be preached among us, and violence taken away by assent on both the sides, I nothing mistrust that the faith of Christ should much more increase than decay." The reason is clear: "We should seem to dishonor God if we mistrusted that His faith preached among other indifferently without disturbance should not be able to prosper." Therefore, if the offer were made for the peaceful preaching of their faiths by Christians and non-Christians, More would not hesitate to accept the proposal because of his reliance upon the inborn strength of truth, because of his conviction of the superiority of Christianity, and because of his concern for the honor of God and the salvation of souls. He concludes: "We should hinder the profit if we would refuse the condition, where there be many more to be won to Christ on that side than to be lost from Him on this side." In view of this attitude, it is no wonder that, when Christianity is preached on the island of Utopia in free and pacific competition with other faiths, not a few of More's Utopians become Christians because of the evidence laid before them.[23]

The situation, however, is altogether different in the case of heretics in a totally Catholic country. "As for heretics rising among ourself and springing of ourself, [they are] in no wise to be suffered, but to be oppressed and overwhelmed in the beginning." Christendom could gain nothing from any "covenant" or agreement with them in regard to free preaching on both the orthodox and the heretical side. "For as many as we suffer to fall to them," argues More, "we lose from Christ. And by all them we cannot win to Christ one the more, though we won them all home again, for they were our own before." In spite of his refusal, More goes far by maintaining that, as a matter of fact, "in the beginning never were they by any temporal punishment of their bodies anything sharply handled till they began to be violent themself."[24]

The practical moral foundation for toleration or nontoleration is clearly stated for this period in history by Angelus Carletus de Clavasio (d. 1495?) in his *Summa*. Under what conditions is toleration good and right? When a person patiently undergoes sufferings which afflict himself alone in bodily or temporal goods, or when a greater evil is thereby avoided. Under what circumstances is toleration wrong? When a person endures things which are to the detriment of his own salvation, or when there is no danger of scandal nor of a greater evil.[25]

The theoretical basis for More's rejection of unrestricted preaching by heretics is his belief in the indefectibility and the infallibility of the visible Church of Christ. This Church had infallibly guarded from error the definitive revelation of Christ (the deposit of faith) and had authentically and unequivocally interpreted His doctrine on what men must believe and on what men must do to attain salvation (faith and morals). It would continue to do so and would last until the end of time on account of the continuing presence of the Holy Spirit and of Christ Himself (John 14:16; Matthew 28:20). Its duty is to transmit to posterity Christ's revelation whole and entire without any addition or subtraction (2 Thessalonians 2:14; 1 Timothy 6:20; 2 Timothy 1:13, 2:2; Colossians 2:8). Hence More can think only of the strong statement of St. Paul: "Even if we or an angel from heaven should preach a gospel to you other than that which we have preached to you, let him be anathema!" (Galatians 1:8). More would have shown himself a weak and unfaithful Christian if he doubted that the Catholic Church of his day possessed the true doctrine! He openly proclaims: "If it so be, as indeed it is, that Christ's Church hath the true doctrine, and the selfsame that St. Paul would not give an angel of heaven audience to the contrary, what wisdom were it now therein to shew ourself so mistrustful and wavering that for to search, whether our faith were false or true, we should give hearing, not to an angel of heaven, but to a fond frere, to an apostate . . . ?" (Here, in retaliation for Luther's own opprobrious name-calling, More applies to the reformer a few choice epithets.) If there were any doubt, however, as to the indefectibility and infallibility of the Church, More would utter the prayer of the pious Utopians, who desired God in His goodness to lead them out of any religious error in which they might be and to let them know a better religion if there were one. This is precisely what he says plainly and logically in his *Dialogue Concerning Heresies:*

> Forsooth, . . . if it were now doubtful and ambiguous whether the Church of Christ were in the right rule of doctrine or not, then were it very necessary to give them all good audience that could and would anything dispute on either part for it or against it, to the end that, if we were now in a wrong way, we might leave it and walk in some better.[26]

In Utopia the identity of the true religion, nay, even the very existence of a single true religion, is "doubtful and ambiguous," and consequently free public discussion is permitted and encouraged. Quite otherwise is the situation in England and Europe. The true religion has been in possession for hundreds of years. There is a body of dogmas which cannot be denied or doubted or left open to heretics for public debate. Utopia, too, has its heretics—those who deny the providential care of God, the immortality of the human soul, or the existence of future retribution. We have already seen how Utopus and the Utopians handle their heretics in our discussions of Situations 2 and 3.

How does Thomas More wish Christian heretics to be handled? It is necessary to stress that heretics, not infidels, are in question. In his *Summa summarum* Silvester epitomizes the position of medieval theologians by saying that the rites of infidels, including Jews, could be tolerated sinlessly in order to avoid greater evil and to facilitate greater good.[27]

It is necessary to decide who a heretic is. He is a baptized person who, keeping the name of Christian, obstinately denies or doubts one of the truths which must be believed. The error, explains Silvester de Prierio, rises in his intellect; the pertinacious adherence to the error comes from his will. Heresy, as Erasmus insists, is not any error whatsoever, but stubborn malice in disturbing the peace of the Church with perverse doctrine. A word like *stubborn, obstinate*, and so forth, is very important in the definition. Thus, when Pico ran into difficulties with the authorities in Rome in posting his nine hundred theses, he insisted in his *Apology* that it is not precisely error of intellect that makes a man heretical, but that malice and perversity in will must be present. He claimed that St. Augustine, St. Cyprian, St. Irenaeus, Origen, and others had held opinions which were contrary to later definition and clarification by the Church, and yet they should not or could not be called heretics because they never *stubbornly* refused to believe an authoritative declaration or interpretation by the Church. He proposes his own theses as true or probable only insofar as the Roman Church judges them true or probable, and submits himself to the judgment of Innocent VIII.[28]

The heretic must submit to the teaching authority of the Church. But is the persuasion of the Utopians that "it is in no man's power to believe what he list" not true and right? Here Thomas More might have in mind a proposition defended by Pico, whom Bremond terms "the Prince Charming of the Renaissance." Like Pico, he wishes to startle his reader, but then the latter upon consideration realizes that the proposition can be interpreted in a perfectly orthodox sense. Rome had condemned the following conclusion of Pico: "As no one thinks something is so precisely because he wants to think so, thus no one believes something is true precisely because he wants to believe it is true." Also condemned was the following corollary: "It is not in man's free power to believe an article of faith to be true when he pleases and to believe it to be false when he pleases." In his *Apology* Pico explained his terms and marshaled many arguments to defend both proposition and corollary in an orthodox sense. His proposition, he claimed, was nothing but a view of Aristotle which was universally accepted; his corollary was nothing else than a restatement of the view of St. Augustine (and theologians) to the effect that one cannot believe at will, that is, at the mere command of the will without conviction and motive on the part of reason. If a man is asked why he believes in the Christian rather than the Mohammedan faith, he does not attribute his belief precisely to an act of the will but rather to one of the eight common arguments of theologians, among which are the uttering of prophecies, the stability of the Church, and the fame of miracles. Since Pico had published his condemned theses "only for the sake of scholastic disputation and under the correction of the Holy See" and in his *Apology* had interpreted them "in a better and Catholic sense," Alexander VI cleared him of the charge of heresy when he perceived his "good and uncorrupted mind, his sincerity of faith, and his devotion and obedience" to the pope and Apostolic See. In passing, it must be noted how careful More is to assign motives of credibility, including the teaching and miracles of Christ and the blood of numberless martyrs, for those Utopians who were converted to Christianity.[29]

Man "would not believe," insists St. Thomas Aquinas, "unless he saw that he must believe on the evidence of signs or something similar." In faith the motive is not the internal evidence of the dogma in itself (otherwise the mind would necessarily have to give assent) but the authority of God, testifying to the truth of something man cannot see. Hence the will must intervene to make the intellect accept revealed truth. "The will cannot make the mind believe anything it chooses," says Canon George D. Smith in discussing the act of faith. "Before the mind can accept a statement, even at the behest of the will, the statement must be 'credible'; it must be attested by a trustworthy witness." The witness to revealed truth is God Himself, who has a right to the obedience of man's will. Hence the will freely causes the mind to assent to truths revealed and testified to by truth itself. God, who in His supernatural providence "wishes all men to be saved and to come to the knowledge of the truth" (1 Timothy 2:4), gives all men sufficient grace to attain salvation. Even to the pagan who must believe at least the two truths that "God exists and is a rewarder to those who seek him" (Hebrews 11:6), He gives "such grace as God keepeth from no man," as More mercifully insists, "but from him that, by his own default, either will not receive it or deserveth to have it withdrawn."[30]

How is the believer, as distinct from the pagan, to know what God has revealed? Christ Himself, More maintains, instituted the means of approach to God's truth, namely, His visible Church, which is the guardian and teacher of divine revelation and which is infallible in its duty because the Holy Spirit preserves it from error. The Church exercises its teaching office extraordinarily through definitions by pope or ecumenical council and ordinarily through the universal consensus of bishops on points of doctrine. The individual is not free to decide what is revealed or not revealed, true or not true. Hence More tells the Messenger in the *Dialogue Concerning Heresies:*

> If a known true man tell you an unknown truth, ye believe not him because the thing is truth, but ye believe the thing to be truth because ye believe the man to be true. And so believe you the Church, not because it is truth that the Church telleth you, but ye believe the truth of the thing because the Church telleth it.[31]

In the eyes of Thomas More heretics refuse to believe God, who is testifying to the truth of dogmas through His Church. Their difficulty lies not in the mind but in the will, which declines to offer homage and obedience to the authority of God as witness to the truth. "I say plainly," declares More, "whosoever, being informed of any article of the faith which God bindeth us to believe, believeth it not, the cause why he believeth not is not because he cannot, but because he will not." If the unbeliever will only do his part—namely, "submit his reason unto faith, with asking help of God for the furtherance of his imperfection"—God "would not fail on His part again," More confidently holds, "but would effectually work with him to perfect in him the faith in which He preventeth him by grace." More never neglects to stress the most important factor in faith, to wit, the supernatural grace of God: "To believe well is no little work, and so great a work, that no man can do it of his own strength without the special help of God."[32]

To resume our discussion of the treatment of heretics. Both Utopus in Utopia and More in England have dogmas which all have the moral obligation to believe. Both draw a distinction between those who obey the laws and those who violate them. Let us see how Thomas More behaves toward heretics who are peaceful (Situation 5) and those who use violent tactics (Situation 6).

Arthur Irving Taft succinctly summarizes More's attitude toward peaceful heretics in the trenchant statement: "I can see no reason to suppose that he would molest any heretic who kept his heresies to himself and did not actually violate the laws." When Rich advised him to conform to the mind of king and parliament, More told him: "Your conscience will save you and my conscience will save me." Like Utopus, More respects private conscience but imposes public silence on the denier of religious dogmas and permits him, it seems, to argue only with learned men. Such, at any rate, was his conduct toward Simon Grynaeus and William Roper.[33]

Roper at the time of his marriage with Margaret More was "a marvelous zealous Protestant" who was not "content to whisper it in hugger mugger" but had "an itch of preaching." Matters went so far that, because of his free manner of speaking and his association with the heretical merchants of the Steel-yard, he was arraigned before Wolsey, who, however, dismissed him with a friendly warning in view of the cardinal's regard for More. Harpsfield in his life of More informs us that the saint "reasoned and argued with him in those points of religion," but in vain. Finally, in the privacy of his garden, he told his daughter, Roper's wife: "I will no longer argue nor dispute with him, but will clean give him over, and get me another while to God and pray for him." Where reasoning failed, prayer won. Roper returned to the Catholic Church. As Roper later phrased it, the followers of heresiarchs begin largely through ignorance, stand fast in holding their own opinion, and end in malice. Toward those who err through ignorance and simplicity, More shows much patience: "I would not they were over-hastily handled, but little rigor and much mercy showed where simpleness appeared, and not high heart or malice."[34]

In his defense of Henry VIII's answer to Luther, Bishop Fisher interprets the current situation as follows. The minds of the commons have ever been light and inconstant, and always ready for the worse course, as is proved by examples from profane and ecclesiastical history and from the Old and New Testaments. How can ordinary people pass judgment on subtle dogmas on which even top-ranking biblical scholars can hardly reach conclusions? The commons have no right to deny matters of faith on which preachers, exegetes, and the fathers are in agreement. To Oecolampadius he later approvingly quotes the statement of Erasmus that there are secrets in Sacred Scripture into which God does not wish us to enter. The deeper our attempted encroachment, the greater our blindness, so that we thereby come to recognize the impenetrability of God's wisdom and the feebleness of man's mind.[35]

More practiced great gentleness and generosity toward Simon Grynaeus (1494?-1541), professor of Greek at Basle, who came in 1531 to inspect the abundance of old texts in England. Grynaeus early subscribed to Lutheran and Zwinglian views, with the result that he had to move his residence at least twice. He extorted letters of commendation from the unwilling Erasmus, who advised him to conceal any inclination toward the English sectaries—something that Grynaeus, according to Erasmus' own words, failed to do. More received Grynaeus into his home. As lord chancellor of England More was overwhelmed with public and personal business, and yet he held literary conversations with Grynaeus, who speaks of himself as being merely a "private and unknown person," placed him at his own table, and took him along on his trips to court. More perceived without the least difficulty that Grynaeus' whole view of religion was different from his own in not a few places, as Grynaeus reports, but he dealt with him in a gentle and kindly manner ("placide benigneque"). A quiet and polite discussion of points of doctrine on which they differed, however much the disputants smoldered underneath the surface, must have been inevitable, yet More helped Grynaeus with his active influence and his counsel and stood the costs. In addition, More gave him his secretary, John Harris, as guide and companion on his fruitful travels, and with his letters, as with a magic wand, opened up for him all the libraries at Oxford. He then sent Grynaeus back to Basle overwhelmed with gifts and benefits. Stapleton speaks as if all these very personal attentions by More and Harris were directed toward the hindrance of any proselytism on Grynaeus' part. More, he says, had warned Grynaeus most strictly never to speak a word on religion to anyone. More and Harris, therefore, were merely helping Grynaeus in fulfilling obligations contracted by charity and generosity. Grynaeus often wrote to More in England in support of Zwinglian views and would have dedicated to More his text of Plato, "corrupt in many places," unless Erasmus had successfully dissuaded him. More was extremely grateful to his friend for rendering this service. Little wonder then that Erasmus at a later date was able to write:

"I know Thomas More, Tunstall, and other scholars are far from well-disposed toward Grynaeus."[36]

Such, then, are More's views on the place of peaceful heretics in a world totally Catholic for centuries (Situation 5). His behavior is curiously like that demanded by Utopus in a pagan country which has dogmas of belief obligatory upon all the citizens (Situation 2). Both impose silence in public upon those persons who will not believe the truths which they should believe; both allow such individuals to discuss their doubts and difficulties in private with orthodox priests and learned scholars. Such agreement between Utopus and More forces upon the student the conclusion and the conviction that Thomas More, chancellor of the realm in his early fifties, is consistent with Thomas More, humanist author of *Utopia* in his late thirties, in his policy toward law-abiding heretics.

But suppose that heretics refuse to keep quiet in the presence of the common people and prove indocile and violent in a world totally Catholic (Situation 6)? The problem of the Catholic is analogous to that of the old-fashioned liberal in a contemporary democracy: What is to be one's attitude and conduct toward treacherous and aggressive communists or fascists whose first act would be the destruction of freedom of speech, assembly, and press? "Most heretics of that time," observes Christopher Hollis, "could not be tolerated, because they were quite frank in their admission that they had no intention of tolerating. Heresy therefore had either to be suppressed or to be allowed to dominate."[37]

More insists that "in the beginning never were they by any temporal punishment of their bodies anything sharply handled till they began to be violent themself." Citing as his authorities church historians and SS. Jerome, Augustine, Eusebius, Basil, Ambrose, Gregory of Nazianzus, John Chrysostom, and other doctors, he unhesitatingly points out that in the first centuries heretics suffered no penalty except a fine sometimes for breaking silence, but they endured "only redargucion [refutation] and reproving by dispycions [disputations or discussions], either in words or writing, . . . or finally excommunications and putting out of Christ's flock." The situation changed when heretics began to use violence. St. Augustine had tried patiently to bring the heretical Donatists to reason by "only writing and preaching in the reproof of their errors" and had resisted any attempt to do them physical harm. But when they took to violence, robbery, torture, and murder, he urged the secular authorities "to repress them with force and fear them with bodily punishment." At the rise of new heresies after the decline of Arianism, "good princes," who remembered the damage and disturbance caused by it, "did of their own good minds for the preservation of the peace prohibit and forbid those heresies upon certain pains." St. Augustine, as has been seen, at first "would have been very glad to treat and use those heretics so tenderly that they should have had no bodily harm." But seeing the injury done to good men and the displeasure given to God, he not only revoked his previous opinion but urged the civil authorities to restrain by fear, repress by force, and punish by pain "such obstinate heretics as to the trouble of good quiet people and disturbing of the Catholic faith, with the peril of many poor simple souls, would stir such schisms and heresies." As a matter of fact, St. Augustine never went to the limit of approving capital punishment or of attributing this power to the Church. Fisher concludes a brief history of the punishment of heretics in his *Confutation of Luther's Assertion:* "Accordingly it was necessary either to remove heretics through the death penalty or to suffer innumerable and daily murders of souls," the latter, of course, through the deadly and loathsome sin of heresy.[38]

Erasmus appears cautiously to concur with More. No matter how much he protests against the abuse of power on the part of some bishops who are intent on subduing, torturing, and committing to the flames instead of teaching, correcting, and healing, no matter how much he insists that only the sword of the spirit was used in battle against heretics in the early ages, he holds with St. Augustine that ambitious heretics who gather followers to seize the rule or aim at other temporal gains must be suppressed in order to maintain the state in time of peril. If the dispute ends in seditious tumults and both sides clamor that they are the defenders of the *Catholic* faith, the prince ought to curb both parties until the final investigation of their claims. In view of this right and duty, "what can keep the prince," asks Erasmus against Protestants who had published an extract from a work of his on leniency toward heretics, "from removing out of the way those *heretics* who disturb the public peace, since our princes (nay, even pagan princes) have the same right toward *orthodox* Christians who do so?" In comparison with More, Erasmus seems slow to realize privately, and to confess publicly, the full social and political implications of Luther's ideas in the first decade or so after 1517. Even the radical nature and import of Luther's religious and doctrinal views appear to have escaped him. To him the questions of justification by faith alone and of free will and grace were significant but not essential to the Christian faith voiced in such documents as the Apostles' Creed.[39]

In his *Confutation of Tyndale* Thomas More protests against the Protestants' doctrine that "it is against the gospel of Christ that any heretic should be persecuted and punished and specially by bodily pain or death." Some had extended this freedom even to theft, murder, and treason. (The Protestants seem to be echoing the earlier doctrine of Marsilius of Padua that no one, *according to the gospel*, could be compelled to observe the commandments of the law of God by any temporal penalty or punishment in the present world.) More points to the inconsistency of the Lutheran claim, for "in Almain now, contrary to their own evangelical doctrine, those evangelicals themself

cease not to pursue and punish by all the means they may—
by purse, by prison, by bodily pain, by death." Little wonder
that, in view of the extreme doctrine on the absolute freedom
of the Christian, they have "refused all good laws, abhorred all
good governance, rebelled against all rulers, fall to fight among
themself, and so many thousand slain that the land lieth in
many places in manner desert and desolate." Such was the fate
which Thomas More hoped to avoid for England by the suppression of heresy. He saw the espousal of heresy was bound
up with the disruption of the social order. He laid the blame
for the Knights' War (1522) and the Peasants' War (1524-
1525) in Germany directly upon the teaching of Luther that
"faithful Christians . . . be in a full freedom and liberty dis-
charged of all governors and all manner laws spiritual or temporal." Violence and ruin had always followed upon heresy.
More could not but agree with the cry of St. John Fisher, bishop
of Rochester: "For God's sake, see what a realm the kingdom
of Bohemia was, and when the Church went down, then fell the
glory of the kingdom." England under Henry V had already
learned the rebelliousness of heretics from its experience with
the Lollards under Lord Cobham, and Parliament had therefore
made "very good and substantial provisions" in view of "the
great peril and jeopardy that the realm was like to have fallen
in by those heresies." In a word, More maintains that the government would have "never indeed fallen so sore to force and
violence against heretics, if the violent cruelty first used by the
heretics themself against good Catholic folk [had not] driven
good princes thereto, for preservation, not of the faith only, but
also of the peace among their people."[40]

The difficulty with permitting the circulation of an heretical
work is that "a simple reader might by delight in the reading
be deadly corrupted and venomed." Simon Fish in his *Supplication for Beggars* might appear only to aid in the attack on
greedy clergy, but "a wise man," like Thomas More, "shall

find the whole book nothing else but falsehead under pretext of plainness, cruelty under the cloak of piety, sedition under the color of counsel, proud arrogance under the name of supplication, and, under the pretense of favor unto poor folk, a devilish device of noyance both to poor and rich; priest, religious, and layman; prince, lord, and people, as well quick as dead." Princes must not allow their subjects to be "seduced and corrupted by heretics." The peril is as great as an invasion by the Turks, since the result is the same: "men's souls withdrawn from God, and their goods lost, and their bodies destroyed by common sedition, insurrection, and open war." The best course of action is expressed in the clause: "Principiis obsta." If the first heretics, who are few in number, are repressed and punished, others will be loath to follow. Nor is the bishop cruel in leaving excommunicated heretics to the secular arm. He does not deliver them nor urge the civil authority to punish or kill them, More claims, but merely abandons and forsakes them as not belonging to Christ's flock. How can the bishop do otherwise? Their "conversation," that is, their consorting with others, is "perilous among Christian men." Should the clergy pity them so much as to have them escape punishment of the body and so be free to effect the loss of other men's souls? No; if the heretic "prove himself obstinate and impenitent, the Church neither is bounden nor ought to receive him, but utterly may forsake him and leave him to the secular hands." More plainly tells the Pacifier (Christopher St. German) that he wishes no new legislation or remedies for heresy, which would be ignored or set aside anyway, but desires "to have the good old provisions kept."[41]

More is referring here to the whole traditional procedure against heretics, not merely to the penalties for heresy. As for the latter, Silvester enumerates fourteen in his *Summa summarum*. The first four are the following: (1) excommunication *ipso facto*; (2) social ostracism, as well as a sentence of exile passed by the secular power; (3) confiscation of goods *ipso facto*

or *ipso iure;* and (4) deposition from all offices, even in the
case of pope or emperor. Excommunication could be a powerful
weapon and, if enforced, could have dire consequences. Fisher
in his *Confutation of Luther's Assertion* observes that Savon-
arola was burned at the stake, not because he taught anything
against Catholic dogma or doctrine (since Fisher could recall
nought reprehensible in his teaching), but for this cause only:
contumacious contempt for the ecclesiastical censure of excommunication. Fisher's judgment on the reformer's death for
reasons of discipline, not faith, is interesting as that of a contemporary and orthodox Catholic.[42]

The priests in Utopia perform an analogous function. The
greatest penalty which they can inflict is excommunication, and
this not for heresy but specifically for evil living. (One must
not fail to note, however, how closely with immorality Utopus
links irreligion, for lawbreaking takes its rise in the denial of
the fundamental Utopian dogmas.) If the evildoer after excommunication does not show prompt reformation in the eyes of
the priests, he is seized and made to pay the penalty of his
ungodliness by the senate. Here, as in Christian Europe, the
secular arm intervenes to chastise the culprit, who has not been
delivered to it for punishment, but merely excluded from divine
worship and abandoned by the Utopian clergy.[43]

In More's eyes "there is no fault that more offendeth God"
than heresy. Here he follows Aquinas, who declares unbelief to
be the greatest sin in the whole range of moral perversity. Consequently he was eager to keep it from spreading. He never
resorted, however, to such unjust measures as were laid to his
charge by his heretical adversaries, namely, that "I used to
examine them with torments, causing them to be bounden to a
tree in my garden and there piteously beaten." He maintains in
his *Apology* that there was only one clear case in which he
inflicted corporal punishment in his own house upon any holder
of heretical opinions. Dick Purser, a child and servant in More's

household, had been educated by his father and George Joye, a priest, in heterodox opinions, especially the denial of transubstantiation in the Holy Eucharist. Dick taught this heretical doctrine to another child in More's household. When he learned of this, More caused a servant of his to whip him like a child before his whole household. The phrase *like a child* seems to be opposed to the phrase *like an adult,* and evidently it meant to refer to a beating which was such as a child could readily endure. The whipping was administered for "amendment of himself" so that Dick would desist from heretical teaching and also for "ensample of such other" so that any other member of the household who had an itch for the spread of heresy would be deterred from endangering the faith and loyalty of orthodox members.[44]

This whole discussion of violent heretics in a world wholly Catholic (Situation 6) can best be summed up in More's important statement: "If the heretics had never begun with violence, though they had used all the ways they could to allect [entice] the people by preaching, though they had therewith done as Luther doth now, . . . [that is], bring up opinions pleasant to the people, giving them liberty to lewdness, yet if they had set violence aside, good Christian people had peradventure yet unto this day used less violence toward them than they do now. . . . [W]hile they forbare violence there was little violence done to them." That this view of More was the view of his contemporaries is evident from history. Pure speculation and theoretical discussion were often of secondary importance and were of value only insofar as they served to upset ecclesiastical authority or social and political order. Vermeersch observes that "in the age in which the Catholic religion was the foundation even of society, the heretical faction appeared simply revolutionary." Just as murder and theft were condemned apart from the private sentiments of the murderer and the thief, so heresy was judged socially apart from the private beliefs of the

heretic. Heresy was viewed as the first step in conspiracy and
treason against authority and society. Since religion, and the
Church in particular, was the basis of society, heresy in the concrete order was both a religious offense and a civil crime, no
matter how they might be distinguished and separated theoretically. Political and social motives justified even capital punishment for heresy.[45]

As the result of treachery and force, More feels that heretical sects can secure control of whole countries. But the faith of
the Catholic Church, which is the faith of Christ, shall never go
down into total defeat on account of the assistance of the Holy
Spirit promised until the end of the world. The Church may
lose some nations, but at the same time it will gain others, just
as the defection of the northern peoples of Europe was compensated for by the conversion of regions in the newly discovered
Americas and in India and the Far East. For this phenomenon
Thomas More uses an apt figure: "As the sea shall never sur-
round and overwhelm all the land, and yet hath it eaten many
places in and swallowed whole countries up and made many
places now sea that sometime were well-inhabited lands and
hath lost part of his own possession in other parts again, so
though the faith of Christ shall never be overflown with heresies,
nor the gates of hell prevail against Christ's Church, yet as in
some places it winneth in new people, so may there in some
places by negligence be lost the old." What a note of sadness
is struck in the word *negligence!* More is here referring to the
overconfidence of those Catholics who are so convinced of the
strength and invincibility of the Catholic faith that they allow
heretics to talk unchecked and who deceive themselves as to the
spirit of heretics. As we have seen above, More had no doubt
that the true faith of Christ was so reasonable and so powerful
that it was bound to prevail in an atmosphere of peaceful discussion. But such was not the method of heretics, who used zeal,
cunning, and violence to carry the day. Hence "it had been

much more wisdom for all good Catholic men to have waxen
warmer afore and to have repressed those heretics in time
before they grew to so many." Fisher, too, in his *Defense of
the King's Assertion* declares that, if officials whose duty it was
to seize heretics at their beginnings had repressed Luther while
he was a little fox *(vulpecula)*, the Church now would not be
suffering a perilous storm and a universal disturbance.[46]

What amazes one, in the light of the history of the past four
centuries, is the novelty and daring of speculation in the fourteenth and fifteenth centuries. Until the Protestant Revolt the
radical thinker, according to Vermeersch, had much less to fear
from the Inquisition than from his colleagues in the university—provided that he confined himself to speculation. The
invention of printing, too, was hailed with enthusiasm by many
churchmen as the means for the increase of piety and learning.
The multiplication of books dangerous to faith and morals, however, made ecclesiastical authorities devise methods of control.
It is indicative of the temper of the times that in May 1515, the
very month in which More set out on his mission to Flanders,
the Council of the Lateran decreed the censoring of all books
by the bishop or his representative to curb evil influences arising
from Latin translations of Greek, Hebrew, and Chaldean books,
as well as from others edited in Latin or in the vernacular,
which contained errors in faith, pernicious opinions opposed to
the Christian religion, and attacks on high personages.[47]

Catholics seemed indeed to be confidently ensconced in the
seats of the mighty. In a conversation with his father-in-law,
Roper urged upon him the happy state of England and rejoiced
especially in Henry VIII, "so Catholic a prince that no heretic
durst show his face." More went even beyond his son-in-law in
praise of all classes and ranks. But he foresaw clearly the steady
spread of heresy until Catholics would be grateful to worship
under conditions of live-and-let-live. "I pray God," said he,
"that some of us, as high as we seem to sit upon the mountains

treading heretics under our feet like ants, live not the day that
we gladly would wish to be at a league and composition with
them to let them have their churches quietly to themselves so
that they would be content to let us have ours quietly to ourselves." In a word, More foresaw a state of affairs in which all
Christian sects would live in a state of mutual tolerance and
would be free to maintain their churches and to preach their
doctrines in peace. This religious toleration would be demanded
by the very *raison d'être* of the state: the maintenance of order
and prosperity for its citizens. This would constitute Situation 7,
that of a state once wholly Catholic but now split into many
Christian sects.[48]

We have seen above that More's policy for Situation 5, that
of peaceful heretics in a world entirely Catholic, is similar to
Utopus' regulation for Situation 2, that of law-abiding dissenters in a pagan country which has a number of necessary
beliefs. Likewise we have discovered that More's remedy for
Situation 6, that of violent heretics in a world entirely Catholic,
is analogous to Utopus' decree for Situation 3, that of violent
dissenters from his obligatory dogmas. Finally, we should like
to equate Situation 7, that of a world once Catholic but now
divided into Christian sects, with Situation 4, that of a pagan
country in which Christianity is now one of many religions. We
cannot do so. Even in Situation 4 in Utopia a person had to
believe in the immortality of the soul, divine providence, and
future retribution. So, too, in Situation 7, which describes the
Christian world after the Protestant Revolt, a person had to
believe, under penalty of political or social sanctions, in Christianity of some form or other: certain restrictions were laid upon
non-Christians, whether Jews, Mohammedans, or atheists. Situation 7, therefore, cannot be compared with Situation 1, that
of a state in which no truths are proposed for the people's belief. In Situation 1, a state in the face of natural and supernatural religions allows its citizens to deny all religious truths

and to defend freely the nonexistence of God, the mortality of the soul, and so forth. In Situation 7 a state in the presence of a supernatural and revealed religion (Catholicism formerly triumphant) does not permit its subjects to deny all Christian dogmas and to preach against the existence of God, the divinity of Christ, and other equally fundamental doctrines. Utopus and More never even considered seriously such a state of affairs as would exist in Situation 1.

It is now possible for us finally to answer the question: Did More alter his youthful views on tolerance, as expressed in the *Utopia*, when he became an important governmental official later in life?

Before we attempt to draw any conclusions, we must point to one fundamental difference between the situation in Utopia and in England which penetrates and permeates every aspect of our comparison. Utopus—and we must insist that More was never in Utopus' position—faces the whole problem of religious toleration as a man who is mainly a searcher for religious truth and the true religion and who asserts the obligation of believing only the most fundamental religious truths, such alone as reason can reach. More confronts the toleration of heresy as one who is secure in the possession of religious truth and the true religion and views himself as the defender of the dogmas which an all-wise Christ had committed once for all to His infallible Church under the guidance of the Holy Spirit to be necessarily believed by all men who hope to be saved.

Bearing this distinction in mind, we are forced to conclude: *More is just as consistent as Utopus in the matter of toleration.*

Both have an eye fixed upon the maintenance of public order. Both have certain fundamental truths, intimately connected with the maintenance of public order, which citizens are obliged to believe. Utopus sponsors the truths of natural religion or natural theology, the only truths which he can logically sponsor, since the Utopians have only reason to guide them.

More espouses the dogmas of the Catholic Church, the only truths which he can logically espouse, since he possesses the revelation of Christ as safeguarded by the fifteen-century-old Church under the Holy Spirit.

Both connect belief in their obligatory truths with public morality and safety. For Utopus the person who does not believe in these truths is debarred from public office as unworthy and suspect of a tendency toward lawbreaking. For More the heretics who refuse to believe Catholic doctrine are thereby suspect of rebelliousness against public authority, since history had always shown them to be guilty of violence and insurrection.

Both use much the same kind of toleration toward persons who cling to their heterodoxy but who observe the law of not speaking before the common people in defense of their non-belief. Both inflict punishment upon those who, against the law, publicly espouse and defend their unorthodox opinions, or use violence against orthodox believers, or incite to lawlessness, tumult, and sedition.

Neither envisages a state in which men might believe privately and defend publicly any belief whatsoever.

We must conclude that the older More is, *mutatis mutandis*, at least as consistent as the Utopus depicted by him a few years earlier in the *Utopia*.

So much for the views of tolerance held by Utopus and Thomas More.

Provided that they believe in the existence and providence of God and in the immortality and reward of the human soul, the Utopians are left free to hold any other religious truth. Beliefs, however, must satisfy two conditions: (1) they must have some foundation in rational argument and (2) they must not be conducive to immoral living. If these requirements are fulfilled, no prohibition is laid upon the defense and preaching of apparently heterodox views. For example, not a few Utopians who have some reason on their side and who lead upright lives err in the maintenance of an extreme view of immortality. Far from upholding the perishability of the human spirit, they think that the souls of even brute animals are immortal. Such souls, of course, are not comparable in dignity to the souls of men, nor are they destined to a future happiness equal to that of human beings. Why does More even mention such an opinion in the *Utopia?* Perhaps in order to show European thinkers that it is more reasonable to extend the concept of immortality too far than to deny it altogether. Such for More, at any rate, was the verdict of the history of philosophy. Consequently More attributes to some of the pagan Utopians an opinion favored by distinguished pagan philosophers, especially the Pythagoreans and the Platonists. In addition, Plutarch notes in his work *The Teachings of Philosophers* that Diogenes, Anaxagoras, and others, too, conceded to brutes a rational soul. Jeronimo Rorario (1485-1556) wrote to defend the proposition: "That brute animals use reason better than man." As far as More himself is concerned, it is interesting to observe that, when in his *Dialogue Concerning Heresies* he makes an appeal for the interpretation of Scripture, not by itself alone, but also by the articles of faith and by reason, he offers the following example: "What if you would upon this text, *Homines et jumenta salvabis, Deus* (God, Thou shalt save both man and beasts), ween that beasts had immortal souls as men have and that man and beast should be both saved at last and so that no deadly sin should be punished with everlasting pain . . .?" The view that brute animals possess rational and immortal souls is opposed to the constant teaching of traditional Christianity.[49]

Death, Euthanasia,
Suicide

Even the Utopians who believe in the immortality of animal souls, as we have seen, hold that their future happiness is inferior to men's. Almost all of them hold as certain and proved that the beatitude of man will be so immense that, though they shed tears over the sickness of all, they utter lamentations over the death of none. This is not true in the case of those persons whom they see to tear themselves away from life in a spirit of anxiety and reluctance. They consider this behavior a very evil omen, as if the soul in despair and with an evil conscience dreaded its departure because of a certain secret premonition of imminent chastisement. God is far from pleased with the coming of the soul which, when summoned, does not run to Him joyfully but has to be dragged in unwilling protest. The spectators of this kind of death feel a cold fear and conduct the obsequies of such a dead person in sadness and in silence. They beseech God to be gracious to his spirit and mercifully to forgive his frailties. Then they cover the body with earth.[1]

In his *Four Last Things* Thomas More points to the solicitations and machinations of the devil, who now has his last chance to win the soul, as the source of both pain and peril to dying men. The enemy of God and man, "when we draw to death, doth his uttermost devoir to bring us to damnation, never ceasing to minister, by subtle and incogitable means, first unlawful longing to live [and] horror to go gladly to God at His calling." In fact, if it is a question of dying for the faith, More declares, "he is truly a brute beast, destitute of true reason, who is so pusillanimous as to yield on account of mere fear, who is conquered before the battle by the mere exaggeration of future hardship so as to be struck down not by a spear but by a blast of the war-trumpet." Ordinarily there are three things, according to the *Dialogue of Comfort against Tribulation*, that make men loath to die: "lack of faith, lack of hope, or finally lack of wit." More then proceeds to discuss each of them. The intention of making amends for one's evil life in the past, however, may before God excuse reluctance to die. For, as Lupset observes in his *Treatise of Dieying Well,* a man fears death either because he has done nothing worthy of reward in heaven or because he has committed deeds certain of future punishment. If he lives, he will have on earth an opportunity to remedy the situation. Ficino uses even this fear of death to testify to the immortality of the soul. Pleasure and pain, he argues, presuppose knowledge. Just as a man longs for the state of life because of the pleasure associated with it, so he fears the state after death because of the pain which he is likely to receive in it.[2]

More, however, is not so indifferent and inhuman as to allow man no reasonable perturbation at the approach of death. Fear can arise less from an evil conscience than from the weakness of nature. If Christ commands us, when necessary, to suffer even martyrdom for His sake, "yet doth He not, for all that, command us so to strive against nature as not once to shrink at death." Christ Himself in His agony in the Garden of Gethsemane, as St. John Fisher declares, felt sadness and fear at the approach of His passion and death on account of "so great an amity between the soul and the body, and so surely a joined knot and bond, that disseverance of them is too painful." Moreover, unless a man, be he ever so perfect, knows by divine revelation that he is in a state of grace, he has reason for "the dread of the judgment of Almighty God . . . for of another manner be the judgments of God than of men." The Christian should fear death less than sin, remain always rational in his view of death, and refuse to be consumed by excessive sadness at its approach. Erasmus knew people who trembled at the very mention of death and yet were pillars of bravery and constancy when death met them face to face. Geiler's *Bark of Penitence* employs a striking simile from St. Gregory's *Morals* to answer the question: How can a man both fear death and rejoice at its approach? He says:

> A stout-hearted man at the approach of battle begins to put on his armor, shakes and yet hastens, trembles and yet rages, seems to grow pale through fear and yet presses forward through wrath. In just the same way, a holy man at the approach of death is troubled on account of the weakness of his nature and yet is made strong on account of the firmness of his hope, is agitated at the nearness of death and yet rejoices exceedingly because of a truer and happier life after death.[3]

If the Utopians bury unwilling sufferers of death in silent sadness, none of them bewail the departure of those who die marked by cheerfulness and filled with good hope. They are far, however, from the unreasonable attitude of the Thracians, who, considering it best not to be born, greeted the birth of infants with tears and the death of persons with banquets and dances. In their cheerful hope the Utopians are like scores of pagans who had borne their death with a high, unbroken spirit. Mantuan, in a fashion typical of a Christian humanist, declares that Zeno, Cleantes, Chrysippus, Cato, and Empedocles committed suicide only to get to the happy life of heaven more quickly, and then asks whether Christians should not forego brief pleasures in order to sustain every struggle manfully and thereby gain eternal felicity. Is it not a disgrace, asks Erasmus, that these pagans should surpass Christians in fortitude of soul? In *The Religious Banquet* he has Chrysoglottus quote Cato (in

Cicero's *De senectute*) and then comment: " 'Oh! glorious day will that be, when I shall leave this rabble rout and defilements of the world behind me, to go to that society and world of spirits!' Thus far out of Cato. What could be spoken more divinely by a Christian?" In the same dialogue Uranius says of another sentiment of Cato: "And what could be spoken more divinely than this, 'I depart as from an inn, and not a habitation.' " Man is but a wayfarer upon earth with his lasting home elsewhere. Erasmus' Franciscan friend, Jehan Vitrier, had caused the reformation of many men and women, "whose death-beds showed how far they differed from the common run of Christians in these days." While the latter drew their last breath tossed between hope and despair, the former "met death with the greatest cheerfulness of spirit, singing a truly swan-like song at its approach." After Christ's victory over the kingdom of hell, Erasmus explains in his commentary on Psalm 38, devout men do not wail at the imminence of death but desire to be dissolved and to be with Christ and sweetly fall asleep with an assured hope of reawakening.[4]

Thomas More was certainly among the number of devout Christians who had no unreasonable fear of death. In Ellis Heywood's *Il Moro*, because More's life corresponded exactly with his words, the audience admires his description of how a brave man gladly bows his head as one who through great fortitude of soul has more hope of life than fear of death. During his imprisonment Margaret Roper wrote to him of her admiration for his "very virtuous and ghostly mind, rid from all corrupt love of worldly things, and fast knit only in the love of God and desire of heaven, as becometh a very true worshiper and a faithful servant of God." His prayer had always been for "the grace so to spend my life that, when the day of my death shall come, though I feel pain in my body, I may feel comfort in soul and . . . part hence into Thy glory." His model, Pico della Mirandola, in the interpretation of Psalm 15 asserted that meditation on our heavenly country makes us ever long for death as departure from a vale of misery. On his own deathbed Pico comforted himself less with the consideration of the end of his sorrows than with the thought that death puts an end to the opportunity and ability to sin. More early translated both Pico's biography and interpretation of Psalm 15. He also translated a Greek epigram on not fearing death: "Is it not stupid to fear death, which is the mother of peace? which banishes disease and dismal poverty? Death alone visits miserable mortals only once . . ." From his prison he wrote to Margaret Roper that an early death was "more than manifold recompensed by coming the sooner to heaven" and to Antonio Bonvisi that heaven means "rest, where shall need no letters, where no wall shall dissever us, where no porter shall keep us from talking together." In his *Four Last Things* he declared that meditation on death, too, was profitable. Plato and other famous pagans had described philosophy as "the meditation or exercise of death." Just as death is the liberation of the soul from the body, "so (said they) doth the study of philosophy labor to sever the soul from the love and affections of the body while they be together." In *The Praise of Folly* Erasmus explains that Plato thus defines philosophy "because it leads the mind away from visible and bodily things, and certainly death does the same." For a true philosopher, therefore, death is far from gruesome and frightening.[5]

Of what sort are the obsequies of that Utopian who meets death full of eagerness and hope? The survivors do not bewail him with cries and trappings of mourning (such is the full force of the Latin verb *lugere* used by More) but they attend the corpse with song. His soul they commend to God with great affection; his body they consign to the flames with greater reverence than grief. They then erect a column with the distinctions of the deceased engraved upon it. But their veneration of the man does not end with a mere monument. Upon their return home they review his character and behavior, but speak of no aspect of his life with greater frequency and pleasure than his joyful death.[6]

If the funeral of a good pagan can be reasonable and noble, how much more should the burial of a Christian be so! The Christian ideal for the survivors of those who die willingly and joyfully with hope in the resurrection is well expressed at this time by Dean Colet: "Over the happy departure, yea and death, of those saints, their friends and relations together rejoice with many congratulations, and pray for a like consummation in Christ of their own lives. . . . Rejoicing through this hope in the departed, and being fully persuaded that he has journeyed to Christ, they carry out the corpse with exultation." He maintains that "nothing is baser and fuller of disgrace, than much weeping for the dead"; that "nothing is more unbecoming our Christian profession . . . than, after the manner of the heathen, to bewail the dead with as many tears, as if our belief were that it had fared ill with them, and not that they were living in the highest bliss with Christ." But this lamentable state now prevails widely among Christians, especially in Italy. "Yet this too," he says, "is what they now practise almost everywhere in the Church, to its discredit; but most of all in Italy, where men shamefully give utterance to womanish outcries at the funerals of their friends and relatives." One suspects a slight anti-Italian bias on Colet's part. An Italian like Polydore Vergil, who resided in England as early as 1502, took special note of the quietness of funerals in England. The inhabitants appeared to think that "it was useless to give a loose to their natural sorrow as men, by any foolish lamentations of God's pleasure to share with us his immortality. And this the more, as by death we bid adieu to the toils and dangers which we enter upon from our very birth."[7]

But the Utopians put Christians to shame not merely by the hopeful restraint of their grief but by the great simplicity of the burial. Both More and Erasmus protest against the excessive display of funeral ceremonies. In *The Funeral,* for example, Erasmus depicts the concern of a dying nobleman and sinner for the details of the funeral pomp: nine members from each of five religious orders, thirty torchbearers, twelve wailers, his horse in mourning, escutcheons on the pall, a marble tomb with his effigy on top in the purest marble, and so forth; yet in Venice a mere cobbler often had six hundred monks in the procession! Thomas More characteristically looks upon this preoccupation of the dying as a temptation of the devil, but just as characteristically he ends upon a note of humor:

> Instead of sorrow for our sins and care of heaven, he [the devil] putteth us in mind of provision for some honorable burying: so many torches, so many tapers, so many black gowns, so many merry mourners laughing under black hoods, and a gay hearse, with the delight of goodly and honorable funerals, in which the foolish sick man is sometime occupied as though he thought that he should stand in a window and see how worshipfully he shall be brought to church.[8]

The manner of funeral among the Utopians presents considerable difficulty for the scholar: they cremate the bodies of those who go to death gladly and inter the corpses of those who die unwillingly. Just why the particular method is designated for each class is not clear. According to Polydore Vergil, who cites Pliny as his authority, Sylla was the first Roman to be cremated, since he feared that his body might later be exhumed and dishonored. Cremation distinguished the Greeks; burial, the Persians. Hythloday himself suspects that the Utopians, whose language is almost Persian but contains Greek words for magistrates and cities, derive their origin from the Greeks. Such descent would explain the retention of cremation as the more ancient and noble form and hence more befitting the virtuous dead. But why burial in the earth, held to be characteristic of the Persians, should be reserved for the unwillingly deceased is hard to explain.[9]

The Utopians' discussion of the good life of the dead serves a twofold purpose: (1) it stimulates the living most efficaciously to the exercise of virtue and (2) it serves as a form of veneration most pleasing to the dead. They opine that the dead are present at these conversations about themselves, although they are invisible to purblind mortals. The reasons for their belief are two: (1) the denial of liberty of moving wherever they wish would be unbecoming the lot of the blessed and (2) the blessed must not be thought to be so unpleasant and unthankful as to have cast off every desire of visiting their friends, to whom they were bound during life by mutual love and charity. Good men after death, in fact, must be thought to experience an increase rather than a diminution of love and charity, as of all other good gifts. The Utopians believe, therefore, that the dead move about among the living as spectators of their words and deeds. In consequence reliance upon such protectors makes the living engage in enterprises more boldly, and the presence of their ancestors deters them from secret acts of shame and disrepute and dishonor.[10]

For the movement and presence of the virtuous dead among the living, Thomas More finds justification in both pagan and Christian sources. In Plato's *Republic*, for example, Socrates asks whether men should not believe Hesiod, who sings that those meeting death gloriously in battle or leading exceptionally good lives become "Hallowed spirits dwelling on earth, averters of evil, / Guardians watchful and good of articulate-speaking mortals." The Athenian in the *Laws* also speaks of "how the souls of the dead have a certain power of caring for human affairs after death." Antoninus in the fifteenth century summarizes the Christian position. Augustine, he writes, expressly denies that the dead know what the living are doing in this life. Gregory, on the other hand, asserts that the souls of those who see God perceive as present everything that is happening here because they are equal to the angels, who, even according to the admission of Augustine, are not ignorant of the activities of the living. Theologians generally have approved the principle enunciated by St. Thomas Aquinas that "the intellect of no blessed lacks knowledge in the Word of everything that concerns it" ("nulli intellectui beato deest, quin cognoscat in Verbo omnia, quae ipsum spectant"). Consequently the blessed see their relatives and friends on earth, perceive the veneration paid them, and hear the prayers addressed to them.[11]

In his declamation on death, in which a dead son addresses his grieving father, Erasmus uses this thought as a source of consolation to the living. The dead person listens to their conversation, and if the heaviness of their bodies did not stand in the way, would administer them a rebuke for their grief over his transference from hardship to happiness, from death to immortal life. In his defense of the intercession of the saints in the *Dialogue Concerning Heresies* More uses almost the same arguments and words which he had employed in the *Utopia*. (1) "When saints were in this world at liberty and might walk about, ween we that in heaven they stand tied to a post?" Such restriction would be unbecoming the happiness which the blessed are granted to enjoy in heaven. (2) "If their holy souls live, there will no wise man ween them worse and of less love and charity to men that need their help, when they be now in heaven than they had when they were here in earth." In the parable of Dives and Lazarus even the rich man in hell was concerned about his five brethren on earth. If this is true, "were it likely that saints, then being so full of blessed charity in heaven, will nothing care for their brethren in Christ whom they see here in this wretched world?" When the Messenger in the dialogue observes that such arguments finally permit one to "pray not only to saints but also to every other dead man," More does not hesitate to answer: "So may ye . . . with good reason if ye see none other likelihood but that he died a good man." The Utopians who die full of eagerness and hope, of course, are

good men and hence after death are aware of the joys and sorrows of their relatives and friends on earth.[12]

This is undoubtedly the place to treat the vexing problem
of voluntary euthanasia in Utopia. The Utopians take extremely
good care of their sick. As for the individual who is ill with an
incurable disease, they sit by his bedside, engage in conversation with him, and use everything they can to alleviate his pain.
Suppose that the disease cannot be healed and is actually the
cause of continual misery and torture to the man? Priests and
magistrates then take matters into their own hands. They tell
the mortally sick person: "You are unequal to all life's duties.
You are a source of trouble to others and a burden to yourself.
You are surviving, as it were, your own death. Therefore make
up your mind not to endure the disease and the light of life a
moment longer. Since your life is torture to you, do not hesitate to meet death. Nay, rather rely upon good hope and release
yourself from this bitter life, as from prison or rack, by your
own hand, or suffer yourself to be rescued from it of your own
free will by the hands of others. Since you sever yourself not
from pleasures but from torture, you would be performing a
prudent act. In fact, you would be performing a pious and holy
act because in the matter you obey the counsel and exhortation
of your priests who are the interpreters of God." The sick man
whom they win by persuasion either ends his life by voluntary
starvation (like Lycurgus, legendary legislator of Sparta, as
Plutarch informs us) or is lulled into an eternal sleep without
feeling the pangs of death (perhaps by a draught of hemlock
as in the famous death of Socrates, perhaps by a large dose of
mandragora, a narcotic described by Erasmus on the authority
of Pliny and Dioscorides). The Utopians never put to death a
diseased person who is reluctant to die and they diminish by
no jot or tittle their solicitous nursing of him. But their persuasion is that death counseled by priests and magistrates brings
honor to its welcomer. Suppose that a man kills himself before

the approval of his reasons by hierarchy and senate? They consider him unworthy of honorable cremation or interment and cast him unburied into a swamp as a sign of his disgrace. Thus, Plato in his *Laws* orders the man who commits suicide without the decree of the state and without compulsion due to unbearable misfortune or disgrace to be buried graveless and nameless in the no man's land on the borders.[13]

No matter how advanced a state of enlightenment and civilization they have attained, the Utopians are still a pagan people and have non-Christian mores. In his *Laws* Plato allows suicide (1) if an individual merely executes on himself the just sentence of the state condemning him to death and (2) if he is "compelled to it by the occurrence of some intolerable and inevitable misfortune, [or] by falling into some disgrace that is beyond remedy or endurance." For those who kill themselves through sloth or pusillanimity "the tombs shall be, first, in an isolated position with not even one adjacent, and, secondly, they shall be buried in those borders of the twelve districts which are barren and nameless, without note, and with neither headstone nor name to indicate the tombs." In the *Republic* he had already spoken of the burial of the impious "in mud in the house of Hades." The second class of suicides is similar to More's, but no permission of the state seems to be demanded by Plato. Unlike Plato, the cynics granted the individual unconditional freedom of committing suicide. The stoics, according to Diogenes Laertius, restricted this freedom to causes similar to Plato's: the needs of country or friends, or overwhelming personal pain, or mutilation, or incurable disease; but for them suicide could become even a duty. Seneca declares that curable illness and mere pain are no excuse for seeking death, but then continues: "But if I find out that the pain must always be endured, I shall depart, not because of the pain, but because it will be a hindrance to me as regards all my reasons for living." The irony of the situation lies in the statement of Diogenes Laertius to the effect that Epicurus, to whose philosophy the Utopians incline, did not view even the loss of eyesight as a reason for withdrawal from life by suicide![14]

The actual policy of ancient states differed widely. In Thebes, for example, suicides incurred the loss of the honors usually paid to the dead. In Cyprus their bodies actually were flung out without burial. On the isle of Ceos, on the other hand, the law permitted or even commanded suicide in certain circumstances. Valerius Maximus notes in Massilia (Marseilles) a custom quite similar to that of the Utopians. The state kept the supply of hemlock and gave it only to those who proved conclusively to the assembly of six hundred their reasons for committing suicide. It was undoubtedly such a regulation which lay at the bottom of four declamations (XXVI, XXIX, XXX, XXXV) of Libanius. According to this writer's imaginative rhetoric, a man should set forth his grievous hardships before the assembly and obtain from it permission for suicide.[15]

The influence of the declamation, a rhetorical composition on an imaginary moral problem in which the exercise of style and talent was the principal end, is glimpsed in this section of the *Utopia* dealing with euthanasia. Thomas More plays first with the definition of suicide. Suicide, of course, must be defined strictly as the direct killing of oneself *on one's own authority*. (This killing is direct when death is intended as an end or a means to an end, whether the actual killing is done by oneself or by another.) The Utopian who lays violent hands on himself *on his own authority* is denied decent Utopian burial, just as a deliberate suicide in the Catholic religion is denied burial from the church and in consecrated ground. But in Utopia the voluntary victim of mercy killing, whether by himself or by others, does not act on his own authority, but on the authority, not only of his government, but also of his official church. Consequently his action is not suicide, not immoral, not reprehensible, but honorable and praiseworthy! It is not the

duty of the rhetorician to point out the flaws in the argumentation in his declamation: his task is to convince and to persuade
and to win his case.

Did Thomas More really believe that church and state had
authority to permit and encourage euthanasia? Hardly! The
Utopians are pagan and need to be set straight by Christian
revelation on this point. They cannot reasonably be expected to
set the pattern for Christians in this matter; otherwise the Christian state would be arrogating to itself illegitimate power over
the lives of the innocent and the Christian Church would be
advocating an action directly opposed to the clear will of God!
Thomas More's views are indicated in *A Dialogue of Comfort
against Tribulation* in chapters which deal expressly with
temptations to self-destruction. His whole argument postulates
the Christian position as set forth, for example, by St. Augustine in his *City of God* and by St. Thomas Aquinas in his
Summa theologica. Among More's contemporaries Erasmus in
his *Colloquies* voices the Christian view when he has one character declare that from the body, which is "the habitation or
house of the soul," "there is no going out before the landlord
calls out," and when he has another character prefer the more
significant comparison of Socrates that "the soul of a man is in
the body as in a garrison; there is no quitting of it without the
leave of the generals."[16]

The state everywhere, as in Utopia, has the right to exact
even the death penalty in order to preserve and vindicate order
against the violation of law. "Of necessity for fear of decaying
the commonweal," enunciates More in the *Dialogue of Comfort,*
"men are driven to put malefactors to pain." Only in the case
of malefactors has God, according to reason and revelation,
been pleased to share with the state His supreme and exclusive
dominion over the lives of men in order to secure the community's peaceful enjoyment of the goods of life. The state has no
such right in regard to the innocent, no matter how much they

burden the community or how little they serve the common good. As for the Church, it never claimed power over human life. Quite the contrary, as More in the person of Anthony declares, "sith there is plain among the ten commandments forboden the unlawful killing of a man, and therefore of himself, as Saint Austin saith, all the Church teacheth." Vincent gives a pat reply: in a private vision, without the intervention of the Church, "God may dispense with that commandment Himself, and both license and command also, if Himself list, any man to kill another man or himself." How is one to convince the would-be suicide that "his vision is but an illusion and not a true revelation"? The distinguishing mark is that a true revelation will not bring one to "the doing or teaching of anything against the Scripture of God or the common faith of the Church." God is unlikely to change His commandment, whereas the devil is likely to speak against it. It is useless to plead the cases of Abraham, Samson, or the virgins who drowned themselves to escape violation. God, says More, never intended Abraham to kill his son, and Samson and the virgins met death, not by their own will, but "by the special instinct of the Spirit of God." Rather, the sources of suggestion to suicide are two: (1) "some devilish fantasy" and (2) oppression by "faint heart and fear." Far from being an act of strength or magnanimity, self-destruction is "plain pusillanimity and impotence of stomach." It is the devil who tempts men to "weariness of themselves after some great loss, some for fear of horrible bodily harm, and some . . . for fear of worldly shame." In fact, the suicide in his attempt to avoid momentary pain in this life falls into everlasting pain in the next.[17]

In his treatment of euthanasia, at least as far as Christians are concerned, More hedges mercy killing about with impossible conditions: (1) The individual must not commit suicide on his own authority. (2) He must secure permission from the state, which, however, possesses no power to grant permission for the self-destruction of the innocent! (3) He must secure the approbation of ecclesiastical authority, which, to be sure, neither claims to have such a power nor would ever allow an act of suicide! If people who are tempted to lay violent hands upon themselves had to get all the permissions necessary for the deed, the number of suicides would be cleverly reduced to nil! Does this mean that More had no serious purpose in this section? More apparently intends to show that, if pagans could even welcome death, Christians should do so no less, since their concept and prospect of a future life with God in heaven are far greater in view of Christ's revelation and grace.

If this treatment of euthanasia does not appear entirely satisfactory, the explanation remains the best that can be offered in the light of present evidence and of the meaning of the *Utopia* as a whole. Self-destruction, even in the case of incurable and dreadful disease, is so opposed to the spirit of Christianity, especially in its teaching on the nobility and salutariness of suffering, that Thomas More cannot, by the farthest stretch of the imagination, be supposed to advocate mercy killing, whether for pagan or for Christian, whether directly by one's own hands or indirectly by the hands of another, even the state.

CHAPTER V

Divination
and Miracles

More passes abruptly from the discussion of dying and the dead to the condemnation of auguries and all the other means by which the apprehensive or curious seek to know hidden facts or to foretell future events. The unusual absence of a transitional word or phrase may perhaps be supplied by the thought: the Utopians enter upon new undertakings more boldly ("res agendas fidentius aggrediuntur") because of their reliance on the protecting spirits of the dead, whereas other peoples will take up no business of importance without the consultation of diviners. At any rate, in the eyes of the Utopians all forms of divination arise from vain superstition. The neighboring nations pay great respect to such practices, but the Utopians make light of them and consider them the legitimate target of ridicule. The form of divination which is singled out for special disapproval in the *Utopia* is astrology. The reasonable Utopians, although great astronomers, have not even dreamed of benevolent and malignant positions of the planets and all the infamous imposture of prophecy by the stars. The marginal note reveals the application to the contemporary scene: the Utopians are ignorant or scornful of astrologers, "but these astrologers have absolute sway among Christians today" ("At hii regnant inter Christianos hodie").[1]

The importance of astrology at the end of the Middle Ages is not exaggerated in the *Utopia*. In the fourteenth and fifteenth centuries, astrologers increased in influence until no pope or emperor, no king or prince, would undertake any significant action without their advice. In the early sixteenth century, there were official astrologers at the courts of Popes Julius II and Leo X. This whole movement definitely marked a regression in human thought and in religion. Several Roman emperors, for reasons sometimes political, had tried to repress astrology, but its practice had survived and continued. Aristarchus of Samos and Sextus Empiricus were its avowed opponents in Greek, Cicero and Juvenal in Latin, but their protests were without success. More might very well have known Cicero's dialogue *De divinatione* (printed as early as 1471), in which he explodes the belief in all kinds of investigation of the future with a view to the avoidance of unpleasant or disastrous events. Since astrology contained many teachings opposed to Christianity, the early Church strongly fought it and, after the triumph of Christianity, caused its disappearance for centuries in the West. St. Augustine in particular attacked it, but tried to distinguish it from the true natural science of astronomy. In the Middle Ages, astrology found its devotees in Arabian and Jewish scholars, whose influence grew steadily in Europe from the time of the Crusades. The discovery of the classical astrological texts by humanist scholars undoubtedly helped to establish and confirm its authority. Petrarch had attacked astrology a number of times, but without making an impression. It remained for Pico della Mirandola, More's ideal, to deliver a telling blow in his *Twelve Books of Disputations against Astrology*. On the appearance of this work, Ficino wrote Poliziano that he agreed with Pico and tried to reconcile statements in his earlier *Life* with it. Erasmus is of one mind with Pico and his friend More on the point. The superstition of augury, he observes, has been exploded among Christians, "but in its place has succeeded an evil almost more pestilential and even doubled, namely, the evil coming from those who announce the future from the stars." These astrologers and their fellow "prophets" impose not only on the vulgar throng but on kings and rulers of the earth. To foresee future happenings, the latter should use a prudence based on knowledge of past and present, and not depend upon prognosticators and astrologers, a race that is false and seditious and noxious to the commonwealth. Alexander Barclay in England had expressed the same thought strikingly in his translation of the *Ship of Fools* (1509):

> Wherefore, have done, just man, note this sentence:
> A man of wisdom, virtue, and science
> Shall guide the stars and they shall him not guide.

Locher in his Latin translation of Brant's *Narrenschiff*, too, had attacked *astrologiae vanitas*. By the time that Albert Pighi published a defense of astrology at Paris in 1519, he lamented the reputation for profaneness and superstition which had been given it of late by scholars, "and especially by our theologians who deem ignorance religion."[2]

More was the implacable foe of astrologers. Against them he wrote a number of clever Latin epigrams. Six were directed against "an astrologer who is the husband of an unchaste wife": the stars are too busy or too helpless to tell him what all men know already. In another he observes: "Not the Cumaean Sybil in the ecstasy of her sacred fury sees more certainly with inspired mind the future than that astrologer of mine, brilliant in the divine art, foresees after an inspection of the stars— the past!" In a topical epigram, a preposterous prognosticator declared that the king of France would enjoy peace that year. When the king died at the beginning of the year, the nonplused astrologer seriously adopted his critics' joking interpretation that the king was really enjoying peace! The reproach of astrology is more solemn and bitter in "A Rueful Lamentation . . . of the Death of Queen Elizabeth" (1503):

Yet was I late promised otherwise:
This year to live in wealth and delice.
Lo, whereto cometh thy blandishing promise,
O false astrology and divinatrice,
Of God's secrets making thyself so wise!
How true is for this year thy prophecy?
The year yet lasteth, and lo now here I lie.

Late in life, in his *Dialogue Concerning Heresies,* More had not changed his views about divination. He views as superstitious necromancers' "circles, within which they think themself sure against all the devils in hell," and this "by reason of foolish characters and figures about it, with invocations of evil spirits and familiarity with devils." In view of More's strong feeling it is little wonder that, on the basis of reason alone without dependence upon revelation, the inhabitants of Utopia reject and scorn all kinds of divination, including astrology, as vain and ridiculous.[3]

The attitude of the Utopians is not the same in the case of miracles. Miracles which occur by no help of nature are venerated as works of, and witnesses to, the presence of the Supreme Power. The diviners in surrounding countries seek to astound their audience with their tricks and wonders, most often with little practical, significant, or edifying result, whereas the miracles obtained by the prayers of the Utopians solve great crises. In fact, profitableness rather than strangeness, declares More in the person of Anthony in the *Dialogue of Comfort,* is "a good mark between God's miracles and the devil's wonders. For Christ and His saints have their miracles alway tending to fruit and profit. The devil and his witches and necromancers, all their wonderful works, draw to no fruitful end, but to a fruitless ostentation and shew." Erasmus, too, finds a true miracle characterized by profit *(utilitas)* and not by wonder *(admiratio).* More's use of the term *miracle* is much more exact than would be expected in a nontechnical work like *Utopia. Miraculum* in

the broad sense is that which inspires wonder ("quod mira-
tionem excitat"), consequently any effect or event which transcends or deviates from the laws of nature. In an exact sense,
Suárez observes, a miracle is "an extraordinary and rare work
deviating from the ordinary law of God and surpassing every
power of natural causes." In the strictest sense, it is an extraordinary work which exceeds the power of all created nature,
whether the creature be human, angelic, or diabolic: it is a
work capable of accomplishment by God alone. When More
characterizes the Utopian miracles as occurring "by no help of
nature" ("quae nullo naturae proueniunt adminiculo"), he
must be taking *nature* in its most generic form as both human
and superhuman, especially since diviners, magicians, and sor-
cerers were supposed to perform their wonders with demoniacal
assistance as well as human ingenuity and since the Utopians
recognize the works as coming from God alone. Unlike the
deists and rationalists of later centuries, the Utopians, by the
light of reason, admit the possibility of miracles. The laws of
nature are contingent and dependent upon a higher efficient
cause. It is not repugnant for God to intervene, on account of
His liberty, wisdom, and omnipotence. The Utopians agree with
what More was to say in his *Dialogue Concerning Heresies:* "If
reason and nature show you there is a God, doth not reason
and nature show you also that He is almighty and may do what
He will? . . . [R]eason and nature doth not show you that . . .
miracles . . . precisely could not be done, but they taught you
only that they could not be done by nature. . . . And they confess both that miracles be possible to God; and they that report
them do report them for things done by God. And therefore they
do report you none impossible tale."[4]

The Utopians not only concede the possibility of miracles
but actually report that they frequently are performed even in
Utopia. Sometimes in important and critical affairs they make
public supplication and with assurance and confidence ("certa

cum fiducia") expect and obtain them. They fulfill the three conditions set down by Suárez for those whose prayers result in miracles: faith in the omnipotence of God in general, a sure belief in God's intervention in this particular instance, and a certain confidence *(fiducia)* which thence results in the will. Their miracles therefore should occasion little surprise.[5]

At this point a difficulty presents itself. In his *Utopia,* Thomas More definitely has miracles being worked in a pagan country; in his later English works, he seems clearly to hold that miracles can occur only in the Catholic Church. "God hath left His miracles," he tells Tyndale in his *Confutation,* "for a mark of His true Church and, by the means thereof, for a mark of His true doctrine too . . . from all the faithless and fained faithful folk, . . . in that God would leave all those congregations void of all miracles, whereby hath been His perpetual custom to declare and magnify His truth." If Tyndale should claim that the Turks also have miracles, More would use a dilemma: (1) Tyndale should prove his claim by the clear words of the Scripture in which alone he trusts or (2) More, conceding the point for the sake of argument, would prove to Tyndale "by plain Scripture that there be neither none such, nor so many done among them as these be that be daily done in Christ's Catholic Church. . . . And therefore am I very sure that neither paynims nor Turks be able to match our Church in miracles." More then delivers a telling thrust: "And of this am I as sure as that the false churches of heretics do no miracles at all!" "And if there had been very miracles of God done for any sect whom we call heretics," More had observed earlier in his *Dialogue Concerning Heresies,* "that sect had been no sect of heretics but the very Church, or else had God by miracles testified the truth of a false faith, and that is impossible." True miracles of God can happen only in the true Church of Christ: "Never hath there been any done for the doctors of any sects of heretics." As for "paynims, Turks, and Saracens, . . . he suffereth the devil sometimes to delude [them] with wonders and marvels."[6]

But in the *Utopia* More credits the miracles to God, not to the devil! Have we later a retractation, a denial, on More's part of what he had held fifteen years earlier? If possible, a reconciliation should be effected in the interests of truth and charity. And an explanation, it appears, is at hand. All Catholic theologians agree that a miracle *performed in confirmation of a divine message* constitutes an absolutely efficacious motive of credibility. "If a true miracle, which is the work of God alone," declares Canon Smith, "is performed by a man *as a sign that his teaching is divine*, it argues an extraordinary intervention of divine power to vindicate his claim, and, since the true God cannot confirm falsehood, the argument is peremptory." This is but an expression of the same view defended by More. An examination of the contexts in the *Dialogue Concerning Heresies* and the *Confutation of Tyndale* from which the passages in the previous paragraph are taken reveals that the controversy centers on the performance of miracles as proof of the true Church of Christ or of true Christian doctrines, such as the veneration of saints. Under this aspect, that is, insofar as they are unmistakable signs of the divine origin of a church or doctrine, no miracles are possible in a non-Catholic denomination. But in addition to using them to set His seal on His true Church and on His saints, God employs miracles, as Ronald Knox observes, also to "prove that He does govern the world"—to prove that divine providence rules the world. The providence of God, as we have seen, is a compulsory dogma of the Utopian religion: Utopus forbade any man to suppose "that the world runneth at all adventures, governed by no divine providence." Their trust in providence is so strong and certain that the Utopians in crises—in the spirit of submission, of course, to the divine will—petition and receive the special exercise of God's almighty power which we call a miracle.[7]

That the distinction just given is not adventitious and arbitrary is seen from the solid authority which can be brought to support it. Theologians maintain that, if God performs miracles among pagans or devotees of a false religion, He never does so in commendation or confirmation of paganism or a false religion but for other ends, such as the defense of virtue or the proof of doctrines held in common with Catholicism. He never does so for a false doctrine as false, but for a true doctrine which happens to be contained in a false religion. In regard to the Vestal virgin who in proof of her chastity drew water in a sieve, for example, St. Thomas Aquinas does not deny that it could have happened by the intervention of God in commendation of her chastity, "because if there were any good things among the pagans, they were from God." In like manner, the miracles among the Utopians do not prove the truth of the Utopian religion as such, but the truth of the doctrine concerning the providence of God.[8]

A miracle in its broadest sense, as has been noted above, may denote whatever excites wonder, especially if it transcends the capacities of merely human or natural causes. Thus, the development of a seed into a plant can be called a miracle since no creature can produce such an effect, but it is not a miracle in the strict sense because it is an ordinary, not extraordinary, occurrence. The Utopians not only venerate unusual miracles occurring "by no help of nature" but esteem the ordinary, everyday miracles of nature. In their eyes, the contemplation of nature and the divine reverence and praise which it engenders constitute a worthy form of worship agreeable to God. This thought is a commonplace in Christian philosophy and scarcely needs much confirmation from other sources. But to cite pertinent instances. Pico in his *Dignity of Man* declares: "Nothing urges man to religion, to the worship of God, more than the assiduous contemplation of God's wonders. When we shall have explored them well through this 'natural magic,' we shall be animated more strongly to the great love of the Workman and shall be compelled to chant that famous refrain, 'The heavens are full, the whole earth is full, of the majesty of Thy glory.' " Having observed that the whole function of the philosopher is to investigate the principles and causes of the universe in its parts and as a whole, Ficino in a letter concludes: "Not only the whole world everywhere shouts to us, but also the interpreter of the world and true philosopher of God assiduously proves to us and exhorts us, that we should acknowledge and love God." Erasmus gives expression to the same thought in many places. In the colloquy *The Epicurean*, for example, Hedonius tells Spudaeus: "What can be a more noble spectacle than the contemplation of this world? . . . [A] godly man, with religious and pure eyes, beholds the works of God his father with great pleasure of mind, admiring everything, finding fault with nothing, but giving thanks for all things, when he considers that all these things were made for man, and so in everything adores the omnipotence, wisdom, and goodness of the Creator, the footsteps of which he perceives in the things created." In the introduction to his *Adages*, he quotes with approval Pliny to the effect that "in the tiniest living things, such as a little spider or gnat, there is a greater miracle of nature than in an elephant." Because of the intimate relation which they perceive between the contemplation of nature and the adoration and praise of God, the Utopians merit the encomium which Ficino pronounced on ancient philosophers: "The whole philosophy of the ancients is nothing else than learned religion."[9]

CHAPTER VI

Asceticism
and Good Works

Not all Utopians spend their time in the investigation of the universe or in the study of the arts and sciences. Individuals who are not intellectually inclined are permitted to use their leisure hours in the exercise of their particular craft and are praised for their pains on account of their usefulness to the commonwealth. The virtue of religion, not personal disposition and propensity, leads others—and these by no means are few in number—not only to pay no attention to contemplation and learning, but to pass not even a single moment in idleness. They are resolved to merit the felicity coming after their appointed day of death in one way—by continual labors and friendly services. Thus, some devote themselves to the nursing of the sick, others to the repairing of roads, the draining of ditches, the rebuilding of bridges, the excavation of turf and stones and sand, the felling of trees, and the transportation of wood, fruit, and other things into the cities by teams of horses. Not only for the state, but also for private individuals, they act the part of servants and thralls lower than slaves; for willingly and cheerfully they take upon themselves without reservation the most dangerous, difficult, and dirty work, from the performance of which the effort required, the loathing aroused, the seeming hopelessness of the task deter the majority. They provide restful leisure for others of the citizenry, but they themselves are engaged in continual work and toil. They are far, however, from blaming or insulting the manner of life of others, or from priding themselves on their own. The more these men take upon themselves the role of slaves, the greater honor they acquire from the whole community.[1]

The section on Utopian ascetics, somehow or other, embodies More's views of monks and friars at the time of the writing of *Utopia*. Thus, in his letter to a monk about four years later, More recalls the ancient monks who would not read even letters from their friends—in complete contrast to contemporary contemplatives who scan books of heretics and schismatics and immense volumes filled with sheer trifles. This statement does not mean that More wants monks to remain ignorant, but that he longs to see them live up to the life of retirement, contemplation, and prayer which they profess. A scholar must be careful, therefore, to tread here warily. On the one hand, he should not ignore the whole passage in *Utopia* as irrelevant to More's real position, nor, on the other hand, be ready to accept it as his final verdict. Instead, a close analysis of the passage in its context and against the contemporary background may enable us to draw some conclusions on More's attitude, especially in 1515-1516. Emile Telle believes that antimonasticism was "the primordial phenomenon of the Pre-Reformation" and that for Erasmus' contemporaries the recurrent and troublesome problem was the dilemma: monasticism or marriage? According to Telle, Erasmus discredited attempts to restore monastic discipline and instead held up the ideal of a "true Christian," living outside the cloister as a married and active man—like Thomas More.[2]

In his life of More, Stapleton explains his failure to become a monk or friar by the simple statement: "Perhaps it was that the circumstances of the time were not propitious to his desire of embracing a stricter life, for our religious communities had

become lax." More's spiritual director, John Colet, too, if
Erasmus' account is trustworthy, longed to leave the cares and
temptations of the world "if he could only have found a frater-
nity anywhere really bound together for a gospel life." As it
was, Colet felt "but very little liking for monasteries,—unde-
serving of the name as many of them now are." Barclay in the
Ship of Fools harshly condemns the religious who have lost the
spirit of their original institute and become hypocrites, hiding
every vice under their habit, but then charitably continues:

> But I shall not so sharply them repreve:
> I am full loath religious men to grieve
> Or discontent; for, if I so do wolde,
> A mighty volume could not their vices hold.

But the more one studies the situation on the eve of the Protestant Reformation, the more one is inclined to accept the verdict of J. S. Brewer on the state of the religious orders:

> That the corruption was either so black or so general as party
> spirit would have us believe, is contrary to all analogy, and is
> unsupported by impartial and contemporary evidence. The gen-
> eral complaint against them is that of ignorance and bigotry;
> and—what an Englishman would now consider as the root of
> all evil—the absence of an ostensible employment.[3]

As an example one might cite the defects noted by Archbishop Warham in his visitation made in 1511: absence from
divine services, conversation in choir, visits outside the monastery sometimes even to questionable places, eating outside the
common meals, lack of care of the sick, failure to educate
novices in Latin grammar, poor serving of food, neglect of lay
servants, failure to take care of lights in the chapels, and so
forth. John Morton, who was a predecessor of Warham's, had
received from Innocent VIII in 1489 a bull for the restoration
of Cistercians, Premonstratensians, and other exempt orders
to their original rule because these religious had gradually left
their first way of life and had grown tepid and because in cer-

tain monasteries the inmates, "giving themselves up to a reprobate sense and setting aside the fear of God, are leading a life
wanton and exceedingly dissolute." In an admonition dated a
year later, Morton accused the abbot of St. Albans not only of
laxity in general but also of tolerating the profanation of sacred
places by the rape of nuns, the effusion of blood, the sale of
church vessels, and so forth. Morton cited in particular the case
of a married woman who against the will of her husband was
residing in a priory and having relations with Thomas Sudbury
and other monks. One must note that these are accusations
leveled against the abbot, not charges substantiated and proved
in court. Nevertheless the monasteries should have been above
even the suspicion of nefarious deeds.[4]

Idleness might well have been the root of the evil. It is noteworthy that even earlier in the *Utopia* monks and friars are
made the object of jokes on this score. To be rid of them,
beggars who are sick or old are to be made lay monks in Benedictine monasteries. When a friar humorously protests that all
beggars will not be shunted off in this way unless some provision is made for the begging or mendicant friars, the hanger-on
of Cardinal Morton enrages him with the barb: "The Cardinal
has made excellent provision for you already when he decided
to curb and put to work all vagabonds, for you are the greatest
vagabonds of all!" Erasmus, too, protests against all those trav-
eling everywhere up and down the country, who have learned
no craft to live by but who carry about with them purchased indulgences and dispensations to be sold for the expenses of their
journey. He attacks especially persons who have the wealth of
satraps at home but who honor themselves in public with the
title of *mendicants*. When Erasmus in 1519 points out to Albert
of Brandenburg the causes of the Lutheran trouble, he inveighs
especially against the mendicant orders: their spirit of proud
tyranny which makes them formidable even to the Roman pontiff, their greed for gain, their sermons on new and shameless

dogmas and not on the teachings of Christ, and so forth. They
are poles from the spirit of the humble, hard-working, and devout ascetics in Utopia. Erasmus declares that he has no quarrel
with religious who live a life actually dependent on the proceeds
of begging, but opines that they would do better if all their able-
bodied members could provide with their own hands the means
for supporting themselves and other poor people. Once upon a
time, he maintains, manual labor was characteristic of monks.
Jerome, whose letters he edited, had written in his *Rule for
Monks:* "Do some work so that the devil may find you always
occupied." Geiler in his *Bark of Penitence* pointed out that the
founders of religious orders, even the Carthusian, had prescribed some manual work, such as copying and binding manuscripts, cultivating little gardens, and so forth. In fact, as
G. Roger Huddleston observes, monks, as distinguished from
mendicants, had to be self-supporting and hence to engage in
manual labor or external work. The oldest monasteries were
located in hitherto uninhabitable places, where "[g]radually
forests were cleared and marshes drained, rivers were bridged
and roads made; until, almost imperceptibly, the desert place
became a farm or a garden"—words curiously echoing the
passage in *Utopia* under discussion. Suppose modern religious,
asks Erasmus, give as a pretext that a trade is demeaning? The
answer is ready: If the working of hides (for tents) did not
demean St. Paul, there is no reason why *they* should fear any
manual work as demeaning. Erasmus returns to the same point
in his defense against Natalis Bedda (Noel Bedier). None of
his strictures have arisen from a hatred of monks. Most lovable
of all men is the monk who is not on the hunt for power and
support but who works with his hands to help the victim of
misfortune and necessity.[5]

This emphasis upon the idleness of religious and their consequent uselessness to the commonwealth helps to explain the
devotion of ascetics to hard manual labor in Utopia. In coun-

tries other than Utopia, "how great and how idle a company is
there of priests and religious men, as they call them"! The
whole monastic state in Europe would be improved if monks
and friars were kept busy with employment profitable to church
and state. The latter, in spite of More's emphasis, does not
necessarily mean only manual work. In his *Answer to "The
Supper of the Lord"* he was to write: "God sent men hither to
wake and work," but "not all men in bodily labor but, as the
circumstances of the persons be, so to be busied in one good
business or other." He himself widens its scope to include all
difficult and unpleasant work which people in general neglect
or shun. Under this aspect, of course, preaching to the poor,
instruction of the ignorant, education of children, and so forth,
are provided for. When the mendicant orders answered the
bishops' complaints at the Lateran Council, they pointed out
that they were charged, not with idleness and laziness, but with
preaching sermons and hearing confessions! (The bishops naturally wished the right to grant permissions for such spiritual
activities in their dioceses.) As a matter of fact, practically
every religious order and congregation has arisen to fill some
crying spiritual or temporal need in the Church. Within two
decades after the publication of *Utopia* the Society of Jesus
would emerge to contribute to the Counter-Reformation by
every possible means. In penning its constitutions the founder,
Ignatius of Loyola, was to emphasize the necessity of some useful pursuit, preferably work from which human nature shrinks
in distaste or desperation. "Every one, so long as he is in good
health," he would write, "must have some spiritual or exterior
occupation, in order that so far as is possible idleness, the root
of all evil, may have no place in our house." And the more
lowly and arduous the occupation, the better it would be for the
individual and his order: "In exercise of abject and mean offices, it is expedient that those be most readily embraced which
are most abhorrent to nature."[6]

At this place in the *Utopia* appears a marginal note: "Active life" ("Vita actiua"). Has the phrase special significance, or is it simply a description of the passage? Does it mean that the Utopians practice the active life only and have not risen to the lofty Christian conception of the contemplative life with its concentration on divine truths (as contrasted with the active ministry and care of souls)? An affirmative answer would be curious because the Utopians love contemplation, especially of nature, with consequent praise of God. What object more worthy of contemplation than the God they praise! The difficulty, of course, is that the number of divine truths which they possess is very few and based only on reason in comparison with the riches of Christian revelation. Consequently the more natural type of asceticism for the Utopians would be the active life rather than the contemplative. At any rate, one is forced to the conclusion that the marginal note has contemporary relevance. Does it imply that all contemplative orders are to be suppressed as socially useless and burdensome? Such would hardly seem to be the view of the orthodox More, who admired at least the contemplative Carthusians. Concretely, the note may boil itself down to an appeal to all orders to make themselves self-supporting and socially serviceable—to eliminate all the abuses of idleness and begging. As a matter of fact, contemplative orders are profitable to society insofar as they take upon themselves the task of penance and prayer to the Almighty in the name of church and state and all mankind. In a word, More wants all orders to shun idleness and to keep busy—and this they will do if they observe their rule and its spirit fervently and faithfully. His friend Colet in *A Right Fruitful Monition* urges his reader: "Every morning, among other . . . meditations and prayers, pray unto thy Lord God that the day following thou . . . mayest use this temporal wretched world in thy thoughts, words, and deeds that by them . . . thou mayest . . . come to the joy everlasting." He declares a little later:

> If thou be religious, remember that the due execution of true religion is not in wearing of the habit but with a clean mind in very deed to execute the rules and ordinances of religion; for so it is that to wear the habit and not to execute the rule and order of religion is rather to be deemed hypocrisy or apostasy than otherwise.[7]

Work, one must hasten to add in order to prevent misunderstanding, is not suggested by humanist reformers as the panacea of all monastic ills. More important, as Erasmus explains, is the gospel spirit in the religious life, which manifests itself also in the refusal of honors, renunciation of all venereal pleasure, contentment with the poorest food and humblest clothing, love of enemies, and prayer and fasting for the salvation of the world. As a matter of fact, Erasmus seems to recommend a return to the free life of the earliest monks, unrestricted by what he considers rigid daily routine, picayunish ceremonies, petty man-made rules, or outlandish garb. As the author of the *Imitation of Christ* had commented earlier: "The wearing of a religious habit, and the shaving of the crown, do little profit; but change of manners, and perfect mortification of the passions, make a true religious man." Many things were more essential to the religious life than work, but work helped to keep the monk from mischief and temptation; for, as the *Imitation* observes, "By useful labor shall his [the Old Serpent's] great approach be barred against him."[8]

The *Imitation of Christ* is the classic embodiment of the New Devotion ("Devotio moderna") and is a manifestation of the early movement of reform in northern Europe. If the author be Gerhard Groote (1340-1384), he was founder of the Brethren of the Common Life; if Gerard Zerbolt (1367-1398), he was the author of their defense entitled *On the Common Life;* if Thomas à Kempis (1380-1471), he was subprior of the reforming Augustinian monastery near Zwolle. The Brethren neither begged nor accepted alms, and labored to support themselves. An early recitation of their rule gives their attitude toward manual labor:

> Daily we labor somewhat with our hands. The individual who is not content to make something daily with his hands, cannot continue longer in his cell, as is narrated in the institutes of the holy fathers [of the desert], of whom blessed Bernard . . . writes: "Our fathers in Egypt and Thebaid, most ardent followers of our way of life, labored with their hands and fed the poor from their labor: they lived from the labor of their hands and dwelt in the labor of their hands. Manual work renders us free of the necessity of coveting the largess coming from others." The same cause moved blessed Paul when he wrote to the Thessalonians: "neither did we eat any man's bread at his cost, but we worked night and day in labor and toil, so that we might not burden any of you." . . . In manual labor, we ought to be faithful and fervent, for "cursed be he who doth the work of the Lord negligently" [Jeremias 48:10].

In particular, the copying of manuscripts is recommended. As in Utopia, three hours before dinner and three hours after it are customarily devoted to manual work. The Brethren took increasingly to education, and by the beginning of the sixteenth century they were managing and teaching in great schools, especially in the Netherlands and in Germany.[9]

The Brethren of the Common Life were not alone in their work of reform. Criticism of the Brethren by members of the mendicant orders made advisable the establishment of a group of them as Augustinian canons regular at Windesheim, which became the center of a congregation which included many houses. The Benedictines, too, had a distinctive reforming organization, the so-called Bursfeld Union. It might have been the members of these three groups for whom even Colet had some respect and admiration. "He was," according to Erasmus' report, "accustomed also to praise certain Germans, among whom there even yet lingered, as he said, some traces of primitive religion."[10]

Colet praised "certain Germans," but Erasmus and More kept their commendation for the Carthusians. The Carthusian order, according to Pourrat, "has always maintained its primitive fervor, and alone has the privilege of never having needed reform." Its type of spirituality exerted tremendous influence on both religious and faithful from the fourteenth to the sixteenth centuries. Especially Denis the Carthusian (d. 1471) "transforms speculative spirituality into affective science." Erasmus' praise of the Carthusians has its reservations, but a single word of praise coming from this inveterate critic of religious is thereby the more remarkable. In *The Praise of Folly*, published five years before *Utopia*, Erasmus explains how "all pursuit of piety" has finally been thrust "upon the Carthusians, among whom, and nowhere else, piety lies hidden—and so lies that it is hardly permissible to find it out" ("in Carthusienses, apud quos solos sepulta latet pietas, & adeo latet ut vix umquam liceat conspicere"). Erasmus clearly concedes the possession of piety by the Carthusians. The latter clause, however, admits of a dubious interpretation. In the favorable sense it might mean that the Carthusians lead a life of such great seclusion that the public catches no glimpse of their genuine devotion to God. A scholion by Gerard Lister, however, in which Erasmus may have had a hand, makes it a statement which damns with faint praise. Erasmus "pays a high compliment to this order," comments Lister, "but lets it hintingly be understood that ceremonies are valued more highly among them than genuine piety—a truth which the more thoughtful members among them admit." The latter seems to be the true interpretation, being substantiated by one of Erasmus' rare defenses—in his own reserved and qualified way—of the religious life, the colloquy *The Soldier and the Carthusian*. The soldier charges the Carthusian with placing "too much confidence in habits, meats, forms of prayer, and outward ceremonies." The Carthusian gives a typically Erasmian defense: "As to myself, I place no confidence in these things, I attribute nothing to them; but I put my confidence in purity of mind and in Christ himself." When the perplexed soldier then wonders at his observance of petty things, the monk gives his reason: "That I may be at peace with my brethren, and give nobody offence. I would give no offence to any one for the sake of these trivial things, which it is but a very little trouble to observe."[11]

In his defense of *The Praise of Folly* addressed to Dorp (1515), More approves the justly merited satire of Erasmus and Noviomagus (Gerard Geldenhauer) against monks and friars guilty of pride, revelling, ignorance, drinking bouts, gluttony, wantonness, and hypocrisy. In his letter "To a Monk" (1519-1520?), More cries out at the great number of religious who apply themselves more diligently to the special ceremonies of their order than to the very commandments of God. Hence the conflicts between orders; hence the dissensions within orders—all on account of the color or cut of a habit or some little point of ceremony. Many consider these minutiae all-important, but think nothing of violations of charity, infractions of their vow of poverty, and rebellion against their legitimate superior. (In an epigram sent by More to Erasmus, November 5, 1517, a friar declares that his monastery contains more than two hundred brethren but not two friends!) They concentrate on their private and peculiar usages, instead of observing, as More ironically observes, "those *plebeian* virtues: faith, hope, charity, fear of God, humility, and others of the same sort." More, however, affirms that, as one accustomed to extol the man poor in riches or noble titles but rich in virtue, he has always loved and revered all religious orders. A few years later he asserted to Bugenhagen that, although some monks had not lived up to the ideals of their order and some orders had degenerated to the morality of the world around them, "nevertheless the most genuine part of the Christian people had ever existed among religious" ("purissimam populi Christiani partem perpetuo fuisse

apud Religiosos"). The latter statement is in agreement with
the observation of Hythloday that the common life still flour-
ished "amongst the rightest Christian companies" ("apud
germanissimos Christianorum conuentus"), namely, the religious orders.[12]

For More, however, ceremonies are also a means to stir up
devotion. He enters actively into the defense of "all the devout
rites and ceremonies of the Church, . . . great part whereof was
from hand to hand left in the Church from the time of Christ's
apostles and by them left unto us as it was by God taught unto
them." They cannot and must not be compared to "superstitious
demeanor and fond fashion of jugglery." And he rises especially to the vindication of the Carthusians: "As for the monks
of the Charterhouse, would God we were no further from very
virtuous devotion than those good men be from unlawful superstition." The meaning of this awkward sentence is simply that
the distance between the Carthusians and vain superstition is
greater than the distance between conscientious Christians and
true zeal; in other words, the Carthusians, far from being superstitious in their observances, are genuinely pious followers
of Christ. As far as work was concerned, the Carthusian lay
brothers cultivated the soil, but the cloister monks copied
manuscripts, usually religious in character.[13]

The ultimate reason for all ascetical practices is found expressed, for example, in Pico's *Interpretation of Psalm XV*,
translated by More and published in 1510: "A perfect man
should abstain, not only from unlawful pleasures, but also from
lawful, to the end that he may altogether wholly have his mind
into heavenward and the more purely intend unto the contemplation of heavenly things." Even the perfect man cannot de-
prive himself of all pleasures. He has but found the highest of
goods and pleasures: "Marvel not though I forsake all thing
to the intent that I may have the possession of God, in whom
all other things also be possessed." He mortifies his senses and

instincts in order to attain the closest possible union with God. All the special observances and penances of the religious orders are but means to this end. Hence, ten years after the publication of *Utopia,* when John Bugenhagen charged that their members placed their confidence in works and cried up works over Christ, More declared that it is pre-eminently they who have always been the most genuine Christians in living according to the norm of the gospel,—they who, selling whatever they possess and giving it to the poor, take up their cross and follow Christ,— they who, dedicating their whole life to watchings, fastings, and prayers, and following the Lamb in chastity, crucify their flesh with its vices and concupiscences. They follow Christ in order to begin, in the least imperfect way, here on earth the life of friendship and union with God which will be consummated in heaven.[14]

This close relation between good works and eternal happiness must mark something basic in More's manner of thinking. Twice in the section on ascetics in *Utopia* he emphasizes the point. Utopian ascetics in general think that continual work and social service earn for them future felicity. The strictest class of them all long to obtain very soon the pleasures of the life to come, precisely by means of their many watchings and great labors. Even earlier in the *Utopia* one learns of the persuasion of the Utopians that God rewards the sacrifice of a brief and small pleasure "with great and everlasting joy" ("ingenti ac nunquam interituro gaudio"). The Utopians, although the noblest of pagans, are nevertheless pagans; and even the most enlightened pagans of classical antiquity emphasized as the reward for good deeds, not the joys of a future heaven, but the testimony of a good conscience, the gratitude of beneficiaries, and the attainment of lasting fame. The Utopians, too, believe these to be the meed of virtue, but also lay uncommon stress on reward in a future life with God. Erasmus gives expression in his *Adages* to the pagan ideal, which, of course, is not his own highest ideal. In his interpretation of one adage, he writes: "Labor for the well-fare and profit of others, and in doing so, look for no other compensation than the satisfaction of having labored in the interest of the greatest possible number of one's fellow-men." In another adage he explains that doing good to others is the path to everlasting fame. In a third he reasons that nature, or rather God, introduces into men a spark of the divine wisdom, namely, the conviction that, even without the prospect of a reward, it is still a pleasure in itself to deserve well of all mankind.[15]

The traditional Christian ideal on the motive of good works finds eloquent voice in the *Imitation of Christ*. A good man's glory and joy is the "testimony of a good conscience" (2 Corinthians 1:12). But a good conscience has a definite relation to the desire and love of the glory of heaven. The voice of the Master whispers: "I am well able to reward thee, above all measure and degree. . . . Are not all painful labours to be endured for the sake of life eternal? It is no small matter, to lose or to gain the Kingdom of God. Lift up thy face therefore unto Heaven: behold, I and My saints with Me, who in this world had great conflict, do now rejoice. . . ." Fundamental to this view is the notion of a meritorious work, that is, a good and supernatural deed which is performed for God's sake and from which arises a right to supernatural reward on account of a divine ordination. To merit, of course, a man must be in the friendship of Christ through grace and love.[16]

For the purity and efficaciousness of a meritorious work Bishop Fisher requires three traditional conditions: no expectation of temporal gain, no seeking after human praise, and no self-complacence in the good deed (vainglory). In his *Tree of Commonwealth* Edmund Dudley devotes much space to the treatment of vainglory or, as he terms it, "subtle glory or gloriation." The remedies are manifold, such as recollection of one's sins, rejoicing in God and His grace "whereby and by whom we have done it," consciousness of having done only one's duty, and awareness that only Christ *deserved* glory.[17]

Many passages in *Utopia* seem to be prophetic or, at least, to contain pithy reference to future controversies, extended and bitter. Thus, More pictures even pagans as conceiving that good works merit everlasting happiness. In a few years Protestant reformers were to object to the Catholic doctrine of merit on two counts. First, merit would make God our debtor, an unseemly and impossible situation. Maintaining that the doctrine was clearly in the New Testament (for example, 2 Timothy 4:7-8; Matthew 5:12), the Catholic theologian answered that the right and claim to a reward for a good action came from the promise of God, not from any service which put Him under obligation to man. Secondly, the Protestants said that man's claim to merit would detract from the sovereign merits of Christ, who alone merited for man the reward of everlasting life. To this objection the Catholic controversialist responded: "We owe it entirely to the merits of Christ that we are able to merit for ourselves. He has won for us the power of meriting; without him we could never do anything which would merit in the sight of God." Hearing the Protestant doctrine, the Utopians might well have exclaimed with More: "What can be a worse belief than to believe that men's good works, been they never so well done, be yet nothing worth, nor the man never the better for them, nor no reward for them coming toward man in heaven?" Stapleton also records More's humorous reply to those Protestants who condemned as mercenary any expectation of a reward or prize for good works: "These gentry are so noble-minded that rather than allow themselves to be hired for work for one penny in the vineyard, they would prefer to be hanged outside!"[18]

In his controversy with Tyndale, More defended the Catholic position and emphasized the performance of good works. Man's works of themselves avail nothing toward salvation and derive their worth only from the goodness of God through the passion of His Son. Hence it is by the promise of the good God that good works done on earth merit a reward in heaven. Confirmation is had in Christ's picture of the last judgment, when the Son of Man will admit men to the kingdom for giving food to the hungry, drink to the thirsty, and so forth (Matthew 25:34-40). His letter to Bugenhagen contains a clear and extensive statement. In brief, the Catholic Church avoids the error of Pelagius by believing that the human will can do no meritorious deed without grace, and it eschews the error of Luther by believing that the human will must cooperate with grace for the performance of every salutary good work. Since, logically, Luther makes God the cause and author of vice and crime as well as virtue and goodness, More interjects: "May I be lost if I should not prefer to be Pelagius ten times over rather than once believe the infamous teaching of Luther!" Bugenhagen knows well the belief and teaching of Catholics that human works do not become good without the merciful grace of God, nor meritorious without living faith in Christ, nor deserving of heaven without the benign and gratuitous appointment of the Father, who was pleased to establish such a high value and precious reward for works which of their own nature are useless and worthless. Faith and charity and grace are all necessary for a salutary deed. Erasmus, too, for all the accusations of Pelagianism leveled against him, maintains that whatever does not arise from faith and charity as sources, even if it has the appearance of great piety, is either a sin or, if not a sin, does not contribute to true salvation. Hence the continence of Zeno, the integrity of Xenocrates, the patience of Socrates, were worthy of praise but, since performed outside Christ, did not confer genuine felicity.[19]

At the end of his life, during his imprisonment in the Tower of London, More returned to the same question. As Anthony, he proposes as one source of comfort the consideration that present sufferings borne patiently produce an increase of merit and reward in heaven. Vincent objects because many hold "that men merit nothing at all, but God giveth all for faith alone, and that it were sin and sacrilege to look for reward in heaven, either for our patience and glad suffering for God's sake, or for any other good deed." Anthony answers that, in view of the possibility of peaceful doctrinal agreement at the time, he will not contend with the Protestants. His exposition is so calm and lucid that it deserves citation here. (1) Catholics concede to Protestants that "no good work is aught worth to heavenward without faith, and that no good work of man is rewardable in heaven of its own nature, but through the mere goodness of God that lust to set so high a price upon so poor a thing, and that this price God setteth through Christ's Passion, . . . and . . . that in all that man may do he can do God no good" (that is, he cannot make God his debtor). (2) Protestants grant Catholics that "men are bound to work good works if they have time and power, and that whoso worketh in true faith most, shall be most rewarded." (3) Catholics and Protestants disagree sharply on whether the reward is given by God to faith alone or to the good works arising out of faith and charity. Unlike the scholarly Erasmus, who is hesitant or neutral on many controversial points, More leaves no doubt that he holds the traditional doctrine, and in the midst of his irenic discourse introduces summary arguments for the reward of good works![20]

The Utopians, as pagans dependent only upon reason, are ignorant of the supernatural order in which they actually live and therefore can philosophize only about the natural order. Consequently they draw no distinction between naturally good acts and supernaturally or salutarily good acts. But they do believe in providence and in a supreme being who has set a sanction upon the observance of that moral law which He has imbedded in human nature and which becomes known through the use of human reason. This sanction, which More describes as "punishments decreed for vices and rewards constituted for virtue," is unobtainable in the present life and therefore consists in the attainment or loss of happiness "after this life." More actually employs the word *merit (promereri)* for the relationship between man's virtuous deeds in this world and God's gift of happiness in the next. Finally, one learns that the religious-minded Utopians are persuaded that God rewards *(rependit)* the sacrifice of some pleasure for the good of others, as in the case of ascetics, "with immense and never-perishing joy." If the differences between the natural and supernatural orders are taken into account as they should be, the consistency of More's position on the meriting of future happiness, whether hypothetically natural or actually supernatural, is evident and indisputable to the fair-minded judge.[21]

Utopian ascetics, who are determined to merit happiness after death by difficult tasks obnoxious to the majority, are divided into two groups with divergent views and ways of life. The first class seems to live in a manner directly counter and opposed to the basic Utopian philosophy of pleasure. They thoroughly and completely reject as harmful all the pleasures of the present life and choose an existence of night watchings and sweaty labors. This renunciation manifests itself especially in two ways: (1) total abstention from all venereal pleasure and (2) perfect abstinence from flesh meat. Some, in fact, may be strict vegetarians since they abstain from all animals, a statement which may include eggs, butter, and milk in its scope. Such rejection of sexual love and animal flesh, however, does not mean mere denial for the sake of denial, for the sake of "a vain shadow of virtue." It rather marks the negative aspect of a positive ideal: union with God in a future life. By means of their watching and perspiration, they look with desire to the pleasures of the future life only. In the meantime they are full of gladness and vivacity on account of their hope of attaining these heavenly pleasures very soon. Consequently these strict ascetics do not really act against the principles of Utopian epicureanism: they forego lesser pleasures in order to enjoy a far greater pleasure. In recompense for their surrender of earthly pleasures for the good of others, they expect the greatest pleasure of all—from God, for "God recompenseth the gift of a short and small pleasure with great and everlasting joy."[22]

In his work against Jovinian, St. Jerome, whose letters Erasmus was editing at this time, cites many examples of abstinence among the heathen philosophers. For example, "Epicurus, the defender of pleasure, in all his books speaks of nothing but vegetables and fruits." Jerome later says: "Eubolus also, who wrote the history of Mithras in many volumes, relates that among the Persians there are three kinds of Magi, the first of whom . . . take no food except meal and vegetables." Much earlier, Tertullian in his work *On Prescription against Heretics* had laid the blame for similarities between pagan and Christian institutions on the devil, who imitated only in order to distort and corrupt. In the course of his argument, he exclaims: "He [Satan], too, has his virgins; he, too, has his proficients in continence." Although the more acceptable interpretation relates this statement to the Vestal virgins, it has been applied also to Mithraicism.[23]

The second class of ascetics are just as eager for hard work as the first. But they act more consistently with the Utopian philosophy of pleasure because they avoid no pleasure which does not retard them in their work. They prize the meat of quadrupeds for the special reason that such food in their opinion makes them stronger for whatever task they have before them. Likewise they prefer marriage to celibacy inasmuch as they do not spurn the contentment and solace which it brings and think that they are under the twin obligation (1) of performing the marital act as a debt to nature and (2) of generating children for the sake of their country ("et opus naturae debere se et patriae liberos putant"). (This seemingly obscure statement will be clarified later.) In his *Praise of Marriage* (1518), Tunstall ingeniously argues that, in comparison with the institutes of Augustine and Benedict and Dominic and Francis, marriage is older, more venerable, established by a greater founder (Christ), and more secure as a rule of human life and behavior.[24]

The Utopians judge the second class of ascetics to be the more sagacious, but the first the more holy. The citizenry would laugh the latter to scorn if they tried to support by rational arguments their preference of celibacy to matrimony and of an arduous life to a comfortable one; but since they confess they are led by the virtue of religion, their fellow countrymen view them with respect and reverence. The reason is the scrupulous observance of the precept that no one should make the least rash statement about any religion. This rule is merely a particular application of one of their most ancient laws, that no person's religion is to be the source of loss or damage to him.[25]

The account of ascetics ends with an explanation of their name: *Buthrescae*. It is not clear from the Latin ("huiusmodi ergo sunt, quos . . . Buthrescas uocant") whether the appellation is conferred upon the holier and stricter ascetics only or upon both classes at once. Insofar as this sentence concludes the treatment of religious or ascetics and the first sentence in the next paragraph passes naturally to the discussion of priests, the designation would seem to belong to all who have been described in the previous section, to wit, both classes. In their own tongue the Utopians therefore call their ascetics by a special name, *Buthrescae*. This word, according to Hythloday, can be interpreted in Latin (and English) as *religiosi (religious)*. Actually the Greek vocable means *prodigiously* or *enormously religious*, since it is compounded of βου- (from βοῦς, bullock, ox, cow), employed to express something *wondrously extraordinary*, and Θρῆσκος, meaning *religious*. The Utopians as a whole are deeply religious but their ascetics are religious to

the point of exciting surprise and amazement. The principal
source of Utopian wonder may be their philosophy, for these
religious surrender pleasures, especially the pleasures of contemplation and learning, and some even those of the body, and
undergo hard, distasteful labor in order to earn a future happiness which most likely would be theirs anyway, although not
in the same degree.

Ascetics in Utopia, who have made themselves the humble
servants of all, deserve their name of "religious" *(religiosi)*.
In his letter to a monk More declares that far too many in
Europe presume that the very name of "religious" raises them
far above the lot of ordinary mortals. In their eyes there is no
holiness outside the cloister. And almost the only cause of their
presumption is superstitious adherence to their peculiar rites
and petty observances. Relying upon these helps, they are
equipped for any villainy. In addition they are too ready to
appeal to papal bulls of excommunication against their critics.
Such in the *Utopia* is the attitude of the wrathful friar against
the parasite who makes him an object of derision—a story
which, More admitted to Erasmus in 1520, he would have
omitted except for the advice of learned and prudent men. Such
in the *Adages* of Erasmus is the behavior of the Franciscan
Henry Standish toward the Italian Servite in a dispute before
the cardinal—an incident which caused great merriment for
all. It is clear that here in the *Utopia* is an exhortation to European "religious" to imitate the humility and other virtues of
Utopian "Buthrescae."[26]

It is noteworthy that on the island of Utopia ascetics do not
seem to band together in monasteries or in orders. They retain
the simplicity and liberty of the monks described by Erasmus
in his life of St. Jerome which formed the introduction to the
great edition of the latter's works in 1516. In Jerome's day the
monk was free to come and go, enjoyed leisure for study or
prayers or fasts not imposed by the petty rules of men but by

personal devotion, lacked any prescribed habit, took no vows except private ones, and suffered no penalty for abandoning the monastic life. Polydore Vergil, too, describes almost nostalgically the simple and independent existence of the earliest monks, who were free from the monastic ceremonies of the present age, free from a rigid pattern of dress, free from restrictions on movement, and free to return to the life of a layman. Erasmus suggested at this time that there be fewer monasteries, that all monks have the same way of life, and that ceremonies be reduced to a minimum, for the latter "can make a man superstitious but cannot make him devout." A Spanish memorandum (1512) of agenda for the Council of the Lateran complains that there are too many religious orders, from many of which the Church derives no profit. To the great scandal of the people, the privileges and exemptions granted them by the Apostolic See was a cause of dispute between them and the secular clergy, especially the bishops. Finally, on December 19, 1516, was read a constitution which modified the privileges of religious orders in relation to the rights of the episcopacy. In Utopia such a conflict could apparently not even arise.[27]

The contemporary problems to which More refers in this section on religious are two: (1) fasting and abstinence and (2) celibacy. There is little reason to point out which religious orders abstained from flesh meat only and which from eggs and *lacticinia* (cheese and milk) as well. The lives of the earliest monks, especially in the desert, reveal that many were strict vegetarians. The Carthusians with whom More lived four years in his twenties had a rule of abstinence from cheese and milk on Fridays and designated vigils and during Advent and Lent and a rule of perpetual abstinence from all flesh meat, even in the case of illness of a professed member. When an Avignon pope, it is reported, wished to get for them a dispensation for the sick, he was dissuaded by a deputation of twenty-seven Carthusians between the ages of eighty-eight and ninety-five years!

In Erasmus' colloquy *The Soldier and the Carthusian*, the soldier marvels at his "eating fish perpetually, so that I wonder you are not turned in a fish." The Carthusian answers: "What signifies it with what food this body of ours is fed, which is satisfied with very little, if we live according to Nature?" Not the quantity and quality of food are important, but the reasons and motives behind one's choice. If virtue on the natural level is, as the Utopians claim, "a life ordered according to nature" ("secundum naturam uiuere") and if nature is seen to demand only a modicum of food without reference to the kind and quality (*pace* modern dieticians!), the Carthusian is acting reasonably in fasting and abstaining from certain foods, and even more so in case that he has religious and ascetical grounds.[28]

What grounds would be insufficient for fasting and abstinence? More himself gives two in *Utopia:* (1) the eagerness to keep up the appearance of virtue to no one's advantage and (2) the desire to harden oneself to future sufferings, which perhaps may never come to afflict one. What reasons are adequate? In his *Confutation of Tyndale* More mentions three, of which the first two are the more fundamental. The first is one which even pagan philosophers have accepted: "As for abstinence, to tame the flesh from intemperance and foul lusts also, this was a thing that many philosophers did both teach and use." This aspect, properly speaking, pertains to mortification, which is the fight against evil appetites and tendencies with a view to their subjection to the will (and, the Christian adds, with a view to subjection of the will to God and His law). At this point Tyndale had been accusing the Catholic clergy of mixing and diluting Christian revelation with pagan philosophy. More's answer is apropos: Truth in one order cannot contradict truth in another order. The union of the two is "a thing that may in place be very well done, sith the wisdom of philosophy, all that we find true therein, is the wisdom given of God and may well do service to His other gifts of higher wisdom than that is."

Like the first, the second reason is one springing from divine revelation: it is atonement for sin (Leviticus 16:29, 23:27, 32; Isaias 58:3-7; Matthew 9:14-15, 17:20). More tells Tyndale: "As for fasting, that is another thing which God hath always among His faithful people had observed and kept, not only for that purpose [of mortification], but also for a kind of pain, affliction, and punishment of the flesh for their sins." This phase, in the strict sense, belongs to penance, that is, expiation for sins which the sorrowing sinner detests as offenses against God and which he resolves to avoid in the future. These same two reasons are offered by Erasmus, that constant censor of contemporary fast and abstinence, as valid and convincing: the subjugation of the lasciviousness of the body lest it grow fierce against the soul and the appeasement of the divine wrath lest God take vengeance on human crimes. And More finally adds a reason which is typical both of himself and of his Utopians: man's home is not here on earth but with God in heaven. God enjoined fasting upon His people in the Old and New Testament "to put us in remembrance that we be now in the vale of tears and not in the hill of joy, saving for the comfort of hope." The example set by John the Baptist and by Paul the Apostle, More was later to argue against Bugenhagen, should prove that all abstinence and fasting are not hypocrisy.[29]

It is in the hope of obtaining future happiness that Utopian ascetics forego legitimate pleasures in order to work hard for the welfare of others. As has been explained above, More in real life does not necessarily restrict the activity of ascetics to manual labor but merely has the general purpose of keeping them from idleness and engaged in some work useful to church and state. Thus, the contemplative Carthusian helps both, not only by his prayers, but also by his penances undertaken in atonement for the sins of his neighbors, whether these be his associate members in the mystical body of Christ or his non-Christian fellow citizens whose conversion, perseverance, and salvation he seeks. His prayer, fast, and abstinence contribute just as much, if not more, to the good of church, country, and individual as the nursing of the sick, the building of roads, and the education of children.[30]

That a spirit of legalism and formality rather than of piety and devotion marked the observance of fast and abstinence among some clergy, religious, and laity at this time appears from the cry for reform. Thomas More seems never to have inveighed against the custom in general. All his pagan Utopians, in fact, fast all day and come to their temples in the evening *(uespere)* on the last day of every month and year—still fasting. His Utopian ascetics do or do not abstain from certain foods according as the spirit of natural reason or the urge of religion moves them. He is undoubtedly pointing to some abuses of his own day when he makes his Utopians contemn only those individuals who fast foolishly in order to toughen themselves to future hardships, perhaps never to befall them, or who fast hypocritically in order to appear virtuous. The same reticence and restraint do not characterize the pronouncements of Erasmus on fast and abstinence. One dictum of his is similar in spirit to the view of the Utopians. "Whoever," he says in his commentary on Psalm 33, "fasts for reasons of health or thriftiness or vainglory or human fear or cold habit, does not praise the Lord. On the contrary, whoever does not fast so that his body may be strong enough for work by which he feeds wife and children, or instructs the people, or undertakes any like task of charity, does praise the Lord even by his not fasting."[31]

Erasmus, however, is not always so reasonable in the expression of his views. He attacks the abuses connected with fast and abstinence so vigorously and bitterly that he seems to be attacking rather the institution itself. He fails to defend fast and abstinence as energetically and extensively as he assaults the abuses. His principal charge is that of superstition and of pharisaism against clergy and laity who in their self-righteousness insist on the strict observance of the letter of the law. Hence, in a lengthy defense addressed to Alberto Pio, Prince of Carpi (1475?-1531), who attacked many of his views as Protestant, he declares his condemnation is not directed against abstinence from flesh meat but "rather against the superstition of individuals who, under pretext of zeal for abstinence, make their neighbor suffer and even allow him to die, and in the meantime appear pious in their own eyes, whereas they are Jews, that is, superstitious creatures." In this respect a number of his *Colloquies* particularly were offensive to many. He had to defend his words in a preface which appeared in 1526 and which contained one of his clearest statements on the subject. Against all liars and slanderers, he declares: "In many places I approve of fasting, and nowhere condemn it." He then points to his words in *The Profane Feast:*

> In a great many circumstances it is not the thing but the mind that distinguishes us from Jews; they held their hands from certain meats, as unclean things that would pollute the mind; but we, understanding that to the pure all things are pure, yet take away food from the wanton flesh as we do hay from a pampered horse, that it may be more ready to hearken to the spirit. We sometimes chastise the immoderate use of pleasant things by the pain of abstinence.

The laws of the Church concerning fast and abstinence are "human constitutions." These ordinances are rejected altogether by some who thereby are guilty of "deviating much from right reason," are extolled by others to the extent that they "prefer them before divine laws," and are abused by still others for their personal profit and lust for power. In his *Ichthyophagia* Erasmus says he wishes to call all parties to moderation and devotion. As a matter of fact, his animosity is directed especially against the Christian Pharisees who prefer human constitutions to divine laws, because people are deceived, not by sins of intoxication and lust, but by "a deceitful show of sanctity" (or, as More would say, by "a vain shadow of virtue"). Here, as in *The Profane Feast*, he exposes "the superstition of some men, who lay more stress on these things than they ought to do, and neglect those things that are more conducive to piety." In their cruelty they force persons really excused by the Church to fast and abstain; in their excessive holiness they condemn their neighbors who take advantage of the Church's clemency. In view of the danger to true piety, "scarce any other admonition is more necessary" than that against fasting in the spirit of superstition, self-righteousness, censoriousness, and insistence on the letter of the law. The proper spirit of fasting is well set forth by the author of the *Priest's Mirror*: "Let us fast also from lechery, from gluttony, from hatred and strife and all wickedness. Let us abstain us from meats but more from vices."[32]

The urgency of the problem of fasting at this very time is revealed by at least two contemporary manuscripts. The one, in France, asks whether, in view of the fact that one can find more transgressors than observers of the lenten fast and abstinence, it would not be expedient to abolish it. The other, in Spain, outlines the points which the king's ambassadors should propose at the Fifth Council of the Lateran. They should ask the question whether the threat of sin should not be removed from the lenten fast and whether instead the faithful should not be encouraged thereto by indulgences. The fate of the proposal at the council is unknown.[33]

CHAPTER VII

Celibacy

Another problem, even more serious than the problem of fast and abstinence, was that of the celibacy of the regular and secular clergy. It is convenient to treat of both classes at this place and time.

In his famous sermon at the convocation of 1512, Colet designates "carnal concupiscence" *(concupiscentia carnalis)* as one of the four ways in which the clergy of England conformed to this world. Yet when he comes to describe carnal concupiscence, there is no reference to sexual aberration. Instead he censures sacerdotal indulgence in "feasts and banquetings . . . vain babbling . . . sports and plays . . . hunting and hawking . . . the delights of the world," for which the Latin terms employed are *convivia et epulationes, vanae confabulationes, ludi et ioca, aucupia et venationes, deliciae huius saeculi.* The last indictment sounds most damning: "Procurers and finders of lusts they set by." But the English words at this time do not bear the heavy connotations of sexual desire and illicit intercourse which they carry at present. The Latin original, too, is far less strong: "Conquisitores et inventores voluptatum in pretio habent," a statement which should be translated literally: "They esteem the collectors and inventors of pleasures." What kind of pleasures? Such as are enumerated in the context: banquets and feasts, jokes and games, hunting and hawking, and

other worldly delights, which in themselves are harmless and
innocent but unbecoming to the clergy, secular and regular.[1]

In Utopia, as has been observed, there are two classes of
ascetics: the first abstaining scrupulously from every sexual
act, the second entering into marriage. The second class offers
little difficulty, being the pagan equivalent of the third orders
secular, the members of which, as far as their station and duty
in the world permit, live up to the spirit and rule of the regular
orders. These lay members, who may wear the habit, share in
the good works of the order to which they belong. The Utopian
motives for marriage, as will be seen later, are noble and interesting. As for priests in the Utopian religion, they enter into
matrimony, taking as their wives the choicest women among
their fellow countrymen.[2]

Clerical concubinage was a problem at this time as it had
been for decades. Roger Aubenas declares that cases of priestly
concubinage were "astonishingly frequent," but public opinion,
characterized by "a disconcerting laxness in such matters,"
appears not to have been scandalized beyond measure. A century before, the Council of Basle had thundered: "Since in
some localities there are ecclesiastical superiors who permit
concubinarii to continue in their crime in return for a monetary
consideration, we command them under penalty of eternal male-
diction that they do not in the future by agreement or in view
of gain tolerate, connive at, or in any way be in collusion with
such transgressions." But the evil continued. The Spanish ambassadors were instructed in 1512 to ask the forthcoming
council whether concubinaries should be punished, not merely
by pecuniary fines, but also by suspension, privation of benefices, imprisonment, and other penalties. At its session of May
5, 1514 the Council of the Lateran called for the severe punishment of concubinaries, both clerical and lay. The Concordat
with France (1516), approved by the council, went into greater
detail on the same matter. In his letter to Dorp, More reports

a discussion at table between an Italian merchant, perhaps Antonio Bonvisi, and a disputatious theologian, newly come from the continent. The latter maintained that it was a worse sin to keep one concubine at home than to maintain ten prostitutes abroad on account of the bad example and proximate occasion of sin. He held this opinion, not so much because he would seem to hate concubinage, but because he hated to agree with anyone![3]

Sacerdotal celibacy is a matter of Western ecclesiastical discipline, not a decree of divine institution. More clearly recognizes this feature: "The Church both knoweth and confesseth that wedlock and priesthood be not repugnant but compatible of their nature and that wedded men have been made priests and kept still their wives." Why, then, does the Church elevate only unmarried men to the priesthood? Because it wishes its ministers to be adorned with special virtues which are pleasing to God, such as chastity. As More observes to Tyndale: "Sith perpetual chastity and the forbearing of the work of wedlock is more acceptable to God than the work of wedlock in matrimony, therefore the Church taketh none to be priests but such as promise and profess never to be married but keep perpetual chastity." Tyndale had claimed that the gift of chastity is extremely rare and the danger of impurity exceedingly great in the priestly state. His statement that "few men can live chaste," according to More, is "plain false; for many have done and doth." In comparison with the vast multitude of men to whom God has not given the grace, the gift of chastity may seem rare but actually many, not few, possess it. A man is always free to choose or not to choose the priesthood, to which is annexed the law of chastity: the Church forces no one into the priesthood and consequently into celibacy. Consequently Aeneas Silvius (later Pius II) wrote to the ecclesiastic John Frunt that, in view of his inability to keep continent, his desire for marriage was laudable; that he should, however, have weighed matters before holy orders; and that therefore Calixtus III refused him a dispensation for marriage in the interests of the common good. When his interlocutor claims that priests in Wales and Germany have wives, More denies his assertion. He transmits the whole question of the married priests of the Greek church, saying: "I will not dispraise them, . . . for I know them not." In this respect it is interesting to note More's complete orthodoxy in the light of the decisions of the Council of Trent and the discussions held during its twenty-fourth session, which restated the traditional and written law of clerical celibacy.[4]

The main philosophical objection to sacerdotal celibacy is not the inability of man to remain perpetually continent but the duty of the preservation of the human race. The classic answer finds expression in Aquinas' *Summa contra gentiles*. The necessary duty of generation, he says, devolves upon the whole human species, not upon the individual. Nature will always urge the vast majority of men to acts of generation and consequently to matrimony. Certain individuals, therefore, may abstain from generative acts in order to be free for other important duties, for example, those of the military life or the contemplative life. The pressure of far more weighty obligations, Erasmus also claims in a sample letter in his work on the art of correspondence (composed *c.* 1498, revised and printed 1522), induced the apostles to practice and recommend a life of celibacy. "Let the Apostles, to be sure, be the example for men with the apostolic spirit, who, in view of their task of teaching and guiding the people, cannot satisfy at one and the same time their flock and their wife." Or, so he argues in another work, "if you have an eye to piety, marriage serves as an obstacle to those hastening to Christ."[5]

This reason and answer, however, did not satisfy Protestants and even some Catholics. Simon Fish in his indiscriminate attack on monks and clergy in the *Supplication for Beggars* pressed the argument that their celibacy was the cause of a

decline in the number of human beings and loyal Englishmen:
the clergy "be the marrers and destroyers of the realm, bringing the land into wilderness for lack of generation by their
abstaining from wedding." To this oft-repeated charge More
in his *Supplication of Souls* gives a simple denial: "If their
abstaining from marriage should make all the land desert and
inhabitable, how happeth it that habitation endureth therein so
long, for the land hath lasted sith the beginning of their abstaining from marriage, ye wot well, many a fair day." Fish's esteem
of marriage cannot be very high, claims More humorously. If
he thought marriage good and noble, Fish would not wish the
clergy "robbed, spoiled, bounden, beaten, and wedded"! But
Fish was not alone. Thomas Starkey's *Dialogue* represents
Thomas Lupset and Reginald de la Pole as objecting to the
celibacy of priests and monks for the reason that thereby "the
generation of man is marvelously let and minished." Pole would
allow secular priests to marry and those desirous of chastity to
dwell in abbeys and monasteries. The *Dialogue* was written
between 1533 and 1535, but the conversation must have taken
place before 1530, the year of Lupset's death.[6]

Such views, of course, are not unusual and are similar to
those used by married ascetics in Utopia. Their reasons for
wedding, as has been seen, are three. The first is personal:
marriage brings solace, help, and contentment to the individual
("nec aspernantur solatium"). The second is natural, that is,
based on the demands of nature: marriage enables them to
fulfill a double debt to nature, namely, appeasement of their
sexual urge and preservation of the human race ("opus naturae
debere se . . . putant"). The third is civic and patriotic: they
contribute to the common welfare by generating children for
the sake of their country ("debere se . . . patriae liberos
putant"). Robinson translates their argument as if they owed
"labor and toil" *(opus)* to nature and "procreation of children"
(liberos) to their native country. The problem is whether *opus*

should be translated in the sense of labor in general or the particular "work" of wedlock, that is, begetting children. Either interpretation is possible. The latter, however, is the more likely for two reasons. First of all, the context definitely deals with marriage. The obligation of marriage rises from a double source, country *and* nature, not merely from duty to country: "et opus naturae debere se et patriae liberos putant." Moreover, work in general, as is stressed throughout the *Utopia*, is due to the common good, nor is any mention made of its obligation as arising from nature. Secondly, the latter interpretation is enforced by a sample missive of Erasmus in *The Composition of Letters* which bears a remarkable resemblance to the arguments employed here in More's *Utopia*. Matrimony, he insists, is a law of nature, not engraved on brazen tables, but deeply implanted in our souls. The individual disobedient to this law must be considered not even a human being, much less a good citizen. If right living, as the keen-sighted stoics argue, consists in following the dictates of nature, what is as consonant with nature as marriage? Nature implants, not only in men but also in the rest of animals, nothing as deeply as the instinct to protect the species from extinction and to effect, as it were, its immortality by the generation of posterity. In fact, the individual untouched by marital love seems to be an enemy to nature and a rebel against its God. Even Socrates took a wife lest he appear deficient in his duty to nature. For he realized that he was born by this law and for this law and that he owed this duty to nature ("hoc se debere naturae"). (Compare *Utopia*: "opus naturae debere se.") Furthermore, no one was even held to be a distinguished citizen who did not work hard at begetting and educating children properly. A state is in peril if it lacks young soldiers to protect it. Its doom is sealed unless the constantly diminishing supply is replenished by marriages and births. Roman laws actually punished bachelors with a fine and excluded them from positions in the government.[7]

St. Augustine in his *City of God,* a work on which More lectured at St. Lawrence Jewry in his youth, shows the relationship between pleasure and virtue, an important consideration at this point because married ascetics shun no pleasure which does not handicap them in their manual labor. Pleasure *(voluptas),* according to St. Augustine, is subject to virtue when the latter uses it as a help. The function of virtue, certainly, includes both living for one's native land and procreating children in behalf of one's country, neither of which is possible without bodily pleasure. For, without bodily pleasure, neither food and drink is taken in order to maintain life, nor is intercourse had in order to propagate offspring.[8]

It is now time to return to the main issue: More's stand on clerical celibacy. There can be no doubt about his later defense of celibacy during his controversies with the Protestant reformers. In this connection it is well to remember that the apparently abusive and bitter invective of More against priests, monks, and friars who married after Luther's revolt is not due to a Puritanical or Manichean hatred of the flesh but to his horror at their violation of the solemn vow of chastity made to Christ as their spouse. Their marriages were illicit and invalid and consequently they were living in continual sin, under the obligation of observing their vow of celibacy and returning to their first love. But what was his opinion at the time of the publication of *Utopia?* His readers will never know. Priests in Utopia are married, but one cannot argue from their marriage to More's advocacy of a wedded clergy in real life. After all, Utopian priests are pagan, not Christian. But this seems to be clear: More does want to air the whole question of clerical celibacy. It is within the realm of sheer possibility that, when the *Utopia* was being written, he might have agreed with Erasmus on the advisability of marriage for priests and monks amid deplorable contemporary conditions. But from what is known of More's lifelong spirit and attitude toward the discipline of the Western Church it would be immeasurably saner and safer to conclude that he favored celibacy.

It is tempting to conjecture that in his later and polemical works More reversed the stand on clerical marriage which he had taken in the *Utopia*. But for such a convenient solution it would appear necessary to produce corroboratory evidence from his precontroversial writings. No such evidence seems to be forthcoming.

But of Erasmus' lifelong attitude toward celibacy there can be no doubt. It might be in deference to Erasmus' opinion that More introduces married priests and religious in his *Utopia*. Even in his specimen letter on matrimony Erasmus contrives to voice his views. Not the worst remedy for the behavior and morality of men would be the concession of the right of marriage to priests and monks, amid the immense throng of whom how few lead a chaste life! How much better to turn concubines into wives, to live in open and honorable marriage, to bring up unblushingly their children in a holy manner! Erasmus then ends on a sarcastic note: the bishops' henchmen would long ago have effected this change if the revenues from concubines were not greater than that from lawful wives! The seriousness of Erasmus' conviction cannot be called in question, as is evidenced by the notes to his *New Testament* (1516). Commenting on 1 Corinthians, Chapter 7, which deals with advice to the married and unmarried, Erasmus wonders whether, on account of changed circumstances, it would not be more expedient even for priests, insofar as they lack self-control, to keep a holy marriage and stainless bed in view of the fact that there are everywhere a vast number of incontinent priests and a great scarcity of those living chastely. His observation on the first part of 1 Timothy, Chapter 3, which is concerned with the qualities required in a bishop, contains the same sentiments. He adds, however, his suspicion that even priests who remain chaste do so not out of piety but out of the fear of losing their ecclesiastical revenues or of failing to increase them. He remarks in his *Method of True Theology* how times have changed. St. Paul commanded *bishops* to rule well their wives and children: now even *subdeacons* are forbidden the right to have a wife! His defense against Bedda is even more explicit. In the age of St. Jerome, French priests married, and even today Greek priests are allowed to have wives. Since celibacy is a human law, a pope or council can abrogate it. The discipline was introduced when priests were infinitely fewer and much holier— and willing, not forced. Now the world swarms with thousands of bad priests. A change of times advises a change in discipline. "I wish for what is best [that is, celibacy]," Erasmus concludes, "but I advise marriage for priests as a lesser evil."[9]

At this time Polydore Vergil, too, cries out that nothing brings greater disgrace to the order of priesthood, greater harm to religion, and greater grief to good Christians than the lewdness of priests. Would that at last the right of open marriage were restored to priests, so that they might lead a holy life in matrimony without ill-fame rather than sully themselves most basely with the vice of impurity![10]

CHAPTER VIII

Priests
and Bishops

The charge that the land swarms with priests, and bad priests at that, can hardly be leveled against Utopia. Its priests are extremely holy and for that reason correspondingly few in number. There are only thirteen in each city, answering to the total of their temples. The reason for the number thirteen is not clear. It may refer to one bishop with twelve priests—on the analogy of Christ with His twelve apostles. In the *Laws* Plato has twelve interpreters of sacred laws for his state. When the Utopians go to war, seven priests set out with the army. In the interval seven others are chosen in their place, but on their return the original seven are reinstated in office. The substitute seven succeed them upon their death and meanwhile serve as attendants of the bishop, who is set over all the other priests. The presence of bishops even in pagan Utopia seems like an anticipatory answer to the reformers who claimed that the Church of Christ was invisible—"some good men scattered here and there unknown till God gather them together and make them known." More's answer is that the constitution of the Church is hierarchical: "Where be also your priests and your bishops? For such must they have if they be the Church of Christ."[1]

The argument for the institution of a priesthood is set forth in Fisher's *Defense of the Sacred Priesthood*. It is consentaneous with reason, he declares, that certain persons be deputed to take care of the whole community in affairs which concern the salvation of souls. The necessity is evident especially from six disadvantages under which most Christians labor: (1) ease of degeneration from the true faith; (2) dullness of understanding; (3) inclination toward every kind of evil, which argues the need for an admonisher; (4) slowness in well-doing, evident from greater zeal for goods of body than for salvation of soul; (5) wiles of the devil; and (6) pestilential doctrines of false teachers. The priesthood, of course, must be composed only of men qualified to carry out their duties prudently, faithfully, and conscientiously.[2]

At this point in the *Utopia* we have a reflection on one of the most serious abuses of the day, a situation well summed up in the succinct complaint of Reginald de la Pole in Starkey's *Dialogue:* "Priests are too many, and yet good clerks too few; monks, freres, and canons are too many, and yet good religious men too few." The complaint was not new. More than three centuries before, Peter Cantor (d. 1197) was crying that "there would have to be fewer churches, fewer altars, fewer and better priests"! The predicament of the clergy in the early sixteenth century was similar to that of the whole Christian community: "a faithful reflection," as Aubenas states, "of lay society." The Church, according to the diagnosis of H. O. Taylor, was "not abnormally bad, but merely permeated with normal human slackness, selfishness, materialism, and ignorance, with occasional instances of a better energy and enlightenment." Gilmore agrees that "the most characteristic abuses in the ranks of the regular as well as the secular clergy had been recurrent throughout the whole late medieval period." Such views are corroborated by the words of More in his *Dialogue Concerning Heresies.* The only reason that the faults and vices of the clergy stand out more than those of the laity is that priests, by virtue of their dignified ministry, are obliged to a greater holiness and perfection than that of laymen. As the *Imitation of Christ*, with which More was familiar, expresses it: "A Priest ought to be adorned with all these virtues, and to give example of good life to others." Hence layman More tells his layman interlocutor: "Now where ye say that ye see more vices in them than in ourself, truth it is that everything in them is greater because they be more bounden to be better." Laymen are no less sinners than priests: "The things that they misdo be the selfsame that we sin in ourself. . . . For undoubtedly if the clergy be nought, we must needs be worse, as I heard once Master Colet, the good dean of Paul's, preach." As More says pointedly in an epigram, even an evil pastor can be to his flock an example—for them to avoid what he does![3]

In his recent history of the Council of Trent, Hubert Jedin declares that the unexpected course of events in Germany was not due to greater negligence in the care of souls, to greater evil among the clergy, to greater religious ignorance or godlessness, or to more greatly strained relations between spiritualty and laity, in Germany than in other countries. The responsibility rested with the laymen, the bourgeoisie, and the intelligentsia, now appearing on the scene as a class, who placed higher demands upon their priests, who perceived the disparity between the ideal and the actual in their regard, and who, above all, were resolved radically to purge all abuses, alleged and real, instead of shrugging their shoulders and putting up with the existing situation as inevitable. From 1520 on, Germans believed that life under previous conditions was impossible—and, says Jedin, "the reformation turned into the revolution."[4]

More maintains that the clergy of England, and especially the secular clergy who serve as the particular object of attack, are the equal of, and even superior to, those in any Christian nation in "learning and honest living." He admits that "many very lewd and nought" are among them. The greater the number of priests, the greater the likelihood of having bad priests:

"Surely wheresoever there is a multitude it is not without miracle well possible to be otherwise." The remedy is easy: choose
only a few men of unquestionable and exceptional sanctity. The
responsibility rests on the bishops: "Now if the bishops would
once take unto priesthood better laymen and fewer (for of us
be they made) all the matter were more than half amended."
But too many bishops, comments More in his *Treatise on the
Passion,* are like the apostles who fell asleep in the Garden of
Olives. There must be, according to the *Dialogue Concerning
Heresies,* "more diligence used in the choice, not of their learning only, but much more specially of their living." The latter
has reference above all to their chastity. Moreover, the super-
abundance of priests leads naturally to failure to appreciate
and honor them. Their great number, argues More, "must min-
ish on our part reverence and estimation toward them which we
never have but in things rare and scarce." To illustrate this
truth he uses a homely figure: "Gold would we not set by if it
were as common as chalk or clay."[5]

In the early Church a handful of holy men, even when chosen
and called, undertook the dignity and responsibility of the
priesthood with the greatest humility and reluctance. "Now,"
notes More indignantly, "runneth every rascal and boldly
offereth himself for able." The "rascal" then supports himself
often enough by acting as chaplain in a private household with
the result that he becomes as much a servant as the groom. "I
would surely see such a way therein," writes More, "that we
should not have such a rabble, that every mean man must have
a priest in his house to wait upon his wife, which no man almost
lacketh now to the contempt of priesthood in as vile office as
his horsekeeper." It was to prevent such humiliation of the
priest that the Church had decreed that no one should be elevated to the priesthood "until he have a title of a sufficient
yearly living, either of his own patrimony or otherwise." In
fact, the universal remedy for the excessive number and unedi-

fying life of priests is the enforcement by bishops of the canons on ordination. "And as for me," declares More, "touching the choice of priests, I could not well devise better provisions than are by the laws of the Church provided already, if they were as well kept as they be well made." The very least that a bishop ought to require in this matter is set forth in Silvester's *Summa summarum:* (1) proper age, (2) sufficient learning, and (3) goodness of life. As for the last requisite, More would undoubtedly not wholly agree with Silvester, who demands nothing higher than freedom from notorious sin and from greater excommunication, suspension, and interdict, because the candidate for orders "must not be judged to be unmindful of his salvation."[6]

The criticisms and remedies of More agree perfectly with those of his spiritual father, Dean Colet. Four or five years before the composition of *Utopia,* in a sermon delivered to the bishops assembled in convocation, he had cried:

> Before everything else, let those canons be revived which warn you, O Fathers, not to lay your hands quickly upon any man or admit them to Holy Orders. For that is the fountain of evils, namely, the door to Holy Orders standing wide open, all who offer themselves are admitted without discrimination and without rejection. From this source streams and spreads that infamous mob of priests, both ignorant and unholy, in the Church. For, in my judgment, composition of a collect, disquisition on a petty theoretical question, response to a sophism, are not enough for a priest. Far more requisite are a good and pure and holy life, approved morals, adequate knowledge of the Scriptures, some information on the sacraments, but, above all else, fear of God and love of heavenly life.

The greatest blemish in the Church, he points out, is the worldly-wise behavior of worldly-minded clerics and priests—in opposition to the Pauline exhortation: "Be not conformed to this world, but be transformed in the newness of your mind" (Romans 12:2). The fight against heresy made the Church only more wise and learned, but the creeping paralysis of the world-liness of ecclesiastics destroyed charity and therewith spiritual wisdom and strength. The mad stupidity of contemporary heretics is not as pernicious and deadly to clergy and laity as the evil and depraved life of priests. The latter, says Colet, quoting St. Bernard, "is, so to speak, a kind of heresy, at once the greatest and most pernicious of all."[7]

Such were the words of the dean of St. Paul's at a council of the clergy of the province of Canterbury. Just as strong and as sad were the expressions used at the ecumenical council of the Lateran (1512-1517) by preachers like Aegidius Viterbenis (Egidio of Viterbo), general of the Augustinians, and Antonius Pucius (Antonio Pucci, 1484?-1544?) on the clergy's corruption and the laity's negligence, even contempt, of sacred persons and things. Praiseworthy decrees were passed on the selection of good bishops, the punishment of blasphemy, the censorship of books, the norms of good preaching, the prohibition of concubinage and simony, and the submission of exempt friars to bishops in certain matters, but the inability of the authorities, high and low, to enforce them nullified whatever good results could be expected from the council. It needed the storm of the Protestant Revolt to bring Catholics to their senses and to reform and amendment.[8]

Colet issued a warning of the approach of the tempest in his exposition of the Epistle to the Romans. He found the greatest single mischief in the Church to be avarice and greed for money—"a disease that . . . is spread so widely throughout the whole Body of Christ, absorbing and infecting the chief members [that is, the clergy] even beyond the rest, that, unless Christ have mercy on his own Body, and aid it in its peril, it assuredly cannot be far off from being doomed to destruction. . . ." His objection is not to possessions and offerings and tithes, but to litigations about them. The liberality which the clergy expect from the faithful will surpass their desires if only shepherds set for their flocks the example of "justice, godliness, faith, charity, patience, mildness" (1 Timothy 6:11) and forbear to make the poor laity feel the rigor of the law "before they understand its meaning." What wonder that "[s]uch a dissension as formerly prevailed between the Jews and Gentiles, now prevails almost everywhere in the Christian Church itself, between the clergy and the laity." Colet pleads for forbearing charity and good example on both sides.[9]

Polydore Vergil points to the cause of the dissension. According to him Urban I (222-230) was the first to decree that priests might receive estates offered by devout people, but he stipulated that nothing should be private property but everything for the common good. Consequently dwellings were common to priests and hospitality open to nonpriests. Gradually the words "for the common good" were blotted out and instead were replaced by "mine" and "thine," those two words always baneful to religion. As the upshot, the priesthood now, he continues, is viewed only as revenue and legacy and ownership. (Erasmus, too, declares that the specific duty of bishops is to teach Christ and His scriptures to the people but that now they are absorbed in the most degrading work: pursuit of litigations and accounts of revenues.) Private interests are far preferred to public, with the result that hatred and dissension have arisen. The fundamental reason is that to make private what is common is always the cause of discord. Bishop Fisher makes much the same analysis before a synod convoked by Wolsey shortly after receiving legatine powers. In a discreet manner he condemned the vanity of the clergy "in wearing of costly apparel, whereby he declared the goods of the Church to be sinfully wasted and scandal to be raised among the people, seeing the tithes and other oblations given by the devotion of them and their ancestors to a good purpose so inordinately spent in undecent and superfluous raiment, delicate fare, and other worldly vanity." Much later he spoke in the House of Lords against the bills passed in the Commons against the clergy, saying: "If the truth were known, ye shall find that they rather hunger and thirst after the riches and possessions of the clergy than after amendment of their faults and abuses." The clergy in their zeal for wealth had set an example for laymen, who learned the lesson and applied it—in their own way.[10]

Bishop Fisher agrees with Dean Colet and other humanists on the dependence of the laity upon the good example of the clergy: "All fear of God, also the contempt of God, cometh and is grounded of the clergy." Even the most hardhearted sinner could not resist grace if every class among the clergy lived as it should—in right order. How far is the actuality of the present from the ideal as realized in the days of St. Paul! "In that time," laments Fisher, "were no chalices of gold, but then was many golden priests. Now be many chalices of gold, and almost no golden priests." In his *Tree of Commonwealth* Dudley declares that the four fruits of the tree are honorable dignity, worldly prosperity, tranquillity, and good example, and then continues: "The fruit of good example . . . is the natural fruit in the which the clergy should feed." Unlike many churchmen of the day, they should "not covet or desire the fruit of honorable dignity which is all at the discretion of their sovereign."[11]

On the plethora and the unfitness of priests and monks Erasmus stands with his friends More, Colet, and Fisher, but, as is to be expected of him, is much more virulent and explicit in his attack. In 1516 he published the following observation on a letter of Jerome to Pope Damasus. Jerome, he says, "shows that the Roman Pontiff ought to be far removed from all haughtiness as the successor of the fisherman and as the vicegerent of the crucified, that is, of the most humble of men." In his explanation of the adage *Sileni Alcibiadis* he launches into a deadly attack on the wealth and worldliness of the clergy, especially bishops and popes, and holds up constantly the apostolic age as the pattern. He extols the primacy of the spiritual

but in an idealistic way which refuses to take heed of reality;
for example, the need of the pope for independence. His *Colloquies* sound the same note. As usual their approach is largely
negative, condemnatory, and satiric, with the result that the
preface of 1526 has explicitly to point out his positive and con-
structive purposes. In *The Abbot and the Learned Woman* he
intends to "incite monks and abbots, who are haters of sacred
studies, and give themselves up to luxury, idleness, hunting, and
gaming, to other kinds of studies more becoming them." His
aim in *The Virgin Adverse to Matrimony* is to castigate those
"kidnappers" and "fishermen" who lure young people into
monasteries, "making a handle either of their simplicity or
superstition, persuading them there is no hope of salvation out
of a monastery." Instead, it is better for a young virgin to
preserve her maidenhead at home with her parents than in a
cloister with lax or corrupt inhabitants. Here Erasmus is referring to the early custom, clear from Jerome's letter to
Demetrias, for a girl who consecrated her virginity to God to
remain in her parents' house. The object of *The Youth's Piety*
is to advise young men who are deliberating about their vocation to reveal the secrets of their souls to their confessors.
Erasmus continues pointedly: "But if so, there will be fewer
monks and priests. It may be so; but then, perhaps, they will
be better, and whosoever is a monk indeed will prove it so." He
sees no reason for regretting his admonition.[12]

Contemporary poets in England naturally joined in the
chorus. In the angry lines of *Colin Clout* (1519-1522?), John
Skelton summarized the abuses charged against the clergy.
Earlier, Alexander Barclay had written a powerful section, "Of
the Abusion of the Spiritualty," in his *Ship of Fools* (1509),
to depict the state of the clergy, secular and regular. He attacks
especially unworthy motives in the numerous candidates for
the priesthood and places the blame squarely on episcopal
shoulders: "The prelates are the cause of this misgovernance"

(Locher: "Pontificis culpa est"). His grief at the state of the
Church is poignant:

> The steeple and the church by this means stand awry,
> For some become rather priests for covetise
> Than for the love of God and His service.[13]

Certainly one of the greatest evils of the day was the passing of the right to appoint bishops from the pope, who had
curbed the power of local chapters, into the hands of kings and
princes. The process had become accelerated since the Great
Schism and reached its climax in the concordat (1516) between
Francis I and Leo X with consequent approval by the Lateran
Council. The king of France now had the right to present to the
pope for confirmation appointees to 93 episcopal sees and 527
monasteries. More than one historian has seen in this concordat
"short-term gains" for the papacy but "on balance" an abdica-
tion by Rome. The higher positions in the Church, which had
become increasingly reserved for the noble or wealthy, were
henceforth even more to be filled only by persons of the highest
social or economic status, not by persons of approved holiness
and solid learning.[14]

The old method of selection of bishops did not pass without
protest. In his *Tree of Commonwealth* Dudley appeals to
Henry VIII: "It were a gracious and a noble act that the Church
of England were restored to her free election after the old
manner and not to be letted thereof by means of you, our sovereign lord, nor by means of any of your subjects." If the king
acquiesces, God will reward him, saying: "Thou hast set my
Church in good order in promoting of virtuous and cunning
men without any point of simony and caused them to keep their
dioceses and cures without disturbance of free election." In
1512 the Spanish ambassadors were instructed to ask the Lateran Council whether a return should not be made to the common law, whereby ecclesiastical dignitaries were chosen "by
way of election, postulation, and confirmation" ("per viam

electionis, postulacionis et confirmacionis"). The common law
is here opposed to special privileges arrogated by princes to
themselves in troublesome times or conceded to princes by
popes, for example, by way of concordat. In a Parisian manuscript dated September 2, 1516 the author marshals "testi-
monials from the Old and New Testament, collected to prove
that the elections of prelates and bishops to the government of
the Church take their source in divine right." Another part
of the same manuscript attempts to show that "the elections of
ecclesiastical prelates are more consentaneous with divine law,
natural and positive, than their presentations by the prince of
the place."[15]

In Utopia the election of priests lies not in the hands of the
prince (or even the bishop) but in the power of the people. They
choose their priests by the same method as the rest of their
public officials—by secret balloting, in order to forestall ambitious campaigning or illegal canvassing. In the *Laws* of Plato
the choice of priests and priestesses is made "partly by election
and partly by lot" and their office endures for only one year.
Once elected, the priests in Utopia are consecrated by their
associates. The Utopians, one must note, draw the requisite and
important distinction between election and consecration. Election is the designation of a person fit for an ecclesiastical dignity
or function; ordination is the sacred ceremony by which the
minister, after his fitness has been determined by election, is
endowed with the sacred power. Thus, in the early Church, as
appears from the Acts of the Apostles and Cyprian's letters,
the people played the role of electors. In commenting on the
former document (Acts 6:5-6) Fisher in his *Defense of the
King's Assertion* explains that, even in case of election by
the people, the person elected has to be properly ordained by
the authorities. In Utopia, too, the people elect; the bishop,
surrounded by his priests, consecrates. The constant teaching
of the Church is that only a consecrated bishop ordinarily can

confer the episcopate and the priesthood. In fact, theologians, except for a handful, agree that a priest cannot be even the extraordinary minister of the order of the priesthood, much less of the episcopate. A priest can offer the holy sacrifice of the Mass and administer the sacraments of baptism, penance, and extreme unction in his ordinary capacity and of confirmation by papal indult or delegation. The ministers of matrimony are the contracting parties. In case of necessity any layman can confer baptism. Utopian converts received baptism at the hands of Hythloday and his companions. Since none of the latter was a priest, the Christians in Utopia still need those sacraments which in Europe only priests confer. They understand, however, the nature and necessity of these sacraments and long for nothing more ardently. In fact, they have begun to take matters into their own hands. They have initiated an earnest dispute as to whether, even if a Christian bishop were not sent for the purpose of consecrating a priest, an individual who was chosen from their own number might not receive the sacerdotal character. ("A character, in the theological sense," explains C. Cronin, "is a spiritual seal or stamp impressed on the soul by God to indicate the consecration of that soul to him in some official capacity. . . . Order bestows the power and office of *dispensing* and *ministering* them [divine gifts] to the faithful.") In other words, they were arguing the point whether a man duly elected might not become a real priest without ordination at the hands of a bishop. And indeed they seemed about to elect someone, but at the time of Hythloday's departure from Utopia they had not done so. It is necessary to note that, while only election is mentioned, the conferring of the sacerdotal character would probably not be automatic but accompanied by rites of consecration, for example, the imposition of hands or the symbolic acceptance of a candle or incense.[16]

More's own view seems to be the orthodox one that sacerdotal consecration without a bishop is invalid. This is clear from his letter to Gilles prefixed to the *Utopia*. More is anxious to know precisely where the island is located, because a certain pious theologian is aflame with desire to reach Utopia. His only purpose is to nurture and spread nascent Christianity there. In order to accomplish his object in the right way ("quod quo faciat rite"), he determined to make arrangements to be sent by the bishop. This sending, or mission in the strict sense, consists in the formal conferring of authority to preach and to administer the sacraments. He wishes even to be created bishop of the Utopians. His ambition arises, not from considerations of honor or profit, but from motives of piety.[17]

One wonders why More ever introduced the question of the validity of lay consecration. That a bishop alone ordinarily could ordain priests was so much a part of Christian doctrine that in the early Church only Aerius (fourth century) went as far as to claim that even a priest could consecrate a priest. Election by the people in a Christian community as ideally virtuous as that of the primitive Church may be a protest against appointment by princely patronage. But lay consecration is another and far more serious matter. It may have been a humorous stroke on More's part to make his Utopians unconsciously heretical by resorting to special consecration as did the Waldensians. If one is to judge from the profession of faith prescribed for them by Innocent III, the Waldensians (or individuals among them) maintained that consecration and unction by the Holy Spirit, independently of any canonical ordination by a visible and tangible bishop, was sufficient to empower a holy person to consecrate the Eucharist and to offer the sacrifice of the Mass. Moreover, one of the propositions of Wyclif condemned at the Council of Constance in 1415, exactly a century before *Utopia*, was that the ordination of clerics was reserved to the pope and bishops on account of greediness for lucre and honor. In the fifteenth century Thomas Netter declared that the upshot of Wyclif's heresy was that a person became validly a priest or a cleric, not by the imposition of the bishop's hands or by a visible sacrament, but by the invisible ordination of God, provided the person led a holy life and taught Catholic doctrine. The implication, of course, was that the power of ordaining ministers pertained to the people at least indirectly. Christians in Europe, naturally, would be horrified by this turn of events in Utopia. Possibly, however, it may have been a theoretical question raised by the scholarly Erasmus as the result of his researches in the New Testament and the fathers.[18]

Less than twenty years later, however, the question began assuming significance other than theoretical. The declaration of Henry VIII as supreme head on earth of the Church of England (1534) made problems connected with the conferring of the priesthood of greater practical importance. There exists a Lambeth Palace manuscript which includes the answers of More's friend, Cuthbert Tunstall, bishop of Durham at the time (1540), to questions on the very point discussed by the Utopians. Perhaps to provide an opening for royal prerogative, purely hypothetical and seemingly impossible cases were proposed, but once the power of the king was admitted, it could be extended, of course, to ordinary circumstances. One pertinent question reads: "Whether (if it fortuned a Christian prince learned, to conquer certain dominions of infidels, having none but temporal learned men with him) it be defended [that is, forbidden] by God's law, that he . . . should . . . make and constitute priests, or no?" Only two clergymen declared that "laymen in no wise can make priests, or have such authority," but Tunstall and some nine others said that "laymen in such case have authority to minister the sacraments, and to make priests." The next question comes closer to home: "Whether it be forefended [that is, forbidden] by God's law, that (if it so fortuned that all bishops and priests of a region were dead, and that the word of God should remain there unpreached, the sacrament of baptism, and others unministered) that the king of that region should make bishops and priests to supply the same, or no?" Three answered that laymen "can make no priests," and three gave an affirmative answer, saying that "in such a case, Necessitas non habet legem." Tunstall is not mentioned by name for this latter question, the document stating merely that "they agree for the most part as they did before." It is only fair to add that another manuscript at Lambeth which summarizes these answers in Latin fails to include the bishop of Durham (Tunstall) by name. The upholders of the lay theory appealed to *Historia ecclesiastica*, Book X, Chapters 10-11. Eusebius' *Church History* ends with Book X, Chapter 9. Chapters 10-11 are really the work of Rufinus (345?-410), whose Latin translation of Eusebius' *History*, with a continuation, was used in the Middle Ages and often reprinted in the early Renaissance. As a matter of fact, while these two chapters relate stories of lay persons preaching Christianity to pagans, in both cases requests are made and granted for the sending of bishop and clergy to them. On one occasion the hardly orthodox archbishop of Canterbury, Thomas Cranmer, went further than all the others by admitting the power of the king and his ministers in ordinary cases. In response to the question as to "whether any other but only a bishop may make a priest," he said: "A bishop may make a priest by the scripture, and so may princes and governors also, and that by the authority of God committed to them, and the people also by their election; for as we read that bishops have done it, so Christian emperors and princes usually have done it, and the people, before Christian princes were, commonly did elect their bishops and priests." Reference seems here to be made not to mere election but to consecration as well.[19]

The people in Utopia, as has been seen above, elect the priests of their official religion by secret ballot. The Christians in Utopia were about to adopt the same procedure for the priest who they decided would thereby receive the sacerdotal character without consecration at the hands of a bishop. Even if they had had a bishop sent to them, they would undoubtedly have elected the priests to be ordained by him. In this respect they would seem to be following the custom of the primitive Church. And this course would be fitting because, as has been observed, the Utopians make as ideal Christians as those in the earliest days of Christianity. But the ancient system gave rise to grave abuses, as Erasmus remarks in his letter to John Slechta (1519) and his *Letter against the Sham-Gospellers*. The election and deposition of bishops by popular voting was full of disturbance, even of bloodshed at times. The result was that the right to designate bishops was restricted to a few definite men. It is impossible to review the history of episcopal election. In the fifty years before the publication of *Utopia* previously existent evils increased in magnitude, such as plurality of sees, episcopal absenteeism, consecration of totally unworthy candidates, retention of wealthy sees for decades by single families, and especially papal surrender to temporal princes of the power to nominate bishops. One of More's epigrams addresses a bishop distinguished by this mark alone—"a more stupid useless choice than you could not be made"! Colet's indignation receives such powerful expression in a treatise on the *Hierarchies of Dionysius* that the passage must be quoted here:

> Wherefore one may here express an abhorrence of the detestable custom, which has now for a long time been growing in the Church, and is at the present time deep-rooted, almost to the destruction of the Christian commonwealth, whereby temporal princes, void of reason, and, under the name of Christians, open enemies and foes of God, blasphemers of Christ, overthrowers of his Church, not with humble and pious, but with proud and rash, minds; not in consecrated and holy places, but in chambers and at banquets; appoint Bishops to rule the Church of Christ; and those too (heinous crime!) men ignorant of all that is sacred, skilled in all that is profane; men to whom they have already shamelessly sold those very bishoprics.

Instead of serving the gospel of Christ and fulfilling their special office of preaching, bishops and prelates serve and prostrate
themselves before temporal kings and princes. "They would,"
Colet scornfully adds, "rather look up to a king in his court,
than to God in His church." What an ironic contrast between
Utopia and Europe does a marginal note in the *Utopia* expose!
If a priest happens to reside in a syphogranty, he takes precedence over the syphogrant in presiding over the dining hall. But
in contemporary Europe even bishops occupy the place of servants in regard to princes! ("Sacerdos supra principem. At nunc
etiam et Episcopi iis mancipiorum uice sunt.")[20]

In his *Defense of the Sacred Priesthood* Bishop Fisher holds
as axiomatic the reasonableness of having special men serve as
representatives and guardians of the whole community in business which relates to the salvation of souls. When priests feed
their flock by word and example, they keep the people from
going astray into many a wrong path, but when they neglect
their duties, the people rush headlong into the abyss of all
evils. And in these official matters Erasmus in his *Ecclesiastes*
names the five chief duties of bishops, that is, those who possess the fullness of the priesthood: administration of the sacraments, prayer for the people, power of judging, faculty of
ordination, and office of teaching. The difference between the
royal and the episcopal dignity is that "between heaven and
earth, body and soul, temporary and everlasting things." If
bishops are now held almost in contempt, it is largely their own
fault. Once they were held in highest honor, not only by the
people, but also by monarchs. Right order demands that the
priest be "the father and nourisher and teacher and censurer
even of monarchs." Toward sinners, whether in high or low
degree, their pastors, whether bishops or priests, have the special obligation of admonition. If pastors fail in this duty,
sinners not only remain as slaves under the yoke of sin, but
have their lot grow worse. Bishop Fisher declares: "They be

also thrast down into a more straiter corner of misery . . . when also prelates and parsons do not correct their misliving and shortly call them to amendment, but rather go by and suffer their misgovernance."[21]

In his *Tree of Commonwealth* Dudley calls upon the clergy to reveal themselves "true priests of Christ's Church," not only in their prayer and virtue, but also in "showing and preaching the word of God truly and plainly to the temporal subjects, and boldly and straitly to punish sin according to their authority and duty." If necessary, the prince must assist: "If there be any sturdy or obstinate persons in his realm that will frowardly disobey their ordinaries in the cause of God, the prince must put to his mighty hand to help and reformation thereof." Alexander the Englishman in his *Destruction of Vices* traces contemporary errors, heresies, and dissensions among the people to the clergy's failure to use the spiritual sword of God's word to kill vices. Moreover, "if prelates, pastors, and priests would use that spiritual sword, the material sword would not kill as many men as it does in modern times." In order to have them perform their duties properly, Dudley would not allow priests to "be in any temporal office nor executors thereof." In this regard St. John Fisher disclosed to an English synod the difficulties encountered by a well-disposed bishop: "Sundry times when I have settled and fully bent myself to the care of my flock committed unto me, to visit my diocese, to govern my church, and to answer the enemies of Christ, straightways hath come a messenger for one cause or other sent from higher authority, by whom I have been called to other business and so left off my former purpose. And thus, by tossing and going this way and that, time hath passed, and in the meantime nothing done but attending after triumphs, receiving of ambassadors, haunting of princes' courts, and such like, whereby great expenses rise that might better be spent otherway." But when Fisher, according to his biographer, was in disfavor at court, "he then fell to his old trade of preaching to his flock and visiting of sick persons, besides an infinite number of other deeds of mercy."[22]

Mutatis mutandis, the bishop and priests of the common religion in Utopia have the same functions as their Christian counterparts: (1) supervision of divine worship, (2) direction of men's consciences (the Latin *religiones,* however, might perhaps refer to the different religions or to the various classes of ascetics or to religious observances), (3) overseeing—or censorship, as it were—of morals and conduct, and (4) education, especially moral, of boys and young men. For anyone to be summoned and taken to task by them as a person of life not upright enough, is considered a great disgrace. For the rest, their special office is solely exhortation to good and admonition from evil. It is the function of the prince and other magistrates to curb and punish criminals. The only penalty which priests may inflict is exclusion from divine worship in the case of individuals whom they discover for certain to be pertinaciously wicked. Yet of hardly any other punishment are offenders more afraid. The reason is that they thereby are branded with the note of deepest infamy (which technically involves the complete loss of one's good name), and are tortured by the secret prick of conscience, fearing lest not even their physical persons be safe for long. To be sure, unless they give proof of quick repentance to the priests, the council seizes them and makes them pay the penalty for ungodliness.[23]

How different is this state of affairs from that in Christian Europe! First of all, with what boldness and self-confidence, asks Erasmus, can a preacher reprehend the vices of his charges when he himself abounds in the same vices or even worse? Who will believe a sermonizer praising chastity and sobriety when he himself keeps concubines at home and frequents drinking parties? Even the most vehement diatribe will have no more effect than sparks of static electricity from an ebony rod in

comparison with bolts of real lightning. A pure heart and
blameless life, concludes Erasmus, impart self-confidence and
authority to the preacher. The great holiness of their lives is
what gives Utopian priests their power and influence in the
correction of their faithful.[24]

Sacerdotal sanctity also provides the inner force of the
excommunication which priests level against evildoers. At one
time in Europe, too, excommunication had been greatly feared
among Christians. Silvester's *Summa summarum* in the early
sixteenth century enumerated twenty-two effects of major excommunication, of which the most important were denial of the
sacraments, elimination from the Church's general prayers, de-
barment from divine services, nonparticipation in private and
public social intercourse, and exclusion from the kingdom of
heaven if the excommunication was just. The excessive use of
excommunication for reasons sometimes worldly had weakened
its might until it ceased to be a really effective ecclesiastical
penalty under many circumstances. Even the efficacy of excommunication by the pope was diminished and sometimes brought
to nought. *The Praise of Folly* speaks of the "weapons and sweet
benedictions" with which the popes are "generous enough":
"interdictions, excommunications, re-excommunications, anath-
ematizations, pictured damnations, and the terrific lightning-bolt
of the bull." And the popes—for example, Julius II—"launch
it against no one with more spirit than against those who, at
the instigation of the devil, try to impair or to subtract from the
patrimony of Peter." In the *Exclusion of Julius* (1513-1514?),
Erasmus humorously has the pope complain about the many
evils and losses resulting from criticism of popes and churchmen by *barbari*, that is, non-Italians. The last straw is that
people tremble at his fulminations less and less. The basic reason for the loss of respect and awe, according to Folly, is evident: "Impious pontiffs . . . by their silence allow Christ to be
forgotten, . . . adulterate His teaching by forced interpretations,

and crucify Him afresh by their scandalous life!" The lesson
is clear: if priests, bishops, and popes wish to regain the esteem
of people and princes for their persons, functions, and penalties,
let them live lives of holy shepherds, as do the priests on the
isle of Utopia.[25]

The Utopian priests excommunicate individuals who are
shamelessly evil. Some scholars have tried to limit their sacerdotal authority to those of depraved lives, but it seems that it
must extend to all those who break the law. Adultery, for
example, is forbidden by law, and yet adulterers surely must
be excommunicated. If one restricts excommunication to minor
violations, there is no reasonable proportion between the light
offense and the grave penalty. Suppose, for example, that one
continues to attack violently another's religion or persists in
denying and assailing publicly the providence of God or immortality of the soul, which all genuine Utopians should believe. Such offenders, too, probably would be first warned by
the priests, then excommunicated, and finally seized by the
secular authorities. In his later controversial works More approves of the "good, reasonable, piteous, and charitable" order
prescribed by the current ecclesiastical law against the heretic
who is determined to preach. In spite of false charges against
them, the clergy desire the death of no one. If he acknowledges
his fault, forswears all heresy, and does the penance enjoined
by the bishop, the heretic is received again into the Church.
"And else, if he prove himself obstinate and impenitent, the
Church neither is bounden nor ought to receive him, but utterly
may forsake him and leave him to the secular hands." If he
relapses into heresy after abjuration, he is excommunicated.
Because his companionship is "perilous among Christian men"
by killing other men's souls, "the Church refuseth him, and
thereof the clergy giveth knowledge to the temporalty, not
exhorting the prince, or any man else either," More explains
carefully, "to kill him or punish him, but only in the presence

of the temporal officer, the spiritualty not delivereth him, but leaveth him to the secular hand, and forsaketh him as one excommunicate and removed out of the Christian flock." At this time there was much complaint against "over-fervent mind or indiscreet zeal, or, percase, an angry and a cruel heart" in the authorities charged with the extirpation of heresies. More says that these failings are only human but do not excuse clerics from sin: hereby "they may offend God in the selfsame deed whereof they should else greatly merit." Utopian usage is thus seen to be curiously parallel to Christian procedure—without the latter's defects.[26]

The restriction of the power of the priests in Utopia to excommunication leads one to wonder whether More does not wish to limit the power of ecclesiastical authorities in Europe to spiritual penalties, such as exclusion from divine services, denial of the sacraments, and so forth. In this way the pecuniary fines which were the source of many abuses would be eliminated and another road opened to genuine reform.

A veritable highway leading to the desired goal of a purified Christianity and enlightened piety is the education of youth. The northern humanists are unanimous on the point. "The reformation of the Catholic Church according to its primitive holy morals," reads a work of James Wimpheling, "must be begun with youth since the latter's deformation proceeds from their improper and wretched education. Since children are less corrupted and less tainted, they are more receptive of salutary teachings." No person deserves better treatment at the hand of the state, maintains Erasmus, than the molder of raw youth, provided he be a man of learning and uprightness. Only stupid people rate as demeaning the task of teaching by which one educates one's fellow citizens immediately from the earliest years in fine literature and Christian morality and by which one consequently gives to one's country men of virtue and integrity. Habits are to be formed at a tender age. The child's natural disposition is to be accustomed to the best when it is like wax soft enough to be molded to any form. Once the years have hardened our inclinations, we unlearn with difficulty the wrong things learned and we grasp with the greatest effort things which we ought to know. The source of all virtue, Erasmus emphasizes, is a careful and holy education. The primary end of education for Erasmus and the humanists, therefore, is the formation of Christian character and social usefulness. To this end the wisdom of Christianity and of pagan antiquity is a means, indispensable and priceless. "Living wisdom," holds Colet, "makes a man worship God in humility, live temperately, and lovingly benefit his fellow men."[27]

In whose hands is education to be? Thomas More here parts company with John Colet. When the latter established St. Paul's School, he insisted upon putting laymen in charge. In this respect, he acted in the spirit of the time, for, as C. P. McMahon has observed: "Probably the most important trend in schools in the fifteenth century was the direction toward lay control, as opposed to the ecclesiastical administration exercised by the secular and monastic authorities." More in his *Utopia*, however, entrusts education to the clergy, probably because their special interest is morality and its defense, maintenance, and encouragement. The priests undertake the instruction, not only of boys, but of young men. (The term used by More, *iuuentus*, refers to the period from the twentieth to the fortieth year in general.) They show no less solicitude about virtue and morality than about intellectual training. It is possible that More is here protesting against the preoccupation of the late medieval school with dialectic and disputation, as evidenced by the youngsters' early use of the *Small Logicals*, to the consequent neglect of moral training. Even if the subjects were to be Greek and Latin classics, great stress was to be laid on virtuous living. Hence the Utopian priests employ the height of diligence in imbuing immediately the still tender and pliable minds of youth with sentiments which are good and noble as well as advantageous to the preservation of the Utopian form of government. When they have taken deep root in children, these sentiments follow them as adults to the grave and contribute a great and useful part in the maintenance of public order and prosperity. The latter never deteriorates except on account of vices which are born of perverse views. The Utopian ideal of education is thus seen to be the humanistic ideal. This attitude toward learning is unlike that of some English clerics toward education; for example, the training of Henry VIII's natural son, the Duke of Richmond, indicated by a letter (1529?) of John Palsgrave to More: "Methinketh that our shaven folk would in no wise he should be learned." More himself has two epigrams on ignorant clerics. One is addressed to a fat priest who keeps repeating the Pauline sentence: "Learning puffs up a man," and who himself has a swollen belly and a mind puffed up, not with learning, but with stupid trifles! The other is directed against an illiterate bishop who declares, "The letter kills": no letter can kill him because he is ignorant of letters but the dictum terrifies him with reason because he does not possess the life-giving spirit![28]

A constitution of Leo X, approved by the Lateran Council on May 5, 1514, insists on training in both knowledge and virtue:

> We decree that masters and teachers instruct their pupils not only in grammar, rhetoric, and other subjects of this kind, but impart to them also religious instruction, dealing especially with the commandments, the articles of faith, hymns, psalms, and the lives of the saints.[29]

After the paragraph on the sacerdotal control of education, Hythloday mentions in passing that the feminine sex is not excluded from the priesthood. Their election, however, occurs rather rarely and even then is confined to women who are widows and advanced in age. Since the pagan Utopians possess merely a natural religion, the presence of priestesses among

them is not at all surprising. They were common enough in the
Greek and Roman religions. The most famous were the Vestals
who preserved the fire on the state hearth in the temple of
Vesta, the goddess of the blazing hearth. The Vestals, however,
were young virgins who retired to private life after thirty years
of service. More again gives a Christian cast to Utopian institutions by making priestesses aged widows. Widows seem to
have enjoyed a special position in the early Church, at least
to the extent of being persons who received regular help from
ecclesiastical bounty. Some of them seem to have played an
official role in the service of the Church, perhaps being in charge
of hospitality and alms. More undoubtedly intended the reader
to apply St. Paul's qualifications for Christian widows to Utopian priestesses: "Let a widow who is selected be not less than
sixty years old, having been married but once, with a reputation
for her good works in bringing up children, in practising hospitality, in washing the saints' feet, in helping those in trouble, in
carefully pursuing every good work." The Apostle advises the
rejection of younger widows because they want to get married
again and "are not only idle but gossipers as well as busy-
bodies" (1 Timothy 5:9-13)! St. Paul mentions, too, his right
to take about with him "a sister woman" (1 Corinthians 9:5),
who, for the sake of prudence and edification, would undoubtedly have the same qualifications. Perhaps More wishes to
remove the slightest suspicion of scandal from the sacerdotal
college by placing Utopian priestesses above scandal.[30]

Priestesses were common in ancient pagan religions, but
traditionally the only prominent Christian sects before More's
time to honor women with the functions of the priesthood were
the Gnostics (according to Irenaeus), the Pepuzians (according to Augustine's *Heresies*), the Collyridians (according to
Epiphanius), the Montanists (according to Tertullian and Augustine), and the Wyclifites. Orthodox Catholics like Fisher
soon made Luther an associate of the Wyclifites. Thus, Fisher

couples Luther with the Wyclifites and views as shameful and
execrable to Christian ears Luther's saying that a boy or a
woman or any Christian could absolve from sin and consecrate
the Eucharist. In his attack on Luther, More says scornfully:
"Luther consecrates for us women as priests." He later chal-
lenges him to point out past Christians among whom women
were believed to be priests, allowed to hear confessions, and
qualified to consecrate the Eucharist. He asks the same question
of Bugenhagen later. Tyndale later attempted to prove that
women "may for necessity minister all the sacraments . . . and
for necessity consecrate also the Blessed Body of Christ"
and proposed the case of a Christian woman cast alone upon
an island. More answered that, in spite of the numberless discoveries of recent years, such an event had never occurred. If
it was God's will to convert a people, He would always provide
"a man or twain."[31]

In Utopia priestesses must be widows advanced in years,
but no explicit restrictions as to age and as to marriage or celibacy are laid upon priests. As a matter of fact, they all seem
to marry. Their wives are the choicest women among their
fellow countrymen. One learns, too, that the priest and his wife
sit at table with the Syphogrant and his wife and preside over
the meal. In having married priests in Utopia, More may be
taking a humorous thrust at the celibate priests of Europe, with
their sometimes ill observance of chastity. Would it not be better
for them to be few in number and to attempt to change Western
discipline in order to allow priests to marry—the most intelligent and beautiful women alive, of course—consequently living
in great honor among their people instead of hiding illicit concubines! But in view of his constant adherence to the lofty
ideals of Christian tradition, More himself must have regarded
celibacy as the state specially suitable for the ministers of the
Church, since it had been praised as such since apostolic times
(1 Corinthians 7:8, 32-35).[32]

Another privilege of priests in Utopia is that the law does not oblige them to manual labor. In other words, they belong to each city's group of less than five hundred whose preoccupation with study or with government entitles them to relative leisure. This exemption is entirely comprehensible in the case of the priests, since their time is taken up, not only with religious services and pastoral duties, but with the education of youth. In fact, they recommend for popular approval the names of outstanding scholars who are to devote their whole time to intellectual pursuits. The priests therefore do not labor with their hands, and yet they are far from idle. A few years after *Utopia,* More was to defend the upkeep of Christian priests. Simon Fish kept pressing home the charge "that they live idle all, and they be all bound to labor and get their living in the sweat of their faces by the precept that God gave to Adam" (Genesis 3:17-19). Thomas More answered that even "among the paynims they had always their priests whose living was well and plentuously provided for," as was evidenced in ancient histories and even in many places in the Bible (especially Genesis 47:22). As for the priests of the Old Covenant, God's "pleasure was that they should live out of labor and upon the labor of other men's hands" (Numbers 18:8-32; Deuteronomy 18:1-8). As for the priests of the New Law, St. Paul affirmed that "he that serveth the altar should live of the altar and . . . also if we sow unto you spiritual things, is it a great thing if we reap your carnal things" (1 Corinthians 9:7-14). More, however, would probably agree with Hythloday that the horde of priests in Europe is too great and too lazy. The remedy for the disorder is to reduce their number, to raise their quality, and to keep them busy with liturgical, pastoral, and educational duties. "God sent men hither to wake and work," More admits in his *Answer to "The Supper of the Lord,"* but "not all men in bodily labor but, as the circumstances of the persons be, so to be busied in one good business or other."[33]

Exemption from manual labor is but one privilege of the clergy in Utopia. "No greater honor," declares Hythloday, "is paid to the highest civil officers." In fact, priests enjoy a form of clerical immunity greater than that in Christendom. In Europe offenders are haled before ecclesiastical authorities and courts. In Utopia priests guilty of any disgraceful or shameful crime are subject to no public tribunal, whether civil or ecclesiastical: they are left to God and to their own conscience ("deo tantum ac sibi relinquuntur"). Divorced from its context, the latter statement might possibly mean that the delinquent priest is left to God and the judgment of his peers, but the lack of later reference to any kind of court or judge and the denial of any human right to correct him favor his immunity from all exterior trial and punishment. He has been rendered sacred to God in a special way as a dedicated being. Consequently Utopians conclude that it is far from lawful to lay the hand of man upon him, no matter how profaned by guilt. This law is easier of observance for Utopians than it would be for Europeans on account of the paucity and exceedingly careful selection of Utopian priests. It does not easily happen that a man who stands out as excellent among good men and who has been raised to the great dignity of the priesthood only because of his virtue, should degenerate into vice and corruption. But suppose it should happen wholesale? No serious consequence by way of a public calamity is to be much dreaded for two reasons: (1) priests are very few in number and (2) they are clothed with no authority except honor. (As a matter of fact, they could work havoc with their power of excommunication!) The Utopians restrict their number to a few extraordinary individuals lest the dignity of the order of priesthood, which is now treated with extreme veneration, become common and cheap because the honor is shared with a host of persons. This is especially true because they consider it difficult to find very many individuals virtuous enough to be deemed suitable for the sublime dignity: a mediocre degree of virtue is not sufficient for holding the high office.[34]

The marginal note for this passage in *Utopia* is such as we would expect: among the Utopians there are only a few priests, "but what a mob of them among us!" The passage itself, however, gives us a clue to More's views, not only on the number and sanctity of priests, but also on clerical immunity, that is, the right of clerics, whether in major or minor orders, who had at least received the tonsure, to exemption from secular judicial jurisdiction. In the course of time grave abuses had arisen from undue extension of the privilege. In 1512 the Spanish ambassadors received instructions to ask the Lateran Council to restrict ecclesiastical immunity by reduction in the number of persons protected by excepting certain crimes and by other ways. As far as England is concerned, a brief historical review would not be out of place. In 1483 the convocation of the province of Canterbury asked and obtained from Richard III the confirmation of ecclesiastical liberties. Innocent VIII in 1485 directed a letter on the same matter to Henry VII. In 1509 Archbishop Warham of Canterbury issued a call to convocation to the prelates and clergy of his province. The language of his missive is most strong, urgent, and alarming. Certain iniquitous men, he declares, have recently disturbed and almost prostrated the English Church, which used to enjoy "many and great liberties and immunities in the times of our forefathers." These men have put a perverted and sinister interpretation on time-honored privileges or have ill-treated and contemned ecclesiastical persons. Lest their enemies find an excuse in their failure to reform the Church, the clergy themselves should apply the proper remedy. In a chapter on ecclesiastical immunity the *Soul of Man*, printed about three years later, says of priests: "To God it longeth only to correct them for their defaults, and so I will it be." Since God has freed them from the "subjection of temporal lords, temporal laws may nothing punish them."

Only God's anointed, that is, those in holy orders, "should correct them under me when they trespass." Hence God has said in Holy Writ, *"Nolite tangere,* etc., to temporal lords: touch not my Christs that be my ministry which be anointed of me, etc." Later, Fisher was to apply this scriptural clause to all Christians, but especially to priests since they are twice anointed and are consecrated by a double imposition of hands. In 1515, the very year of *Utopia,* the proposal in Parliament to lay restrictions on this "benefit" met with opposition from the clergy as being against the liberties of the Church. Relying upon More's statement, Gasquet concludes that the problem "did not apparently reach any very acute stage." In 1528 Clement VII conceded to Wolsey the right to degrade clerics, secular and regular, and to hand them over to the secular court for more atrocious crimes.[35]

More's position on immunity is far from clear in its details. He makes his few and holy Utopian priests exempt even from spiritual tribunals on earth! But it is evident that he wanted some sort of exemption, at the very least from secular jurisdiction, to be given to those in holy orders. If Utopia frees its priests from all human judges, whether secular or spiritual, European states should at least allow the spiritualty to be judged by the spiritualty alone. If one is to infer from his general attitude, More would have retained "benefit of clergy," but removed all its abuses and insisted upon the condign punishment of offenders by ecclesiastical courts. In his *Apology* he gives his practice and reputation in regard to criminal clergy: "Priests and religious, running out of religion and falling to theft and murder, had at my hand so little favor that there was no man, that any meddling had with them, into whose hands they were more loath to come." One remedy attempted by the Council of the Lateran, in May 1515, was to strengthen the power of episcopal courts over clerics who abused the privilege of exemption from the authority of the local bishop.[36]

The issue of immunity was not idle or useless. Historically
it is important in regard to the question as to whether the secular or the spiritual authorities should undertake and accomplish the needed reformation of the Church. If the clergy
sparked the reform, the old system of faith and discipline would
remain safe and intact at its core. If the laity effected the reform, there was more danger that nonreligious motives might
operate. Actually, on the eve of the Reformation people were
accustomed to regarding ecclesiastical reform as the task of
secular lords, especially since the latter had achieved some
notable results, for example, in Spain. The difficulty, as Hubert
Jedin and many other historians have noted, was that the secular
authorities were naturally inspired, not only by zeal for discipline and piety, but by a fiscal concern in the taxability of
ecclesiastical property. For reasons such as these Fisher in his
Confutation of Luther's Assertion expressed his desire that, if
the life of the pope and his court were not in keeping with
Christ's teaching, they should reform themselves and remove
stumbling blocks from the souls of the weak. Unless they did
so, he feared that divine vengeance would overtake them (a
prophecy many saw fulfilled in the sack of Rome in 1527). It
was far from fitting that the emperor or lay princes should
attempt the task and reduce them to a less luxurious standard
of living. Ten and more years of investigation for Thomas More
had failed to reveal any approved author who held that a secular
prince could be head over any church or over ecclesiastical persons and possessions. On the contrary, all these years of study
had persuaded More that the primacy of the pope had been
"provided by God" and "begun by the institution of God"; it
had not been "instituted by the corps of Christendom." Consequently God alone could bring His vicar and Church to account.
Immunity from secular jurisdiction at this time meant spiritual
independence for the pope and clergy so that they might reform
the Church and keep intact the deposit of faith.[37]

That the crime-hating and justice-loving Utopians should grant their priests absolute immunity is the most significant token of the esteem which they tender them. But the estimation in which priests are held among their own citizens is no greater than the reverence which they command even among foreign nations. Hythloday thinks that the source of the veneration is easily discernible. When the troops are trying to decide the issue in battle, the priests stand aloof and, not very far away, settle upon their knees, clothed in their sacred vestments. With hands stretched out toward heaven, they pray first of all for peace and then for victory for their soldiers, a victory without much bloodshed on either side. If their men happen to conquer, they rush to the battle line and try to restrain their ferocity toward the vanquished. It is enough for the latter merely to glimpse and to call upon the priests in order to secure their lives. To touch their flowing garments is sufficient to preserve the rest of their possessions from all loss due to war. On account of their holy conduct their persons are treated with extreme veneration by all nations. The result has been that they have saved their fellow citizens from their enemies as much as they have saved their enemies from their fellow citizens. The explanation is simple. At times, as is common knowledge, when the Utopians' battle line was broken, when the situation was hopeless, when they had turned their backs in flight, when the enemy was rushing forward to their butchery and spoliation, the priests intervened to halt the slaughter, to separate the armies, and to arrange and establish peace on favorable terms. There was never a nation so savage, cruel, and barbarous as not to venerate their persons as sacrosanct and inviolable. It is interesting to note that one of Erasmus' *Adages* mentions the custom of ancient peoples of having a soothsayer precede the advancing army, crowned with laurel and bearing a torch. This held in check the fury of war because both sides considered it an impious deed to draw one's sword against a sacred person.[38]

The same scruple does not trouble Christian soldiers, who do not hesitate to kill prelates in battle. Witness the number of bishops, abbots, and others slain at the battle of Flodden Field only two years before. The fault lay less with laymen than with the prelates themselves. Alexander VI and Julius II had lately furnished an example in Italy, no matter how justified their warlike maneuvers might have been or how defended by learned theologians of the day. Even loyal hearts, Cardinal Gasquet comments, would have seconded the following words of von Hutten, addressed to Leo X in a preface prefixed to Valla's treatise on Constantine's donation: "Would to God . . . that this horrible saying may no longer be heard: 'the Church fighteth and warreth against the Perugians, the Church fighteth against the people of Bologna.' It is not the Church that fights and wars against Christian men; it is the Pope that does so." Erasmus in *The Praise of Folly* is at a loss to say who first set the fashion: whether the popes or certain bishops in Germany. "These bishops," Folly declares, "personally acted as colonels, laying by their garb, forgetting about benedictions and other such formalities, as though they esteemed it cowardly and lacking in decorum for a bishop to return his soul to God from any place but a battlefield." A prime example was the life and career of Diether von Isenburg, archbishop of Mayence.[39]

The whole nature of their office and the long tradition of church history was against the active participation of prelates in war. St. Thomas Aquinas had answered negatively the question as to the liceity of clerical and episcopal participation in battle. He gives, as St. Antoninus of Florence explains, two reasons: first, the conduct of war keeps clerics from the contemplation, prayer, and leisure for divine services for which they are deputed and, secondly, killing or shedding blood is unbecoming to the minister who at Mass represents the Passion of Christ, since he ought rather to be prepared to suffer death in real imitation of the action represented on the altar. In a note in his edition of Jerome's letters Erasmus declares that apostolic men ought to conquer by shedding their blood, not by arms as in the case of Julius II. Bishop Fisher says that he can approve the intrusion of bishops in affairs of war only when extreme necessity demands their activity or presence. Clerics, however, may in a just war be present to help by spiritual exhortation and administration of the sacraments. Suárez maintains that the obligation of desisting from battle binds persons in holy orders under pain of mortal sin. Bishops who are the supreme heads of states, however, may licitly declare a just war. Not divine law but ecclesiastical law, nevertheless, forbids the active prosecution of even just wars by prelates in person. The pope, of course, is above ecclesiastical law, but a great council of French bishops which was called at Tours in 1510 by Louis XII in reprisal for Julius II's endeavors to drive the French from Italy unanimously declared that the pope neither could nor ought wage war against temporal princes in lands outside the Patrimony of Peter. An addition by Ludovicus Ballius comments that this statement must perhaps be understood of the pope actively participating in his own person, as did Julius II, who said that he was using the sword of St. Paul, since his predecessor had used enough the keys of St. Peter (that is, excommunication, interdict, and so forth)! The acts of this council were later disavowed by its participants.[40]

Julius himself, on July 25, 1511, called a general council which met in the Lateran Basilica for the first time on May 3, 1512. The bull of convocation declared one of the five purposes of the council to be the promotion of peace among Christian princes. Julius died on February 21, 1513, but Leo X continued his work. During the eighth session, December 19, 1513, a papal constitution, *Ad omnipotentis,* was read on the establishment of peace in Christendom. At the tenth session, May 4, 1515, a sermon was preached which fierily urged the pope to command a universal peace for ten years at least, to bind kings in the fetters of the great King, and to restrain nobles by the iron manacles of censures, because all power in heaven and on earth is given to the pope. Even earlier, in 1514, Erasmus mentions the presence of Bishop Caraffa, later Paul IV, in London on the mission of peace. His comment is caustic and unjust: "He will be more concerned, unless I am mistaken, about his own interests rather than ours." Thomas More, however, must have welcomed all attempts to secure peace. One of the three things which he wished were "well established in Christendom" was: "That where the most part of Christian princes be at mortal war, they were [all] at an universal peace." Of Erasmus, too, one scholar has said: "The beginning and the end of the political designs of Erasmus was the desire for peace." In these designs for a Europe which would enjoy permanent friendship and peace, prelates play an important role.[41]

What is this role? A letter of Erasmus to Antony of Bergen, abbot of St. Bertin at St. Omer, written in March 1514, states plainly: "It is the function of the Roman Pontiff, of the Cardinals, of Bishops, and of Abbots to compose the quarrels of Christian princes, to exert their authority in this field, and show how far the reverence of their office prevails." A missive in 1518 to Paul Volz, Benedictine abbot of Hügshofen near Schlettstadt, is even more explicit. As Christ draws the priesthood to Himself and makes it pure from worldly defilement, so priests, especially prelates, have the duty of summoning princes to purgation. Wherever the violence of war threatens, advises Erasmus, let bishops strive after the settlement of the affair without bloodshed, or, if that is impossible, let them endeavor to make the action less bloody and to shorten the duration of the war. How close the matter was to Erasmus' heart is seen even in a comparison of his in *Similia*. Just as kingfishers *(halcyones)* are very rarely visible but, as often as they do appear, they either create or announce a halcyon calm, so abbots and bishops ought rarely to go forth into the courts of princes except to compose by their authority the disturbances of affairs and the tempests of wars.[42]

Such is the theory and the ideal: what the practice and actuality were we have already seen. Some notes to the New Testament reveal Erasmus' bitter mind. In commenting on 2 Corinthians 10:4 ("the weapons of our warfare are not carnal, but powerful before God to the demolishing of strongholds"), he writes: "Now one can see some who, at the demands of circumstances, have troops, swords, lances, and cannons, and whatever becomes a hardy warrior. But when the forces of vice are to be shattered by the sword of God's word, they have neither tongue nor hands." He had expressed the same sentiment four years before in a letter to Peter Gilles when he saw the gradual entanglement of Henry VIII and Maximilian in the Holy League against France: "O inarticulate divines! O mute bishops! who can gaze upon such plagues of human affairs with silent lips!" Even in the midst of his eloquent eulogy of Alexander, archbishop of St. Andrews, who perished at Flodden Field, in his *Adages,* he laments: "Tell me, what had you to do with Mars, . . . you who had been enrolled in the army of Christ? . . . What had you, a bishop, to do with weapons?" His remarks on two passages in the gospel according to St. Luke (3:14, 22:36) are more direct. "Now bishops wage war," he declares, "and they do almost nothing else but wage war." And what is the purpose of this constant campaigning? "We priests ourselves wage war," he cries, "and that for civil dominion, for booty, for earthly glory."[43]

His advice to princes runs along the same lines. In a panegyric addressed to Philip the Handsome, Erasmus argues that, just as a quiet voyage is better for a pilot than a stormy one and just as the treatment of a slight disease is better for a physician than that of a serious one, although crises and perils test more the skill of both pilot and physician, so a peaceful victory won without bloodshed is more glorious for the prince than a conquest gained by bloody war. In *The Education of a Christian Prince*, dedicated to Philip's son, the future Charles V, he points to arbitration by prelates or learned laymen as the means for bloodless triumph: "There are plenty of bishops, abbots, and learned men, or reliable magistrates, by whose judgment the matter could better be settled than by such slaughter, despoliation, and calamity to the world." In the same work he cannot refrain from pointing out some bishops who are "the very firebrands of war." They bring Christ's cross and Christ's Eucharist into the very camp and "in such bloody discord produce the symbols of the greatest charity." His *Method of Prayer* reveals that, in the preparation of Christians for war on Christians, it is disgraceful for the offerer of the holy sacrifice of the Mass to petition a glorious victory for his side and disaster for the enemy, since sometimes the petitions of both sides displease God.[44]

The same ideas are repeated in two other important works of Erasmus: *The Complaint of Peace* and *Adage 3001: Sweet Is War to the Uninitiated*. Here he adds more explicitly other arguments: for example, (1) the very nature and name of *man* should teach *men* to try to agree; (2) the doctrine of Christ, more powerful than the teaching of nature, inculcates especially peace and mutual benevolence among Christians—"the Spirit of God accomplishing," as Colet asserts, "what human nature failed to do"; (3) the trivial accident of birth and life in a mere *place* like England and France should not make Englishmen and Frenchmen enemies when they are united by the stronger bonds of nature and chains of Christ; (4) no matter how unjust the peace, it is better than even the most just war; and (5) if the voice of the supreme pontiff was obeyed when calling to war, why is it not hearkened to when calling to peace? And again he cannot refrain from an attack on every ecclesiastical representative of the Christian religion who has become the author and firebrand of war, the thing Christ detested most heartily. "Art thou not afeard," he tells him, "lest that that [that which] was said and spoken of Christ's messengers—how goodly be the feet of those that show forth peace, good tidings, and health—be turned clean contrary? How filthy is the tongue of priests exhorting unto war, inciting to evil, provoking to death and murder!" Among many other humanists Josse Clicthove (Jodocus Clichtoveus), too, in his work *War and Peace* maintained that ecclesiastics in their counsel and in their sermons to the people ought to incite princes not to war but to peace.[45]

The thorough reform of the Church, therefore, was to embrace the establishment of peace among all Christian princes.

CHAPTER IX

Religious Devotion
and Holydays

It is natural for More to pass from a description of priests, their duties and their privileges, to a sketch of holydays, churches, and rites in Utopia. But it is impossible to grasp the full implications of this section without some knowledge of the religious background.

More is heavily indebted neither to the New World nor to the ancient world. As far as the ancients are concerned, Plato in the *Republic* admired and imitated by More is content to leave the settlement of religious matters to the Apollo of Delphi and makes no attempt to set up an ideal religion in his ideal commonwealth. As for the newly discovered Americas, in the first of his *Four Voyages* Vespucci on insufficient evidence proclaims that the Indians are "far worse than the gentiles themselves or the pagans, for we could not discover that they performed any sacrifices nor that they had any special places or houses of worship." And in his *New World* he seems to shrug his shoulders as he asks: "Beyond the fact that they have no church, no religion and are not idolaters, what more can I say?"[1]

For Thomas More, the Christian and the humanist, the possibility of reasonable men being religionless was inadmissible. Here humanists and scholastics were at one. Aquinas had asserted that the dictates of natural reason obliged men to perform acts in reverence to the supreme being, although the particular acts to be performed were determined by divine or human law, not by the dictates of natural reason. Scotus had declared that in every law, therefore in the law of nature also, men used sacrifices or rites or genuflections in token of reverence toward God as the supreme Lord and of submission to His dominion on their part. From the viewpoint of the humanists, for example, of Ficino, no brute animals gave signs of being religious; in fact, religion was almost as proper to men as neighing to horses or barking to dogs! Disregard for divine worship would make the human race less happy and more wretched than brute creation. "When religion is neglected," agrees Colet, "men sink most lamentably into every kind of wickedness." For, as Erasmus observes, "religion is an inborn power which guides men by the reverence and rites of the gods." But Erasmus goes further than Ficino; for in his *Explanation of the Creed* he declares that religion is so much according to nature that some religious feeling is believed to exist in elephants and other brute animals.[2]

More than anything else, the humanist reformers sought to reintroduce or to strengthen the spirit of devotion in religion. True devotion does not consist alone in the recitation of many prayers, nor in bodily austerities, nor in philanthropic charities, nor in exalted feeling and imagination, nor in spiritual consolations, nor in ecstasies and visions. "Devotion," says St. Thomas Aquinas, "seems to be nothing else than a certain willingness to give oneself promptly to those acts which pertain to the service of God" as the sovereign master of man and the universe. The principal interior acts are adoration, thanksgiving, atonement, and petition. The chief exterior acts, the function of which is to manifest interior sentiments, are sacrifice and public prayer. All acts of devotion, internal and external, have as their primary end the love of God and union with Him and as their secondary end the love of one's neighbor for God's sake and one's own salvation and perfection. External or sensible works must not be slighted. Prostrations, genuflections, songs, and vocal prayers, according to Aquinas, are means, not to arouse God, but to animate and inspire man to communion with the divine. Since God is omniscient and His will immutable, He does not need such things: He does not accept, as if they were to His advantage, the soul's feelings or the body's gestures. No, insists the Angelic Doctor in his *Summa contra gentiles,* we perform such sensible acts on our own account to serve as means to direct our intention to God and to enkindle our love for Him. "At the same time," he then comments on the obligation of exterior or bodily as well as interior or spiritual worship, "in this way we acknowledge God to be creator of our soul *and* body, to whom we offer *spiritual* and *bodily* works of submission." Thus, the Utopians use candles, incense, and so forth, in worship, not as if they were ignorant that these things contribute nothing to the divine nature—just as the very prayers of men do not—but because this harmless form of worship is a source of pleasure to them and because as a result men in some unaccountable fashion feel themselves elevated and join in the worship of God with greater animation. Sensible signs, insists Colet, are "reminders to us, and inducements to the things which are not seen. . . . For as long as we are in the body, our sacraments and ecclesiastical system must be in some degree corporeal." Ronald Knox has expressed the same idea under another aspect: the Catholic Church "does not make the silly Puritan mistake of trying to outlaw the pagan part of our nature, she adopts it, and hallows it, and turns it to her own ends." Thomas More gives full recognition to the external or "pagan" aspects of religion in his *Utopia.*[3]

But a blight had descended upon the religion of the time. And no blight upon religion, declares Erasmus, is more fresh and vigorous than superstitious reverence for ceremonies, since

it commends itself chiefly under the guise of religion. His exclusive purpose in composing the *Handbook of the Christian
Soldier* at an early date, he tells Colet, was to heal the wide-
spread error of those who placed the essence of religion in
almost more than Jewish ceremonies and observances of corporal things, while outrageously neglecting the things which
belong to true devotion. This attack he continued throughout
his life. In his *Colloquies,* for example, he returns to the abuse
again and again. One instance is provided by the words of
Chrysoglottus in *The Religious Banquet.* "If you look at Christians in common," he asks, "don't you find they live as if the
whole sum of religion consisted in ceremonies?" From birth
to death the Christian undergoes ceremonies: baptism, confirmation, confession, communion, marriage, fasting, hearing Mass,
extreme unction, and so forth. "Now I approve of the doing of
this well enough; but the doing of them more out of custom
than conscience I don't approve; but to think that nothing else
is requisite for the making of a Christian I absolutely disapprove." And then Chrysoglottus makes an almost universal condemnation: "The greatest part of men in the world trust to
these things, and think they have nothing else to do but get
wealth by right or wrong to gratify their passions of rage, lust,
malice, ambition." Even the monk in *The Soldier and the Carthusian,* putting his trust "in purity of mind and in Christ himself," speaks of all outward observances as "trivial things." Nor
are his *Adages* free from criticism and condemnation of those
Christians who, like philosophers who are wise only in their
wearing of pallium and beard, place perfect holiness of life,
not in mind and morality, but in ceremonies and rites. In his
important adage *Sileni Alcibiadis* he begs his reader not to
think that his comments are contumelious to anyone. "We
censure the thing or abuse, not men or individuals" ("Rem
notamus, non homines"). This is only partially true. In assailing
the abuse he seems to be assailing the proper use too much.

Although refraining from attacking individuals, he does nevertheless attack Western Christendom as a body.[4]

It need occasion little wonder that Erasmus himself should
become the target for criticism and censure. His only defense
is a repetition of his previous stand: approval of rites insofar
as they add symbolism and majesty to divine worship, but condemnation for the burial of Christian life under a weight of
formal ceremonies. In fact, in a later addition (1523) to the
Method of True Theology (1518) he declares that the great
disturbances, wars, spoliations, and schisms of the past fifteen
years draw their origin from the abuse of ceremonies. Again,
in his *Apology against Certain Spanish Monks* (1528) he declares his often-repeated approbation of the moderate and
earnest use of ceremonies—his frequent reproof of those who
rely on ceremonies to the neglect of essentials. More weighty
were the censures of his *Colloquies* by the faculty of theology
of the University of Paris. In his response Erasmus points to
St. Jerome, who characterized as superstitious the simplicity of
foolish women carrying on their persons a page of the gospel
or a fragment of the cross, not because the practices were in
themselves impious, but because they relied more on those external things than on interior sentiments. Continual prayering
without corresponding affection, or fasting for its own sake without any other motive, is irrational and superstitious.[5]

When one makes a survey and study of all Erasmus' pronouncements on fasting, holydays, vows, indulgences, pilgrimages, sacramental ceremonies, and so forth, one is inclined
to consider him either guilty of rash judgment insofar as he
assigns hypocritical or superstitious motives to Christians in
general or a reformer who has gone so far in his doctrine that
he unreasonably but unconsciously attacks not only abuses but
legitimate usages. For one statement of qualified approval there
are a hundred condemnations. His approach is so spiritualized
and intellectualized that his reform falls on the other side in

failing to make proper provision for the physical or sensitive aspects of man's nature and their expression in external or visible form. The chief fault may lie in Erasmus' hyperspirituality and hyperintellectuality, which some would term a liberal rationalism and which left him insensitive to the religious feelings and emotions of ordinary people. Certainly Huizinga's judgment of Erasmus appears to be correct: "Intellectualist as he is, with his contempt for ignorance, he seems unaware that those religious observances, after all, may contain valuable sentiments of unexpressed and unformulated piety." And one is tempted to conclude that the intellectuality of Erasmus is not that of a thinker but of a scholar. Unlike More, he was relatively out of contact was the mass of passionate, struggling, ordinary humanity. More knew better than Erasmus what was in man, and consequently More's judgments appear more comprehensive, more sane, more human.[6]

Thomas More in the eyes of Erasmus, as is clear from the latter's epistle to Hutten, diligently practiced true piety but remained most free from all superstition. In this respect More was like his model Pico, in the translation of whose life he wrote: "Of outward observances he gave no very great force. We speak not of those observances which the Church commandeth to be observed, for in those he was diligent; but we speak of those ceremonies which folk bring up, setting the very service of God aside, which is (as Christ saith) to be worshiped in spirit and in truth." Yet More's views on ceremonies, indulgences, pilgrimages, and other pious works are definitely sane and middle-of-the-road views which safeguard both the spiritual intention and its external manifestation, whereas Erasmus' opinions are extreme and offensive to pious ears. If the decrees and canons of the Council of Trent be accepted as norms, Thomas More, not Desiderius Erasmus, has the true and orthodox doctrine on these sensible aids to religion and devotion. And this genuine doctrine More has exemplified in the religion of his reasonable Utopians. Here, therefore, is another instance of the positive attitude of More as contrasted with the negative or neutral viewpoint of Erasmus. Both are reformers, both regret abuses. Erasmus ridicules and attacks abuses so that he is mistakenly judged to condemn ceremonies and observances themselves; More depicts such simplicity and purity of intention in his Utopians that they can serve as models for Christians.[7]

A classic defense of ceremonies is to be found in the controversial writings of St. John Fisher. In his *Confutation of Luther's Assertion* he enunciates the principle that, on the one hand, the person who places his hope of salvation in ceremonies is grossly deceived, but, on the other hand, one must not view ceremonies as useless. Abolish such ceremonies as genuflection, striking of the breast, standing during the reading of the gospel, and so forth, and you extinguish the worship of God and the spirit of devotion in the majority of Christians. For the spark of devotion which still exists in the hearts of a few Christians is nourished by ceremonies. Later, in his *Reality of Christ's Body and Blood in the Eucharist,* Fisher declares that one should distinguish between persons strong in faith and persons weak in faith. Ceremony and pomp are necessary for strong Christians, not absolutely but because of the ordination of the Church guided by the Holy Spirit. They are necessary for weak members in order to inflame them, for example, to love of the Blessed Sacrament. In the first age, when Christ's blood had just recently been shed, the faith and the ardor of Christians were so great that they were happy in Christ's presence alone and needed no devotional helps. At the present time people have grown so cold that, unless aided by ceremonies and displays, the vigor of faith would die away in many. In the times of the apostles, Fisher claims, songs were not heard in church, but later were introduced by the fathers to incite torpid souls to greater devotion. "What has ever been so good and holy," questions Fisher, "that no one could ever find occasion to abuse it?"

But the abuses which Oecolampadius mentions, far from being derogatory to faith in the Blessed Sacrament, rather strengthen it. The gold and the silver, the gems and the flowers, the banquets and the plays, are an easy way of drawing the uncultured crowd to piety. "And certainly," Fisher continues, "one must connive at many things on account of weaker members." Nevertheless he has no praise for false trappings or for the omission of more useful pursuits. But provision, he insists later, must be made for weaker members: lighted torches and sounding cymbals incite their sluggish hearts more to the things of God.[8]

It is logical for More to begin his treatment of rites and ceremonies with an enumeration of the days which they keep holy. They compute the cycle of the year by the revolution of the sun. They divide the year into months which they determine by the revolutions of the moon. The first and last days of each month and of each year are celebrated as holydays. The first days are termed *Cynemerni*, a word translated by More into Latin as *primifesti* and by Robinson into English as *first feasts*. The last days are called *Trapemerni*, a word signifying in Latin *dies finifesti* and in English *last feasts*. In his explanation of Utopian names the scholar Gerard John Vossius (1577-1649), "the greatest 'Polyhistor' of his age" according to Sandys, makes no attempt to explain the two terms, since More claims that only the names of cities and magistrates are derived from the Greek. The second element in both words, however, seems to be clear: ἡμερινός, an adjective derived from ἡμέρα, *day*. Lupton derives the first element of *Cynemerni* from κυν-, a combining form meaning *of a dog*, and claims that "the word is meant to suggest κυν-ημερινός, 'the dog's day of the month,' strictly the night between the old and new, when food was placed out at the cross-roads, and the barking of the dogs was taken as a sign of the approach of Hecate." He derives the first syllable in *Trapemerni* from τραπ-, second aorist root of τρέπω, *to turn*, and thus "τραπ-ημερινός would express the turning or closing

day of the month." On the *Trapemerni* or last feasts the Utopians fast until their religious rites in the evening *(uespere)*
and therefore have little time for other activities after services.
"Evening" should probably be interpreted in the broad sense,
that is, some time after three o'clock in the afternoon. Thus, in
the Middle Ages, the fast was broken after Vespers, "which in
the Lenten season," according to Aquinas, "is said after the
ninth hour." On the *Cynemerni* or first feasts they worship before the midday meal, have dinner, and then spend the rest
of the day in games and the practice of the art of war. The
nature of the games is not revealed. They are probably more
strenuous than the recreation in which they indulge after supper
every evening: music, conversation, battle of numbers, and
battle of virtues and vices. Dice playing and other gambling
come in for specific condemnation.[9]

Hythloday makes no mention of days equivalent to the
Jewish sabbath or Christian Sunday. If the Utopians have no
free day each week, they celebrate only twenty-six holydays
each year. This paucity must be deliberate on More's part. The
European Christian would be astounded to learn that much less
than one tenth of the year is devoted to holydays in Utopia. In
Europe one fourth to one third is free from work and sup-
posedly consecrated to divine worship. The multiplication of
holydays, in addition to the fifty-two Sundays of the year, had
begun early. Fifty holydays, of which twenty-five permitted a
half-day's work, were celebrated at Oxford by 1222. More than
forty, plus a dozen half-holydays, were observed at Worcester
by 1240. The situation was the same all over Europe. The Council of Szabolch in Hungary mentions thirty-two in 1092. There
were fifty-four at Cognac in 1260, forty-seven at Pont-Audemer
in 1305, and so forth. Efforts to reduce their number were
made in the fifteenth century but were unsuccessful until the
sixteenth. At the provincial council of Rheims in 1408, John
Gerson, the great religious leader of the early fifteenth century,

argued against the multiplicity of holydays on the score that they kept workmen from earning a livelihood and that they were the occasions of grave moral danger, particularly idleness with its deadly consequences of drunkenness, dangerous games, dances, prodigality, and other similar evils. The result is that "what was wisely instituted for the honor of God and for the salvation of souls has been changed into His vilification and the loss of salvation." The same ideas are repeated often by the reformers who followed him, including Erasmus, as we shall see.[10]

A picture of the abuse of Sundays and holydays in England in the early sixteenth century is found in Alexander Barclay's *Eclogues* (published 1515, but written earlier). In a passage in Eclogue V for which there is no counterpart in Mantuan's Eclogue VI, he deplores the visiting of stews on holydays in the city and the corrupt ways of the country as well:

> On the holyday, as soon as morn is past,
> When all men resteth, while all the day doth last,
> They drink, they banket, they revel, and they jest—
> They leap, they dance, despising ease and rest.
> If they once hear a bagpipe or a drone,
> Anon to the elm or oak they be gone.
> There use they to dance, to gambol, and to rage:
> Such is the custom and use of the village.

His *Ship of Fools* notes the excessive drinking which marks the holyday, for the "tavern is open before the church be." The section "Of fools that keep not the holyday" does not suggest that the number of holydays should be decreased, but merely enjoins the dedication of the holydays to the purpose for which they have been instituted:

> Cease, fool, and leave off worldly business
> Upon the holyday, and rest of the labor
> Of thy hands, applying the whole to holiness
> With word and deed to laud thy Creator.[11]

Idleness or leisure, for Erasmus, is the source of all danger
and all wickedness for everybody, but especially for young men
and for women. In the days of old the Christian people were
granted freedom from work in order to devote themselves to
works of piety, but now they abuse their leisure by drinking
parties, by visits to prostitutes, by dicing, by brawls, and by
fights. At no other time are more foul sins committed than on
the holydays when it is most fitting to shy away from them.
Never do people imitate pagans more than on days when they
ought to be most Christian. Instead of daily increasing the
number of holydays, bishops ought to follow the example of
prudent physicians who change the remedy according to the
changed condition of their patients. Since the innumerable holydays now mean the ruin of piety, Erasmus recommends a return
to the few established by early Christians and a careful observance of these few in the spirit of piety. "To true Christians," he
concludes, "every day is a holy day, but to bad Christians, the
majority of people, holydays are less holy than godless and
unholy." The same plea is found in a note to the *New Testament.*
Finally, in his irenic work on church unity and harmony
(1533), Erasmus descends to details. He would abolish various
feasts of the Blessed Virgin Mary, such as those of the Immac-
ulate Conception, the Nativity, and the Presentation in the Temple. As for feasts established by the private authority of various
confraternities and guilds, he would have the feasts, as well as
the organizations themselves, abolished by the government since
they are nothing else than associations of Comus and Bacchus.
Instructions were given the Spanish ambassadors in 1512 to
ask the Lateran Council to reduce, on account of abuses, the
number of feasts to those of Christ, the Blessed Virgin Mary,
the apostles, and a few others. Tunstall, the friend of More and
Erasmus, issued a measure for practical reform in 1523 in his
capacity as bishop of London. He ordered all feasts for the
dedication of churches to be transferred to and celebrated on

October 3. His reason is typical: human weakness excessively abuses these feasts by devoting the days free from business and labor, not to prayer and fasting and meditation, but to gossiping, dancing, drinking, even drunkenness, and often to quarrels and brawls, and sometimes even to murder and other dreadful sins and crimes.[12]

More's basic agreement with Erasmus can be surmised from the passage on holydays in *Utopia,* but there seems to be no particular reference to the multiplicity and abuse of holydays in his other works. More, however, concurs with his friend in the fundamental principles from which Erasmus argues. In the *Answer to "The Supper of the Lord"* he states that "an evil and a perilous life" is led by those that "live either in idleness or in idle business, driving forth all their days in gaming for their pastime, as though that else their time could never pass . . . but if they drave away the day with dancing or some such other goodly gaming." As for "sleep and gaming," they "must serve but for a refreshing of the weary and forwatched body to renew it unto watch and labor again." More then uses a homely comparison, such as is quite typical of him:

> For rest and recreation should be but as a sauce. And sauce should, ye wot well, serve for a faint and weak stomach to get it the more appetite to the meat and not for the increase of voluptuous pleasure in every greedy glutton that hath in himself sauce malapert already enough. And, therefore, likewise as it were a fond feast that had all the table full of sauce and so little meat therewith that the guests should go thence as empty as they come thither, so is it surely a very mad-ordered life that hath but little time bestowed in any fruitful business, and all the substance idly spent in play.

More would certainly have objections to spending more than a quarter of the year in idleness and its evil concomitants. If the holydays were actually spent in a devout manner, with pleasant and innocent secular pursuits as their sauce, he would probably not be adverse to their great number.[13]

Common Religion

Because of the great diversity and unparalleled freedom of Utopian religions one would expect each sect to have its own priests and its own churches and temples. But religion for More and the Utopians was not merely a private affair but a matter of public or state importance. Consequently on the social and political level there was a religion of the state which included only elements common to all the religions. The established religion had a bishop and twelve priests and presumably thirteen temples in each city. But whether the temples had been official or denominational, More would still have insisted on their necessity. If all churches were abolished in Christendom, for example, "we were like," says More in his *Dialogue Concerning Heresies,* "to have few good temples of God in men's souls, but all would within a while wear away clean and clearly fall to nought." Experience attests, moreover, that "those which be the best temples of God in their souls, they most use to come to the temple of stone." In public services in church everyone helps everyone else spiritually. As More explains in the *Confutation of Tyndale,* "the whole company prayeth for the whole presence, and so is every each the better for other's prayer, and all people the better both for the prayer and the sacrament and every devout observance used in the church at the divine service." Social aspects are not negligible![1]

189

Erasmus protests at this time against the formal devotion which puts its trust in exterior works rather than in change of heart. According to a note to Jerome's epitaph for Paula the saint's words will probably not please some people because he seems not to give sufficient credit to persons who erect or adorn sacred buildings at their own expense. Today very many Christians esteem the latter to be the height of piety. Some princes, to say nothing of bishops, suppose that numberless wars, killings, sacrileges, villainies, and shameful crimes are properly expiated if only they undertake the construction of a sacred chapel—even with other people's revenues. Jerome prefers alms, for these are expended upon the living temples of God, that is, upon the poor of Christ.[2]

The Utopian temples are extraordinary buildings to look at, not only on account of their painstaking workmanship, but also on account of their capacity for holding immense throngs of people. The latter, of course, is necessary in view of their relative paucity. All temples are somewhat dark on the interior. They say that this obscurity arises, not from ignorance of architecture, but from the advice of the priests, on account of their opinion that excessive glare scatters one's thoughts, but rather little and somewhat uncertain light makes the soul recollected and intent upon religious devotion. The Carthusian recitation of the Divine Office with which More was familiar relies upon the use of dim light or darkness for devotion. A candle in a lantern casts enough light upon the folio antiphonary for the needs of the three monks assigned to each book, but "leaves all the rest in shadow, so that a semi-darkness always prevails." During parts of the Office known by heart, all lights are covered and even extinguished in order to rest the eyes. "This also aids devotion," observes one Carthusian, "and favours holy poverty." The use of "dim and doubtful light" as an aid to "religion and devotion," therefore, is introduced into Utopian churches because it is a feature verified by More's own experience.[3]

Because the Utopian religion is not the same for all citizens and because, Hythloday comments, all forms of religion, no matter how varied and multiple, converge by different routes on one goal, namely, the worship of the divine nature, one can see or hear in their temples nothing which does not appear to square with all the religions in common. If a religion has a rite peculiar to itself, its devotee attends to it within the walls of his own home. The Utopians conduct the public services by means of observances which in no way detract from anyone's private ceremonies. In their invocations they use no special appellation for the deity except Mithra, the name of the Persian god of light and truth. The choice of this name is natural, since the Utopian language is almost like the Persian except for titles of officials and cities. All Utopians agree in employing this word to designate the one divine nature, whatever it may be. Prayers are formulated in such a way that they can be recited by everyone without prejudice to his personal religion. No effigy of the gods appears in the temple and consequently everyone is free to conceive the deity imaginatively according to the highest religious aspiration. Moreover, in antiquity Strabo in his *Geography* had reported that "the Persians do not erect statues or altars." The latter fact is mentioned at this time by Polydore Vergil in his *Inventors of Things.*[4]

This prohibition of images in the state church would seem to be but common sense, since nature and reason, knowing the deity is a pure spirit, have no means of depicting Him visually. Not possessing revelation, the Utopians have no conception of the Incarnation, the union of the divine nature with the human nature in visible bodily form. According to Polydore Vergil man invented and fashioned statues to remember persons who were dead or absent; but, in view of God's omnipresence, man from the very day of his creation did nothing more stupid than to fashion a likeness of God. St. Augustine in his *City of God,* upon which young More had given lectures, quotes Varro to the effect that the ancient Romans worshiped the gods without an image for more than one hundred and seventy years. "If this custom had survived," says Varro, "the gods would be honored more piously." The individual who imposed images of the gods on the people added to the common errors about the deity and took away the fear of the gods because it is easy to contemn them in the form of stolid statues. More's friend, John Colet, follows St. Paul in connecting immorality with idolatry or the worship of an image as God. In commenting on Romans 1:22-28 he writes: "For *professing themselves to be wise,* and to know God, *they became fools* really and in fact, under the obscuring influence of idolatry, and the gloom of image-worship. *And changed the glory of the uncorruptible God . . . for the likeness of an image*—for the false worship of an image, by doing to images what they would do to God. . . . In leaving God, they are themselves left to their own lusts, *to vile affections, to a reprobate mind. . . .* In idolatry the world found its ruin." Since More makes his Utopians models of reason and virtue, he can hardly make them worshipers of idols for fear of what befalls idolaters.[5]

But Thomas More would seem to have an ulterior motive in banishing images from temples. A clue to his intention is found in an abuse attacked by the humanists: the improper veneration of saints and images. For example, Folly in Erasmus' *Praise* is far from asking for worship in the form of stone and colored images. The latter "would but hinder the worship of me, since by the stupid and dull those figures are worshiped instead of the saints themselves. And it would come about with me exactly as it usually does with the saints—they are thrown out of doors by their substitutes." Saints and their images, moreover, have taken the place of pagan heroes and their statues. Hercules has found a successor in St. George, "whose horse, piously decked out with trappings and bosses, they all but worship, often commending themselves to him by some little gift." On these passages Lister's comments are illuminating. Once upon a time the churches of Christians had nothing sculptured or painted in them, but now even the horse of St. George, arrayed in real armor, takes up a good part of the church. Almost all the ancient saints, as is seen in many texts and especially in St. Jerome, condemned the use of images in churches for fear of idolatry. Erasmus, according to Lister, does not intend to reproach any legitimate usage of Christians, but the stupidity of those who venerate images not as signs but as sentient beings and who trust in the images rather than the saints themselves. This kind of idolatry ought to be removed as the occasion of sin for the ignorant.[6]

Erasmus returns to the subject in several other works. In his open *Letter against the Sham-Gospellers* he repeats his assertion on the prohibition of images in the early Church on account of both the Jews, who were inclined to idolatry, and the gentiles, who might still be under some influence of their idol-worshiping religions. The introduction of Christian images has developed to the point where their veneration now exceeds both moderation and decorum. Paintings which would appear out of place even in galleries or restaurants are displayed in churches. There is no need for removing all paintings altogether, since they serve a threefold purpose: pleasure, ornament, usefulness. Abuses, however, must be corrected. In his *Explanation of the Creed* he suggests that in the place where God is solemnly adored (presumably in the sanctuary or even in the church proper) no image except that of the crucified Christ should be placed. At any rate, as he writes in his commentary on Psalm 85, Christian churches should fittingly have few images, and these few should be pure and simple and evocative of religious feeling. In this same commentary Erasmus approaches the reasoning of the Utopians, who debar images so that every man can conceive God according to his highest religious sentiment. He recommends that the Christians adore God without reliance upon any sensible image, since no human utterance, no human thought, can picture God as He really is. If a true portrait represents a man inadequately, how can any image represent God? Erasmus has no objection to fixing the eyes of the body upon an image, provided the eyes of the soul are intent upon God, but the person who can contemplate God only with the aid of an image is lamentably obtuse. A reasoned defense of images appears also in his *Letter to the Brethren of Lower Germany* and in his plea for peace in the Church. "Mere superstition, of which I admit there is much in the worship of the Saints, must be refuted," he concedes in the latter work; "but simple piety may be accepted, even when it is combined with some degree of error."[7]

Thomas More is much more acutely aware of the dependence of the mind upon the senses, and of their interdependence, than Erasmus. He is much more cognizant of the reason for, and the fact of, the Incarnation—"what we have heard, what we have seen, what we have looked upon and our hands have handled" (1 John 1:1). Even the most devout and the most learned, he declares, have their feelings deepened by the contemplation of the crucifix; otherwise their feelings toward Christ's Passion are suspect or "very faint." "And albeit," he writes in his *Dialogue Concerning Heresies*, "that every good Christian man hath a remembering of Christ's passion in his mind and conceiveth by devout meditation a form and fashion thereof in his heart, yet is there no man, I ween, so good and so well learned, nor in meditation so well accustomed, but that he findeth himself more moved to pity and compassion upon the beholding of the holy crucifix than when he lacketh it."[8]

In the very same *Dialogue* More denies outright that contemporary Christians pay homage to the images, not to the saints represented, for example, the Blessed Virgin Mary. Here More definitely parts company with Erasmus in his interpretation of the motives and impulses of ordinary Christians. "Nor the flock

of Christ is not so foolish as those heretics bear them in hand,"
he asserts, using a homely comparison, "that whereas there is
no dog so mad but he knoweth a very coney from a coney carved
and painted, Christian people that have reason in their heads,
and thereto the light of faith in their souls, should ween that the
images of our Lady were our Lady herself." Christians are not
"so mad but they do reverence to the image for the honor of
the person whom it representeth, as every man delighteth in the
image and remembrance of his friend." The Church venerates
saints not as God Himself but as "God's good servants": the
honor paid to them redounds to the honor of their Master. The
Old Testament, claims More, prohibited only the making of
images of false gods because they were devils and forbade also
the worship of an image as God. In the New Testament, Christians are forbidden to worship saints or their images with the
honor and reverence due to God. "But I suppose neither scripture nor natural reason," More concludes, "doth forbid that
man may do some reverence to an image, not fixing his final
intent in the image, but referring it further to the honor of the
person that the image representeth." The reason is that "in such
reverence done unto the image there is none honor withdrawn
neither from God nor good man, but both the saint honored in
his image and God in His saint." The immense popularity of
Dives et Pauper, a book of instruction on the ten commandments, during More's lifetime substantiates his claim that the
faithful received the proper instruction on the veneration of
the saints and their statues. In summary, one may say that More
agrees with Erasmus in the basic doctrine, in the necessity of
propriety, and, most probably, in the need for fewer images. He
disagrees with him by interpreting favorably the motives and
knowledge of ordinary Christians and by stressing the need of
aids for the senses in religion.[9]

CHAPTER XI

Confession, Sacrifice,
Accouterments

U topians, as has been seen, come to their imageless temples upon the first and last days of every month and year. The observance of these days is varied in purpose and in rite. On a "last feast" the people assemble in the temple at sundown, still fasting, in order to give thanks to God for the prosperity of the month or year of which that day is the last. In former ages it was customary to fast until nightfall or at least until Vespers or Evensong, but Vespers was gradually anticipated until by the early sixteenth century, as More reveals in his *Apology*, it was recited in Lent before noon, at which hour a full meal could be taken. On the next day, which, of course, is a "first feast," they flock to the temple in the morning in order to pray together for a fortunate and happy issue to the following month or year which they begin that day under good auspices.[1]

On last feasts the pious Utopians have a custom which appears strangely Christian. Before their trip to the temple wives cast themselves at the feet of their husbands, children at the feet of their parents. They confess their frailties, whether the commission of a fault or the neglectful omission of a duty, and ask forgiveness for their failings. In this way, if any little cloud of dissension surrounds the home, it is dispersed by these amends, so that all can be present at the sacrifices with pure and tranquil heart. Attendance with a conscience not at peace is a sin. For this reason individuals conscious of hatred or anger toward anyone, unless they get rid of their base feelings and reconcile themselves to their enemy, do not intrude themselves on the sacrifices out of fear of swift punishment.[2]

At first this avowal of faults and sins seems to be advocacy of lay confession, but actually, as is seen from the context, it is, on More's part, but a pagan adoption and application of the admonition of Christ against anger and hatred in His sermon on the mountain. Speedy and severe punishment, in accordance with the gravity of the offense, comes from the local court or the high court and even may result in the capital sentence and burning in Gehenna. "Therefore, if thou art offering thy gift at the altar, and there rememberest that thy brother has anything against thee, leave thy gift before the altar and go first to be reconciled to thy brother, and then come and offer thy gift" (Matthew 5:23-24). Even according to the natural law pardon must be asked and reparation made for contumely and wrath. More in his *Confutation* agrees with Tyndale that "if I have hurt my neighbor, I am bound to shrive myself unto him [that is, to confess my offense to him] and make him amends if I have wherewith, or, if not, then to ask him forgiveness, and he is bound to forgive me." The Utopian custom is not of sacramental origin, nature, or efficacy. The inhabitants of Utopia, like the ancient Greeks, are non-Christian, and, as More says, "in Greece before Christ's days they used not confession, no more the men then than the beasts now." Scotus sums up the traditional doctrine when he states that the law of nature does not oblige men to the sacramental confession of their sins to priests but only to confession to God as the just judge in petition for forgiveness. Relying upon Jerome's epitaph for Fabiola, Erasmus concludes that confession was once public and concerned only with open sins and that secret confession of all sins to the priest was not yet instituted in Jerome's age. It was the Church which later salutarily introduced secret and private confession.[3]

The avowal of faults in *Utopia*, as has been asserted above, is not to be taken as a plea for the revival of lay confession. It may be useful, however, to discuss briefly the practice so that the differences may appear. Lay confession was found in the Middle Ages in two forms: acknowledgment of minor sins or faults which did not have to be confessed to the priest and confession of serious sins which were revealed to a layman in urgent cases in the absence of a priest. The first form was practiced in monasteries and religious houses and clearly covers the situation in Utopia. The principal basis for the custom was St. James's advice: "Confess, therefore, your sins to one another" (James 5:16). Exegetes, such as W. H. Kent, hold today that "since there is mention of confession of sins which is evidently to be made before priests, it seems more likely . . . that 'to one another' indicates in the concrete the priests, considered as a part of the community." In former times other interpretations prevailed. The comment of the Venerable Bede on this scriptural text was often quoted:

> It should be done with discernment; we should confess our daily and slight faults mutually to our equals, and believe that we are saved by their daily prayer. As for the more grievous leprosy [mortal sin], we should, according to the law, discover its impurity to the priest.

As for the second form, confession of grievous sin to a layman in the absence of a priest was made more or less obligatory in two influential works: in the pseudo-Augustinian *True and False Penance* and in Peter Lombard's *Sentences*. Albert the Great and Thomas of Aquin even saw a certain sacramental value in this form of confession. Scotus rejected the obligatory nature of the practice and found certain perils in the custom. All held that the confession had to be repeated to a priest later. Lay confession fell increasingly into disuse, until at the end of the fourteenth century Gerard Zerbolt complained that it was scarcely ever practiced. A very famous late incident was the confession of the dying Bayard to his *maistre d'ostel* in 1524. Bossuet, quoting Pylicdorf, points to the Waldensians who "began, being laymen, to hear confessions, to enjoin penances, and give absolution." Luther claimed that a layman had the same power as a priest to absolve from sins. His condemnation brought lay confession into further obloquy. By 1564 Dominico Soto is said to have found difficulty in believing in the existence of the custom. For the Brethren of the Common Life, Zerbolt specifically allowed the confession of venial sins and failings to laymen at any time and of mortal sins in case of necessity. He appealed to Peter Lombard but admitted that contemporary theologians and canon lawyers were against the Master of the Sentences. The practice, however, if not obligatory, was at least licit. It was the Brethren of the Common Life who educated Erasmus, the friend of More. The custom in Utopia secures an atmosphere of necessary peace in the family and a state of friendship among fellow citizens. At most, it can be considered as the introduction of the monastic confession of faults into the Utopian family.[4]

After the confession of faults at home and after their arrival in the temple, the Utopians follow a very old Christian custom. The men betake themselves to the right side (Epistle side), the women to the left side (Gospel side). The members of the household do not separate altogether. The males, including the boys, take their station in front of the father of the household; the females, including the girls, in front of the mother of the household. Provision is thus made for having the persons whose power of ruling and training prevails at home keep an eye on every gesture of every person away from home. Special precaution is taken to join the younger members with the older and not to trust children alone with children, lest they pass in tomfoolery the very time in which they ought especially to develop religious reverence toward the gods. Such reverence, observes Hythloday, is the most powerful and almost the only stimulus to the acquirement of virtue. This axiom is altogether in keeping with the intimate and inseparable union which the Utopians believe exists between religion and morality.[5]

Now what happens? The people, men and women, young and old, are assembled in the temple. The priests also are present. Sacrifices, too, have been indirectly mentioned earlier in this same chapter in *Utopia*, where one learns that individuals with hatred or anger in their heart dare not to be present at the sacrifices *(sacrificia)*. As John Fisher was later to observe in his vindication of Henry VIII's defense of the seven sacraments: "No law has ever been without priests, and no priests we read about have ever been without sacrifice." Sacrifice is an act of homage toward God which has as its purpose closer union with Him as Creator, providence, and end of man: it involves the oblation of a gift symbolizing interior consecration to Him. The gift in the Utopian religion, the reader is expressly told, does not consist in animals sacrificed to God. The opinion of the Utopians is that the divine clemency takes no pleasure in the blood and slaughter of the animals to which God has granted life in order to have them live. Neither, strangely enough, do they offer to God an unbloody sacrifice of the fruits and vegetables of the earth. Theophrastus and other ancient philosophers believed that the oldest sacrifices were unbloody and vegetarian. This type of sacrifice, in fact, persisted dominant throughout antiquity, not merely because of its venerable age and of tenacious tradition, but especially because a basically vegetarian diet prevailed among the Romans and the Greeks. After all, one was to sacrifice one's means of subsistence to the gods upon whose power one's existence depended. Erasmus in his *Adages* calls attention to the disciples of Orpheus, who would not stain the altars of the gods with the blood of herds but offered sacrifices of cakes and fruits.[6]

The gifts of the Utopians to the deity, however, are incense and candles. They burn frankincense and other fragrant spices: they light wax tapers in great abundance. They understand that odors, lights, and ceremonies are not necessary for God but are helpful to man in elevating his mind and making his spirit more prompt in the divine service. More was much pained when the Protestants mocked "the setting up of candles" and demanded "whether God and His saints lack light or whether it be night with them that they cannot see without candle." The observation of Aquinas on the sensible aspects of worship and sacrifice is here most apt. Because it is connatural to man to receive his knowledge through the senses and most difficult for him to transcend sensible objects, God provided that even the man whose mind is not strong for the contemplation of divine things in themselves should have his attention focused on these divine things by the use of sensible objects in divine worship. For this reason God instituted sensible sacrifices for man to offer to Him, not to satisfy any need of His own, but in order to give man a symbolic representation of the truth that he ought to refer himself and all he has to God as his last end and as the Creator, governor, and Lord of all things.[7]

In Utopia the consecration of man to God is sufficiently symbolized in the burning of candles and incense. The dedication expresses itself especially in a pure and upright life—in the endeavor "to present your bodies as a sacrifice, living, holy, pleasing to God—your spiritual service" (Romans 12:1). The comment of Colet on this text offers a clue to the exclusion by More of bloody sacrifices from the Utopian religion. In this exhortation, Colet asserts, St. Paul is "covertly reproving the sacrifices of all those who slew and offered cattle; especially the Jews who . . . were accustomed to make oblations of victims on festival days by slaughtering thousands of sheep, and to glut the whole temple with blood; thinking that by this act they gave great pleasure to God." After citing God's rejection through

Isaias of bloody sacrifices without good intentions and good deeds (Isaias 1:11-16), Colet continues: "For this is the sacrifice that is pleasing to God, a victim fat and without blemish; namely, a man cleansed from evil. . . . For in truth God is not gratified by dead, but by living offerings."[8]

As one reads of unbloody sacrifices, incense, candles, and vestments in the Utopian temple, one cannot help feeling that here is the external setting for the unbloody sacrifice of Christian revelation—the divine sacrifice, as the Council of Trent is later to declare, in which is "contained and immolated in an unbloody manner the same Christ who once offered Himself in a bloody manner on the altar of the cross." But the Church, like the Utopians, realizes that "the nature of man is such that he cannot without external means be raised easily to meditation on divine things." Therefore use is made of "ceremonies, such as mystical blessings, lights, incense, vestments, and many other things of this kind, whereby . . . the minds of the faithful [may be] excited by those visible signs of religion and piety to the contemplation of those most sublime things which are hidden in this sacrifice." Grace builds upon nature. The introduction of the Christian sacrifice of the Mass would not abolish or change radically, but rather bring to perfection, what is contained in the Utopian service in a rudimentary and natural form. The Utopian incense and candles would seem to be but preparations for the Mass. The Christian who stepped into the Utopian temple would feel that this was all a kind of setting for the visible, unbloody, true sacrifice which was about to begin at any moment. This sacrifice, as the Council of Trent explains, "was prefigured by various types of sacrifices during the period of nature and of the law" and "comprises all the good things signified by them, as being the consummation and perfection of them all." Consequently the transition from Utopian worship to the Christian sacrifice of the Mass would be easy. There is no need to expatiate on Thomas More's own assiduous attendance at Mass. The author of the *Relation of the Island of England* writes of Englishmen in general about 1500: "Although they all attend mass every day, . . . they always hear mass on Sunday in their parish church." In his *English History*, which probably existed in manuscript by 1513, Polydore Vergil declares his opinion that no contemporary nation pays more devout and diligent attention to everything concerning divine worship than the English. On account of magnificent churches in every village, precious shrines of saints, and constant attendance of crowds at sacred services, "the English must receive praise for this cause above all, that they are by far the most Christian and the most religious of men."[9]

Within less than fifteen years after the publication of *Utopia,* More was forced to the defense of the external aids to devotion against "the madness of these heretics that bark against the old ancient customs of Christ's Church, mocking the setting up of candles and with foolish faceties [facetiousness] and blasphemous mockery demand whether God and His saints lack light or whether it be night with them that they cannot see without candle." He points to Christ's approval of His anointing by the woman at Bethany (Matthew 26:6-13, Mark 14:3-9, John 12:1-8) and adds: "By these words of our Savior, learn that God delighteth to see the fervent heat of the heart's devotion boil out by the body and to do Him service with all such goods of fortune as God hath given a man." Why should heretics object to the use of gold, candles, and so forth in the Christian church when the Lord Himself caused immense wealth to be expended in the ornamentation of the Jewish temple, altar, and priestly vestments? God designed these rich decorations not for His own sake but for His people's. "What was Himself the better for all this?" questions More like the Utopians. "What for the beasts that Himself commanded to be offered Him in sacrifice? What for the sweet odors and frankincense?" God has given men enough wealth both for the relief of the poor, who are "the quick temples of the Holy Ghost made by His own hands," and for the embellishment of churches, "the temples of stone made by the hand of man." Consequently heretics like Friar Barnes should not condemn as evil "the things that are very good and which, devoutly done, . . . are greatly pleasant to God," such as "bells for calling folk to God's service, . . . vestments, candles, books, and chalices." More's friend Erasmus, in his reply to an attack by Alberto Pio, characteristically approves of a moderate use of candles and disapproves of any superstitious use. Quoting St. Jerome, he holds that a lit candle has a mystic meaning. The lighting of a candle is superstitious in itself unless one strives to feel interiorly what the use of a candle signifies exteriorly. The censure by Alberto Pio was provoked by such statements as that in *The Praise of Folly*, to the effect that plenty of Christians "will burn a little candle to the Virgin Mother, and this at noon when it is unnecessary." Lister in a note points out that the latter words were added by way of a joke and that Erasmus wishes people who light a candle to "burn with zeal to imitate her in chastity of life, temperance, love of heavenly things." According to a note of Erasmus published in 1516, Jerome apparently viewed as superstitious the lighting of candles during daylight in honor of the saints, whence it seems that the practice was tolerated rather than stamped with approval in Jerome's age. Erasmus could hardly have found fault with the Utopians, since they use candles and incense, not as ends in themselves, but as means to the arousal and increase of religious devotion.[10]

When the people pour into their spacious and darkling temple filled with incense and lit with many candles, they wear shining white garments. There is hardly any need to pause over the significance of the color. More again uses Christian symbolism for Utopian customs. In the rite of baptism the priest lays a white linen cloth on the individual to be baptized, saying: "Receive this white garment, which mayest thou carry without

stain before the judgment seat of our Lord Jesus Christ, that
thou mayest have life everlasting." In his *Handbook of the
Christian Soldier* Erasmus explains: "If the exterior man is
veiled in a white tunic, let also the garments of the interior man
be white as snow," that is, the baptized Christian is to be clothed
in innocence and purity. Hence Colet in his exposition of the
letter to the Romans comments: "By this sacrament [of bap-
tism] you die to the world, and begin to live to God; advancing
along the path of Christ in sweetness, whiteness, and light. This
methinks is the meaning of the white christening-robe and the
candle, which you received in baptism. Let none look back; let
none fall away." White is also the color of the Carthusian garments, and hence the Carthusian in Erasmus' colloquy defends
his habit against the soldier by saying: "What colour is more
becoming Christians than that which was given to all in baptism? It has been said also, 'take a white garment'; so that this
garment puts me in mind of what I promised in baptism—that
is, the perpetual study of innocency." The use of the white
garment is associated likewise with the New World in a curious
incident recounted by Peter Martyr d'Anghiera in the First
Decade (1511) of his *New World:*

> One of our archers went off in the woods to hunt. He there
> suddenly encountered a native, so well dressed in a white tunic,
> that at the first glance he believed he saw before him one of the
> Friars of Santa Maria de la Merced, whom the Admiral had
> brought with him. This native was soon followed by two others,
> likewise coming out of the forest, and then by a troop of about
> thirty men, all of them clothed. Our archer turned and ran shout-
> ing, as quickly as he could, towards the ships.

No further trace was ever found of these natives in white
tunics—except in More's *Utopia.*[11]

The white garments of the congregation may have their
origin in the Christian rite of baptism, not in any costume observed in the New World, but the vestments of the priests seem

definitely to have their source in accounts of America. The latter are not white but parti-colored, remarkable for their shape and workmanship but not made of costly material. They are not interwoven with gold thread or inlaid with rare gems. They are nevertheless wrought with variegated feathers of birds so ingeniously and artistically that the preciousness of no material can counterbalance the value of the exquisite craftsmanship. More undoubtedly obtained the hint for this sacerdotal apparel from the Indians. Vespucci had described their neglect and even scorn of gold and gems and their admiration and appreciation of "variegated birds' feathers." In one of the very earliest English books on America a translator had written that "the men and women have on their head, neck, arms, knees, and feet, all with feathers bounden for their beautiness and fairness." The works of Plato, too, have been mentioned—for example, by Lupton—as furnishing the suggestion for the feathery garments, but, it seems, with far less probability. In the *Timaeus* birds are transformations of "harmless but light-minded" human students of the heavens who naively suppose that "the most solid proofs about such matters are obtained by the sense of sight." In the vision of Er in the *Republic*, Orpheus becomes a swan from hatred of women, Agamemnon an eagle from hatred of human nature, and Thamyras a nightingale, perhaps in order to regain his gift of song. The *Birds* of Aristophanes, with its Utopian features, might also have provided a hint in some remote way. But the fact that Hythloday was a companion of Vespucci on his voyages of exploration should tip the balance heavily in favor of an Indian, rather than a classical, source for the vestments made of feathers.[12]

Thomas More, as usual, is not content to use a source without adaptation or transformation. The feathers and plumes of the birds, as well as the definite rows in which they are set, are carefully assorted and marked off on the priestly garb. The Utopians say that the arrangement expresses certain secret mysteries, the interpretation of which the offerers of the sacrifices assiduously transmit and reveal to the people. In general, the various colors and rows and birds which are used serve to remind them of the benefits of God toward them, of their reciprocal devotion toward God, and of their mutual duties toward one another. If More had entered into detail upon the mystical significance of the birds, he would perhaps have had them approach Christian meanings, but without revealing the similarities directly. Thus, the dove represented peace (Genesis 8:11), rest (Psalm 54:7), love and purity (Canticle of Canticles 5:2, 6:8), and guilelessness (Matthew 10:16), as well as the Holy Spirit (Luke 3:22). The eagle symbolized Christ and His divine nature insofar as it alone could look unblinkingly at the sun and the regenerated Christian insofar as it was said to renew its youth by bathing three times in a font of lucid water (Psalm 102:5). The pelican, which was reputed to sacrifice itself for its young to feed on, was the symbol of atonement and redemption by Christ. The peacock signified the resurrection on account of the supposed incorruptibility of its flesh, and the fabled phoenix symbolized immortality on account of its resurgence from its own ashes. These emblems certainly embody God's gifts to man and man's consequent obligations to love God and his fellow man.[13]

One cannot help feeling that, by calling attention to the mystical significance of the priest's garb, More intends to reawaken Christians, laity and clergy, to a consideration of the symbolism of vestments and ceremonies. Thus, Thomas à Kempis had said of the priest's chasuble: "He beareth the Cross before him, that he may mourn for his own sins; and behind him, that he may with sympathy and tears lament for the faults of others also, and know that he hath been placed in the midst between God and the sinner." Even more germane is the section in *The Praise of Folly* in which Erasmus calls bishops and cardinals to the study of the meaning of their garments.

The alb of the bishop represents sincerity and blamelessness of life; his miter, "perfect knowledge of the Old and New Testaments"; his gloves, "a clean administration of the sacrament and one unsullied by any taint of human concerns"; his crozier, "most watchful care of the flock put under his charge"; and the cross borne before him, "a victory over all carnal affections." As for the cardinal, his crimson lower vestment symbolizes "a burning love of God" and his immense outer robe "charity ample enough to embrace all men in its helpfulness, by way of teaching, exhorting, chastising, admonishing, ending wars, resisting wicked princes, and freely spending blood—not money alone—for the flock of Christ." And in *The Complaint of Peace* later, Peace declares of priestly garb: "The white garments, nobilitated [ennobled] with my own color, do please me" ("Arrident vestes candidae meoque colore insignes").[14]

As soon as the Utopian priest presents himself at the entrance, not attired in any symbolical Christian vestments but bedecked in his feathery garb, the whole congregation at once falls prostrate to the floor in such reverence and in such deep silence on every side that the very external appearance of the action strikes a certain fearful awe into a person as though at the presence of some divine power. After they have continued prone on the ground for a little while, they stand up at the signal given by the priest. In this respect, too, the reverence and silence of the Utopians in their temples is in marked contrast with that of Europeans in their churches. The Latin version of Brant's *Ship of Fools*, for example, attacks men who by their barking, shouting, or whispering desecrate the house of God during the recitation of the Office or the chanting of Mass. The English version by Barclay goes into greater detail in a long corresponding section entitled "Of them that make noises, rehearsing of tales, and do other things unlawful and dishonest in the church of God." Special censure is made of the fool who goes to church with his hawk resting on his wrist and his hounds

running at his heels. Others meanwhile take care of their legal
business, making purchases and sales, "chatting and babbling
as it were in a fair" instead of a church, "while the priest his
Mass or matins sings." There is giggling and laughing and
staring at girls—and married women—with little attention to
the service. In fact, at the very pronouncing of the words of
consecration by the priest, a knave walks by the altar with "his
bonnet on his head" and fools keep up their gossiping and
blabbing. In an envoy to his readers at the end of this section,
Barclay recalls that such behavior for Christians is a sin and
disgrace, and then concludes:

> But this one thing causeth me oft to muse
> That the false paynims within their temples be
> To their idols much more devout than we.

The deepest shame, for both Brant and Barclay, is that even the
priests in the choir do not keep silent during the divine service
but unblushingly exchange news about battles, all the way from
Britain to the Black Sea and the fierce Turks. In the memorial
of his visitation in 1511, Archbishop Warham counseled the
monks to reform by keeping better silence in choir.[15]

Erasmus the reformer, as might be anticipated, attacks in
the *Adages* those who chatter away, instead of praying, during
religious ceremonies. In fact, the higher his state, the more
pleasant the dignitary finds the practice—and even supposes
it polite to yelp in his neighbor's ear during the holy sacrifice.
What purity, what reverence, Erasmus declares in his commentary on Psalm 85, is requisite for the adoration of God, and
yet men in church and even at the altar entertain trifling or
impure thoughts, besides being as disorderly in their bodily
posture as in their mental attitude! Budé, too, can find nothing
more abhorrent and less consentaneous with Christian innocence
and simplicity than the picture of a priest offering Mass at the
altar while his audience, silken, prettily ornamented, curled,
shining in parti-colored suits, girded with the sword, one hand

resting on the pommel and the other carrying a hawk, delighting in wanton gesticulation, crowds into the sanctuary and ousts the clerical ministers. Budé is often forced to turn his eyes away from the unworthy spectacle. The Utopians, however, not only are innocent of misconduct in their temple but actually can set the example for Europeans in their Christian churches. At the entrance of their officiating priest, as has been seen, they "fall down incontinent everyone reverently to the ground with so still silence on every part that the very fashion of the thing striketh into them a certain fear of God as though He were there personally present." For Catholics like More and his contemporaries their God is personally present. Hence, "what reverence and devotion," as the author of the *Imitation of Christ* exclaims, "ought now to be preserved by me and all Christian people, in the presence of the Sacrament"; for, "behold, Thou art Thyself here present with me on Thine altar, by God, Saint of saints, Creator of man, and Lord of the Angels."[16]

Music
and Prayer

After the feather-clad priest has signaled the congregation to rise, they sing hymns of praise to God, connected by passages from musical instruments. The musical forms are in good part different from those followed in the Eastern Hemisphere. Very many surpass in sweetness those forms in use in Europe, but on the other hand some by comparison are inferior to the European. There can be no doubt, nevertheless, that in one thing Utopians far outdistance Europeans. Whether performed on instruments or sung by human voices, all their music imitates and reveals the natural emotions, accommodates the sound to the subject matter, and lucidly expresses the meaning of the theme to such a marked extent that it influences, penetrates, and inflames the souls of its audience to a marvelous degree. This holds true whether the mood of the particular prayer is one of petition, propitiation, anger, disquiet, mourning, or joy. The description of Utopian hymns shows that they correspond more or less to the psalms of Jews and Christians.[1]

Plato in the *Republic* had twice emphasized that in music, as in poetry, "the sound must seem an echo to the sense" (Pope). Socrates says that "the music and the rhythm must follow the speech" and "the rhythm and harmony follow the words and not the words these." In More's own day the Carthusians faithfully exemplified this principle. The following passage from their statutes gives the spirit of their chanting:

> Since the business of a true monk is far more to weep than to sing, let us use our voices in such a way as to arouse in the soul that deep joy which comes from tears, rather than the emotions produced by a harmonious blending of notes. To this end, we will, by God's grace, suppress those methods of producing sensations which when not sinful are always worthless, as, for example, what are called *fractio vocis, inundatio vocis, geminatio puncti*, etc.—variations having nothing in common with simple devotional singing.

Petrarch found Carthusian psalmody "angelic." St. Bridget of Sweden was told by Christ in a revelation that her "Sisters should imitate the Carthusian chant which breathes tranquillity of soul, humility and devotion rather than a tendency to ostentation." "Ostentation" in ecclesiastical music—Erasmus uses the same term *ostentatio*—was a growing evil in the early sixteenth century. In his *Dialogue* Starkey has Pole declare that the manner of church music was more suited to minstrelsy in taverns or at plays than to divine service. If Augustine, Jerome, or Ambrose had reproved the far simpler singing of their day, they would cry out against "our curious discanting and cantering in churches" as exciting minds to worldly pastime and vain pleasure rather than to piety and love of heavenly things.[2]

On October 2, 1498 the Sorbonne had condemned the proposition of Jean Vitrier, the friend of Erasmus, that "the musical chant which is sung at Notre Dame is only lewdness and provocation to lewdness." The most powerful expression of opinion by Erasmus on church music was written, according to his own admission, in England (1511-1514?), and consequently is marked by occasional references to English customs. The criticism takes the form of a note to 1 Corinthians 14:19, in his *New Testament* (1516): "In the church, I had rather speak five words with my understanding, that I may also instruct others,

than ten thousand words in a tongue." (Erasmus' translation:
"Sed in ecclesia volo quinque verba mente mea loqui, ut et alios
instituam, potius quam decem millia verborum lingua."—Vul-
gate: "In ecclesia volo quinque verba sensu meo loqui, ut et
alios instruam, quam decem milia verborum in lingua.") By
way of brief explanation it is sufficient to observe that the miracle of speaking new languages, which needed to be interpreted,
seems to have been directed rather toward praising God than
preaching. Hence "tongue" often refers to the sounds of strange
languages, unintelligible to the hearers, which were uttered in
spiritual ecstasy. Erasmus makes a particular application of
the text by declaring that in some regions whole days are consumed in song without moderation and without end, but in six
months one scarcely hears a single salutary sermon exhorting
one to true devotion, something which St. Paul calls "speaking
with understanding." The custom is so attractive that monks,
especially among the British, do nothing else. Their chants
ought to be expressions of mourning (compare the Carthusian
attitude above), and instead they believe their frolicsome neigh-
ings and warblings are pleasing to God. For this purpose, even
in the communities of Benedictines among the British, youths
and boys and vocal artists are maintained to sing the Office and
Mass of the Virgin Mother. Bishops are forced to support such
choirs at home. Totally absorbed in their occupation, the chor-
isters never get a good education nor learn in what the true
religious spirit consists. Almost every ecclesiastical edifice is
filled with boisterous voices. But in the age of St. Paul, Erasmus
asserts, there was no chant but only careful enunciation of the
text. Paul's successors reluctantly admitted chant, but a kind
of chant which was nothing else than clear and rhythmical pro-
nunciation. There is a survival of the latter in the intonation of
the Paternoster during the Canon of the Mass.[3]

Erasmus' strictures on contemporary ecclesiastical music
naturally attracted criticism, especially by Alberto Pio years

later. In his answer Erasmus declares that his remarks pertain above all to the English who are forever singing, and in such a way that the words are unintelligible; nevertheless the people are warned under pain of hell to attend the morning services and all the canonical hours. "Now, which is holier," demands Erasmus, "to support with manual labor children in danger of hunger or to listen the whole day to singing which is not understood and therefore useless?" As for himself, Erasmus says: "By all means let churches have their solemn song, but let it be moderate." Alberto Pio condemns polyphonic music in church, and yet this type of music—but no sermon—is heard in the chapel of the pope and the court of the emperor and kings. Erasmus censures only music which is excessive or unworthy of churches. He makes the same historical observations and takes the same reasonable stand in his *Letter against the Sham-Gospellers* as in his answer to Alberto Pio and in his note to the *New Testament:* music is not to be banished from churches but freed from abuses and restored to pristine simplicity.[4]

Types of abuses are mentioned also in his other works. (1) Instead of echoing the sense with a kind of chant which does not obscure the sense but rather impresses it more effectively on the minds of its hearers, churches now resound with the din of clarions, pipes, and trumpets, with a varied babbling of voices, and with a type of music more difficult and lascivious than that formerly heard in pagan theaters. (2) In addition to the introduction of music typical of dances and carousels into church, sacred words are adapted to most wicked tunes with no more decorum than if one were to deck out Cato the Censor in the costume of Thais the courtesan, and sometimes even shameless words are not suppressed according to the license of the songsters. (3) On account of extended renditions of singers or instrumentalists or prolonged cadences at the end of each verse, very important parts of the service are omitted or curtailed; for example, almost an hour is taken up with the Prose or Sequence with the result that the Creed is cut short and the Paternoster omitted. (4) Far from the voice being soft, certain persons in church, with extraordinary ostentation of voice, thunder more truly than sing, but meanwhile their mind is idle. Melody is pleasing to God only if one's feelings harmonize with the words, if the same desires are in the soul as in the song, and if the whole man is in tune so that the inner man corresponds to the outer. Consequently the music itself, whether vocal or instrumental, must be temperate, sober, and worthy of divine worship. But because God is wonderful always and everywhere, the Christian must never cease from "psalms and hymns and spiritual songs" (Ephesians 5:19).[5]

Polydore Vergil makes much the same criticism and offers much the same remedy as Erasmus. Even Augustine in the tenth book of his *Confessions,* he points out, begs pardon of God for paying more attention to the melody than to the weighty meaning of the sacred words. In contemporary Europe church singers roar so loud that only their shouts can be heard. Their auditors care very little about the sense of the words; in fact, a good part of the congregation go to divine service as to a theater. The more artificial and intricate the singing, the more pleased the people are. The Church should decree that singers should pronounce words articulatively and distinctly, almost like readers, with that type of melody now employed in the Preface and the Paternoster of the Mass, that is, Gregorian chant.[6]

In 1519 Wolsey issued salutary statutes for monasteries of canons regular of St. Augustine. One statute was concerned with music. The canons are to sing the psalms, and so forth, neither too fast nor too slow, with perfect enunciation of the words. The plain melody, the unpretentious gravity, and the sweet and quiet rhythm would incite and invite the souls of listeners to spiritual delight and to desire of the harmony of heaven. In express terms Wolsey forbids prick song in the canons' choir. On Sundays and saints' feasts the canons may use a more elaborate melody, but must not neglect the clear expression of the words. But Wolsey's reform stops here. Masses intended for the people may be celebrated with the use of the organ and lay men and boys, even to the singing of prick song.[7]

In addition to the views of More on music and prayer implicitly contained in the *Utopia,* an explicit statement appears in his letter to a monk (1519-1520). He protests against "certain rhythmical prayers," foolish and absurd, by which the monks think they can win all the saints to their side. The abuse has crept into churches and grown in influence from day to day, especially on account of the accompanying music. As a result the congregation is much less well disposed toward the sober and earnest prayers ordained by the holy fathers of the Church. Unless bishops interdict all this tomfoolery, as they undoubtedly will at some time or other, the flock which Christ wished to be wise as well as guileless (Matthew 10:16) will gradually accustom itself to embrace foolishness instead of piety.[8]

In view of disorderly behavior and worldly music in church, it is little wonder that the Council of Trent later ordered bishops to "banish from the churches all such music which, whether by the organ or in the singing, contains things that are lascivious or impure; likewise all worldly conduct, vain and profane conversations, wandering around, noise and clamor, so that the house of God may be seen to be and may be truly called a house of prayer." The original form of the canon, proposed for discussion on September 10, 1562, insisted upon a style of music which would permit all to understand the words and would raise all hearts to the desire of heavenly harmony and the contemplation of the joys of the blessed.[9]

In their house of prayer the Utopians, priest and people, conclude the service by uniting in the recitation of solemn prayers which consist in fixed formulas, but so composed that each man may apply privately to himself what all rehearse together. The prayers are those of praise, thanksgiving, and petition. First of all every individual recognizes and praises God as the source of creation, of providence, and of all other good gifts as well. Next he gives thanks for the whole multitude of divine benefits, especially for the fact that, by the grace of God, he has chanced to be born in the happiest of all commonwealths and has been destined to hold the truest, as he hopes, of all religions. Finally he offers up his petitions. If his government or religion suffers from any defect or if some other is better and more approved by God, may His goodness bring it to his knowledge, for he is ready to follow whithersoever God may lead him. But if the Utopian form of government is the best and the Utopian religion the most genuine, may God give him perseverance and lead all other mortals to the same way of life and to the same belief in God, unless it be His inscrutable will to delight in a variety of religions. Last of all the individual beseeches God to grant him an easy passage to Himself, but how early or how late he does not presume to prescribe. Nevertheless, if it might happen without offense to His divine majesty, it would be much more according to his heart's desire to join God's company by a most painful death than to be kept separated from Him any longer by a most prosperous life. At the end of this prayer the Utopians again prostrate themselves on the ground. After a little while they rise and go to dinner.[10]

The most remarkable characteristic of these prayers is the extent to which they are permeated by the spirit of submission to God's will. This attitude is especially evident in the petition discussed earlier in this treatise: their desire for union with God through death as soon as possible but according to His will in regard to time and manner. Detachment from self-will and attachment to divine will manifests itself also in those all-important subjects for Utopians: politics and religion. They show precisely the same healthy attitude and behavior which More advocates in his *Confutation of Tyndale*. Suppose Tyndale should try to convert to true Christianity Mohammedans, Jews, or pagans—like the Utopians—who believe in "one almighty God" but reject the Trinity, the Scriptures, and the Holy Eucharist. What counsel and advice would Tyndale proffer them?

> Would he not advise and counsel them to pray unto God and to call for aid of Him that it might please Him to help to lead them in the way of the right belief and that He would with His grace help them to incline their hearts into the following of that thing that should be unto His pleasure and the salvation of their own souls, which kind and prayer they might assent unto without any prejudice of their own faith.

In addition to such receptivity of spirit toward God, would Tyndale not urge his unbelieving auditors to a tolerant willingness to hear the arguments of Christianity—just as the Utopians listen to the peaceful and reasonable defense of all religions—and encourage them to a sure hope that God will give them His grace and salvation?

> Would he [Tyndale] not also counsel them to be not willful nor obstinate, but conformable and willing to hear and learn the truth and, upon the hearing thereof, gladly to print in their hearts those things that most make toward the moving and inclination of their minds toward the credence thereof? And would he not tell them that through such toward and willing demeanor on their part . . . God would lead them and go forth with them and never leave them nor forsake them till He would, with their own good endeavor walking and working with Him, bring them first into the right belief and good hope and godly charity, with other many virtuous and good works proceeding thereupon, and finally by that mean, after this transitory life, into the perpetual bliss and eternal joys of heaven?[11]

Erasmus enunciates the general principle of such appeal—in fact, of all petition—when he writes in his *Handbook of the Christian Soldier:* "God must always be petitioned to deign to draw us on to the better things." In fact, a person ought to seek nothing except what is simply and wholly good, although people

in general seek a well-dowered wife, riches, honors, ruling position, or long life, as if prescribing to the deity what He must
do. But God knows best what is good for us, and what not. Especially reprehensible are the petitions of superstitious Christians
"who will promise themselves any and every thing," says Folly,
"relying upon certain charms or prayers devised by some pious
impostor either for his soul's sake or for money, to bring them
wealth, reputation, pleasure, plenty, good health, long life,
and a green old age, and at last a seat next to Christ's in
heaven—but they do not wish to get it too soon." St. Paul himself desired "to depart and to be with Christ, a lot by far the
better" (Philippians 1:23), just as the Utopians longed to go
to God, but his wish was dependent upon the need which his
Christians had of him. The devout man, says Erasmus in a
summary of Christian doctrine, may lawfully pray to be freed
from persecution, incurable disease, war, and pestilence, but he
should pray as follows: "Lord, if it is Thy will, if it is expedient, if it is to Thy glory and my salvation, snatch me from
these evils; if not, do what is good in Thy sight." More in his
prison was going to display even greater Christian perfection.
To his daughter Margaret Roper, to whom he had revealed "the
very secret bottom" of his soul, he wrote: "I assure you, Margaret, on my faith, I never have prayed God to bring me hence
nor deliver me from death, but referring all thing wholly unto
His only pleasure as to Him that seeth better what is best for
me than myself doth."[12]

Erasmus points out other evils no less worthy of blame. For
example, some Christians will superstitiously repeat the same
little prayers without ceasing; in fact, they view these prayers
as the height of devotion. Others engage in *unduly* verbose and
prolonged prayers—against the injunction of Christ: "In praying, do not multiply words, as the Gentiles do" (Matthew 6:7).
The word *unduly* is important because, as Erasmus observes,
Christ told His disciples that "they must always pray" and He

Himself, "falling into an agony . . . prayed the more earnestly" (Luke 18:1, 22:43). St. Paul, too, said, "Pray without ceasing" (1 Thessalonians 5:17). Thomas More also realizes that "your Father knows what you need before you ask him" (Matthew 6:8). In an epigram on what the Christian should petition from God in few words, he begs God to grant good things and to deny evil things, whether or not He is asked for them. It is characteristic of More and his consistency that his earliest extant letter, addressed to John Holt (1501?), should contain the following statement: "We are living according to our desires: may God therefore grant that we may always have good desires" ("Ita viuimus vt volumus, donet ergo Deus vt bene velimus"). Christ Himself taught the manner in which one should pray— according to the model of the Paternoster (Matthew 6:9). In his *Method of Prayer*, therefore, Erasmus demands that a Christian ask for nothing which cannot be referred to one of the seven parts of the Lord's Prayer. Such was the opinion of the fathers of the Church. Moreover, one learns from the Paternoster that there is an order to be observed in one's petitions. First one should seek for what pertains to the glory of God and salvation of men; thus, the Utopians acknowledge God as Creator, governor, and giver of good gifts, and beg Him to lead all men to the government and the religion most pleasing to Him. Next one should petition for what contributes to the public welfare; likewise, the Utopians thank God for their government and religion and wish to be guided to better ones if they exist. It is last of all that one should ask for what is to one's own advantage; in like manner, the Utopian requests a swift journey to God if He wills it: "he would be much gladder to die a painful death and so to go to God than by long living in worldly prosperity to be away from Him." Barclay in his *Ship of Fools* holds the same view of the Our Father:

> Pray your Pater Noster with devout heart and mind,
> For therein is all that is needful to mankind.[13]

With the description of the temple filled with incense and candlelight and echoing with the simple service of hymns and prayers, Hythloday closes his account of the Utopian religions in general and of the state religion in particular. Thomas More, speaking in his own person at the very end of his *Utopia*, looks upon not a few Utopian laws and customs as extremely absurd. Among these absurd institutions he places religion and the divine services. But just what specific elements would he find absurd? As a matter of fact, there would not be many: (1) the multiplicity and variety of religions, (2) the priestly vestments made of feathers, (3) the substitution of incense and candles for animals, fruits, vegetables, and so forth, in the divine sacrifices, and (4) the appearance of the whole service as merely a setting and preparation for the sublime Christian sacrifice of the Mass. In spite of these few drawbacks and of the nature of the Utopian state religion as something defective and incomplete to be made whole and perfect by Christianity, the Utopians remind Christians of their own lofty Christian ideals and can even set the example in the industry of their ascetics, holiness of their few priests, peacemaking role of their clergy, tolerance and forbearance toward one another, reverence in church, simplicity of music, and fervor of prayer. In general, the religious-minded Utopians, in their limited way, furnish patterns for the reform of the Church. They point out the spiritual direction in which the reform of the Christian Church should move.[14]

Deformation
and Reformation

Long after the title of this chapter had been chosen, it was discovered in a statement, already quoted here, in James Wimpheling's work entitled *Youth*. "The *reformation* of the Catholic Church according to its primitive holy morals," he declares, "must be begun with youth since the latter's *deformation* proceeds from their improper and wretched education." The need for reform no Christian, not even the most worldly churchman, could deny. From the end of the Great Schism to the revolt of Luther and, more precisely, to the Council of Trent, *Reform!* was "a veritable leitmotiv," as Aubenas and Ricard declare, for all the members of the Church. The desire of More, Erasmus, and their circle was for a general reform which, according to Dermenghem, was to be "liberal and humanistic, but orthodox and schismless."[1]

The friend of the humanists, Archbishop Warham, called a convocation of the clergy of the province of Canterbury in 1512, with a view to the extirpation of heresy and the correction of other evils. Dean Colet delivered what might be called the keynote address. In passing, it is interesting to note that Bishop Burnet had intended to publish it in his history of the English Reformation "as a piece that might serve to open the scene, and to show the state of things at the first beginnings of the Reformation." His patrons dissuaded him because "it might have been judged that I had inserted it on design to reflect on the present, as well as on the past state of things"! In his discourse Colet declared that reform was never more necessary, for the spouse whom Christ wished to be without stain or wrinkle was ugly and deformed, and "nothing hath so disfigured the face of the Church as hath the fashion of secular and worldly living of clerks and priests." The latter is evident especially in four ways: (1) pride of life, that is, greediness for honor and high rank; (2) carnal concupiscence, that is, indulgence in banqueting, hunting, and so forth; (3) covetousness, that is, desire for rich benefices and preferments; and (4) worldly occupation, that is, service of men in secular positions rather than of God in the apostolic life. To pride of life Colet opposes humility; to carnal concupiscence, soberness or temperance; to covetousness, charity; and to secular occupation, spiritual occupation. The practical remedies are many: careful admission of men to the priesthood; bestowal of benefices on worthy men; war against the sin of simony; personal residence of clergy in their churches; and clerical abstention from merchandising, interest taking, hunting, carrying of weapons, haunting of taverns, suspect familiarity with adventuresses, and rich and gaudy apparel. Monks and religious should not become involved in secular or ecclesiastical business, but should give themselves to prayer, fasting, and their monastic rule. Bishops should be chosen by just and canonical election. They should reside in their dioceses, employ the patrimony of Christ for the right purposes, and suppress the avariciousness of their curias. Finally, provincial and general councils should be held frequently. Like Thomas More, John Colet sincerely believes that no new legislation or sanction is necessary: "There are no trespasses but there be laws against them in the body of the canon law. Therefore it is no need that new laws and constitutions be made, but that those that are made already be kept. . . ."[2]

The difficulty is that Christians have done to canon law what they have done to Christ's doctrine. In regard to the latter, Hythloday in the *Utopia* declares: "They have wrested and wried His doctrine and like a rule of lead have applied it to men's manners that by some means at the least way they might agree together." By precisely the same method, according to Budé, the holy canons, enacted in better times in order to regulate clerical life and (so to speak) to form offspring by their fathers' precepts, have been turned into soft leaden rules. By the clever manipulation of ecclesiastical superiors they have become as flexible as wax. As a result the time-honored laws and penalties are not used for regulating human behavior but are almost made to lend the weight of their authority to the banker's profession. In a word, the canons are being utilized only for the profits which can be derived from them.[3]

And Fisher cries out in his *Seven Penitential Psalms:*

> None order, none integrity, is now kept. It seemeth almighty God to be in manner in a dead sleep, suffering these great enormities so long. Now we must do as the disciples did then in the ship. They awaked Jesu their Master from sleep with crying and great noises that they made, saying: "Magister, non ad te pertinet quod perimus? Master, is it Thy will, longeth it unto Thee, to see us perish?"[4]

The call for reform was even stronger at the Fifth Council of the Lateran (1512-1517). The Augustinian general, Egidio of Viterbo, described by Richard Pace in 1517 as "that famous fount of theology, who has frequently sounded off in church pulpits, even against the Sovereign Pontiffs themselves," delivered the very first sermon. It was a trumpet call. He asked God to bestow upon the clergy the strength necessary for recalling religion "to its old purity, to its ancient light, to its native splendor, and to its sources." Unless the cupidity for worldly things, which is the root of all the evils, is compelled to yield to love of heavenly things, "it is all over with religion, it is all over with the very resources which our forefathers begot by the fostering of divine worship and which we on the contrary will lose by its neglect." At the first session of the council Bernard Zane reinforced Egidio's prophetic remarks by fastening on two evils: (1) heresy and infidelity and (2) desire for dominion, luxury, and ambition on the part of princes. If the latter are forced to be content with their own country and to restore alien territory, Christians will not be guilty of rage, threats, and plots toward Christians, nor faithful toward faithful, nor brothers toward brothers.[5]

As far as princes are concerned, Ferdinand the Catholic wrote to his viceroy in Naples early in 1513 that "as long as the Church is not thoroughly reformed, wars will never cease." Later in the same year he wrote to his ambassador in England that the allied rulers of Spain, England, France, and Germany "ought to see that general and radical reformation of the Church be carried out, with the cooperation of the whole of Christendom, by a general council and by the Pope himself." Second on the agenda should be "a common war of all Christians with the Infidels." Ferdinand voiced the same sentiments to the Emperor Maximilian. Almost four years passed and then the latter expressed to Wolsey on February 3, 1517 his grief at the condition of Christendom now that Leo X had decided to dissolve the Lateran Council. Historically this council marks the last general effort at reform before the revolt of Luther. The greatest obstacle to reform was to be found in "private interests" on the part of both individuals and nations.[6]

It is worth while here to describe the viewpoint of Mantuan, a Carmelite poet of great vogue and influence at the time. In a poem addressed to Julius II he praises him for regaining the lands of the Church and begs him now to turn his attention to bad morals. With faith, hope, and charity dying away, the ecclesiastical structure, once mighty but now shaken by age and disease and gaping with fissures, must needs crash to the

ground. In verses directed to Leo X he finds three tasks worthy
of the pope's concern and effort: the cessation of war in Italy,
the reform of the Roman curia which is spreading its poison to
all lands, and the rescue of Christian populations from the
Turks. In conclusion he makes a double appeal: (1) help for
the collapsing Church of Christ and for faith which is sick even
unto death and (2) diversion of war from the Italian states to a
crusade against the Turks, who are hostile to Christ's precepts.[7]

Fisher's use of such material in his controversies is interesting. To Ulrich Wellen (or Willen), for example, he points
out that the infidels have occupied the sees of all the apostles
except Peter, and yet Rome deserved to be destroyed on account
of its unspeakable crimes and heinous offenses. What conclusion can one draw except that Christ, in spite of the injuries to
His name, has kept His promise to abide forever with Peter and
his successors? In another book Fisher, who has never been to
Rome, tells Luther that he must know better than he the kind
of life and morality of pope and curia—whether "they pursue
pleasures, riches, glory, that is, the world and the flesh." It is
enough for Fisher to observe their teaching, not their behavior,
according to the advice of Christ in regard to scribes and pharisees sitting upon the chair of Moses.[8]

In regard to reformers Etienne Gilson acutely remarks that
"the real reformer is not the man who sees that a reform is
needed; nor is he the man who, in season and out of season,
preaches the necessity of that reform; the true reformer is the
man who achieves it." All the Christian reformers preached the
need for a return to the pristine spirit of the apostolic age and
early Christianity—in a word, to the sources, which, interpreted
concretely, meant Scripture and tradition. The Protestant reformers were to seize upon only one of these sources of revelation as the basis of reform: the Bible. They were to make little
or no allowance for progress, growth, and development of
dogma and discipline. As Monceau observes in his *Literary*

History of Christian Africa, "Schism and heresy have almost always, for their point of departure, a regret for the past, the claim or the dream of going back to the fountain-source of a religious idea, to the discipline or the faith of an apostolic age." Even Erasmus with his constant cry to return to the sources— classical, patristic, and scriptural—finally had to confess that there had been some development for the better in the Christian Church. In his *Letter against the Sham-Gospellers* he assumes that the Church, like all human institutions, has its beginnings, its development, and its consummation or perfection. To recall it suddenly to its first beginnings is no less absurd than to wish to drag an adult person back again to his cradle and infancy. Times and circumstances carry many things away with them, and they change many things for the better.[9]

CHAPTER XIV

Family
and Marriage

The cry for reform applied to every aspect of the whole Church, head and members, but especially to religion and morality. The last chapter of *Utopia* is directly concerned with religion. But there are in *Utopia* problems so intimately connected with religion that a discussion of them is imperative. These are moral problems. Some center about the family, especially adultery and divorce, and others about international relations, especially war and peace. Since he was a humanist interested in reform, it was inevitable that More, directly or indirectly, should treat these problems in a work concerned primarily with abuses and reforms.

The fundamental difficulty with contemporary morality, according to the humanists, was the adulteration of the pure doctrine of Christ. This is well described by Hythloday: men had suffered the conformation of their behavior to the rule of Christ so unwillingly and grudgingly that religious preachers, slyly and cunningly, had molded the teaching of Christ to the current morality of men. The result had been, not an improvement in human conduct, but a feeling of security in wrongdoing on the part of Christians. In two works published in 1516, Erasmus expresses the same sentiments. There are persons, he observes, who forcibly accommodate Holy Scripture to the morality and passions of the people and who, instead of taking Holy Scripture as the norm of conduct, manipulate its authority to justify the low behavior of the general public. It should not be necessary to twist Christ's teaching to contemporary morality and human traditions; "instead, let us adapt our whole life and all our institutions to that true and genuine prototype: Christ." Many bishops, and especially Leo X, wish reforms but fear greater evils, "rather desiring what is best than demanding it" ("magis optantes quod optimum sit, quam exigentes"). Like St. Paul, "they prescribe, not what is most Christ-like, but what they can extort from these times."[1]

Thomas More assigns marriage and the family an exceedingly honorable and fundamental role in his ideal republic. Here he parts company with his friend Dean Colet, whose views on marriage and celibacy, as voiced in his commentary on St. Paul's first letter to the Corinthians, are extreme. Paul, says Colet, wished all men to live single like himself (1 Corinthians 7:7). The only reason for allowing marriage is the alleviation of incontinency. (According to the Catholic Church, the remedy of concupiscence is only a secondary end of marriage: the primary end is the procreation and education of offspring, future citizens of heaven.) Even in marriage continence ought to be practiced "as far as human weakness allows." Moreover, "in a case where that weakness [incontinency] is not felt, no use ought to be made of this license to marry." How, then, is the number of souls destined for Christianity and heaven to be maintained and increased? Colet's answer is simple, even naive: "If all that were called to the faith had remained single, there would still have always been a surplus from heathendom, to supply materials of grace to the Spirit of Christ." Suppose that all gentiles had been converted and had remained single? If "the whole multitude of heathens had been converted to the worship of Christ, . . . all mankind . . . would have come to an end in this state of sanctity. . . . Than which end, what could have been happier for men, or more acceptable to God on their part?" In *A Right Fruitful Monition,* however, Colet adopts a much more reasonable attitude toward sex and matrimony. He allows not only for the primary end of marriage but even for its secondary end. His advice to the married is direct: "Have in remembrance that the intent of marriage is not in the beastly appetite or pleasure in the thing, but the intent thereof is to eschew the sin of the flesh or else to have children."[2]

What is the view of marriage on the part of Colet's friend, Erasmus? Insofar as he recommends marriage for clergy and laymen, he would seem to have a higher esteem for the state than Colet. On the other hand, he refuses to raise matrimony to the dignity of a sacrament. What his attitude was in 1516 can be determined from his editions of the New Testament and Jerome's letters.

Erasmus points out that many things in Jerome's opus against Jovinian can grievously offend the present generation, which numbers matrimony even among the seven sacraments. Erasmus finds it strange that neither Jovinian in his praise of matrimony nor Jerome in his refutation should mention its sacramental status. Even Christians have discovered their own Epicurus in Jovinian, that great champion of flesh eating and weddings (as opposed to abstinence and virginity). Erasmus continues: "Matrimony is such a miserable thing that not even Epicurus who placed the supreme good in pleasure found it pleasant; nevertheless, the ordinary run of men marry a wife chiefly for the sake of pleasure." In the scholia to another letter he expresses his opinion that certain contemporary theologians were giving too much license or freedom to married people in their sexual relations. Jerome, on the contrary, interprets the expression "marriage-bed . . . undefiled" (Hebrews 13:4) as referring to husband and wife who imitate virginity in marriage out of zeal for chastity. In the comments on still another letter Erasmus writes: "[Jerome] means that coitus belongs to corrupt nature, not to nature as originally established by God." This statement, as well as many another of Jerome's, would seem to disagree with the common view of theologians, who make marriage one of the seven sacraments.[3]

Edward Lee clashed with Erasmus over the latter's interpretation of Mark 10:8 in his *New Testament:* a man and his wife "shall become one flesh." Erasmus had noted that some "sordidly" *(sordide)* apply the expression to coitus. Lee declared that he saw no reason for calling coitus sordid, since St. Paul had termed the marriage bed holy and undefiled: "What God has cleansed, do not thou call common" (Acts 10:15). According to his reply Erasmus had not called conjugal coitus obscene or unclean but had labeled as sordid the interpretation which judged marital union by its most ignoble element. Lee, however, could see no reason why the interpretation should be labeled sordid when the union itself was not sordid. At any rate, although he uses also the argument from the silence of Christian antiquity, a fundamental reason for Erasmus' refusal to consider matrimony a sacrament seems to be his low opinion of the marital act.[4]

So much for Colet and Erasmus. As for More in the *Utopia,* he differs from Plato, who advocated in his *Republic* the extreme measure afterwards abandoned in his *Laws:* a community of wives and children. By way of declamation, More in his youth, Erasmus informed Hutten, had defended Plato's communism, even that of wives, but like his model abandoned it in his *Utopia,* undoubtedly as being against his reforming purpose. At least one Christian sect, however, that of the Nicolaitans, as More could have learned from Augustine, Pecock, and Erasmus, held their wives in common. But instead of looking upon the family as an impediment to perfect care of the common welfare, More sees it even as the foundation of the state and the source of civil administration and political responsibility. For example, thirty families elect annually the Syphogrant or Philarch.

Moreover, the council of Syphogrants, before deciding upon any matter of great moment, consult their families and report the result of their deliberations to the senate. There are other instances of the importance of the family in public affairs. One need mention only the fighting of the family as a unit in battle, "that they whom nature chiefly moveth to mutual succor, thus standing together, may help one another."[5]

The Utopian family is characterized by a form of patriarchy, the oldest male holding the supremacy. If the oldest suffers from senile dementia, the next oldest takes the reins. Male children and grandchildren continue to dwell in the family and, when married, bring their wives to live with them. Although his appreciation and esteem of the family would be sufficient to account for the adoption of patriarchy, More may have taken the custom from the pre-Mosaic patriarchs of the Bible or even from Plato's *Laws*. Of the patriarchal polities the Athenian says: "Did they not originate among those people who lived scattered in separate clans or in single households, owing to the distress which followed after the catastrophes [for example, Deucalion's Flood]; for amongst these the eldest holds rule owing to the fact that the rule proceeds from the parents, by following whom they form a single flock, like a covey of birds, and live under a patriarchal government and a kingship which is of all kingships the most just?" Each family in Utopia consists of no fewer than ten nor more than sixteen adults *(puberes)*, that is, persons who have reached or passed the age of puberty, commonly interpreted in law as twelve for girls and fourteen for boys. No limit is set upon the number of children under the age of puberty. If adults in a family surpass the count of sixteen, the surplus is added to a small family. There is little need to defend More against the charge of lack of affection on the score that it was the English practice of the period to send children at or before the age of seven or nine to receive training in another household. As is clear from the *Utopia* itself, which declares that children *(impuberes)* cannot be involved in calculations, only adults, including married couples apparently, are transferred from their own family to a smaller household.[6]

In Utopia children minister to their parents, and wives to their husbands. The commands of parents and husbands are obligatory, Vitoria succinctly explains, because "it is necessary to the existence of the family that there be one Head, whom the other members of the family are bound to obey; and this is the husband, who is the head of the household and of the wife, as we read in *Ephesians*" (5:23). Civil laws, moreover, determine the nature and extent of wifely obedience and "also whether or not the husband may inflict corporal punishment upon his wife." Erasmus in his *Instruction on Christian Marriage* mentions the power of life and death which the husband used to have over his wife, and parents over their children. More does not go to such an extreme length. He says simply that husbands punish their wives, and parents their children, unless they have committed a heinous crime prosecuted by the state. The nature of punishment which may be inflicted by husbands or parents is not specified, whether corporal, verbal, or both. More's own policy is clear. Erasmus wrote Hutten that More obtains greater obedience from his wife by way of cajolery and jesting than another man by way of command and sternness. His behavior toward his children is evident from a poem, written perhaps in 1517 and addressed to them: "You know . . . how often I kissed you, how seldom I whipped you. . . . [Y]ou know well how gentle and devoted is my manner toward you, for I have always profoundly loved my own children and I have always been an indulgent parent—as every father ought to be." Bishop Fisher's manner of admonition was much more rigorous, if one is to credit his anonymous biographer. If on personal investigation he found any member of his household at fault, he "would for the first time but punish him with words only, but it should be done with such a severity of countenance and gravity of speech that whosoever came once before him was very unwilling to come before him again for any such offense."[7]

Both Erasmus and More single out silence as a virtue in woman. "Nothing," declares Erasmus, "dignifies woman, who by nature is a loquacious animal, more than silence." And More in his *Treatise on the Passion* advises: "A woman . . . should learn of him [her husband] *in silentio,* that is, in silence, that is to wit, she should sit and hear him and hold herself her tongue." The fault, of course, may often lie with the husband who is excessively critical of his wife and defames her by calling her a shrew. The husband should rather look to his own faults. Thomas More quotes his father with approval: "He saith plainly that there is but one shrewd wife in the world; but he saith indeed that every man weeneth he hath her; and that that one is his own." It is a humanistic commonplace that virtues of the mind are much more important in a wife than comeliness of body. But, as More observes in the *Utopia,* physical beauty serves to enhance moral virtue. He is careful, however, to preclude any abuse by decreeing the same cut of dress for all married women in Utopia. Against excessively ostentatious dress Eulalia declares in Erasmus' colloquy *The Uneasy Wife:* "We are well enough dressed if we but please our own husbands." In his *Handbook of the Christian Soldier* Erasmus admonishes husbands not to love their wives for carnal pleasure but in a spiritual way: "You love her for this special reason that you behold the image of Christ in her, e.g., piety, modesty, sobriety, and chastity; and you love her not in herself but in Christ, nay, you love Christ in her, and thus at last you love her spiritually." More himself could have set the example for such a lofty Christian ideal, for Erasmus wrote Faber in 1532 that "he loves and cherishes this [wife of his], although she is sterile, although advanced in age, not otherwise than if she were a girl of fifteen years." The epitaph, probably composed about 1516, on the grave of his first wife, Jane, appears humorous or distasteful to many, but it shows that More unselfishly loved each wife "as Christ also loved the Church" (Ephesians 5:25). He admits: "I cannot decide whether I did love the one [Jane] or do love the other [Alice] more." There will be no embarrassment when the grave and heaven unites husband and both wives, for "at the resurrection they will neither marry nor be given in marriage, but will be as angels of God in heaven" (Matthew 22:30).[8]

It is therefore clear, as Erasmus notes, that if wives must have great respect for their husbands, husbands in their turn must have some respect for their wives. Wives are the help-mates, not the slaves or servants, of their husbands. This is certainly true of women in Utopia. Making allowances for monogamy instead of community of wives, one perceives that More allows them almost as much equality with men in his *Utopia* as Plato does in his *Republic,* whose "guardians and female guardians must have all pursuits in common." They may go to battle and fight side by side with their husbands. They share in the knowledge and exercise of agriculture. In the additional trade or craft which everyone must learn, however, women engage in the lighter tasks, such as the spinning of wool or flax. As far as government is concerned, Syphogrants consult their families, presumably including their wives. The senate does not grant a divorce until they and their wives have care-fully examined the whole case. If any husband wishes to take a trip through the agricultural districts surrounding his city, he must first obtain leave, not only of the head of the household, but also of his wife. In regard to the latter permission, More is apparently very anxious to keep husband and wife together. From his foreign embassies he realized how much he needed the family and how much the family needed the father. It is just possible that the wife's permission here may be suggested as an antidote to indiscriminate pilgrimages during which the husband abandoned his wife and children. Erasmus calls atten-tion to the evil in the scholia to one of Jerome's letters. "Today," he complains, "very many individuals, even from the number of those who seem to have sense, run to Jerusalem and holy places from the ends of the earth, at exorbitant expense, at the peril of their life and sometimes their morals, their wife and children left deserted at home."[9]

More departs from Plato in his *Republic* not only in the substitution of monogamy for community of wives but also in the establishment of a closer link between mother and child. Plato makes maternity "a soft job for the women of the guardians" by having the children carried to nurses in a common "pen or crèche" and by forbidding the mothers themselves to "suckle too long" or to take upon themselves "the trouble of wakeful nights and similar burdens." One must take "the greatest possible care that no mother recognizes her own child." More, on the contrary, has every mother nurse her own offspring. Only death or disease excuses from the obligation. In this case the wives of the Syphogrants provide a nurse. There is no difficulty in the matter, for the task is considered extremely honorable, and this for two reasons: (1) the mercy of the nurse is rewarded with great praise and (2) the nurse is acknowledged by the child as his own mother. In antiquity wet and dry nurses were used in Greece and Rome, and their devotion and trustworthiness was recognized in literature and law. Plutarch and Gellius, however, inveighed against the practice. In the Renaissance, Filelfo expressed the opinion that mothers who refused the duty of breast feeding ought to be called savage and inhuman rather than delicate and dainty. Erasmus adds no new argument, but no one surpasses him in denouncing mothers who thus transgress the laws of nature and God. The strongest statement of his position is found in the colloquy *The Lying-In Woman.* "Fashion" cannot be pleaded as an excuse for the use of a wet nurse, since "it is the fashion to do amiss—to game, to whore, to cheat, to be drunk, and to play the rake." As nature grants the power to conceive, so also it grants the power to give

suck: every animal feeds its own offspring. Moreover, even if
the nurse is healthy and virtuous, the milk of the mother is
"natural and familiar." Eutrapelus, the spokesman for Erasmus, is "of that opinion that the genius of children are [*sic*]
vitiated by the nature of the milk they suck, as the juices of the
earth change the nature of those plants and fruits that it feeds."
Consequently even the mind is affected by the type of milk,
since "the soul affects the body, and is affected by the body."
Finally, the child could with reason call his mother only half-
mother since she "refuses to feed what she has brought into the
world." In fact, he will divide his natural affection between
two mothers with a resulting lack of obedience to his real mother
later on. For reasons such as these More makes Utopian
mothers give suck to their own children.[10]

Utopian females may not marry before the age of eighteen,
nor males before the completion of their twenty-second year. In
designating these as the earliest ages for marriage More differs
from Plato, who sets the minimum age for union in his *Republic*
at twenty for women and thirty for men, and in his *Laws* at
sixteen for women and thirty (or, in another passage, twenty-
five) for men. In the latter work Plato foreshadows a custom
of the Utopians by declaring: "The suitability or otherwise of
the time of marriage the judge shall decide by inspection, view-
ing the males naked and the females naked down to the navel."
By establishing ages rather advanced for his era More may have
been protesting, less against the era's dynastic espousals and
marriages of royal children of extremely tender years, since
these were easily broken unless consummated, than against
abuses existing among the laity in general. Erasmus in his
Instruction on Christian Marriage reveals some of these evils. In
France, he says, it is not rare for a girl to be a wife at ten and
a mother at eleven. In England and Italy a septuagenarian often
marries a young girl in a union which will not succeed—unless
they offer a special sacrifice of atonement to Venus! A guardian

in England profits from the possessions of his wards unless the latter marry the wives chosen for them. They remain wards until their twenty-second year (the age for men in *Utopia*). Erasmus recalls that Aristotle in his *Politics* designated eighteen as the age for a girl (the age for women in *Utopia*) and thirty-seven for her husband. The best procedure, however, is not to reckon their age but their bodily maturity. In Erasmus' colloquy *The Old Men's Dialogue* Glycion, who used judgment in his choice of a wife, married at the age of almost twenty-two (the age for males in *Utopia*). The canon law of the time declared for the validity of marriages between those who had reached the age of puberty, that is, boys of fourteen and girls of twelve. When the Church finally passed on the matter at the Council of Trent after long and intricate debate, it condemned those who maintained that the marriages (even clandestine) of minors without the consent of their parents were invalid, but, to remedy the evil which it had always detested and prohibited, it declared that marriages which did not take place before the pastor and at least two witnesses were null and void.[11]

In an annotation to the *New Testament* Erasmus had inveighed against the ease, not to say heedlessness, with which people rushed into marriage, contrary to old custom and to natural equity. The pope, he says, must have the power to declare invalid marriages contracted by young boys and girls, intoxicated and unadvised, on the instigation of panders and bawds, and thus keep them from entanglement in wretched bonds. The consent of parents was required for marriage among Romans, Greeks, and Jews: perhaps it would be expedient to observe the same restriction at the present time also. He returns to the subject in his *Instruction on Christian Marriage*. In the choice of a wife, as in the conduct of war, one is not allowed to make a mistake the second time—because there is no second time. Canon law leaves no hope of dissolving a marriage once entered. In other contracts, where there is great risk or danger

of financial harm, people use the utmost care to avoid deception
or loss, but they rush headlong into the contract of marriage
upon which depends the happiness of their whole life and, in
great part, the salvation of their soul. In buying a horse people
look round repeatedly for a hidden defect, they stipulate for
its return on the discovery of such a hidden defect, they investigate the local custom or law in the matter, they even call in a
horse specialist, and yet tender girls and boys contract indisso-
luble matrimony by three words of consent whispered during an
embrace. Formerly a long interval elapsed between betrothal
and nuptials so that an unknown boy could not be matched
with an unknown girl. The ancient custom of bodily inspection
to see if they were ready for marriage was dropped in deference
to modesty and respect for age or sex. Since marriage is a union
of bodies as well as minds, some attention should be paid to
physical considerations. A genuine philosopher, of course, will
make light of the most homely appearance in a girl provided
the absence of charm is compensated for by gifts of the soul.
The man who has not enough philosophy to be content with
mental goods should choose a girl with moderate beauty, which
will not cause weariness or detestation on the one hand nor
attract adulterers on the other. Erasmus advises people who are
unhappily married to acknowledge their fault and patiently to
suffer the misfortune in case the marriage was due to heedlessness on their part. In case they were not at fault, they should
smile and bear their lot since God, who knows better than they
what is expedient for their salvation, has permitted the unhappy
marriage for hidden causes. In both the *Instruction on Christian
Marriage* and the colloquy *The Unequal Marriage* Erasmus
utters severe strictures against permitting men with syphilis
(*scabies vulgo dicta Neapolitana*) to marry.[12]

The care with which the Utopians choose their wives would
meet with the approval of Erasmus, even if the method of choice
would not. They are far from choosing blindly and from being

in the predicament in which Thomas More's father humorously described every man as being placed—"in the case that . . . every man is at the choice of his wife, that ye should put your hand into a blind bag full of snakes and eels together, seven snakes to one eel, . . . a perilous choice to take up one at adventure though ye had made your special prayer to speed well." Under carefully supervised conditions, to be described later, man and woman in Utopia are shown naked to each other. At least two classical authors may have given hints for this practice. Plutarch in his life of Lycurgus mentions that the maidens in Sparta wore scanty clothing in games and processions to develop their health, beauty, and dignity, and to serve as incentive to marriage. Plato in the *Republic* completely denudes women, as well as men, for gymnastics. In his *Laws* judges inspect "the males naked and the females naked down to the navel" to determine their readiness for marriage. For the prospective husband and for the father of the future bride Plato in the same work uses a less direct method and allows the young people a rag of clothing. But Plato's purpose is the same as that of the Utopians.

> In view of the fellowship and intercourse of marriage, it is necessary to eliminate ignorance, both on the part of the husband concerning the woman he marries, . . . and on the part of the father concerning the man to whom he gives his daughter; for it is all-important in such matters to avoid, if possible, any mistake. To achieve this serious purpose, sportive dances should be arranged for boys and girls; and at these they should both view and be viewed, in a reasonable way and on occasions that offer a suitable pretext, with bodies unclad, save so far as sober modesty prescribes.

Pontano in *The Dignity of Marriage* describes what he terms a shameless custom of the Taxilli in Asia. When a girl is poverty-stricken, her relatives lead her in the flower of her youth to the market place with brass band and great display. She then bares first her back and then her front to the prospective suitors, the most pleased of whom marries her. More's method, of course, is more human, more prudent, and more modest.[13]

More's primary purpose is to make certain that every possible objectionable feature, moral and physical, in a marriage which cannot be broken except by death should be brought to light and be faced before the knot is tied, not afterwards. His secondary purpose, subordinate to the primary, is to secure bodily wholesomeness in both parties. In particular, he may want both to be free from the relatively new disease, syphilis, which Colet at this time describes as "the abominable great pocks, daily appearing to our sights, growing in and upon man's flesh; the which sore punishment, everything well remembered, cannot be thought but principally for the inordinate use of the flesh." He does not wish Europeans to adopt the Utopian custom but, like Erasmus and Plato, he desires men and women to enter upon marriage with deliberation and caution. This spirit animates his poem "How to Choose a Wife," published in 1518, which outlines the requirements for the ideal spouse of the Renaissance. The similarity of this section of *Utopia* to the *Instruction on Christian Marriage* shows the closeness of the views of Erasmus and More.[14]

Both More and Erasmus may be assumed to approve the spirit, not the method, of the people of Utopia. In the choice of their mate the Utopians in all seriousness and strictness observe a practice which appeared the height of absurdity and ludicrousness to Hythloday and his companions. Whether the woman be virgin or widow, a dignified and virtuous matron shows her naked to the suitor, and some honorable citizen in turn shows the suitor naked to the girl. Hythloday and his associates had laughed at and found fault with the custom as absurd, but the Utopians on their part marvel at the extraordinary stupidity of all other peoples. In their argumentation they employ a common analogy used by Erasmus. Non-Utopians, in purchasing a horse, where a few pennies are at stake, are so careful that they refuse to buy unless the seller strips the saddle and every bit of equipment from an already almost nude horse to discover any sore hidden under the trappings. But in choosing a mate, a business which will make either pleasure or disgust fill their whole future life, they behave in an extremely heedless way. Leaving the rest of the body wrapped in garments, they judge the whole woman from scarcely the space of one hand, for they see only her face, and bind her to themselves not without grave danger of an unhappy union if they afterwards discover something repulsive in her. The Utopians, like Erasmus, hold that physical attractiveness is not to be scorned. Not all men are wise enough to take account only of virtues in a woman. In marriages even of wise men themselves, bodily comeliness adds and contributes not a little to mental qualities. At any rate, it is certain that such an ugly deformity can lie concealed under pretty clothes that it can completely alienate the affection of the husband from the wife— when they are not allowed to separate even physically. If a hideous deformity should chance to happen *after* the wedding, every man must necessarily bear his lot, but laws ought to be passed to prevent anyone from being deceitfully taken in *before* the wedding. The matter, the Utopians feel, had to be provided for with the greatest possible solicitude because they alone of all the peoples in that hemisphere hold, first, to monogamy and, secondly, to the indissolubility of marriage.[15]

CHAPTER XV

Divorce, Adultery, Fornication

Marriage in Utopia, as a matter of record, is hardly ever dissolved except by death. But, in spite of this fact, divorce is permitted, and this for three reasons: (1) adultery, (2) intolerable perversity of conduct, and (3) mutual incompatibility. The second is difficult of translation since it excludes adultery: "moral turpitude" is too strong and "wayward manners" too weak. At any rate, in the case of adultery or unbearably perverse behavior, the innocent party obtains from the senate of Tranibors permission to change his or her mate, but the guilty party must forever lead a life of legal infamy and forced celibacy. Under no circumstances do Utopians tolerate divorce from an unwilling wife whose only crime is some bodily misfortune that has happened to her. Their reason consists in the conviction that abandonment of anyone in the hour of greatest need of solace is an act of cruelty and that old age, which brings sickness and is itself a sickness, would see and suffer a wavering and weak fidelity in addition to the other hardships. There is, as has been mentioned, a third ground for divorce. It happens now and then that two people separate by mutual consent and contract new marriages when their ways of thinking and acting do not agree reciprocally and when they have found other partners with whom they hope for a more pleasant life. This separation, however, never takes place without the authority of the senate, who grant a divorce only after a diligent investigation of the case by themselves and their wives. Even after thorough examination they do not grant a divorce easily because they realize that the hope of easy new nuptials entertained by men is something very little calculated to strengthen the love which is essential between husband and wife.[1]

Since divorce was permissible and common in Greece and Rome, it is hardly necessary to find classical antecedents for the practice in Utopia. Both Cuthbert Tunstall and Polydore Vergil note that Spurius Carvilius was the first Roman to secure a divorce 523 years after the founding of the city. His reason was the sterility of his wife, but he was subjected to much adverse criticism because he had preferred the desire for children to the vow of conjugal fidelity. Of particular interest, moreover, is a passage in Plato's *Laws* which mentions women as connected with the granting of divorce.

> If a man and his wife, being of unhappy dispositions, in no wise agree together, it is right that they should be under the constant control of ten members of the Board of Law-wardens, of middle age, together with ten of the women in charge of marriage. If these officials are able to bring about a reconciliation, this arrangement shall hold good; but if their passions rage too high for harmony, the officials shall, so far as possible, seek out other suitable unions for each of them.[2]

The indissolubility of marriage, according to Scotus, is one of the more difficult precepts of the natural law about which men very often live in ignorance, doubt, or error. The natural law really extends to the indissolubility of the marital bond but not in a way evident and manifest to all. "Hence it was expedient," Scotus concludes, "that the necessity of this precept should be determined by the positive law of God."[3]

After the spread of Christianity the dissident Eastern churches, as well as a few local Western synods, allowed adultery as a cause for divorce on the strength of the scriptural passage: "Moses, by reason of the hardness of your heart, permitted you to put away your wives; but it was not so from the beginning. And I say to you, that whoever puts away his wife, *except for immorality* [literally, *fornication*], and marries another, commits adultery; and he who marries a woman who has been put away commits adultery" (Matthew 19:8-9; see Matthew 5:31-32). The texts in Mark (10:11), Luke (16:18), and Paul (Romans 7:3, 1 Corinthians 7:10) mention no exception. The constant approved teaching of the Roman Catholic Church declared for the absolute indissolubility of a ratified and consummated marriage. A classic statement of the doctrine may be found in the postils of Nicholas of Lyra (1270?-1340?). Stapleton notes in connection with More: "At table a passage of Sacred Scripture was read with the commentaries of Nicholas of Lyra or some other ancient writer." In his comment on Matthew 19:8-9 Lyra asserts that divorce did not exist in the beginning but was permitted to fallen men in order to avoid a greater evil (the murder of unwelcome wives), therefore permitted not as something legitimate but as a lesser evil. In case the wife is guilty of fornication, the husband must dismiss her lest he appear to be an abettor of her wickedness. This divorce, Lyra insists, must be understood in regard to cohabitation and the matrimonial debt, not, however, in regard to the bond, which is dissolved only by death. But the indissolubility of matrimony, according to Lyra, arises not only from the divine law promulgated by Christ but also from the natural law. Just as male and female among animals and birds mate and stay united for as long a time as is requisite for the training of their young, so, too, nature dictates that man and wife remain joined during their whole life, since a very long time—in fact, a whole lifetime—is necessary for the proper education and instruction of their sons and daughters. Lyra repeats the same interpretation in his note to 1 Corinthians 7:10-11.[4]

In general, the schoolmen argue (1) that divorce interferes with the primary end of marriage, the orderly propagation and proper education of children, who need both parents, (2) that the prospect of divorce renders unstable the mutual love necessary for cooperative development of husband and wife and spoils the moral atmosphere of the home, and (3) that the possibility of divorce, easy or hard, weakens marriage as the remedy for concupiscence since it offers incentives for adultery in the hope of another marriage. Aquinas has a passage, much like that in the *Utopia*, in which he argues against divorce on grounds of natural equity. A man, he reasons, takes a woman as wife with a view to a primary end of matrimony, the necessity of generation. When her beauty and fecundity are at an end, the woman, who by nature tends to lean upon man's greater wisdom and virtue, is handicapped in securing another husband. If, therefore, a man could marry a woman in the blossom of her youth when she possessed fertility and comeliness and then could cast her off when she was advanced in years, he would inflict upon her an injury contrary to natural equity.[5]

In reading the passage on divorce in *Utopia*, it is absolutely necessary to bear in mind the firm stand of the Western Church on the indissolubility of a marriage between two baptized persons which had been ratified (that is, really a sacrament) and consummated (that is, really completed by the physical act in which two are made one). If the marriage was not ratified or not consummated, it could be dissolved in certain cases. The scriptural texts in Matthew which seemed to favor divorce on grounds of fornication or adultery were interpreted as referring to divorce from bed and board, not to perfect separation with the right to remarriage. Since the Utopians are pagans, their marriages are not sacramental unions. If they are converted to Christianity, they may remarry according to the conditions of the Pauline privilege (1 Corinthians 7:12-16). But the indissolubility of marriage is not merely a matter of the positive law of Christ: it is based upon the natural law which is obligatory on all men, Christian and non-Christian, including the Utopians. In granting divorce to persons in intolerable situations, the Utopians stress too much the individual good and ignore the general good, which demands stable unions, without exception, for the good of society. Consequently More may merely be reflecting in his Utopian commonwealth the practice of pagan antiquity, with special precautions, at least verbal, against easy divorce. But he may have had an eye upon marriages in Christian Europe. This may be gathered from the observations of his friend Erasmus upon the indissolubility of marriage, some of them being written just before or during the composition of *Utopia* by More.

An extremely important statement of Erasmus is found in his lengthy comment on 1 Corinthians 7:39: "A woman is bound as long as her husband is alive, but if her husband dies, she is free." An epitome of this annotation is contained in his gloss on Matthew 19:3: "Is it lawful for a man to put away his wife for any cause?" Erasmus acknowledges that the indissolubility of marriage was defended by Chrysostom, Augustine, and early Latin fathers, then confirmed by episcopal statutes and the decretals, and finally established fully by unanimity of opinion in the schools of theology. If change to a better opinion, however, is dear to good men and if laws like medicines are to be applied according to the nature and the stage of the disease, "might not certain marriages be licitly dissolved, not rashly but for serious reasons, not by anyone but by the Church's authorities or legitimate judges—and be dissolved in such a way that both, or certainly the one who gave no cause for divorce, be free to marry whom they please?" Even according to the *Sentences* of Peter Lombard, Pope Zachary told the husband who had had relations with his sister-in-law that he had to lead a penitential life without hope of remarriage but that his wife was free to marry whom she pleased. The interpretation of

Lombard, it seems to Erasmus, is farfetched when he says that the phrase "whom she pleased" is to be understood as "after the death of her husband." Moreover, is it equitable that a husband should be forced to live with a wife whose shameful and disgraceful behavior he neither caused nor can mend? Is it equitable that, in case he puts her away, he should be compelled to spend his whole life abandoned, forsaken, and, as it were, castrated? The guilty party whose shameless conduct supplied grounds for the divorce could in all fairness be deprived of the right to remarry. What valid and unbiased reason, however, could be alleged for punishing the husband whose only fault happens to have been the unfortunate choice of a wife that has later been unmasked as lewd or wanton?

What Erasmus desires is a divorce from the bond with the right to remarry, at least for the innocent party. Who of the ancient divines or lawyers, asks Erasmus indignantly, ever called separation from cohabitation with perseverance of the bond a *divorce?* Christ restricts grounds for divorce to adultery, not because some other crimes are not worse than adultery, but because adultery by its very nature conflicts with, and breaks up, the union by which two are made one. In calling His own back to the state of original innocence, He does not wish divorce because He does not wish hardheartedness, and yet Paul is often indulgent to human frailty and relaxes the Master's command. "Why could not the Roman Pontiff," demands Erasmus, "do the same?" Why could not the pope allow divorce for serious reasons? Erasmus denies any desire to open the window to frequent divorces: he affirms that his only intent is the salvation of unhappy and weak persons. Even the pagans who honored marriage conceded a mutual right to divorce, but not heedlessly. If divorce is to be rare, care must be taken to prevent easy marriages.

Toward the conclusion of this note to 1 Corinthians 7:39 Erasmus sums up his argument and plea:

I was sorry for the persons whom I saw entangled in inextrica-
ble chains of this sort and whom I knew to be very many in number, especially among the English, where I first organized this
work. I saw that once upon a time men of approved doctrine and
holiness had not been frightened by the word of the gospel or of
Paul from admitting divorce. I saw that the Roman Pontiff was
granted to have the power to interpret the teaching of the gospel
and the apostles, to limit it, to relax it, to dispense from it, and,
according to some, even to abrogate it in some respects.

Among the men of learning and holiness Erasmus cites Origen,
Tertullian, Pollentius, and Ambrose, of whom the last was
"beyond controversy a man not only orthodox but also of proved
sanctity." In the defense of his views on marriage and divorce
against the animadversions of Edward Lee, future archbishop
of York, Erasmus develops at length the historical background
in general and the patristic evidence in particular. It is interesting to note that More in his letter to a monk (1519-1520?)
mentions the disagreement of Augustine and Ambrose on the
right to remarry: "When a wife has been put away for fornication, Augustine denies that another wife may be wed as long as
she is alive, but Ambrose affirms that remarriage is licit." Today
the work of Ambrose on which More and Erasmus rely is considered spurious.[6]

Erasmus is perfectly willing to yield to the judgment of the
universal Church in regard to the relaxation of ecclesiastical
discipline on divorce. He repeats the claim of submissiveness
in his *Response to the New Notes of Edward Lee*. In commenting on hardness of heart as God's and Moses' reason for permitting divorce among the Jews (Matthew 19:8), Erasmus had
questioned: "Since there is nearly equal hardness of heart in us,
why is not the same divorce allowed us to whom even brothels
are allowed?" Lee appeals to Paul's letter to the Ephesians
(6:32) and to Augustine and Jerome to prove that matrimony
is a sacrament and hence cannot admit divorce. Even the pope
cannot dissolve a ratified and consummated Christian marriage

because "it depends upon the decree of God Himself." Silvester in his *Summa summarum* holds the same view as Lee. In his *Apology against Bedda* Erasmus defends his annotation to 1 Corinthians 7. Here he again returns to the point that the interpretation of the term *divorce* as merely *separation from bed and board* is strained and farfetched.[7]

In his *Instruction on Christian Marriage* Erasmus extols the sanctity of marriage. He claims that even pagans like Aristotle, Xenophon, and Plutarch never wrote in a more holy and religious strain than when treating of marriage. The very mention of divorce at a wedding is the worst of omens. Even among the peoples who allow it, the universal consent of mortals has labeled divorce as ingratitude and betrayal of friendship. Marriage, insofar as it is perfect charity and union of souls, persists even beyond the death of the body. The fathers restricted the right, apparently granted by the gospel, of divorcing an adulteress to separation from bed only, not to the liberty of contracting a new marriage. Yet Erasmus again proposes for serious consideration, but not as his tenaciously held opinion, a relaxation of contemporary matrimonial legislation. If the laws spare the adulterous husband from death and if the wife cannot bend her mind to living with him again, it would not seem absurd to hold for dead the husband who deserves death and so to let the innocent wife go free.[8]

Does More agree with his friend Erasmus? The passage on divorce in his *Utopia* is curiously similar to Erasmus' views as expressed at about the same time in his *New Testament*. Matrimony is sacred and lifelong for both. For both, divorce for adultery breaks the bond completely and permanently. As for reasons apart from adultery, Erasmus admits others but remains general; More specifies intolerable perversity of conduct. By both, only the innocent party is allowed to remarry. More goes beyond Erasmus in permitting husband and wife in the case of mutual incompatibility to secure a divorce and to wed more

congenial partners already at hand. Both declare that divorces
are to be difficult and rare. Both assign the power to grant
separation and remarriage only to the highest authorities—
More to the Utopian senate, Erasmus to ecclesiastical superiors.
The coincidence is so striking that, if one had no other source
than the *Utopia*, one would conclude that the two men hold
much the same opinion on divorce.

But one has no other source than *Utopia* for More's viewpoint. One cannot adduce, as proof of disagreement, More's
opposition to the separation of Henry and Catherine, since this
was a question not of divorce but of the nullity of the marriage
from the beginning.[9]

But one difficulty will remain even in regard to the *Utopia*.
Utopian marriage is not a sacrament which, when ratified and
consummated, can be dissolved by no power on earth. It is a
contract and bond between unbaptized persons, and such a contract and bond the Catholic Church can dissolve according to
the Pauline privilege. More's real and undisputed mind on divorce at the time of the *Utopia* perhaps ought not even to be
made the subject of inquiry, since he is writing about pagans
and in a fictitious account at that. After all, no independent
evidence exists to show that he ever held any other than the
traditional doctrine. This is especially true because the outbreak
of the Lutheran revolt, with the Protestants granting divorce for
adultery, would undoubtedly cause More to keep to himself
any personal opinion of his own. In the latter respect he was
unlike Erasmus. Nor should one conclude *a priori* to perfect
agreement between the two men; that is, one should not tenaciously hold the position that More agrees with Erasmus unless
there is evidence to the contrary. Friendship might keep More
from voicing his opposition to Erasmus' opinions, especially
since the latter was always willing to submit to the final judgment of the Church. But this much seems certain about More's
thought: if divorces were to be granted to validly married Cath-

olics, they were to be granted with the approval of the authorities in the Catholic Church.

Is it possible that in the section on divorce in the *Utopia* one must see at once a safeguard and a joke—a safeguard insofar as More could always claim and plead that all divorces in Utopia are referred to the highest authorities in the matter, which in Christendom would be the hierarchy, and a joke insofar as in Christendom cases of divorce from a ratified and consummated marriage would be taken up before a court which never grants a perfect divorce! This explanation, it is true, is far from being satisfactory. Even as speculation, it is highly tenuous. The most that can be said for it is that it lies within the realm of possibility.

Adultery, which is the principal ground for divorce in Utopia, is subject to a severe penalty. The guilty party incurs public disgrace and loss of character and must forever lead a life of celibacy. In addition, defilers of the marriage bed are punished with the most grievous form of slavery. If both the adulterers are married, the innocent parties after divorce from the guilty are themselves joined in matrimony to each other— an ironic turning of the tables! This situation, of course, obtains only if the innocent are willing to have each other; otherwise they may marry whom they wish. But if either of the injured parties perseveres in love toward the ill-deserving spouse, he or she is not forbidden to use the rights of marriage, provided he or she agrees to follow the condemned party into hard labor. Occasionally it happens that the repentance of the guilty and the dutiful assiduity of the innocent move the prince to pity and effect their liberation from bondage. For the rest, if the adulterer falls into the same crime again, he is punished with the sentence of death.[10]

Slavery for the first offense, death for the second—how different is the attitude toward adultery in Utopia from that in Christian Europe! Philip the Good (1396-1467), duke of Burgundy, is reported to have left sixteen bastards behind him. Rodrigo Cardinal Borgia, later Alexander VI, acknowledged and legitimized his many natural children. Aeneas Silvius, later Pius II, had written calmly in his *History of Frederick III:* "In our time the majority of reigning princes were born outside wedlock." It is little wonder that the period has been labeled the "Era of Bastards." The severe legal penalties were rarely inflicted: small fines were imposed. The Latin version of Brant's *Narrenschiff* laments the universal transgression of marital vows, the lack of any serious penalty like the Lex Iulia, which allowed the husband to kill the adulterer and decreed exile to a tiny island as punishment for adultery, and the detestable view held by many that the violation of another's marriage bed is noble and praiseworthy. Barclay in his *Ship of Fools* makes the same complaint and dramatically suggests that, since Christ confirmed the Old Testament by the New, adulterers should now receive the punishment meted out to them in the Old, namely, stoning or burning![11]

Erasmus comes even closer than Brant and Barclay to the spirit of the *Utopia.* The reader will recall how in the first book of *Utopia* Hythloday passionately argues that there is no proportion between crime and punishment, between stealing and hanging—"to kill a man for taking a little money." God's commandment is: "Thou shalt not kill." If the extent of permissible killing is to be defined by human law, what will keep men from agreeing among themselves as to the extent that rape, adultery, and perjury are allowable? In *The Education of a Christian Prince* Erasmus asks: "Why is it that everywhere simple theft is punished by death and adultery goes almost unscathed (which is in direct contradiction to the laws of all of the ancients)?" After making the same observation in a scholion to a letter of Jerome's, he concludes: "We consider theft to be a great evil because we deem money to be the highest good." Human laws, he declares in his *Instruction on Christian Marriage,* show a

topsy-turvy clemency when they hang a simple thief, even one
making his first attempt, from the gibbet and let go scot free
the man defiled by numerous adulteries. The gravity of adultery
is evident from the death penalty decreed by Moses for both
parties (Leviticus 20:10) and demanded even by the pagans.
In view of the stern attitude of Jew and heathen, how does it
happen that adultery is a sport and a joke among *Christians?*
The person who has just once committed a theft does not dare
to show his face. Why should the man who has been rendered
distinguished by many adulteries take first place among his
peers? In his *Exomologesis* Erasmus reports the assertion of a
Franciscan in a public sermon that if the ancient law on the
stoning of adulteresses were still in force, a whole mountain of
rocks would not suffice for the stonings.[12]

In his *Adages* Erasmus returns to adultery, its prevalence,
and its punishment a number of times. At Cumae an adulteress
was exposed to public scorn in the forum, conveyed about the
city on an ass, and finally declared forever infamous. Matrimony is a sacrament among Christians, and yet adultery is considered a sport. Nothing remains but the decreeing of awards
to those who violate the most wives! "At one time even uncon-
secrated virgins were buried alive if found unchaste: today the
violation of a virgin dedicated to Christ is an act of virtue."
Tenedos, he observes, had a law ordering adulterers to be
hacked to pieces and applied it even in the case of the king's
son. Radishes were used as a singular form of punishment in
another state. An especially humorous punishment is related by
the innkeeper in the colloquy *The Franciscans; Or, The Rich
Beggars* about a newly discovered "island of a very temperate
air, where they looked upon it as the greatest indecency in the
world to cover their bodies." The inhabitants, who are very
religious, punish adultery more than any other vice: "They forgive the women, for it is permitted to that sex; but for men that
are taken in adultery this is the punishment, that all his life

after he should appear in public with his privy parts covered."
Polydore Vergil concludes that in Christian Europe "the gentleness of the punishment is an enticement to the sin."[13]

In Utopia slavery is the penalty for adultery, that is, sexual
intercourse between a married man and another than his wife
or between a married woman and another than her husband.
What is the penalty for fornication, that is, sexual intercourse
between unmarried persons? If the case is proved, the guilty
parties receive a severe punishment the nature of which is not
specified, and then are forever forbidden to marry unless the
prince pardons the offense. Both the father and the mother in
the household where the sin was committed incur great loss
of reputation as having failed in the diligent fulfillment of their
duties. The Utopians mete out such a severe punishment to all
concerned because they foresee that, unless single persons are
carefully kept from random intercourse *(vagus concubitus)*,
very few will unite in the love of matrimony. For young people
know that they would have to spend their whole life with one
person alone and would have to put up with the troubles which
marriage brings. A Spanish memorandum (1512), prepared
for the Lateran Council, deplores contemporary conditions. The
bad example everywhere of prelates who practice concubinage
and strive to secure lucrative positions in church and state for
their bastards has caused the lower clergy to imitate them and
lay people to think that simple fornication is no sin.[14]

More kept a watchful eye on the morals of his own household. Stapleton, for example, notes: "To ward off danger of
unchastity he arranged that his men-servants and maid-servants
should sleep in separate parts of the building, and should rarely
meet together: only in cases of necessity were the women
allowed to enter the part of the house in which the men lived."
P. S. Allen, the editor of the letters of Erasmus, asserts that, in
the matter of celibacy, "Thomas More as a young man was not
blameless." He uses as his authority a statement of Erasmus

to Hutten in 1519. For Allen "it is surprising to find that Erasmus . . . stated the fact in quite explicit, though graceful language; and further, that More took no exception to the statement, which was repeated in edition after edition." More took no exception because Erasmus specifically declares that his relations with girls were blameless (*citra infamiam,* that is, not of the nature to bring him into any kind of bad repute). At the proper age he naturally enjoyed the companionship of girls. When the latter offered him their attentions, he relished them, but did not go out of his way to win them. Common likes and dislikes, rather than any hankering after sexual intercourse, attracted More to them. Boy and girl are naturally drawn to each other, and the enjoyment which they have in each other's company can be entirely innocent and chaste if the proper safeguards are employed. Erasmus is paying More the compliment of saying that his youthful relations with girls were characterized by the virtue of modesty, the golden mean between prudishness and pruriency. This interpretation, far from being apologetic or gratuitous, is confirmed by a poem, written probably in 1519, in which More recalls how, as a lad of sixteen, he had fallen ardently in love with a girl of fourteen. He describes how her face had inspired him with innocent love ("innocuo amore") and states that their love had been pure ("Castus amor fuerat"). The behavior of young More could well serve as an example of normal conduct even for single Utopians, male and female, in their dealings with one another.[15]

So strict are the Utopians in matters of sexual immorality that the very solicitation to illicit intercourse is no less in danger of serious punishment than the actual perpetration of the act. Robinson translates the Latin *stuprum* by *aduoutrye (adultery),* but in the general sense, in which it is used here, *stuprum* refers to any kind of lustful deed. *Stuprum* technically is the illicit deflowering of a virgin and is distinguished from *raptus,* the violent carrying away of a girl with a view to ravishing her and keeping her as wife or concubine. The reason for Utopian conduct is their conviction that in every crime the certain and determined attempt is no less heinous than the execution itself. For they think that the failure to accomplish the wicked deed ought not to excuse the culprit, who after all is only accidentally and unwillingly responsible for his lack of success. Robinson's translation, especially in the use of the words *intent* and *purpose*, leaves the reader under the impression that the Utopians can read hearts and can punish the interior act of intention. But Robinson's *intent* and *purpose* is really More's *conatus (attempt)*. As More declares in his *Debellation of Salem and Bizance:* "Though the farther deed be not done, . . . none advoutery done in deed, though the laws of the world for lack of power to look into the heart cannot punish the bare intent, . . . yet our Savior . . . saith that Himself taketh their wills for their deeds" (see Matthew 5:28). In the same work he humorously applies the distinction between mere wishing and attempted deed to the accusation that the clergy wished for more money: "To make now so great a matter of this and call it an heinous name of confederacies is, as seemeth to me, somewhat like to him that would needs have an action against his neighbor because his neighbor's horse stood and looked over his hedge. For he said that he saw by his countenance that he would have eaten his grass if he could have gotten to it; for, as for that [fact] that the hedge letted him was little thank to him, for his will was never the less." Human law, whether civil or canonical, can judge and punish only exterior acts. God alone can pass on the evil intentions of the interior man. As for the relationship between exterior act and interior act, "the exterior act," according to moral theologians, "does not increase the guilt unless it renders the interior act of the will more intense."[16]

Slavery

Adulterers, as has been noted, are punished with the most severe form of slavery. In fact, almost every heinous crime is subject to the penalty of slavery. The Utopians consider the latter as no less painful than death to sinners and as much more advantageous to the state than if they immediately got rid of offenders by a hurried execution, for (1) criminals help the state more by their labor than their slaughter and (2) they deter others from a like crime by the example of their punishment. But if convicts prove rebellious and recalcitrant in their bondage, they are finally killed as wild beasts, as creatures whom it would be foolish to think mere prison or fetters could curb. Slaves who bear their lot patiently are not deprived of all hope of release. Those whose spirit has been rendered docile by long-endured hardships and whose repentance manifests and proves that they detest their sin more than their penalty have their slavery either mitigated or canceled, sometimes by the special power of the prince, sometimes by the vote of the people.[1]

But Utopian criminals constitute only one class of slaves. There are really three classes in all. The first consists of prisoners taken in war waged by Utopia itself. The second comprises criminals of two kinds: Utopians for whom shameful crime in their native land has merited slavery and aliens whom a vicious deed in foreign cities has made deserve capital punishment.

The latter group is by far the more numerous, for Utopia harbors many, sometimes bought at a cheap price, more often obtained even for nothing. Both kinds of criminal slaves are not only kept at perpetual hard labor but also bound in chains, but Utopians are treated more rigorously. They are judged to be in a more deplorable plight and to be deserving of worse exemplary punishment for the reason that even an outstanding education aimed at training them in virtue could not restrain them from crime. The third class of slaves is made up of foreigners who, after leading a life of drudgery, hardship, and poverty in their native land, have chosen freely to live as slaves in Utopia. They treat these persons honorably and not much less mildly than their own free citizens, except that they impose a little more work on them, as being hardened to it. They do not detain unwillingly those who wish to depart—an infrequent occurrence—nor do they dismiss them empty-handed. The Utopians specifically exclude three classes of slaves: (1) captives taken in the wars of nations other than their own, (2) the children of slaves, and (3) even slaves already serving in foreign lands whom they could acquire.[2]

Not much is said about the treatment of slaves on the island of Utopia. The thick fetters with which they are shackled are made of gold and silver, as are the chamber pots, to show in what contempt Utopians hold these precious metals. Because the hunting and the butchery of animals are not suitable for free men and are destructive of natural mercy and clemency, they are left in the hands of slaves. The latter also take care of the heavier and dirtier work in the dining halls. The Utopians view eating as a necessary and low pleasure. Contrary to expectation, however, cooking and the preparation of food are not considered servile tasks and are assigned to free women by turns.[3]

In view of these meager particulars about the life of slaves, it is natural to suppose that More intended to have some details supplied from Hythloday's account of the system used by the

Polylerites for thieves in Book I. Only if the theft has been enormous does the thief wear fetters or is he locked in prison barracks. Otherwise, the convicts go loose and free as they labor at public works. Those who refuse to toil or who are slack in their efforts are not bound in chains but are urged on by whips. Those who perform their tasks briskly are spared all rough words and only at night, after roll call, are locked in their cells. Apart from their constant labor, their life is not unpleasant. Among the Polylerites the convicts are hired out to private persons to work by the day—something that cannot happen among the Utopians, since the individual citizen has no money of his own and all work in a sense is public. The Polylerites have elaborate means to prevent escape and rebellion: a special haircut, clipping the tip of one ear, a distinctive garb for prisoners of each county, death for touching money or arms, and rewards for informers. As in Utopia, everyone has held up before him the hope of recovering his freedom through obedience and patience and evident promise of leading a better life in the future. As a matter of fact, every year some are restored to liberty for bearing their punishment without complaint or discontent. This procedure, explains Hythloday, is both more humane and more useful than the system of hanging thieves used in England. The legislation of the Polylerites is directed against vices, not men, and aims to destroy the vice and save the man by having him make amends and become a good and trustworthy citizen.

One important difference between the terminology used in the section on the Polylerites and that in the section on the Utopians must be noted. During the whole first half of the rather long description of the Polyleritic system, More appears to be trying sedulously to avoid the use of the term *servi* to label the convicts, but finally seems to give up in despair since Latin has difficulty in distinguishing sharply between *slave* and *servant*. He explains parenthetically and almost apologetically that the

Polylerites call their convicts slaves: "servos . . . (sic enim damnatos vocant)." The whole context, however, shows that the punishment for thievery is penal servitude rather than strict slavery. Robinson realizes this fact and in his translation of the passage constantly employs the term *serving men* and carefully avoids the term *bondmen,* his usual name for slaves. In the section on Utopian slavery, however, More is unhesitant in the use of *servi* and Robinson in the use of *bondmen.* Therefore one must draw the conclusion that the Polyleritic system is one of penal servitude; the Utopian, one of strict slavery. This distinction is important in view of the whole discussion of slavery in Utopia. It is the Polyleritic system of penal servitude which Hythloday urges the English to adopt in their treatment of thieves.[4]

Utopian "bondage" has provoked a great deal of disagreement. Michels and Ziegler, editors of a Latin edition of *Utopia* (1895), see in the enslavement of war captives a positive inconsistency in More, who apparently should not have introduced slavery into a free Utopia. Oncken, too, in his influential introduction to Ritter's German translation of *Utopia* (1922), sees the enlightened political theory of the king who will rule only over free men abandoned practically in favor of the eudaemonistic philosophy of the Utopians. The answer that More is merely following his ancient model is inadequate, since Plato, as Oncken observes, after all found slavery already existing as a social institution in his native city, whereas More, living in a Christian slaveless environment, was under no compulsion to introduce it among his Utopians. In 1928 Bendemann published an elaborate critique of Oncken's position. More, he claims, had no intention of having his Utopians live on the "exploitation" of penal slaves but rather the purpose of keeping usefully busy the convicts with which they were saddled. After all, every Utopian citizen, except for a handful, has the duty of daily manual work. Only a few less dignified and honorable tasks humorously are assigned by More to convicts who must be kept occupied anyway. Bendemann approves the assertion of Dietzel that Utopia quite evidently has no real slave class in the sense of a sociological stratum of the population. As for prisoners of war, More wanted to avoid the gruesome slaughter of military captives by licentious soldiery which was common during the period, and yet he had not attained to the concept of modern international conventions on prisoners of war. Consequently, according to Bendemann, the only course open to him was that of forced labor for prisoners, which had to be lifelong since war-mad mercenaries like the Swiss were involved.[5]

Chambers independently stresses the same points as Bendemann: in Utopia all citizens must work and bondmen do not constitute a distinct social class. "Bondage in Utopia is penal servitude—a humane substitute for the death penalty." Donner, too, asserts that Utopian bondage would be termed "penal servitude" in modern times. Bondmen constitute only five per cent of the population according to Donner, who relies undoubtedly on Hythloday's statement that every farm household of forty persons has two bondmen.[6]

This whole discussion is not a mere quarrel about words— no petty *lis de verbis*. It is important and interesting to know whether More espoused a modern method of penal servitude or an ancient system of slavery. As often happens in the interpretation of *Utopia,* a glance at the historical background throws light upon the problem.

In Athens and Rome the numerous slaves constituted an essential element in the social structure and consequently slavery was everywhere regarded as a just and indispensable institution. The hostility of stoicism and Christianity to slavery effected a great decrease in the number of slaves or an amelioration of their condition until it disappeared altogether or evolved into a much superior and more humane serfdom. In his *City of God* St. Augustine traces all slavery to sin. He mentions the conjectural etymology of the Latin *servi (slaves)* as being based on the fact that captives were *preserved (servabantur)* and made *servants (servi)*. "Every victory, even when it falls to the wicked, humbles the vanquished by the divine judgment, either by correcting or by punishing sin." The position of the medieval schoolmen and their successors was that it was impossible to prove the repugnance of slavery with the natural law and that slavery was sanctioned by the law of nations *(ius gentium)*, but that it was not becoming his dignity for a Christian to be totally subject to a Christian. "What is more shameful," exclaims Erasmus in resuming the doctrine in his *Instruction on Christian Marriage*, "than that among Christians, all of whom Christ equally redeemed at the cost of His blood, one person should treat another, not as his brother and fellow-inheritor of the kingdom of heaven, but hardly as a human being, buying him with money just as a beast of burden and reselling him at pleasure, . . . yea, sometimes handling his brother in religion more harshly than his horse!"[7]

The position of Duns Scotus upon the legitimate causes of slavery in the strict sense is especially significant because of its coincidence with that of Thomas More. Duns Scotus names three: Thomas More names the same three. In his commentary on the *Sentences* Scotus maintains that slavery is just: (1) when a man voluntarily subjects himself to slavery, although such a renunciation of one's freedom would be foolish and perhaps even against the law of nature; (2) when legitimate authority, seeing that some men are so criminal that their freedom injures themselves and the commonwealth, punishes them with slavery, just as it can justly execute them in certain cases for the common good; and (3) when the victor in a just war, who could have killed his captives, preserves them from death and keeps them as slaves. The justice of the third case is not patently evident ("non apparet manifeste justitia hic") because it would be unreasonable to kill the vanquished if their aggression were at an end and they were to use their freedom rightly. Another famous Franciscan philosopher of approximately the same time or a little later, Aureolus, admits the justice of the enslavement of captives without any hesitation. He appeals to an implicit agreement and convention of the belligerents that slavery be the price of sparing one's life; in other words, slavery is an institution of the law of nations *(ius gentium)*. According to the fifteenth-century Dominican archbishop of Florence, St. Antoninus, slavery in the proper and strict sense was introduced not only by the law of nations, canon law, and civil law, but also by divine right when Noe cursed his son Cham, saying, "Cursed be Cham [Canaan], a servant of servants shall he be unto his brethren" (Genesis 9:25). The reduction of war captives to slavery results from the law of nations. Actually, Antoninus continues, this practice is not observed in wars between Christians, whether these wars be just or unjust. Especially interesting in the light of the punishment of sexual offenders in Utopia is his statement that canon law makes a slave [serf?] of anyone who rapes a woman. In his *Summa summarum* Silvester adds a condition: "The rapist becomes the slave of the girl raped unless he should wish to buy himself off."[8]

It is significant that slavery assumed a new importance in the second half of the fifteenth century and the early decades of the sixteenth, especially on account of the discovery of new regions first in Africa and then in America. The following account of the revival of slavery in Christendom is necessarily sketchy. Antam Gonçalves of Portugal took captive some Moors in 1442 and, when ordered by Henry the Navigator to restore them, took in exchange some gold and ten Negroes. Excited by his success, the Portuguese erected forts on the coast of Africa from which they exported blacks to Spain. As early as 1462 Pius II condemned slavery as "a great crime" *(magnum scelus)*, but the traffic continued. In 1495 Columbus was about to have almost five hundred Indian prisoners of war sold at Seville, but

Queen Isabella, after consultation with theologians who disagreed on the justice of their sale and acting under the influence
of Fra Hernando de Talavera, archbishop of Granada, sent
them back to America. In the account of the first voyage in
Vespucci's *Four Voyages* read by More, the Europeans in their
war with the Indians are reported to have planned "to capture
as many of them as we could and make and keep them as our
slaves forever." Of the twenty-five prisoners they gave seven to
their Indian allies and kept the rest until they reached Cadiz,
"where we sold all our prisoners."

In order to protect the Indian natives the governor of Haiti
in 1502 was allowed to carry to the island Negro slaves born in
Spain and instructed in Christianity. In 1510 and later King
Ferdinand sent Africans to Haiti to work the mines. In 1516,
while still in the Netherlands, Charles V licensed his courtiers
to import slaves into the colonies, but Cardinal Jiménez, regent
of Castile, forbade the practice. Bartolomé de las Casas began
in 1514 to fight against the slavery of the Indians. He urged the
importation of Negro slaves in their stead. One of the notable
deeds of Leo X (1513-1521) was a bull directed against the
enslavement of the Indians. The contemporary attitude toward
the Negro might be illustrated from Pontano. Negroes alone, he
says, are the slaves of all nations. The reason is that, since they
live without law and custom, they become first the prey of the
neighboring nations and then the slaves of all the others. "Nay,
even parents themselves," he exclaims, "sell their children to
our merchants and very often barter them for grain."[9]

In the early sixteenth century Spaniards were much exercised over the moral problems connected with conquest and
enslavement. When the Cortes was held at Burgos in 1512,
Ferdinand the Catholic was anxious to silence the protests of
missionaries coming from the Indies. He set up a commission
of theologians and jurists to study the conditions under which
conquest, government, and evangelization of the new lands

might be achieved. As a member of this group Matías de Paz, O.P., wrote an illuminating treatise entitled *The Lordship of the Kings of Spain over the Indians (De dominio regum Hispaniae super Indos)*.[10]

Matías is careful to draw the proper distinctions on the word *servus*. In the broad sense a *servus* is any person who is subordinate to a lord or to jurisdiction, for example, a subject to his king, a citizen to his state, and a Christian to his bishop. In a more specialized sense a *servus* is one who has a special obligation of service to another in specified ways but who retains liberty and full legal capacity, for example, a vassal or a mercenary. In the proper and strict sense a person is a *servus* when he does not possess full legal capacity nor freedom of any sort but works and profits for his master, not for himself. The rule over him, according to Aristotle, is called a despotic dominion. The last sense can be taken in two ways: (1) when the condition is permanent and (2) when it lasts an interval of time and through the greater part of the year. (Silvester at this time says that, though a serf is bound to the soil, he properly is not a slave and can perform legal actions.)[11]

Matías de Paz enunciates three principles for the guidance of the Spanish king and his successors. First of all, "Christian princes may declare war against infidels, not from lust for power nor from avarice for wealth, but only armed and fortified by zeal for the faith so that the name of our Redeemer may be exalted and magnified throughout the world." Hence they may not invade the lands of infidels if the inhabitants are gladly willing to listen to Christian preachers and are prepared to receive the Catholic faith. The natives, if conveniently possible, must be warned of their obligation to embrace and revere the faith of Christ. The second principle is the following: If the proper warning has not been given beforehand, the Indians may justly defend themselves even against a king who is armed by zeal for the faith and fortified by papal authority. The Indians conquered in such a war do not become slaves *ipso iure* but only after persistent and stubborn refusal to obey the king and to subject themselves to the sweet yoke of Christ. If they freely wish to receive baptism after being captured, they are by no means to be ruled according to despotic dominion. The third and final principle is that only the supreme pontiff can give the king of Spain the right to rule the aforesaid Indians according to royal or political authority, never according to despotic dominion, and so to keep them forever under his lordship. Consequently whoever suppresses convert Indians to the point of despotic dominion is bound strictly to make restitution for the damage caused and the gain made through such slavery, but for no other reason. Even after their conversion to the faith, it is allowed to exact from them certain services, perhaps greater than those demanded of other Christians in those regions, provided they are consonant with the faith of Christ and the just dictates of reason, in order to defray expenses and costs of government and to keep the land in peace and good order.[12]

When Vitoria shortly came to write on the question as to "whether or not captives taken in war are slaves," he declared that the law of nations *(ius gentium)* which allowed the enslavement of captives in a just war had been abrogated among Christian nations and therefore "in our times Christians may not be made slaves, even in a just war in which it is assumed that they have licitly been captured." But the law of nations still obtains among non-Christian peoples. "I hold," Vitoria said, "that, in the case of other persons,—for example, in that of pagans and Moors,—captives made in war are slaves. That is to say, they are slaves if a just war is waged against them; for if a war is not just, the captives may not be made slaves."[13]

Against this background it is now possible to answer, with some degree of probability, the question: Do the Utopians practice penal servitude or slavery in the strict sense? If it were only a matter of convicted criminals, the response would be "penal servitude." But Thomas More includes two other classes: voluntary bondmen and war captives. And the three classes which More mentions, as has been seen, are precisely the three classes of slaves allowed by Scotus. The only reasonable conclusion is that the Utopians have a system of slavery, not penal servitude.

There exists, of course, the possibility that the case of voluntary bondmen is an example of Morean humor and satire. The lot of prisoners at compulsory labor in Utopia might be better than that of free workingmen in other countries, just as Carlyle in *Past and Present* finds the feudal condition of a medieval serf under Cedric the Saxon superior to the position of a free worker exploited by a socially irresponsible nineteenth-century capitalist. But this touch is too bitter: it is hardly worthy of the humane Utopians to subject poor freemen to the lot of penal servitude, however much milder, instead of admitting them to citizenship. To accept them into a system of slavery, however, is at least consistent in the light of their social institutions, although the introduction of slavery itself into Utopia is to be lamented. Much the same answer must be given to the possible explanation that the Utopians regard their captives as war criminals (although no hint is given of this persuasion) and therefore persons deserving of penal servitude. But in view of the principle of enslavement of war prisoners in the law of nations as witnessed by Augustine, Scotus, Aureolus, Antoninus, and Vitoria, the more immediate, obvious, and likely answer is that the Utopians have accepted the law of nations on this point. Far too often the upholders of the theory of penal servitude simply ignore the Utopians' enslavement of captives in war.[14]

The people of Utopia, after all, are not a perfect Christian people: they are enlightened pagans. Even as pagans, however, they will not admit slavery by birth or by purchase, except the purchase of alien criminals. More may have adopted slavery from his classical background without much thought. This surmise may be bolstered by the consideration that he makes no defense of slavery and even no special comment on it, although it is his custom thus to treat mooted questions. Even so, the introduction of slavery into Utopia does not necessarily imply More's approval of the institution. In the light of the theoretical and historical background, however, one may conclude that More first examined the question of slavery; then agreed (with Scotus) that theoretically, at least among non-Christians, voluntary submission, criminal activity, and capture in war were just causes of enslavement; and finally rejected birth and purchase as legitimate methods of acquiring slaves. The whole controversy on bondage has arisen because More, in view of the purpose of the *Utopia*, had to emphasize slavery, rather than death, as a punishment for thievery. In addition he wanted a severe but not harsh penalty for adultery and other criminal deeds. On account of More's great stress on crime and his mere mention of voluntary and war slaves, scholars have been led to hold that bondage in Utopia is not slavery but penal servitude. But if one takes all three classes and the whole historical background into consideration, one must conclude that there prevails in Utopia a system of slavery—mild, humane, permissive of manumission, and not very extensive—but still slavery in the strict sense of the word.

Just War

It is impossible to believe that More intends to advocate among Christians the revival of the enslavement of war prisoners based on the law of nations. But he would probably agree with Vitoria that this phase of the law of nations in regard to war was still in force among non-Christian peoples such as the Utopians. At this point it is necessary to enter into a discussion of the section on warfare in *Utopia*. The problems are many and vexing. Only those, however, which have a direct bearing on morality, Christian and pagan, will be treated.

Like true humanists, the Utopians abominate war *(bellum)* as an activity manifestly and wholly brutish *(res plane beluina)*. Yet they perceive that no kind of brute makes more continuous use of the practice than man himself. Cicero in *De officiis* had declared that, of the two forms of struggle, parley was proper to man; violence, to beasts *(beluae)*. This etymology passed into popular usage. Before 1264 Vincent of Beauvais was writing in his *Speculum doctrinale* that *bellum* is derived from *bellua* because "people in war *(bellum)* often imitate the ferocity of wild beasts *(bellua)*." Erasmus in his adage *Sweet Is War to the Uninitiated* refers to this etymology and continues: "To me, to be sure, a conflict of arms appears worse than wild, worse than brutish." One would think that Christians were different. But the enemies of Christianity, he says in *The Complaint of Peace,* see and insult Christians fighting one another for reasons more frivolous than those of pagans, with greater cruelty than the impious heathens, with weapons more abominable than they. "Whose invention was the cannon? Was it not of Christians?"[1]

Clicthove in his *War and Peace,* published a few years later, finds that the ancient pagans, wandering far from the true faith and path of salvation, waged their wars with much more moderation, justice, and clemency than Christians, who now conduct them among themselves to their mutual destruction. Strong voices were raised at the Lateran Council in protest against the terrible conditions of war and against the armed attacks on the prestige and freedom of the Church. Calling war the most serious, perilous, and deplorable evil of the times, Egidio of Viterbo declared that princes and armies had almost succeeded in extinguishing her canonical authority and God-given liberty. The change in the Christian attitude toward war and its methods, however, had been observed by St. Antoninus even in the middle of the fifteenth century. He exclaims:

> The whole science of warfare has been turned into brigandage, and there is no faith or piety in the men who pursue martial service. They are full of treachery, theft, sacrilege, perjury, blasphemy, cruelty toward even innocent prisoners, drunkenness, gambling, and sodomy. They pay no attention to the justice of the war on the part of him who hires them, but look only to plunder and higher pay.[2]

As for the concept of a just war, it is impossible to give its history in these pages. The concept has a continuity stretching from antiquity to the present. St. Augustine took the ideas of Cicero especially and developed them to new noble, enlightened, and Christian heights. They found their way into Gratian's *Decretals,* into the doctrine of schoolmen from Aquinas to Suárez, and finally into the treatises of Grotius. The following synopsis by J. K. Ryan of the scholastic teaching on war will help the reader to keep his perspective:

1. Peace, which is a positive condition, not a mere negation, is the natural, normal and necessary good of civil society.

2. War derives its moral and social validity insofar as it is an instrument designed to maintain or recover peace.

3. Since peace is the end and war only a means, it is correct to emphasize the right to peace rather than the right to war. The right to peace is coactive. Purely defensive war does not present an ethical problem.

4. Aggressive war can be justified insofar as it is an act of vindicative justice.

5. Objectively speaking, war is always wrong. That is, it cannot be both formally and materially just on the part of both belligerents.

6. Both defensive and just aggressive wars are acts of necessity, a last resort against an actual evil.

7. In every just war there must be a just, proportionate and known cause; lawful authority; proper motive; right use of means.

8. There is an essential distinction between combatants and non-combatants in war.[3]

A humanist like Clicthove might make a sane yet spirited exposition of the traditional doctrine in his *War and Peace*. But this was not true of all humanists. When Henry VIII was preparing his expedition against France in 1513, Colet declared in his sermon on Good Friday "how few entered on a war unsullied by hatred or love of gain; how incompatible a thing it was, that a man should have that brotherly love without which no one would see God, and yet bury his sword in his brother's heart." Just how Colet explained to the king in a private interview his words that "for Christians no war was a just one" it is difficult to see. But he did so to the satisfaction of Henry, who asked only for a clearer explanation to be made later to his rough soldiers who might misinterpret his statement. Colet, however, did not desist from attacking wars among Christians. In *Letters of Some Learned Men* (1520) appears a letter of a canon of Mainz to Dean Colet (d. 1519) which speaks of a recent antiwar speech of the latter. "You treated the topic with such great authority," the canon writes, "that I might truly say that the power of Christ shone out of Colet. By His power you safely dispersed the darkness of your treacherous adversaries; you conquered, by almost apostle-like composure, men raging against the truth; and you quietly turned aside their insane onslaughts." His support must have pleased Colet.[4]

Erasmus was even more ardently opposed to military force and war, but it is a mistake to consider him a pacifist in the strict sense of the word, that is, a person opposed to all war. But one of the notes to *The Praise of Folly,* in which notes Erasmus had a hand, terms the use of weapons and war one of the corrupt worldly opinions which are as compatible with the doctrine of Christ as fire with water. In general Erasmus holds, as in *The Education of a Christian Prince,* that Christ and the apostles were against war, but figures like Augustine and Bernard were for it in some cases. "If the whole teachings of Christ do not everywhere inveigh against war," he writes in challenge, "if a single instance of specific commendation of war can be brought forth in its favor, let us Christians fight." In the scholia to a letter of Jerome's he writes that Jerome viewed war as licit under the Mosaic dispensation but not under the gospel, because Christ ordered Peter to sheathe his sword and wished men to conquer by long-suffering, not by arms. In the notes to his *New Testament* he takes much the same attitude, not hesitating to disagree with Augustine in interpretation of pertinent texts on war. He makes a very grudging concession: if it must be so, let war be classified among necessary evils provided it be lawful, but there is no need to search for this right to war in the precepts of the gospel, since it cannot be found there. Princes are to undertake no war which can be avoided, are to keep bloodshed to a minimum during its duration, and are to end it as soon as possible.[5]

Two other important works of Erasmus on war and peace appeared within a year or two of the publication of *Utopia.* *Sweet Is War to the Uninitiated* was added to the *Adages* in the

Froben edition of 1515, being printed separately in 1517, the year in which *The Complaint of Peace* first saw the light. (A decade or so later the imperial orator of Charles V, perhaps maliciously, told Edward Lee, who had just given the usual reasons against a declaration of war, that anyone was wasting his effort in attempting to set forth arguments against war more lucidly than Erasmus in these two masterpieces.) In the former work Erasmus lays his finger upon what he believes to be the source of infection in the Christian body: the contamination of the whole pure doctrine of Christ by the writings of pagan dialecticians, sophists, mathematicians, orators, poets, philosophers, and lawyers. The principal offender is the authority of Aristotle, which is almost more respected than that of Christ. But Roman law is also responsible, since it extols war as something admirable, provided it be just: "A just war is . . . one which has been declared by the prince, however youthful or stupid." Exact investigation reveals that the outbreak of almost all wars of Christians is due to stupidity or malice. Matters have gone so far that anyone who attacks war as criminal and wretched is labeled a heretic. Not Bernard of Clairvaux, not Thomas Aquinas, but Christ, who forbade His followers to resist evil, should move the lawyer or theologian. The true Christian teacher never approves a war, although he might permit it somewhere, but unwillingly and sorrowfully. The principal doctrine of Christ, according to *The Complaint of Peace*, concerns "peace and mutual benevolence" or, at least, the will "to forget this so wicked and so cruel madness of making war." The most criminal and evil of men become leaders in war: "Their works whom in time of peace thou wouldst crucify and hang up, in war are chiefest and most regarded." A similar statement on the chief players in "this famous game of war" is found earlier in *The Praise of Folly*.[6]

But Erasmus never dares to condemn war outright and categorically as fundamentally forbidden to Christians. His failure, however, to relate his opinion clearly to the traditional doctrine was bound to draw attacks. When he answered Alberto Pio, he explained: "I have never said unconditionally that Christians may not wage war, although the wars which we have seen hitherto are completely pagan." His purpose in writing strongly was to frighten people away from war as the greatest source of evil to the Christian commonwealth of nations. But war, he has to admit, was licit in cases of great necessity or outstanding and just usefulness. His apparent inconsistency is merely that of Jerome and Augustine on this point. Erasmus takes the same stand in his *Explanation of the Creed.*[7]

The difficulties of Erasmus, especially on the incompatibility of war with Christ's doctrine, find their traditional answers in the Renaissance treatise of Suárez on charity. War, writes Suárez, is neither intrinsically wrong nor forbidden to Christians, since God in the Old Testament, which is an integral part of Christian revelation, praises the wars of those holy men Moses, Joshua, Samson, Gideon, David, the Maccabees, and others. According to the natural law war is necessary for the preservation of peace, the repelling of foes, and the prevention of acts of injustice. "The law of the gospel repeals no part of the natural law and has no new divine precepts, except those of faith and the sacraments." When Christ ordered Peter to sheathe his sword (John 18:11), He was speaking of the person who wishes to draw his sword on private authority, especially against the will of the prince. War is not against peace as such, but against an unjust peace, and is rather a means for securing a true and just peace. It is not contrary to the love of one's enemies, since the just wager of war hates not the persons but their works. It is not opposed to the forgiveness of injuries, since vengeance or punishment can sometimes be sought without unlawful injury. But what of the objection that war is always the occasion for an infinite number of sins? Suárez answers with Augustine that war must be avoided as far as possible and waged only in case of extreme necessity. As for the evils which always accompany war, they happen *per accidens* and, moreover, still greater evils would follow if war were never licit. If the enemy offers condign satisfaction upon request before the war, the prince, of course, is bound to accept, since otherwise the war would be unjust.[8]

Three centuries before Suárez, Aquinas, in giving voice to the conditions for a just war, requires not only the authority of the prince and the justice of the cause but also a right intention, namely, the promotion of good or the avoidance of evil. If the intention is wrong, the war is illicit. He cites the wrong intentions mentioned by Augustine: the desire to inflict injury, cruelty in seeking revenge, an unreconciled and irreconcilable mind, a lust for dominion, and so forth. In respect to one prince's seizure of territory long possessed by another, Silvester agrees with Antoninus in his inability to see how the prince can justly keep it; or how confessors can palliate even notorious sins, or accept alms and possessions from him, or absolve him; or how such deeds can be viewed as licit in Italy. Vitoria later contributes valuable additions to Antoninus' and Silvester's doctrine and makes applications especially pertinent to the *Utopia*. Hythloday, who has been urged to become the councilor of some king, asks his advisers to picture him at a meeting of the French king "to discuss by what craft and means the king may still keep Milan and draw to him again fugitive Naples." The question posed by Vitoria is: "What should be done when the justice of war is doubtful, that is, when there are apparent and probable reasons on both sides?" He answers that the French king may *not* "seize Naples or Milan, if there be doubt who is entitled to it." The reason is that "in doubtful matters the party in possession has the better position." He insists, moreover, that, since "wars ought to be waged for the common good," an apparently just war can become unlawful if greater evils come from waging it than from desisting from it.

For it is clear that if the King of France, for example, had a right to retake Milan, but by the war both the Kingdom of France and the Duchy of Milan would suffer intolerable ills and heavy woes, it would not be right for him to retake it. This is because that war ought to take place either for the good of France or for the good of Milan. Therefore, when, on the contrary, great ills would befall each side by the war, it could not be a just war.[9]

In both books of *Utopia* More shows that he shares with Erasmus the hatred of war and bloodshed. But there is no chance for confusion and misinterpretation, such as reigns in the case of Erasmus, as to his view on the liceity of war for Christians. No matter how bestial a thing war may be, More apparently takes it for granted in the *Utopia,* and elsewhere, that war is licit. He concentrates rather on just causes for war. But first he levels an attack against a cause which was proving to be the bane and ruin of Christian Europe in the early sixteenth century: the winning of glory. The Utopians are just like the humanists of Europe: "Contrary to the custom almost of all other nations, they count nothing so much against glory as glory gotten in war." Almost two decades later More in his *Dialogue of Comfort* was to reaffirm the view expressed in *Utopia:*

As for fame and glory desired but for worldly pleasure, [it] doth unto the soul inestimable harm. . . . This maketh battles between these great princes, and with much bloodshed to much people, and great effusion of blood, one king to look to reign in five realms, that cannot well rule one.[10]

Vitoria simply asserts: "[The truth that] extension of empire is not a just cause of war . . . is too well known to need proof." Suárez declares that the declaration of war merely to acquire name and wealth is an error of pagans which is most absurd even according to natural reason. Christian princes, of course, would not accept such a patent error. Rather, as Erasmus points out to Antony of Bergen in 1514, they insist upon the maintenance of their rights—with the result that immoderate right *(summum ius)* becomes immoderate wrong *(summa in-*

iuria). Stimulated by ambition, some princes first decide what they want and only then seek to invent some title, obsolete and rotten, to cover up their real purpose. Especially pertinent is Erasmus' explanation of the adage: "You have obtained Sparta: now adorn it" ("Spartam nactus es, hanc orna"), which contains the following observations. The itch to get abroad hardly ever ends happily. Since nature has differentiated nations according to temperament, language, or geographical barriers, a sovereign should be content to adorn, not extend, whatever country he rules. When he is active abroad and pants after others' territories, he exhausts the resources of his subjects and submits himself and his whole fortune to the vicissitudes of war just in order to annex one or two small towns to his realm. To such a ruler one should say: "You have obtained Sparta: now adorn it." The field of activity proper to a king as a source of praise is within the confines of his own kingdom. Erasmus employs a quaint image: While the rest of the bees wander hither and thither in their flight, the king bee alone lacks a sting and has much smaller wings so that he is unfit for flying abroad. As examples of rulers who left their own kingdoms with disastrous results Erasmus cites James IV (1488-1513) of Scotland and Charles VIII (1483-1498) and Louis XII (1498-1515) of France. "France," Erasmus writes in *The Education of a Christian Prince*, "is obviously by far the most prosperous of all countries, but it would be much more flourishing if it had refrained from attacking Italy."[11]

Francis I (1515-1547) does not meet with Erasmus' censure, if one is to judge from two letters written in February 1517, the first to Stephen Poncher, bishop of Paris, and the second to Francis himself. The French defeat of the Swiss at Marignano (1515) during the invasion of Italy had merely made clear that Francis had both the courage and the equipment requisite for war if necessary, but actually his whole endeavors were directed toward the betterment of his kingdom and the promulgation of perpetual peace among Christian nations. This view of Erasmus, of course, is far from agreeing with that of Hythloday in his fanciful description of the council meeting of the French king. But the events of 1515-1516, especially the treaties of Geneva and Fribourg and the concordat of Bologna, would induce an observer in 1517 to conclude to the peaceful intentions of the young king. Much the same can be said of Henry VIII. Chambers speaks of "the purposeless wars into which the restless ambition of Henry or of Wolsey was constantly plunging his country," but Pollard, more justly, calls attention to "the fundamentally pacific character of his reign." Henry, declares the latter, realized the impossibility of winning the crown of France, but used his antiquated claim as often as the European balance of power demanded a break with France. In the *Utopia* the warning for a ruler to be content with one kingdom is directed expressly toward France, but actually the union of the German and Spanish dominions in the person of Charles V, however peacefully it had been effected by marriage, gives much point to the advice. Charles's inability to bestow his undivided attention on advantages gained in one country deprived his achievements of more lasting results. According to justice, of course, as Vitoria notes, "there is no obstacle to many principalities and perfect States being under one prince."[12]

But the Utopians hold to the principle: "One king, one kingdom," and look upon the glory sought in war, especially in the annexation of new territory, as something "inglorious." Yet this attitude toward war does not mean that they are strict pacifists and a prey to ambitious neighbors. Both men and women diligently exercise themselves in military training on stated days so that, when occasion demands, they will not be unfit for war. But they are far from being rash in undertaking a war. Just causes of war for them are four in number: (1) the defense of their country, (2) the expulsion of hostile invaders from the lands of their friends, (3) the rescue of a people from

tyranny, and (4) vengeance for injuries done to themselves or
their friends. More apparently considers the first two causes so
evident as to need no word of explanation or proof. The second
cause came into play for More especially in the case of Turkish
invasions. The first session (1512) of the Fifth Council of the
Lateran heard an appeal for war against the Turks by Archbishop Zane of Spalato, who had been an eyewitness of their
atrocities. In fact, the bull of convocation announced as one of
the five purposes of the council the consideration of ways and
means to organize a crusade against the Turks. During and after
the council Leo X strove to launch a crusade against the aggressive and conquering Turks, but the contest of sovereigns over
the imperial crown in 1519 put an end to all hopes. Poets made
appeals for the crusade. In an elegy (1515) Janus Damianus
begged Leo X to bring peace to war-ridden Italy and to lead
Christians victoriously against the Turks. In a fervent poem
which was at once a reprimand and an exhortation, Mantuan
made individual appeals to the great princes of Europe, including Henry VIII, whom he compliments on his virtue and
noble ancestry, for example, Arthur, Alfred, and Edward. In
1509 Barclay included in his *Ship of Fools* a magnificent old
appeal to save Europe. The section, which was entitled "Of the
ruin, inclination, and decay of the Holy Faith Catholic and
diminution of the Empire," eulogized Henry VIII of England
and James IV of Scotland and then went on to say that, if the
"English lion" unites with the "Scots' unicorn,"

> Then is no doubt but all whole Christianity
> Shall live in peace, wealth, and tranquillity,
> And the Holy Land come into Christian hands
> And many a region out of the fiend's bonds.

Later on, More as chancellor complained of "the blindness of
Christian princes who refused to help the Emperor [Charles V]
against so cruel and implacable an enemy as the Turk." A cause
contributing to this situation in some degree was Luther's prop-

osition: "To battle against the Turks is to resist God, who is visiting our iniquities through their instrumentality." In his *Confutation of Luther's Assertion* Fisher attempts to answer him and points to the vast number of Christians whom the Turks have slain or reduced to most harsh servitude.[13]

The Turk might also be assailed under the third cause of war allowed by the Utopians: the suppression of tyrants in other countries. The Utopians take pity on many a people that has been crushed by tyranny and with all their forces they free it from the yoke of the tyrant and from slavery. The Utopian motive is a sense of humanity. Their action is not without precedent or justification. Under Lycurgus, Sparta "put down illegal oligarchies and tyrannies in the different states." The methods and weapons, both spiritual and temporal, used against tyrannical rulers in the Middle Ages are too well known to rehearse here. Vitoria clearly sets forth the reason why foreign rulers may go to war to help a people suffering unjustly from their king: "The reason . . . is that the people in question are an innocent people, and that, by natural law, princes may and can defend the [whole] world, lest injury be inflicted upon it." More and Utopians are not indifferent to the cries of oppressed peoples, nor do they believe that the doctrine of noninterference in the internal affairs of another nation must take precedence over feelings of a common humanity and justice.[14]

The fourth cause of war is vengeance and retribution. Utopia does not restrict the help given to its friends always to circumstances which involve their self-defense: sometimes it assists them also in retaliation and vengeance for injustices committed against them. But Utopia moves cautiously. Its advice must be asked before a decision is reached on the matter. In addition, the case must be proved. Finally, the enemy must be asked to make restitution. In case the enemy refuses, Utopia itself initiates the war to be waged. Vitoria proves the justice of an avenging war by an appeal to the authority of St. Augustine, who had written: "Those wars are described as just wars which are waged in order to avenge a wrong done, as where punishment has to be meted out to a city or state because it has itself neglected to exact punishment for an offence committed by its citizens or subjects or to return what has been wrongfully taken away." Allies and friends may justly join in the war because the wronged state is, as Vitoria declares, "quite properly able, as against foreign wrongdoers, to summon foreigners to punish its enemies." Suárez terms the demand for satisfaction as a just cause of war an opinion that is "common," that is, universally accepted. He adds a cautionary word: a friendly country may undertake a war of vengeance only if its ally may avenge itself justly and in fact intends to do so.[15]

Utopia enters upon such an offensive war for its friends, not only when the enemy has carried away booty, but also whenever the friendly countries' merchants undergo a malicious prosecution, cloaked under the appearance of justice, but actually engineered under the cover of wicked laws or by the manipulation of good ones. In fact, it shows itself more fierce and ready in the latter case. This zeal was demonstrated especially in Utopia's violent and complete overthrow of the Alaopolitae because they had committed an injustice against the merchants of the Nephelogetae under the pretense of justice. More's indignation at the wrongs done to merchants undoubtedly takes its rise in his experiences in the Netherlands in 1515. In fact, the very purpose of the embassy was to keep Charles and his council from carrying out their threat: to "suddenly arrest the English fleet and cast on the merchants' necks all the arrearages of the Sewestoll and the toll of the Hound, which amounteth to a marvelous great sum, not able to be paid by our merchants without their utter undoing."[16]

The Utopians are extremely solicitous about the welfare of merchants of other nations, but if they themselves suffer the loss of their goods only, they do not go to war but merely break off relations with the guilty nation. The reason is that in one case the merchants suffer great loss personally whereas in the other, on account of the communistic system and resultant plenty, no Utopian suffers and therefore there is no proportionately serious cause for the declaration of war. The situation is altogether different when an Utopian citizen is unjustly disabled or killed in a foreign country, whether on public or private authority. Unless the criminals are handed over to them to be punished with death or slavery, Utopia declares war on the spot.[17]

There is actually a fifth just cause which is not mentioned in the section on warfare but in the earlier one on social life. When the island of Utopia has a surplus population, the authorities settle it in a district on the mainland wherever the natives have a superfluity of land which has remained uncultivated. The settlers make fruitful the soil which has hitherto seemed barren and poor. If the natives refuse to become citizens of the new colony, they are driven from the region staked off. If they set up a fight, they have war declared against them. Under the circumstances the Utopians consider that they have a most just cause for war: a people in the possession of unoccupied and untilled land which it does not use itself should not prohibit its use and possession by others who are supposed to support themselves on it according to the law of nature. This general principle, susceptible to abuse, is just and honorable in itself. One Christian writer states pertinently:

> All sovereign states have a right to self-preservation and self-development. The right of self-development may justify a state in occupying a territory which is sparsely inhabited and lacking an organized government. Since the earth was created to satisfy the needs of man in general, so that a portion of it cannot exclusively belong to a people which does not adequately develop it, a superior state may develop it. The superior state, however, must respect the rights of the natives and provide for their development. In general, the right of a state to self-development must be exercised with proper regard for the rights of other states.[18]

Socrates in Plato's *Republic* does not seem to be troubled or exercised by the moral principle behind the necessity of taking alien territory for excess population. When the original territory becomes too small to feed the population, he says simply: "We shall have to cut out a cantle of our neighbor's land if we are to have enough for pasture and ploughing." To do so, of course, renders war inevitable. Two thousand years later, Europeans discovered the vast expanses of the Americas, Africa, and Asia. Little wonder that More could say: "I am sure there have been more islands and more part of the firm land and continent discovered and founden out within this forty years last passed than was new founden, as far as any man may perceive, this three thousand year afore." Moral justification was necessary for their colonization and conquest. On the more popular level, D'Anghiera reports in his *New World* that, in the struggle for colonies, the Castilians urged against the Portuguese that "everything existing on the earth since God created the world is the common property of mankind, and . . . it is, therefore, permissible to take possession of any country not already inhabited by Christians." But the most reputable sixteenth-century theologians—like Cajetan, Vitoria, Soto, and Bañez—insist that pagan princes or sovereigns are legitimate rulers and cannot be deposed merely because they are infidels but only for just reasons. On the theoretical level Vitoria is a representative spokesman. He devotes the first third of his treatise *On the Indians* to prove that "the conclusion stands sure, that the aborigines in question were true owners, before the Spaniards came among them, both from the public and the private point of view." By what lawful title, then, have the Indians been made subjects of the Spaniards? Vitoria appeals especially to the title of "natural society and fellowship." According to the law of nations Spaniards have a right to travel, sojourn, and trade on Indian lands, and the Indians may not hinder them. If the Indians object, the Spaniards ought to use reason with them and show that they mean them no harm. If the Indians persist, the Spaniards may build the forts necessary for protection. If the Indians use force, the Spaniards may seize their cities and reduce them to subjection in order to secure peace and safety. If the Indians remain aggressively hostile, the Spaniards "can make war on the Indians, no longer as on innocent folk, but as against forsworn enemies, and may enforce against them all the rights of war, despoiling them of their goods, reducing them to captivity, deposing their former lords and setting up new ones." The Spaniards thus wage war justly.[19]

Vitoria, however, dares neither to support nor to condemn as a just title the proposed civilization of the aborigines who are reported to be almost wholly savage and barbarous. He does find a possible title in the tyranny of Indian rulers or laws allowing the slaughter of the innocent for sacrificial or cannibalistic purposes. In this case war is justified according to the third Utopian reason: the rescue of a people from tyranny. Vitoria proves its justice by "the fact that 'God has laid a charge on every individual concerning his neighbour' [Ecclesiasticus 17:12], and they are all our neighbours. Therefore, any one may defend them from such tyrannical and oppressive acts, and it is especially the business of princes to do so." This view of the interest of governmental heads in the maintenance of national and international peace and order reveals the humanistic concern for a common nature and humanity superior to all merely regional considerations.[20]

Conduct of War

After the discussion of the nature, liceity, and just causes of war, More turns naturally to the methods of warfare. The Utopians, of course, would prefer to conquer by peaceful rather than bloody means. As Erasmus observes in his *Panegyric of Philip,* the glory gained in war may be conceded to be more splendid, but the victory secured by peaceful tactics is certainly more desirable and beautiful. The skill of a pilot is more evident in a fierce tempest, that of a physician in a grave illness; but who is so foolish, asks Erasmus, as not to prefer a quiet voyage or sound health? More could have found an example of the prince victorious in peace in Henry VII, whom Fabyan praises for his "subduing of his outward enemies of the realms of France and Scotland by his great policy and wisdom more than by shedding of Christian blood or cruel war." If the Utopians cannot conquer by peaceful means, they use the least bloody method possible to achieve victory. A bloody victory fills them, not merely with regret, but also with shame, for they consider it stupid to purchase an article, no matter how precious, at too high a price. They pride themselves much more on conquering and crushing their enemy by skill and guile. If they succeed, they hold a public triumph and erect a monument as for an exploit sturdily executed. The reason for their behavior lies in their brag that they have acted manfully and worthily—

that they have conquered in a way in which no animal could, except man, that is, by the powers of one's wits. They assert that bears, lions, boars, wolves, dogs, and all other brutes battle by using their bodies and that, just as most are superior to men in brawn and ferocity, so men are superior to them in reason and ingenuity.[1]

Thomas More, who refers to Chrysostom in his letters to the University of Oxford (1518) and to John Frith (1532), might have read in his *Treatise on the Priesthood* an apology for well-timed deception. In this defense occurs a statement especially pertinent to the *Utopia:*

> And, if you care to seek those generals who, from all time, have enjoyed high esteem, you will find most of their triumphs have been won by deception, and that these victors are praised above those who have conquered in open action.[2]

When the Utopians boast of conquering by "skill and guile" *(arte doloque)*, they are not referring only to the ordinary stratagems of war. They practice these also, of course. Such are (1) the hiring of mercenaries, (2) the choice of a select corps of young soldiers who concentrate on slaying the general of the enemy, (3) the holding in reserve of a portion of their army to attack the pursuing enemy from the rear in case the Utopian army is routed, (4) the laying and avoidance of ambushes, (5) the pretense of fleeing when nothing is further from their intention, (6) the stealthy removal of their camp at night in case that they are outnumbered or disadvantageously situated, (7) the invention and use of secret weapons, and so forth. Whether the Utopians use such "hellish instruments" as the cannon, which Erasmus in *The Complaint of Peace* finds hard to believe was an "invention of man," is not stated. It would be altogether characteristic of the Utopians to accept the invention of printing and to reject that of gunpowder. The use of the ordinary artifices of war has always been considered morally licit. Thomas Aquinas, for example, quotes with approval

Augustine, who declares that it makes no difference in justice whether the just wager of war conquers in open fight or by ambush. Augustine proves his proposition by the authority of God, who ordered Josue to lay an ambush for the inhabitants of Hai (Josue 8:1-29). Antoninus agrees with Aquinas but draws a further distinction: it is illicit to lie or to fail to keep one's promise but licit not to reveal one's intentions or secrets as one strives to trap the enemy.[3]

The primary principle of the conduct of war by the Utopians would hardly meet with the approval of the sixteenth-century supporters, real or feigned, of the chivalric or feudal system. The Utopians ungallantly care less for the winning of praise or fame than for the careful avoidance of all perils. In fact, European gentlemen and noblemen would definitely pronounce the outlook of the Utopians as degenerate and ignoble. According to Ortolan, who cites Pliny, Valerius Maximus, Tacitus, and Quintus Curtius as his authorities, even pagan civilized antiquity had interdicted placing a price on the enemy's head, arranging for his traitorous assassination, and so forth. There are three successive steps in Utopian strategy: (1) assassination of the prince and his chief adherents; (2) if assassination fails, the support of a pretender to the throne; and (3) if the civil war miscarries, the incitement of neighboring nations to declaration of war and to invasion.[4]

The moment that war is declared, the Utopians connive to have posted in the most prominent places in enemy territory a large number of placards bearing the Utopian great seal. The proclamation promises immense rewards to subjects who kill the prince and other fomenters of the war, and a double amount if they surrender them alive. The result is mutual suspicion and betrayal among the enemy. There is no possible villainy, observes Hythloday, which bribery cannot effect. On this point Erasmus in an adage approves of Cicero's true dictum against Verres: "Nothing is too holy for the power of money not to violate, nothing is too secure for it not to capture." As has been said above, this "custom of buying and selling adversaries among other people is disallowed as a cruel act of a base and a cowardish mind." The Utopians, on the other hand, find in it a source of great praise for themselves: (1) on account of their shrewdness, for they win the war without a single battle, and (2) on account of their humaneness and pity, for they buy off the loss of numerous innocent lives on both sides by the murder of a few criminals. The common people of the enemy, they know, would not have undertaken the war of their own free will but had been driven to it by the mad actions of their princes. The constant presumption of the Utopians apparently is that only the governors of their foes are in favor of war.[5]

The section in *Utopia* on the assassination of enemy leaders, and on other dubious means to be mentioned later, has exercised Morean scholars a great deal. As often in controversial matters, More has given the reader a clue—in fact, two clues, each of which yields a possible explanation.

The first clue lies in the view of Utopian practice held by other people: it is nothing but "cruel villainy springing from a degenerate soul." Yet plots much like those engineered by Utopians (but without the benefit of official placards!) were laid in the game of war between the princes of Christian states. Every prince must have believed heartily in the words addressed to Charles by Erasmus in *The Education of a Christian Prince:* "You judge it an infamous crime, for which there is no punishment terrible enough, for one who has sworn allegiance to his king to revolt from him." But the European prince who thought so did not hesitate to suborn his enemy's subjects to treachery and murder. Even pagans had been too noble and proud to use such means. According to Tacitus, when the Roman senators had heard a letter from a chief promising the death of Arminius if they sent him poison to do the work, they replied "that 'it was not by treason nor in the dark but openly and in arms that the

Roman people took vengeance on their foes': a high saying intended to place Tiberius on a level with the old commanders who prohibited, and disclosed, the offer to poison King Pyrrhus." But Christian rulers did not hesitate to use every means, whether fair or foul, to attain an end which seemed good to *them*. Too often this end was territorial expansion or winning of glory in war. The means under the circumstances appeared to them indifferent or amoral. There can be no doubt that the end of their war seemed good to the Utopians—and actually was good in itself. It was nothing else than winning a war, in which all the justice was on their side, with the least possible bloodshed and slaughter, especially of the common people, the innocent but great sufferers in every war. This is the point at which Utopian reason becomes unreason. Their end is so excellent that the employment of absolutely any means must be legitimate. Subjectively, therefore, the Utopians may be committing no crime, but objectively they seem to be instigating citizens to treason and assassination. The loftiest of ends cannot justify means which are neither good nor indifferent, but bad.[6]

But are the means used by the Utopians evil in themselves? Killing in itself is not wrong, but killing an innocent man or on one's private authority is illicit. Here the second clue furnished by More comes into play. The common people of the enemy, according to the Utopians, do not wage war of their own free will but are impelled to it by the fury and madness of their princes. By this act do the rulers become tyrants? Is tyrannicide on the part of the citizens permissible and even laudable? Do the Utopians merely incite the subjects of their enemies to the exercise of their rights? The explanation is tempting in its simplicity and in its exoneration of More and the Utopians. The interest of More and his friend Erasmus is evident from the declamation which each composed in connection with tyrannicide. Both translated and, at More's suggestion, both wrote replies to Lucian's *Tyrannicide*. In addition a number of More's epigrams deal with tyrants. The history of the controversy over tyrannicide from the appearance of John of Salisbury's *Policraticus* (1159) is long and complicated. Just one hundred years before the composition of *Utopia*, however, the Council of Constance in general terms had condemned on July 16, 1415 the following proposition: "Any vassal or subject may lawfully and meritoriously kill, and ought to kill, any tyrant; he may for this purpose have recourse even to secret plots, flattery, or feigned friendship, regardless of any oath of fealty to him or pact made with him, and without any judicial decree or command." The condemnation grew out of the great orator Jean Petit's public defense of the Duke of Burgundy's share in the assassination of the Duke of Orleans. A short time later the Dominican John Falkenberg declared it lawful to kill the king of Poland and his allies in the struggle of Prussia and the Teutonic Knights against Poland and Lithuania. A commission at the Council of Constance condemned the book but spared the life of its author, who subsequently suffered various degrees of imprisonment and custody. The whole affair flared up again at the end of the sixteenth century with the publication of Mariana's book and a series of political assassinations, especially in France, to say nothing of the Gunpowder Plot in England (1605). The temptation to view the Utopians' instigation to the ruler's assassination as an incitement to legitimate tyrannicide is great, but a number of considerations militate against this interpretation. First of all, the whole tone of the passage in *Utopia* is realistic in its appeal to the venality of the agents. Secondly, if More had intended to excuse and defend the behavior of his Utopians, he would have been much more careful to make clear that the rulers among their enemies were viewed as tyrants and hence worthy of death.[7]

If the assassination of their principal opponents is not effected, the Utopians proceed to the second step: they sow and foster the seeds of dissension among their enemy. They do so by instilling into a brother of the prince or into a nobleman the hope of mastering the kingdom. This Utopian stratagem is so obviously a reflection of contemporary European politics that no great delay on the point is necessary. In Hythloday's description of the council of the king of France the advisers plan to hold the king of England in check by deciding "to make much of some peer of England that is banished his country, which must claim title to the crown of the realm and affirm himself just inheritor thereof." In 1512, for example, Louis XII had recognized Richard de la Pole as king of England. An undated dispatch (May 1516?) of this decade reports the words of the French king to Richard de la Pole: "I know that the King of England is my utter enemy . . . and because [I] know your title to be good to the crown of England, I shall . . . assist you both with men and money for obtai[ning of your] said right, and shall not forsake you in that behalf w[hile I] have one crown to expend." Richard's brother, Edmund, had been promised the support of the emperor Maximilian I, but had been delivered to Henry VII by Philip the Handsome in the treaty of 1506. He was beheaded by Henry VIII in 1513. Not only Charles VIII of France, but also Maximilian I of Germany and James IV of Scotland, had furthered the earlier and disastrous schemes of Perkin Warbeck (1474-1499), the subject of an historical play by John Ford. Foreign help, too, had been given the English impostor Lambert Simnel who, after his defeat at Stoke (1487), was fortunate enough to be pardoned and to become royal falconer. Nor were the schemes of Henry VIII more praiseworthy in his relations with Scotland. Brewer asks: "Were the intrigues of Henry VIII and his minister Dacre against Scotland more moral than these [of the Utopians]? Were not their attempts to sow treason and disaffection among the Scotch lords an exact exemplification of this Utopian policy?" Almost every European state might see in Utopia an image of itself in this regard.[8]

If neither the murder of the ruler nor the support of a pretender to the throne is successful, the Utopians stir up and embroil the neighboring countries in the struggle. For this purpose they dig up any old title, such as kings never lack. Of this sort was the hereditary claim of the English king to the French throne, extremely useful whenever it was expedient to declare war on France. In the imaginary council meeting of the French king it is decided that "the Scots must be had in a readiness, as it were in a standing ready at all occasions, in aunters the Englishmen should stir never so little, incontinent to set upon them." The same dispatch which mentions the French king's recognition of Richard de la Pole as legitimate king of England contains the news that the "French King intends to send men and money to the Duke of [Albany] that he may make war upon England." The duke was John Stewart (1481-1536), who had been brought up in France, made regent of Scotland in 1515, and proclaimed heir to the throne in 1516 instead of the future James V. Even more devastating than the account of the meeting of the French king's councilors, however, is Julius II's revelation of his own international manipulation and intrigue in Erasmus' *Exclusion of Julius*. All Christian rulers, from petty prince to pope, seemed to be using Utopian tactics.[9]

The whole section in *Utopia* on bribes, assassins, pretenders, and traditional enemies, of course, is not to be taken as expressing More's real opinion on international politics. Without doubt he himself would wholly disavow Utopian practice as "a cruel act of a base and a cowardish mind." But he paints a picture which he knows the Christian of Europe will abhor. And then he cries: "Wherefore, thou art inexcusable, O man, whoever thou art who judgest. For wherein thou judgest another, thou dost condemn thyself. For thou who judgest dost the same things thyself" (Romans 2:1).

When Utopia persuades neighboring countries to attack its enemy, it promises them and furnishes them with all the moneys and supplies of war. But it is exceedingly reluctant to send even a few of its own citizens to help them. Utopians love and cherish one another so much that they would not exchange a single Utopian even for the prince of their enemy. This is totally unlike the conduct of Christians in Europe. On one occasion Henry VIII visited More unexpectedly, had dinner with him, and walked for an hour with his arm on his shoulder. When Roper congratulated him on his familiarity with the king, More acknowledged the royal favor and then added: "Howbeit, son Roper, I may tell thee I have no cause to be proud thereof; for, if my head [could] win him a castle in France (for then was there war between us), it should not fail to go."[10]

Another means which one is surprised to find the humane and merciful Utopians using against their enemy is the hiring of the Zapoletes, the fiercest of all mercenaries. One must admit, however, that the Utopians professedly do not "use" them *(utuntur)* but rather "abuse" them *(abutuntur)*, for they wish to rid the world of them by promising them great rewards and then exposing them to the greatest perils. By the Zapoletes Thomas More obviously means the German and Swiss mercenaries of the period. He seems to devote a disproportionate amount of space to them, but an explanation is readily found in the events of 1515.[11]

First of all, the French in a brilliant triumph had forced the Swiss to withdraw at the battle of Marignano, September 13-14, 1515. Of this maneuver which amounted to a defeat, Erasmus at Basle wrote in jubilation to Andrew Ammonius, October 2, 1515, describing the anger of the Swiss against the French who had not "politely" yielded in battle to them as they once had yielded to the English at the Battle of the Spurs, 1513. "They have returned home," he continues, "somewhat fewer than they had gone forth, maimed, mangled, wounded, with torn standards; instead of paeans of victory, they are uttering dirges for the dead." The report found its way also into the *Letters of*

Obscure Men: "But, to come to the news: The Swissers and the Landsknechts have been mightily waging war, and slaying one another in thousands; and it is to be feared that none of them will go to heaven, because they fight for pelf, and one Christian ought not to slay another. . . . [T]he soldiers are but lewd folk, and they fight because they list."[12]

On October 24, 1515, when More was returning to Calais after his recall from Bruges, he met Richard Pace on the highway. Pace, chief secretary of Henry VIII, who had just made a defensive alliance with Ferdinand of Aragon on October 19, 1515, was on a mission to secure the services of Swiss mercenaries in order to expel the French from Italy. In a report to the Council of Ten, dated June 3, 1516, Giustinian relates how he remonstrated with Henry and "delated on the inhumanity of the Germans, who burn, destroy, and kill in all directions; the ferocity of the Swiss was notorious, and no sex or age was exempt from their inhumanity." Three years before, Machiavelli in a letter to Vettori had written an appraisal of the Swiss and said: "I believe you completely deceive yourself in the case of the Swiss, and about whether they are to be feared much or little. I feel sure they are very much to be feared." In his *Prince* he sees mercenaries as the cause of the downfall or near-downfall of states, including Carthage and Rome. He voices his objections to hired soldiers and his predilection for citizen troops. It is noteworthy that Hythloday in the *Utopia* calls hired standing armies, even of native troops, the ruin of the Carthaginians, Romans, and Syrians in the past and of the French in the present, and then proceeds to praise the warlike courage of the sturdy English yeomen in their battles against the French. He pays his audience the high compliment of saying that the "new-made and unpractised soldiers" of England have often been victorious over even "the French soldiers, which from their youth have been practised and ured in feats of arms." But Ferdinand the Catholic gives a more unbiased opinion of the

English army in 1512 and 1513. The English "are strong,
stout-hearted, stand firm in battle, and never think of taking
flight." On account of long years of peace, however, they hate
to perform the routine drudgery of the camp. After drill and
experience, "the English troops would excel those of any other
nation." For greater efficiency a larger number of pikemen is
necessary. Otherwise the French army, reinforced with German
troops, might have the upper hand. Ferdinand recommends that
English archers be merged with German pikemen, since "it is
not probable that English archers alone could resist German
troops in a pitched battle." He concludes: "German infantry has
deservedly acquired a high reputation."[13]

But Thomas More did not have to look far south to the
Swiss to perceive the ravages committed by mercenaries. The
Landesknechte, who had been organized by Maximilian early
in his career into almost irresistible infantrymen, had spread
terror through the Netherlands in the last decades of the fifteenth century and had been the cause for much agitation and
resistance to Maximilian, especially in Flanders. In 1514 the
governor of Friesland, Duke George of Saxony, had used the
"Black Band" to repress rebellion. In 1515, the very year in
which More was in Flanders, George promised to dismiss the
Black Band in exchange for a large sum paid in redemption
of unhappy Friesland. But these mercenary troops kept seeking
employment wherever they could find it. Their depredations in
Holland continued until their dispersal and partial massacre
in 1518. Thomas More, therefore, had right at hand testimony
and evidence of great evils done by mercenary troops. The
details of the description of the Zapoletes, however, fit the Swiss
best: the distance of five hundred miles from Utopia (England)
to the native land of the Zapoletes (Switzerland), the moun-
tainous and wooded nature of their country, and so forth. Is it
possible that More is here paying Henry VIII the same dubious
compliment which he pays the Utopians? Is Henry VIII, like

the Utopians, not merely *using* mercenaries against his enemies but *abusing* them, that is, occasioning their deaths in the name of mercy and humanity? Most probably not, since Henry was likely to have in mind only the expulsion of Francis and the French from Milan and Italy.[14]

As might be expected, Erasmus has much to say on the subject of mercenaries, especially in his *Adages*. He is horrified at the existence of a German people which boasts of the great number of mortals its natives have slain with the sword—behavior the more detestable because they do so hired for money, just as any old hangman paid for executing people. There are many others, kinsmen of one another and subjects of the same prince, who, for the sake of paltry gain, fly to the armies of opposing parties and kill one another in battle. When they return home, they are not treated as deserters of country and family or despoilers and murderers of the innocent, but as honorable and upright citizens! In antiquity the Carians, according to Pomponius Mela, Herodotus, and Strabo, were a barbarous, war-mad, and pelf-seeking people. Suidas writes that they were the first of mortals to war for wages, as persons who held life cheap, and therefore those who hired them were wont to place them first in the battle line so that they would be the first to bear the full shock of the enemy attack, or used to expose them where the fortune of war seemed most perilous. The similarity of these tactics to those of the Utopians is evident. The contemporary counterpart of the Carians, affirms Erasmus, are the Swiss, a people born for war, but otherwise upright and the least evil of men, who would be outstanding in literature and all honorable pursuits if only they turned their minds to them away from war. In another adage Erasmus observes that the seeds of plants and the habits of men correspond to the nature of the terrain: mountaineers are almost always wild and inhumane—like the Zapoletes, More would add. In *The Complaint of Peace* Erasmus tells a prince not to insist upon every iota of his rights for fear of dulling the luster of his majesty a little bit, since if he hires mercenaries to help him, his majesty will suffer much more:

> But how much more abjectly dost thou despise thy majesty when that now and then thou shalt be compelled to please the barbarous companies and vilest dregs of all scelerate [wicked] and mischievous persons, the which shall with gold never be filled nor satisfied; while that thou as meek and with prayers dost send ambassadors unto the Carians, a most vile and hurtful people; whilst thou committest thy life and thy people's goods and substance to their faith that have neither consideration nor holiness.[15]

In the background of the section on war in the *Utopia* is the doctrine of the humanist and Christian. This is given clearly in Erasmus' colloquy *The Soldier and the Carthusian.* The Carthusian calls it an "unhappy way of living, for a poor pay, to murder a fellow Christian, who never did you harm." The soldier protests that "it is lawful to kill an enemy." The Carthusian answers: "Perhaps it may be so, if he invades your native country. Nay, and it is pious too to fight for your wife, children, your parents and friends, your religion and liberties, and the public peace. But what is all that to your fighting for money? If you had been knocked on the head, I would not have given a rotten nut to redeem the very soul of you." Vitoria in his treatise on war holds much the same view and actually cites the Swiss as an example:

> I also maintain that those who are prepared to go forth to every war, who have no care as to whether or not a war is just, but follow him who provides the more pay, and who are, moreover, not subjects [of that person], commit a mortal sin, not only when they actually go to battle, but whenever they are thus willing. I further contend that, when the case is doubtful, allies—for example, the Swiss—may not, when they themselves are not subjects, furnish aid to the other side.[16]

Suárez later examines the various opinions on mercenaries at greater length. The common opinion as expressed by Silvester

(1460-1523) and Cardinal Cajetan (1470-1534), both Italian
Dominicans, seems to be that mercenaries are bound to examine
into the justice of the war before they enlist. A mercenary who
looks only to the pay, according to Silvester, cannot be absolved
unless he renounces his calling or enlists only in a war which
he knows to be just or, at least, believes to be probably just.
Cajetan, however, qualifies this general principle: this is true
unless mercenaries receive pay also during peace time and are
pledged to answer every call of the prince. In the latter case,
continues Cajetan, they may bear themselves as subjects since
they are really subjects because of their pay. After a careful
examination of Cajetan's arguments Suárez concludes to no
real distinction between subjects and nonsubjects in this matter.
But morality is involved. If the doubt is purely negative, it is
more probable that mercenaries may go to war without an
investigation and may cast the whole moral burden on the
prince, who, of course, must enjoy a good reputation in the eyes
of all. If the doubt is positive and the reasons for justice on both
sides are probable, mercenaries are obliged to learn the truth.
If they cannot reach the truth, they ought to follow and help
the side which is more probable and more just. The reason is
that probabilism, which teaches that one may follow a probable
opinion when supported by solid reasons even though the opposite opinion may have stronger reasons, may *not* be used when
the harm of one's neighbor or the defense of the innocent is
involved. In such a case one is bound to choose the safer course.
The mercenary Zapoletes are to be condemned, since they pay
no attention to the justice of the cause served but look only to
the size of their pay.[17]

The Utopians, like Hythloday, disapprove of all soldiers,
whether native or alien, who fight for pay. In a word, they dis-
like a professional army and rely upon the citizen militia.
Here More's *Utopia* departs from Plato's *Republic*, because,
acting on the principle "one man one task," Socrates would

have a professional army. Lycurgus, too, had separated the military class from other classes in Sparta, perhaps in imitation of the Egyptian system. But Utopia trusts to the bravery of all its ordinary citizens, men and women, who receive military training on stated days. On the battlefield, however, More adopts a practice taken from the *Republic*. In the latter work Socrates observes that "when it comes to fighting, every creature will do better in the presence of its offspring." Consequently it is plain that men and women "will march out together, and, what is more, will conduct their children to war when they are sturdy, . . . and in addition to looking on they will assist and minister in all the business of war and serve their fathers and mothers." The Utopians go even further. Although they do not blame women who do not accompany their husbands to war, they exhort and stimulate with praise those who do. In battle every Utopian is supported by those whom nature intended to help one another: his children and his relations by blood and by marriage. The spouse who returns without spouse, the son who returns without father, falls into the deepest public disgrace. The Utopian does not fear death, for he is aware that his loved ones will be well taken care of by the communistic system. He would agree with what More was to write later in his treatise on the passion: "Marry, for dread of death or torment, either to run quite away when need requireth a man to abide by his tackling, or desperately to yield himself into his enemy's hands, this, lo, is by the law of arms reputed a very shameful and traitorous act." The custom of families fighting as units in battle was true of ancient peoples, such as Teutons, Gauls, and Britons. In 1515 Jehan Le Veau wrote to Margaret of Savoy: "The Swiss have arrived, . . . a fine body of men, promising, if he [the Duke of Milan] wants soldiers, their women and children shall come from Switzerland to maintain him in his duchy." Only the practice of fighting by families had died, not the spirit![18]

Whenever the Utopians strike a truce with the enemy during the war, they keep the agreement as a most sacred pledge. In fact, even under provocation they will not break the truce. On the other hand, Utopia never concludes an alliance or treaty with its neighbors, who are always making and breaking treaties. The greater and the holier the ceremonies, the more quickly the latter break a treaty by discovering some frivolous defect purposely and deceitfully worked into it from the start. How unlike, More ironically cries out, the holy and inviolable observation of treaties in those parts of Europe where the faith and morality of Christ holds sway, where princes are just and good, and where pope and bishops are revered and feared for keeping their own promises and forcing lay rulers to keep theirs! The Utopians believe that the mutual good feeling which *nature* causes to spring up in all men is better than any mere treaty. Men, they hold, are united more strongly by good will than by pacts, more by kinship of mind than by the written and sworn word.[19]

More, as has been seen, deplores the European attitude toward agreements. The lament is found in other contemporary documents. John Skelton in *Speak, Parrot* exclaims: "So many truces taken, and so little perfite truth; / . . . Since Deucalion's flood the world was never so ill." Later, in the *Gouernour*, Thomas Elyot finds pagans better observers of their word than Christians. He undertakes to "show how the Gentiles, lacking true religion, had solemn oaths in great honor and how terrible a thing it was among them to break their oaths or avows insomuch as they supposed that there was no power, victory, or profit which mought be equal to the virtue of an oath." Even Mohammedans show greater mutual faith than Christians: "Alas! what reproach is it to Christian men and rejoicing to Turks and Saracens that nothing is so exactly observed among them as faith consisting in lawful promise and covenant. And among Christian men it is so neglected that it is more oftentimes broken than kept." Much earlier, in his *Tree of Commonwealth*, Dudley had told Henry VIII about his daily prayer that "your Grace will truly keep and observe all leagues and promises . . . though they should be to your loss; for, [of] all worldly losses, and specially in a prince, honor and credence is the most."[20]

The Utopians, as good pagans, find a sufficient substitute for treaties in the bond of a common nature. Erasmus, as a good Christian, finds it in the ties of a common religion. "Among all Christian princes," he explains in *The Education of a Christian Prince,* "there is at once a very firm and holy bond because of the very fact that they are Christian. Why, then, is there a need to conclude so many treaties every day as if everyone were the enemy of everyone else and human agreements were essential to gain what Christ could not [accomplish]?" Wise and good rulers find a confirmed friendship better than a treaty, whereas a wicked or stupid monarch makes a treaty the cause of war by claiming the violation of some hitherto insignificant clause. If the mere promises of princes should be more holy than the oaths of common men, is it not ignoble of them "not to live up to those agreements which they made in solemn treaty, with those ceremonies included which are the most sacred of all among Christians?" Yet the moral atmosphere of Christian Europe was so corrupt on this point that a pope could be designated as the master of all deceit. Machiavelli writes: "Alexander VI did nothing else than deceive men, and had no other intention. . . . There never was a man more effective in swearing that things were true, and the greater the oaths with which he made a promise, the less he observed it." Nor were Alexander's successors, Julius II and Leo X, much behind him in filling this unenviable role when need required. The ironic stricture of More in the *Utopia* on the behavior of "great bishops" *(summi pontifices)* is so clear that he must be judged to have recent popes in mind. The supreme pontiffs, he declares with irony, "like as they make no promise themselves but they do very religiously perform the same, so they exhort all princes in any wise to abide by their promises, and them that refuse or deny so to do, by their pontifical power and authority they compel thereto."[21]

If the Utopians happen to gain the victory in battle, they do not proceed to the violent and unrestrained slaughter of the fleeing enemy. They would rather capture them alive than strike them dead. In their mercy toward the vanquished, they imitate the policy of the Spartans toward their fellow Greeks. Plutarch in his life of Lycurgus reports that when the Spartans "had conquered and routed an enemy, they pursued him far enough to make their victory secure by his flight, and then at once retired, thinking it ignoble and unworthy of a Hellene to hew men to pieces who had given up the fight."[22]

The Utopians follow other Greek ideals, described by Plato in the *Republic:*

> They will not, being Greeks, ravage Greek territory nor burn habitations, and they will not admit that in any city all the population are their enemies, men, women and children, but will say that only a few at any time are their foes, those, namely, who are to blame for the quarrel. And on all these considerations they will not be willing to lay waste the soil, since the majority are their friends, nor to destroy the houses, but will carry the conflict only to the point of compelling the guilty to do justice by the pressure of the suffering of the innocent.

Nor were the Greeks alone in this respect. In his *War and Peace* Clicthove notes with approval a custom of the Asiatic Indians, narrated by Diodorus Siculus. In time of war farmers might cultivate their lands without the slightest anxiety, for they were left unscathed and unmolested as servants of the common good. The fields of the enemy were left unburned, their trees unfelled. In addition Clicthove reports that ancient generals sternly forbade their soldiers to seize forcibly the crops and goods of farmers and villagers and punished them if they did not obey orders. The Utopians live up to this ideal. They do not lay waste the territory of the enemy nor burn out his fields. They keep the grain even from being trampled on by horses' hooves or men's heels, firm in the belief that it is being grown for their own use. They harm no defenseless man. They safeguard the cities surrendered peacefully, and do not plunder even those taken by assault. They leave the whole civilian population untouched. In a word, the Utopians live up to the highest possible pagan ideals. How much more should Christians surpass them in humanity and mercy since the Christian standard of perfection is immeasurably superior to the pagan![23]

Just what was the Christian norm at the time, not according to the highest theoretical principles of Christian counsel, but according to the limits of commandment below which Christians could not fall without serious sin? The common doctrine is summarized well by Vitoria, who was a contemporary of More. In respect to the slaughter of the fleeing enemy, Vitoria asks whether it is permissible for the victorious Spaniards, who now fear no danger, to follow and kill them. He answers in the affirmative. The king has power both to regain his possessions and to punish his enemy; otherwise, "it would not be possible to avoid wars, [for the enemy] would come back forthwith." As far as nonbelligerents are concerned, it is not permissible to kill children and women (not even of Turks and unbelievers! says Vitoria), nor inoffensive farmers, nor "the rest of the peaceable civilian population," since all these persons are innocent unless the opposite is clear. Vitoria bases his view on the same ground as Silvester, namely, "War is founded on a wrong done, and therefore the rights of war may not be enforced against the innocent if the wrong can be redressed in another quarter." Suppose the latter course is not possible? Then it is certainly licit to despoil the innocent, not only of the weapons of war, but also of money, grain, and horses, if this procedure is necessary to sap the strength of the enemy. Suppose even this policy does not work? Vitoria concludes that "if the war goes on for an indefinitely long time it is lawful utterly to despoil all enemy-subjects, guilty and guiltless alike, for it is from their resources that the enemy is feeding an unjust war, and, on the other hand, his strength is sapped by this spoliation of his citizens." He insists that the purpose of war is not the ruin of the enemy but the obtaining of one's rights, the defense of one's country, and the winning of peace and security. Consequently for the Spanish wantonly to set fire to the cities and fields of the French is "diabolical; this fire is the fire of hell; for such an act is not needful in the attainment of victory." Suárez agrees substantially with Vitoria: if the end is licit, the necessary means are licit, and therefore all necessary damages inflicted on the enemy, except the death of the innocent, are lawful. Unlike the Utopians who spare the fields and cities of the enemy, Henry VIII in 1523 availed himself of the privilege of pillage. The incident is narrated in a letter of More to Wolsey. Charles, Connétable de Bourbon (1490-1527), who after a quarrel with Francis I had allied himself with Henry, had advised that "the king's army shall in the marching proclaim liberty, sparing the country from burning and spoil," but Henry decided otherwise. The king thinks, reports More, that "sith his army shall march in hard weather with many sore and grievous incommodities, if they should also forbear the profit of the spoil, the bare hope wh[ereof], though they got little, was great encouraging to them, [they shall have] evil will to march far forward and their captains shall have much ado to keep them from crying 'Home! Home!' "[24]

When the Utopians capture a city, they do not pillage it but they do slay those who prevented its surrender. Their reason probably is that such men have prolonged the siege and thereby caused unnecessary suffering and bloodshed. They reduce the armed defenders of the city to slavery, but spare the innocent civilian population. At the end of the war they force the enemy, as the guilty party responsible for the war, to bear its whole cost. Reparations take the form, not only of money, but also of rich landed estates among the vanquished, the revenues of which remain forever in their possession. The conquered country, it must be noted, does not become a tributary or subject nation in an Utopian empire: Utopia simply collects the revenues coming from its estates as a foreign investor. The distinction is fine but justifiable.[25]

The conduct of the Utopians is in accord with the law of war in the sixteenth century. Vitoria enunciates the general principle that, even after the winning of victory and redress and peace, the wronged party may licitly avenge injustice and punish the enemy. By "the law of nations and by the authority of the whole world . . . [and, it seems, even] by natural law also," rulers have lawful authority, "not only over their own subjects, but also over foreigners, so far as to prevent them from committing wrongs." The peace and safety which are the end of war would not be secure "unless evils and damages be visited on the enemy in order to deter them from the like conduct in the future." Therefore the Utopians may lawfully kill the guilty perpetrators of wrongs committed against them. Vitoria follows Cicero in upholding the claims of equity and humanity and insists that the public good militates against the killing of *all* the guilty. If a city capitulates without laying down conditions for the safety of its defenders, it is not unjust to put to death "the more notorious defenders." Since the aggressor is bound to restitution, the innocent party may seize enemy property to pay for all expenses and all damages. In addition it may impose a tribute on the conquered enemy, not only by way of reparations, but also by way of punishment and revenge. Thus, the Spaniards, according to Vitoria, may (1) appropriate a hundred thousand ducats in enemy goods if the French have despoiled them of that amount, (2) seize enough enemy property to pay for all the expenses of the war, and (3) punish the French to the amount, say, of twenty thousand ducats. Suárez insists upon the observance of a just proportion between the punishment and the crime. But to this whole procedure there is a serious objection: it is against the law of nature for the same person to be both accuser and judge in a case. Suárez declares that this double role is seen in God, to whom public authority is similar. This act of vindictive justice is necessary to the human race. A more natural, human, and suitable way is not at hand at present. The presumption is that the guilty party, insolent and unwilling to make satisfaction, is the one responsible for his own subjection to the wronged party.[26]

To conclude, the Utopians' love of peace and detestation of bloodshed, as well as their humane conduct of inevitable wars, can set a basic pattern for Europeans, who can and must improve upon it to the extent that a divinely inspired Christianity surpasses the enlightened humanism of paganism.

CHAPTER XIX

Praise of Wisdom

During the close study of the sections on religion and morality in More's *Utopia* one is amazed, first, at the great number of topics on which he touches and, secondly, at their relevancy to actual conditions in the Christian West on the very eve of the Protestant Reformation. There is hardly an important issue of the day which does not appear in the pages of *Utopia*. On some problems, of course, it is impossible to surmise More's real mind at the time of its composition and publication. But the number of these is relatively few. The results of this whole study are confirmatory of the humanistic theory on the interpretation of the *Utopia*.

Utopia is the praise of wisdom—not so much of the wisdom of Christian revelation as of the wisdom of classical antiquity. It is, therefore, the praise of reason. The book is an act of humanistic faith in the ability of reason to construct an intellectually satisfying religion and morality upon which Christianity can build with minimal destruction of pre-existing elements. Human nature, even in Utopia, is a fallen nature, but if it follows the guidance of reason, it can enter a land of sweetness and light, preparatory to being called into the kingdom of God, overflowing with spiritual milk and honey. To change the figure, the Utopian temple with all its accouterments stands ready as if waiting for the Christian liturgy to begin. The Utopians have

advanced in religion and morality as far as it is possible for
rational creatures, unassisted by supernatural grace, to go.

In fact, Utopian intellectuals put some Christian philosophers to the blush. The former admit the ability of human reason to prove God's existence and attributes and at least to
follow the lead of religion in regard to the immortality of the
soul and future retribution. The latter sometimes derive from
reason truths diametrically opposed to the truths of Christian
revelation. In Italy especially, the great freedom of expression
permitted to professors encouraged teachers to espouse unorthodox philosophical opinions, often veiled as historical disquisi-
tions which purported to determine Aristotle's true doctrine. To
the humanists the Utopians, like the virtuous pagans of Greece
and Rome, certainly seem more likely, somehow or other, to
attain salvation than professed Christians like Pomponazzi and
the Averroists. The contemplation of the wonders of earth and
sky lead Utopian scientists and philosophers to God and His
praise. In fact, they even expect from Him miracles in time
of crisis.

As far as the religious problems of the individual person
are concerned, More stresses two in particular. First of all, the
Utopians have no use for astrology, that pseudoscience dominant
in Europe. No diviner tries to foretell future events by the positions and aspects of the stars. Secondly, the Utopian attitude
toward death and burial puts to shame unenlightened Christians.
So full of hope and so devoid of fear are Utopians that they
welcome the dread visitor—even to the point of submitting to
euthanasia. How unlike the terror and reluctance of Christians
to die! Utopian burials, too, are conducted with simplicity, consolation, and joy, in contrast to the foolish ostentation and mel-
ancholy grief of Christian funerals.

When it comes to the choice of his vocation, the Utopian
acts with prudence and deliberation, whether this calling be to
the lay state, the ascetic ideal, or the priestly dignity.

Suppose the Utopian plans to marry. Before his wedding he is assisted, as it were, by stringent laws to keep himself free from fornication—and consequently from the new and terrible disease, syphilis. He is permitted to make sure that his wife, too, is physically healthy and fit. He may never marry in haste, nor too young. He must wait until his twenty-second year when he is sure of bodily and emotional maturity. Once tied in wedlock, he knows that divorce is all but impossible. The threat of severe punishment tends to keep him from adultery. Finally, the spirit of love which prevails in his family is manifest in the mutual confession of faults before departure to religious services. What a sharp contrast to many a European: marrying in secrecy and in haste after barely attaining the age of puberty or after many extramarital adventures, and then degrading his marriage with concubinage and adultery! There is little social disapproval for his conduct and perhaps only a slight fine for his misdemeanor. But there is no hope of divorce for him in his unfortunate and ill-fated union.

If the Utopian decides to lead an ascetical life, whether within or outside the married state, he knows that he must devote himself to hard, unpleasant manual work as the self-denying servant of all. Here More may be showing the influence of Erasmus as affected by St. Jerome's works: the desire for a return to the spirit of early monasticism. At the very least, he wants monks and friars to follow the primitive rule of their founders. There must be less stress upon the religious garb and ceremonies peculiar to each order and far more attention to practical spirituality. The life of the Christian ascetic should not be one of pride, ease, and idleness, but of labor, industry, poverty, and humility.

An Utopian would encounter great difficulty in becoming a priest and, of course, much more in becoming a bishop. The clergy in Utopia are very few in number and very holy in life. As the result of their sanctity they enjoy special immunities. In war they are peacemakers. In peace they have care of the education of youth and charge of the morals of adults. Even the mere threat of excommunication frightens offending laymen and leads to their speedy amendment. In Europe there are far too many in holy orders. As a result their moral level is low. Many priests and bishops are worldly-minded and even concubinary in direct opposition to their serious obligations and to their duty of setting a high example for laymen. Their privileges of immunity, on account of abuse and subterfuge, are threatened by the civil power. Their excommunications become less effective as they become more numerous. Far from working to establish peace, popes and bishops and clerics seem to countenance, and even foment, wars.

Wars between Christian nations are a crying evil of the day. Many are waged for the sake of territorial expansion and vindicated on the score of dynastic claims. More has in mind kings like Francis I of France with designs on Italy, Henry VIII of England using an antiquated title to France when expedient, and Charles, ruler of the Netherlands and Spain and heir of Germany. Like the Achorians, the Utopians must believe that a king has his hands full with one kingdom and lacks the capacity to rule two well. For this reason a dynastic war is unjustifiable and hence unjust. Every war of the Utopians is just, for it satisfies the conditions of a just war. They consider morally vindicable a war for the colonization of sparsely settled regions by their excess population—a much better reason than those excuses, if any, proffered by many a European nation for its imperialistic exploitation. The period of discovery, in addition, had brought with it a recrudescence of slavery, which the Utopians strive to keep within narrow and humane limits. They would undoubtedly approve the call of Leo X and the Lateran Council to a crusade to resist the aggression of the Turks and to rescue the peoples groaning under their tyrannical yoke. As for the conduct of war, the Utopians use some methods as reprehensible as those which Europeans use: assassination of the enemy ruler, recognition of a rival claimant to the enemy's throne, and so forth. If Europeans grow angry at such Utopian tactics, More can turn the accusation against them: you do the same! Like Western governments, the Utopian state employs the services of mercenaries—but with the idea of ridding the face of the earth of the inhuman wretches. The Utopians observe truces scrupulously and do not break them even under provocation. As far as alliances are concerned, they refuse to enter into them, since they hold the bond of common humanity and friendship to be sufficient. They would abhor the behavior of European princes, including the popes, who used flimsy excuses to break the most solemn pacts.

Designs for the reform of religious accouterments and services, too, are sketched in the *Utopia*. Grave abuses, such as drunkenness and lechery, connected with the observance of Sundays and holydays are to be eliminated. Perhaps the number of holydays should be reduced. At any rate, holy festivals are to be kept in a holy spirit. In regard to churches, many unbecoming statues and paintings must be removed. A distinct improvement in the conduct of the faithful in church is to be desired. Silence and reverence should mark the house of God. The church is not a tavern or a music hall but a house of prayer. Improper and ostentatious music is to be eliminated. The music should pray and the prayer should sing. Finally, the clergy as the representatives of Christ should be more ready for teaching than condemnation, more prepared for peaceful persuasion than excommunication and the stake. For truth, if it is not suppressed by violence and rancor, will always win over error. Such is More's humanistic conviction.

At the end of *Utopia*, it is true, More declares that not a few things in the religion and rites of the Utopians, as in their warfare and their communism, seem extremely absurd.[1] But in regard to Utopian customs and laws, Europeans are to behave

as they ought toward the pagan classics: take the good and leave
the bad. The good things are many and point the way to a
practical religious renovation. If the Utopians, by the light of
reason alone, could keep even a natural religion on a high
plane, how much more, with the help of revelation and grace,
should Western Christianity, head and members, institute a
reform that would present to the world the Church of Christ
"in all her glory, not having spot or wrinkle or any such thing,
but . . . holy and without blemish" (Ephesians 5:27).

Chapter I

1 Joseph H. Lupton, editor, *The "Utopia" of Sir Thomas More* (Oxford, 1895), pp. xciii-xciv, 33, 307-08; James Mackintosh, "Life of Sir Thomas More," in *Miscellaneous Works*, new edition (London, 1854), I, 425; Myron P. Gilmore, *The World of Humanism: 1453-1517* (New York, 1952), pp. 34-35. Lupton's edition will be designated henceforth simply as *Utopia*, but, as announced in the Preface, the spelling and punctuation will be modernized.

2 Jack H. Hexter, *More's "Utopia": The Biography of an Idea* (Princeton, 1952), p. 56; Gilbert Burnet, *The History of the Reformation of the Church of England*, edited by Nicholas Pocock (Oxford, 1865), III, 95.

3 *Ars poetica*, ll. 343-44, translated by the Earl of Roscommon, *Horace's Art of Poetry* (London, 1680), p. 24. For a recent competent and comprehensive survey of scholarly views of the problem which centers about the relations of religion to humanism and the Renaissance see Roger Aubenas and Robert Ricard, *L'église et la Renaissance (1449-1517)*, in Augustin Fliche and Victor Martin, editors, *Histoire de l'église* (Paris, 1934—), XV, 201-10.

4 "De Utopia," in *Utopia*, pp. 320-21; Victor Michels and Theobald Ziegler, editors, *Thomas Morus: Utopia* (Berlin, 1895), p. xxxv. See also Thomas Stapleton, *The Life and Illustrious Martyrdom of Sir Thomas More (Part III of "Tres Thomae," Printed at Douai, 1588)*, translated by P. E. Hallett (London, 1928), p. 34.

5 Facsimile of title page, *Utopia*, opposite p. lxxvi. For a detailed treatment of the following section see the present writer's "Interpretations of *Utopia*," *Catholic Historical Review*, XXXVIII (1952), 156-74.

6 Ronald Knox, "The Charge of Religious Intolerance," in *The Fame of Blessed Thomas More* (London, 1929), pp. 43-44; Christopher Hollis, *Thomas More* (Milwaukee, 1934), p. 92; William E. Campbell, *More's Utopia and His Social Teaching* (London, 1930), pp. 24, 116. For Jules Michelet's severe stricture on even the literary merits of *Utopia* see *Histoire de France* (Paris, 1852-1867), VIII, 414.

7 Karl Kautsky, *Thomas More and His Utopia*, translated by H. J. Stenning (London, 1927), pp. 249-50; Hermann Oncken, Introduction to Gerhard Ritter's translation of *Utopia*, Klassiker der Politik, Band I (Berlin, 1922), pp. 22*, 40*; John D. Mackie, *The Earlier Tudors: 1485-1558* (Oxford, 1952), p. 263; Russell Ames, *Citizen Thomas More and His Utopia* (Princeton, 1949), pp. 5-6. See also Arthur E. Morgan, *Nowhere Was Somewhere* (Chapel Hill, 1946), pp. 33-78; Thomas Maria Zigliara, *Summa philosophica*, sixteenth

315

edition (Paris, 1919), III, 179; Reinhold Baumstark, *Thomas Morus* (Freiburg im Breisgau, 1879), pp. 106-09. For an analysis and refutation of Oncken's influential views see Oswald Bendemann, *Studie zur Staats- und Sozialauffassung des Thomas Morus* (Charlottenburg, 1928), *passim*, and Henry W. Donner, *Introduction to Utopia* (London, 1945), pp. 55-57, 60-66, 98-106.

[8] *Utopia*, pp. 73-78; Philip Sidney, *The Defense of Poesy*, edited by Albert S. Cook (Boston, 1890), pp. 11, 17.

[9] *Utopia*, pp. xciii-xciv, 210-11; letter of Beatus Rhenanus to Willibald Pirckheimer, in More, *Omnia Latina opera* (Lovanii, 1565), fol. 19^v; Johann Valentin Andreae, *Christianopolis*, translated by Felix Emil Held (New York, 1916), *passim*; Francis Aidan Gasquet, *Cardinal Pole and His Early Friends* (London, 1927), p. 70.

[10] Franciscus Suárez, "De gratia," in *Opera omnia* (Parisiis, 1856-1878), VII, 207, 215, 357, 359, 364, 404, citing the following theologians who lived before or contemporaneously with Thomas More: Thomas Aquinas (d. 1274), Bonaventure (d. 1274), Albert the Great (d. 1280), Duns Scotus (d. 1308), Giles of Rome (d. 1316), Marsilius of Padua (d. 1328), Durandus of St. Porçain (d. 1334), Gabriel Biel (d. 1495), Cajetan (d. 1534), Conrad Koellin (d. 1536), and Soto (d. 1560). For Aquinas see *Summa theologica*, I-II, q. 109, aa. 1, 2, 6; II-II, q. 10, a. 4; *Contra gentiles*, III, 147. A very explicit statement of the goodness but nonsalutariness of acts of infidels appears in Silvester de Prierio, *Summa summaru que Siluestrina dicitur* (Bononie, 1514), fol. 340^r. Bishop John Fisher declares himself, not for the scholastics, but for the fathers of the Church, who require the special help of God for every morally good action (*Assertionis Lutheranae confutatio* [Coloniae, 1525], p. cccclxxxi).

[11] *Utopia*, p. 268; Joannes D. Mansi and others, *Sacrorum conciliorum nova et amplissima collectio*, second edition (Paris, 1899-1927), XXXII, 842; Charles-Joseph Hefele and others, *Histoire des conciles*, translated and edited by H. Leclercq (Paris, 1907-1952), VIII, 421. Merely as one representative of the common doctrine, see Aquinas, *Summa theologica*, I, q. 1, a. 1; II-II, q. 5, a. 3; *Contra gentiles*, I, 2, 5, 6, 9; *De veritate*, q. XIV, a. 10, ad 11; *In Boetium de Trinitate expositio*, q. II, a. 3. On revelation as an extrinsic norm for philosophy see Etienne Gilson, *Reason and Revelation in the Middle Ages* (New York, 1938), p. 83; Louis De Raeymaeker, *Introduction to Philosophy*, translated by Harry McNeill (New York, 1948), pp. 20-26; Iulius Dávila, *Introductio ad philosophiam, et logica* (Mexici, 1945), pp. 98-104.

[12] For further and important explanation and bibliography see the following articles: E. Magnin, "Religion," *Dictionnaire de théologie catholique* (henceforth cited as *DTC*), XIII, 2182-2306; N. Iung, "Révélation," *DTC*, XIII, 2580-2618; A. Michel, "Surnaturel," *DTC*, XIV, 2849-59; C. F. Aiken, "Religion," *The Catholic Encyclopedia* (henceforth cited as *CE*), XII, 738-48; G. H. Joyce, "Revelation," *CE*, XIII, 1-5; J. F. Sollier, "Supernatural Order," *CE*, XIV, 336-39.

[13] Aquinas, *Summa theologica*, I, q. 1, a. 1; II-II, q. 2, a. 4; *Contra gentiles*, I, 4; *De veritate*, q. XIV, a. 10. For a more detailed explanation see Henricus

Denzinger, *Enchiridion symbolorum*, twenty-third edition, edited by Clemens Bannwart and Ioannes Bapt. Umberg (Friburgi Brisgoviae, 1937), Nos. 1786, 1807-08; George Smith, editor, *The Teaching of the Catholic Church* (New York, 1949), I, 4-6; and especially Hermannus Dieckmann, *De revelatione Christiana* (Friburgi Brisgoviae, 1930), pp. 212-41.

14 Raymond W. Chambers, *Thomas More* (London, 1935), p. 127.

15 Desiderius Erasmus, *The Education of a Christian Prince*, translated by L. K. Born (New York, 1936), p. 152.

16 Budé to Lupset, *Utopia*, p. lxxxvii; Gilles to Busleyden, *Utopia*, p. xcvii; Robinson, "The Epistle of the Translatour," *Utopia*, p. 17; Busleyden to More, *Utopia*, pp. 316-17; Noviomagus, "De Utopia," *Utopia*, pp. 320-21; Grapheus, "Ad lectorem," *Utopia*, p. 322; Paludanus to Gilles, *Utopia* (Paris, 1517), sig. b. iii^v-iv^r; Erasmus to von Hutten, *Opus epistolarum Des. Erasmi* (henceforth cited as *Eras. Ep.*), edited by P. S. Allen and others (Oxford, 1906-1947), IV, 21; Nicholas Harpsfield, *The Life and Death of Sr Thomas Moore*, edited by E. V. Hitchcock (London, 1932), pp. 102-03; Lily, in Paulus Iovius, *Virorum aliquot in Britannia . . . elogia* (Venetiis, 1548), fol. 53^v, quoted and translated in Stapleton, *More*, p. 33.

17 *Utopia*, pp. 187-88; Erasmus, "The Epicurean," in *The Whole Familiar Colloquies of Erasmus*, translated by Nathan Bailey (London, 1877), p. 409; "De contemptu mundi," in *Opera omnia* (Lugduni Batavorum, 1703-1706), V, 1257.

18 *Utopia*, pp. 188-95, 202-11. For a more detailed discussion of Utopian Epicureanism see the present writer's articles, "The Defense of Pleasure in More's *Utopia*," *Studies in Philology*, XLVI (1949), 99-112, and "Epicurus in Utopia," *ELH, A Journal of English Literary History*, XVI (1949), 89-103.

19 More to Budé, in *The Correspondence of Sir Thomas More*, edited by Elizabeth Frances Rogers (Princeton, 1947), p. 246.

20 "Confutation of Tyndale," in *The Workes of Sir Thomas More* (London, 1557) (henceforth cited as *Works*), pp. 422-23; Prefatio Caroli Patini, "Moriae encomium," *Opera*, IV, 385-86.

21 More to Bugenhagen, in *Correspondence*, p. 351. On More's "inconsistency" see Chambers, *More*, pp. 351-77.

22 John Fisher, *Convvlsio calvmniarum Vlrichi Veleni Minhoniensis* (Parisiis, [1522?]), sig. Gi^r; Gerardus Geldenhauer Noviomagus, *Collectanea*, edited by Jacob Prinsen (Amsterdam, 1901), p. 72; Edward Lee, *Apologia . . . contra quorundam calumnias* (Parisiis, [1519-1520?]), sig. AAij^v; More, "Ad Edu. Leum epistola," in *Epistolae aliquot eruditorum uirorum* (Basileae, 1520), p. 59; Philip Hughes, *A History of the Church* (New York, 1934-1947), III, 466, following Pierre Mesnard, *L'essor de la philosophie politique au 16me siècle* (Paris, 1936), pp. 86-87; Gilmore, *World of Humanism*, p. 223. Catholic estimates of Erasmus have been swinging from the adverse and denunciatory attitude of Johann Janssen and Charles-Joseph Hefele (see the latter's *Conciles*, VIII, 586) to the cautious or favorable views of Francis Aidan Gasquet, *The Eve of the Reformation* (London, 1913), pp. 137-83; Hughes, *History of Church*, III, 466-73; and Aubenas and Ricard, *L'église et Renaissance*, pp. 240-46.

[23] "Confutation of Tyndale," in *Works*, pp. 421-22; *Eras. Ep.*, XI, 221; Emile Dermenghem, *Thomas Morus et les utopistes de la Renaissance* (Paris, 1927), p. 179; Stapleton, *More*, p. 39; Henry De Vocht, editor, *Acta Thomae Mori* (Louvain, 1947), p. 78.

[24] *Eras. Ep.*, III, 592; John Donne, "The Ecstasy," ll. 25-26. In *Erasme et l'Italie* (Genève, 1954), pp. 103, 126, Augustin Renaudet affirms the complete agreement of idea on the part of More and Erasmus in *The Praise of Folly* and *Utopia*.

[25] *Eras. Ep.*, II, 13; Renaudet, *Erasme*, pp. 179-81. In Rhenanus, *Veterum aliquot de arte rhetorica traditiones* (Basileae, 1521), pp. 210-12, there appears in Latin "The Praise of Wisdom" ("Sapientiae laudatio") by Aphthonius, a Greek rhetorician (fourth-fifth century A.D.), which begins: "The height of happiness is the attainment of wisdom. . . ."

Chapter II

[1] "Four Last Things," *Works*, p. 76; "Dialogue Concerning Heresies," *ibid.*, pp. 128, 156; "Confutation of Tyndale," *ibid.*, p. 585; Pecock, *The Reule of Crysten Religioun*, edited by W. C. Greet (London, 1927), pp. 23, 227, 229, 430; *The Donet*, edited by E. V. Hitchcock (London, 1921), pp. 14-15; *The Folewer to the Donet*, edited by E. V. Hitchcock (London, 1924), pp. 9-10. On Pecock's important case see Ronald Knox, *Enthusiasm* (New York, 1950), p. 115; James Gairdner, *Lollardy and the Reformation in England* (London, 1908), I, 202-38; and Aubenas and Ricard, *L'église et Renaissance*, pp. 247-48.

[2] Gilson, *Reason and Revelation*, pp. 85-87, and *La philosophie au moyen âge*, second edition (Paris, 1947), pp. 602-03. For distinctions to be made in Scotus' doctrines see Frederick Copleston, *A History of Philosophy* (London, 1946—), II, 527-29, and Parthenius Minges, *Ioannis Duns Scoti doctrina philosophica et theologica* (Ad Claras Aquas, 1930), II, 34-44. Consult also Minges, *Das Verhältnis zwischen Glauben und Wissen* (Paderborn, 1908), pp. 122-203. On Ockham see Copleston, *History of Philosophy*, III, 80-88, 96-101.

[3] *Utopia*, pp. 188-89, 266-67; More to Ruthall, *Correspondence*, p. 12; Copleston, *History of Philosophy*, III, 221.

[4] Antoninus, *Summa sacrae theologiae* (Venetiis, 1581-1582), III, 485ᵛ-486ʳ; Erasmus, *Adagiorum opus* (Lugduni, 1541), No. 69 *(Homo homini Deus)*, col. 63; Cuthbert Lattey, *The Psalter* (London, [1944]), pp. 185-86; *The Complete Bible: An American Translation* (Chicago, 1939), p. 552. See Pecock, *The Repressor of Over Much Blaming of the Clergy*, edited by C. Babington (London, 1860), I, 242-51, "for to know how idolatry came up" and how men gained their concepts of supreme beings. It might be well to mention as a curiosity that St. Augustine in a passage in his tractate on John's gospel, now used as a lesson for the Saturday during the fourth week of Lent, upbraids the foolish Manicheans for believing the visible sun to be the Lord Christ.

[5] Peter Martyr, *De orbe novo*, translated by F. A. MacNutt (New York, 1912), I, 167 (but "this supreme being was himself brought forth by a mother who

had five names" [I, 168]) ; Colet, *Super opera Dionysii: Two Treatises on the Hierarchies of Dionysius*, edited by J. H. Lupton (London, 1869). On the ineffability of the nature of God see Erasmus, "Ecclesiastes," *Opera*, V, 1088, and "Explanatio symboli," *ibid.*, V, 1143.

6 More, "Passion," translated by Bassett, *Works*, p. 1363; Colet, *Opuscula quaedam theologica*, edited by J. H. Lupton (London, 1876), pp. 54, 65-66; Erasmus, "Ecclesiastes," *Opera*, V, 1092; "The Religious Banquet," *Colloquies*, p. 83; Copleston, *History of Philosophy*, III, 248, 259-61.

7 Raphael Holinshed, *The Chronicles of England, Scotland, and Ireland* (London, 1587), I, 19-20. On what More's contemporaries considered to be the opinions of nations and philosophers on the gods, see Polydore Vergil, *De rerum inventoribus* (Argentorati, 1606), pp. 1-6.

8 *Utopia*, pp. 214, 267; Erasmus, "Explanatio symboli," *Opera*, V, 1143; *Adagia*, No. 626 *(Omnia octo)*, col. 304; No. 2215 *(Plures adorant solem orientem, quam occidentem)*, col. 878; No. 3755 *(Mithragyrtes, non daduchus)*, col. 1261; "In epistolam ad Laetam de institutione filiae scholia," *Hieronymi opera omnia* (Basileae, 1516), I, 24^r; Jerome, *Letters*, CVII, 2, translated by W. H. Fremantle in *A Select Library of the Nicene and Post-Nicene Fathers of the Christian Church*, Second Series (1890-1900), VI, 190; Strabo, *Geography*, translated by H. L. Jones (London, 1917-1932), VII, 175. See H. Leclercq, "Mithriacisme," *Dictionnaire d'archéologie chrétienne et de liturgie* (henceforth cited as *DACL*), XI, 1498-1554.

9 "Dialogue Concerning Heresies," *Works*, p. 128.

10 *Ibid.*, pp. 128-29.

11 Joseph Rickaby, *St. Augustine's City of God* (London, 1925), p. 2; Ambrose, *Letters*, XVII-XVIII, in *Nicene and Post-Nicene Fathers*, Second Series, X, 411-22 *(Patrologiae cursus completus: series Latina* [henceforth cited as *PL*], XVI, 961-82).

12 *Utopia*, pp. 268-69. See S. Harent's exhaustive article, "Foi," *DTC*, VI, 55-514.

13 More, "Dialogue Concerning Heresies," *Works*, p. 183; Vitoria, "De Indis," translated in James B. Scott, *The Spanish Origin of International Law: Francisco de Vitoria and His Law of Nations* (Oxford, 1934), pp. xxix-xxx. Vitoria relies on Aquinas, *Summa theologica*, II-II, q. 1, a. 4, ad 2, and a. 5, ad 1.

14 Valla, "Oratio . . . habita in principio sui studii," *Opuscula tria*, edited by Vahlen, pp. 97-98, quoted in Paul Mestwerdt, *Die Anfänge des Erasmus* (Leipzig, 1917), p. 39, n. 3; Erasmus, "Antibarbari," *Opera*, X, 1712-13; "Ecclesiastes," *ibid.*, V, 1093; Ficino, Prooemium, "In Plotinum," *Opera omnia* (Basileae, 1576), II, 1537. On the composition and publication of "Antibarbari" see *Eras. Ep.*, I, 121, n., 587-89; IV, 277-80.

15 Ficino, Prooemium, "Theologia Platonica," *Opera*, I, 78; Letter to Ioannes Nicolinus Archiepiscopus Amalphiensis, *ibid.*, I, 855. See Pico, "Apologia," *Opera omnia* (Basileae, [1601]), I, 82, and Erasmus, "Enchiridion," *Opera*, V, 7-8. See Augustine, *De civitate Dei*, Lib. VIII, Cap. i-xiii, *PL*, XLI, 223-38.

16 More, "Dialogue Concerning Heresies," *Works*, pp. 153-54; Erasmus, "Dialogus Ciceronianus," *Opera*, I, 1026; "Enchiridion," *ibid.*, V, 7-8, 15, 25; "Ratio verae theologiae," *ibid.*, V, 92; "Paraclesis," *ibid.*, VI,*4^r; "Hyperaspistes,"

ibid., X, 1294; "Antibarbari," *ibid.,* X, 1711-12; "Hiernonymi vita," *Opuscula,*
edited by W. K. Ferguson (The Hague, 1933), p. 151; "De libero arbitrio,"
edited by J. von Walter (Leipzig, 1910), p. 23, quoted in J.-B. Pineau,
Erasme: sa pensée religieuse (Paris, 1924), p. 55, n. 34.

[17] Johannes Dominici, *Lucula noctis,* edited by E. Hunt (Notre Dame, 1940),
passim; Salutati, *Epistolario* (Novati, 1896), III, 539 ff., quoted in Mestwerdt,
Anfänge, pp. 38-39, n. 2; Mansi, *Conciliorum collectio,* XXXII, 842-43;
Pico, "Heptaplus," *Opera,* I, 33.

[18] "Dialogue Concerning Heresies," *Works,* pp. 256-57; "Confutation of Tyndale,"
ibid., pp. 368, 408-09. On the dethronement of the speculative intellect in
converts to fanaticism, whether Catholic or Protestant, see Knox, *Enthusiasm,*
pp. 585-87.

[19] "Dialogue Concerning Heresies," *Works,* pp. 152-53. For Pecock's excessive stress
upon the role of reason see Pecock, *Crysten Religioun,* pp. 23, 229, 430;
Donet, pp. 14-15; *Folewer to Donet,* pp. 9-10.

[20] Colet, *Enarratio in epistolam S. Pauli ad Romanos,* edited by J. H. Lupton
(London, 1873), pp. 83-84; More, "Letter Impugning Frith," *Works,* pp. 837,
839, 841; "Answer to *Supper," ibid.,* pp. 1052, 1125-26; More to Frith,
Correspondence, p. 457; More to Bugenhagen, *ibid.,* p. 336. (Italics not
in original.)

[21] *Education of Christian Prince,* p. 150.

[22] Colet, "Exposition of Epistle to Romans," in *Opuscula quaedam theologica,*
pp. 51-52; Raymond of Sabunde, *Theologia naturalis* (Lugduni, 1541), p. 3^r;
Viola anime (Coloniae, 1501), sig. Giiij^{r-v}. *Viola anime* is a compendium of
Theologia naturalis in the form of a dialogue.

[23] *Utopia,* p. 269.

[24] *Utopia,* pp. 188-89; Scotus, *Opus Oxoniense,* I, d. 2, q. 3, n. 7 (*Opera omnia*
[Parisiis, 1891-1895], VIII, 499), quoted in Minges, *Scoti doctrina,* I, 523
(see *ibid.,* III, d. 37, q. un., n. 13 [*Opera,* XV, 851]); Aquinas, *Contra
gentiles,* I, 4 (see *Summa theologica,* I, q. 1, a. 1).

[25] *Utopia,* pp. 112, 268; "Supplication of Souls," *Works,* p. 315; Roger Bacon,
Opus tertium, c. xxiv (Brewer, p. 81), cited in Harris, *Duns Scotus* (Oxford,
1927), I, 125, n. 1.

[26] *Utopia,* pp. 188-89; Scotus, *Opus Oxoniense,* IV, d. 43, q. 2 (*Opera,* XX, 34-65).
See the fine discussion in Minges, *Scoti doctrina,* I, 121 ff.

[27] More, "Passion," *Works,* p. 1282; Erasmus, "De puritate tabernaculi," *Opera,*
V, 293; "Explanatio symboli," *ibid.,* V, 1133; Thomas Starkey, *A Dialogue
between Cardinal Pole and Thomas Lupset,* edited by J. M. Cowper (London,
1871), pp. 19-20. For a discussion of Erasmus' views on the salvation of noble
pagans see C. Thompson, editor, *Inquisitio de fide* (New Haven, 1950), pp.
101-21, and Hans Baron's review and additional note, "Der Humanismus und
die thomistische Lehre von den *gentiles salvati," Archiv für Reformationsgeschichte,* XLIII (1952), 254-63. For the whole background see Louis
Capéran, *Le problème du salut des infidèles* (Toulouse, 1934), and S. Harent,
"Salut des infidèles," *DTC,* VII, 1726-1930.

[28] Colet, *Enarratio in epistolam ad Romanos,* pp. 71-72; "Exposition of Epistle to
Romans," in *Opuscula quaedam theologica,* pp. 86-88; Erasmus, "Epistola ad

Romanos," *Opera*, VI, 573; Prefatory Letter to Lucian's "Toxaris," *ibid.*, I, 213-14. Budé asserts that "Christ left among His followers a Pythagorean communion and love" (*Utopia*, p. lxxxvi).

Chapter III

1 Arthur I. Taft, editor, *The Apologye of Syr Thomas More* (London, 1930), Introduction, pp. lxxvi-xxxvi; Chambers, *More*, pp. 129-31, 264-67, 274-82. For definitions, kinds, and degrees of tolerance see Vermeersch, *La tolérance* (Louvain, n. d.), pp. 1-9, 115-19.

2 All references to *Utopia* in this chapter on toleration and heresy are to pp. 270-76 unless otherwise noted.

3 Ficino, "De Christiana religione," *Opera omnia*, I, 4; Symmachus, "Memorial," in *Nicene and Post-Nicene Fathers*, Second Series, X, 415 (*PL*, XVI, 969); Ambrose's response in Letters XVII-XVIII, *ibid.*, 411-14, 417-22 (*PL*, XVI, 961-66, 971-82). In the light of *Utopia* it is interesting to examine the variety of reasons by which men have tried to base tolerance on absolute principles, either religious or philosophical, in Vermeersch, *Tolérance*, pp. 217-30.

4 Henricus Cornelius Agrippa, *De occulta philosophia* (Coloniae, 1533), p. ccxvi.

5 Erasmus, Latin translation of "Icaromenippus," *Opera*, I, 207; Ficino, *Opera*, I, 817-18, 853-54; Antoninus, *Summa*, I, 208ʳ. For Augustine's position see *De civitate Dei*, Lib. V, Cap. xi, *PL*, XLI, 153-54; for Aquinas see *Contra gentiles*, III, 75-76, and *Summa theologica*, I, q. 22.

6 *Utopia*, pp. 187-88; Plato, *Philebus*, translated by H. N. Fowler (London, 1925), pp. 261-63; *Republic*, translated by P. Shorey (London, 1930-1935), II, 39, 487; Lucretius, *De rerum natura*, translated by W. H. D. Rouse (London, 1931), pp. 130-31; Ficino, "De quatuor sectis philosophorum," *Supplementum Ficinianum*, edited by P. O. Kristeller (Florentiae, 1937), II, 9; Erasmus, *Adagia*, No. 3331 (Μονόγραμμοι), col. 1149; Latin translation of "Icaromenippus," *Opera*, I, 207, 213; "Explanatio symboli," *ibid.*, V, 1148.

7 Erasmus, *Adagia*, No. 762 (*In diem vivere*), cols. 359-60.

8 "Dialogue Concerning Heresies," *Works*, pp. 129-30. See Arthur O. Lovejoy, *The Great Chain of Being* (Cambridge, 1936), pp. 73-79, and especially the criticism by Anton Pegis, *St. Thomas and the Greeks* (Milwaukee, 1939), pp. 34-35, 44-56, 80-82.

9 "Supplication of Souls," *Works*, p. 315; Lupset, "A Treatise of Dieying Well," in John A. Gee, *The Life and Works of Thomas Lupset* (New Haven, 1928), p. 275; Erasmus, "In Ps. IV," *Opera*, V, 253; *Republic*, Introduction, II, lxiv-xv, and the places cited there; A. C. Pearson, "Ethics and Morality," *Encyclopedia of Religion and Ethics*, V, 495.

10 *Utopia*, p. 188; Erasmus, *Adagia*, No. 3001 (*Dulce bellum inexpertis*), cols. 1078-79. On Pomponazzi see Charles Sturge, *Cuthbert Tunstal* (London, 1938), pp. 9-10; Copleston, *History of Philosophy*, III, 222-26; Aubenas and Ricard, *L'église et Renaissance*, pp. 213-14; F. Bonnard, "Pomponazzi," *DTC*, XII, 2545-46. On Scotus see Pecock, *Crysten Religioun*, pp. 26-27; Gilson, *Philosophie au moyen âge*, p. 603; Minges, *Scoti doctrina*, I, 121-29. On Cajetan see Gilson, *Reason and Revelation*, pp. 84-85.

[11] "Dialogue Concerning Heresies," *Works*, pp. 251, 256, 261; "Supplication of Souls," *Works*, p. 315; *Utopia and A Dialogue of Comfort*, revised edition (London, 1951) (henceforth cited as *Dialogue of Comfort*), pp. 149-50; Ep. 999, *Eras. Ep.*, IV, 21; *Republic*, II, 491; Epistle VII, *Timaeus, etc.*, translated by R. G. Bury (London, 1929), p. 511; Constitutio "Apostolici regiminis," Mansi, *Conciliorum collectio*, XXXII, 842. For a brief, accurate account of the proceedings of the council see Hefele, *Conciles*, VIII, 419-21.

[12] *Laws*, translated by R. G. Bury (London, 1926), II, 299, 379-83.

[13] More, "Passion," *Works*, p. 1285; Scotus, *Opus Oxoniense*, IV, d. 43, q. 2, n. 3 (*Opera*, XX, 35), cited in Minges, *Scoti doctrina*, II, 729-30; Pecock, *Crysten Religioun*, pp. 122-27; Fisher, "Month's Mind Sermon of Princess Margaret," *The English Works of John Fisher*, edited by J. E. B. Mayor (London, 1876), I, 303.

[14] *Utopia*, p. 267; Aeneas Silvius, Epistle to the Sultan Mohammed, *Opera* (Basileae, 1551), pp. 879-80, quoted in Mestwerdt, *Anfänge*, p. 40, n. 1.

[15] More, "Passion," *Works*, pp. 1282, 1288; "Confutation of Tyndale," *ibid.*, p. 449; Stapleton, *More*, p. 97; Suárez, "De fide," *Opera*, XII, 344-60; Aquinas, *Summa theologica*, II-II, q. 2, a. 7, ad 3; Starkey, *Dialogue*, pp. 19-20. The future Hadrian VI (Hadrianus Florentinus de Traiecto) in *Questiones quotlibetice* (Lovanii, 1515) holds that everyone is obliged to believe *explicitly* all articles contained in the creed and the truths preceding them, for example, the existence of God and His just and loving government of the world (fol. xxv^r).

[16] *Laws*, I, 35, 37; II, 299, 379-81.

[17] "In librum secundum adversus Iovinianum scholia," *Hieronymi opera*, III, 44^v.

[18] *Utopia*, p. 68; Robert P. Adams, "Philosophic Unity of More's *Utopia*," *Studies in Philology*, XXXVIII (1941), 46-47.

[19] Soto, *In quartum sententiarum commentarii* (Venetiis, 1569), I, 301-02; Suárez, "De fide," *Opera*, XII, 444-48; Ficino, "De Christiana religione," *Opera*, I, 11. Antoninus of Florence declares that Christians are not obliged to admit Mohammedan preachers because the cases are different: "Mohammedans are wandering in the path of error, but Christians are on the right road of truth" (*Summa*, III, 54^{r-v}).

[20] "Ratio verae theologiae," *Opera*, V, 99; "Novum testamentum," Notes, *ibid.*, VI, 501, 896; Ruskin, "Fors Clavigera," *Works*, XXVII, 480, cited in Chambers, *More*, p. 396.

[21] Hollis, *More*, p. 68. Hollis compares the fault of the conservatives to that of the "ill-mannered Christian" in *Utopia* (p. 270) on this point.

[22] Erasmus, *Adagia*, Introduction, cols. 12-13; No. 1317 (*Tempus omnia revelat*), col. 588; Fisher, *Confutatio secundae disceptationis* (Parisiis, 1519), fol. iii^r; Paul O. Kristeller, *The Philosophy of Marsilio Ficino*, translated by Virginia Conant (New York, 1943), p. 319; Reginald Pecock, *Book of Faith*, edited by J. L. Morison (Glasgow, 1909), pp. 130-31.

[23] More to Ruthall, *Correspondence*, p. 13; "Dialogue Concerning Heresies," *Works*, pp. 275-76. For Pecock's use of the same approach against the Lollards see *Repressor*, I, 99-100.

[24] "Dialogue Concerning Heresies," *Works*, p. 276.

25 Angelus Carletus de Clavasio, *Summa angelica de casibus conscientiae* (Lugduni, 1512), fol. cccxlvi^v.

26 *Utopia*, pp. 297-98; "Dialogue Concerning Heresies," *Works*, p. 247.

27 Silvester, *Summa*, fol. 340^r.

28 *Codex iuris canonici*, can. 1325, par. 2; A. Michel, "Hérésie-Hérétique," *DTC*, VI, 2208-57; Vermeersch, *Tolérance*, pp. 43-44, n. 1; Erasmus, "Ecclesiastes," *Opera*, V, 1081; Pico, "900 Conclusiones," *Opera*, I, 56; "Apologia," *ibid.*, I, 140-41; Silvester, *Summa*, fol. 296^v.

29 Pico, *Opera*, I, a2^{r-v}, 63, 148-53, 158; Henri Bremond, *Sir Thomas More*, translated by H. Child (London, 1904), p. 18. See the condemnation in *Bullarum . . . collectio* (Romae, 1733-1762) (henceforth cited as *Bullarium Romanum*), III, Pars III, 210-11.

30 More, "Passion," *Works*, p. 1288; Aquinas, *Summa theologica*, II-II, q. 1, a. 4, ad 2; Smith, *Teaching of Church*, I, 19.

31 "Dialogue Concerning Heresies," *Works*, p. 205.

32 "Confutation of Tyndale," *Works*, p. 601; "Answer to *Supper*," *ibid.*, p. 1048. See Campbell, *More's Utopia and His Social Teaching*, p. 138.

33 *Apologye*, Introduction, p. lxxxiv, n. 5; "Causae iudiciales et sententiae capitales nunc primum ex originalibus asservatis in tabulario nationali Angliae (Baga de secretis, Pouch VII, Bundles 2 et 3) editae," *Canonizationis beatorum martyrum Iohannis Card. Fisher . . . et Thomae Mori . . . informatio* (Typis Vaticanis, 1944), p. 30.

34 "Dialogue Concerning Heresies," *Works*, p. 279; Harpsfield, *More*, pp. 84-88.

35 John Fisher, *Defensio regie assertionis contra Babylonicam captiuitatem* (Coloniae, 1525), foll. 108^v-15^r, and *De ueritate corporis et sanguinis Christi in eucharistia* ([Coloniae], 1527), fol. 1^v.

36 Letter of Grynaeus to John More, *Correspondence*, pp. 478-79; Stapleton, *More*, pp. 62-64; Erasmus to Viglius Zuichemus, Ep. 2878, *Eras. Ep.*, X, 316-17. For Grynaeus' life see *Eras. Ep.*, VI, 244-45.

37 Hollis, *More*, p. 141. Hollis concludes: "In a sixteenth-century European society there was room for only one religious faith" *(ibid.)*.

38 "Dialogue Concerning Heresies," *Works*, pp. 275-76; "Confutation of Tyndale," *ibid.*, p. 794; Fisher, *Assertionis Lutheranae confutatio*, pp. ccccxxiii-vi, ccccxxxii-iii; on the history of the coercive power of the Church, especially of the right of the sword (capital punishment), see Vermeersch, *Tolérance*, pp. 47-50, 65-113 (especially pp. 82-85, 313, on St. Augustine). For a contemporary history of the punishment of heretics from St. Paul to More's own day see Polydore Vergil, *De inventoribus*, pp. 471-73.

39 "Novum testamentum," Note to Acts 19:9, *Opera*, VI, 507; "Apologiae in Beddam," *ibid.*, IX, 580-83; "Ep. in pseudevangelicos," *ibid.*, X, 1586. On the last-mentioned work see *Eras. Ep.*, VIII, 283, 303-04, and Preserved Smith, *Erasmus* (New York, 1923), pp. 393-94. See also Thompson's introduction to Erasmus' *Inquisitio de fide*, especially pp. 41-48. In 1511, when Ammonius reported no wonder at the rise in the price of wood because many heretics were being burned and even more were springing up, Erasmus facetiously replied that he was hostile to heretics also on the score that they had raised the price of wood at the approach of winter (*Eras. Ep.*, I, 481, 483).

[40] "Dialogue Concerning Heresies," *Works*, pp. 257-58, 275-76, 284; "Confutation of Tyndale," *ibid.*, p. 352; More to Bugenhagen, *Correspondence*, p. 328; Fisher, quoted in G. Constant, *The Reformation in England*, translated by R. E. Scantlebury (New York, 1934), I, 22. On Marsilius of Padua see Paul Janet, *Histoire de la science politique dans ses rapports avec la morale*, fourth edition (Paris, 1913), I, 461; Copleston, *History of Philosophy*, III, 168-80; and Gasquet, *Reformation*, pp. 91-92, which mentions William Marshall's English translation of *The Defence of Peace* published in 1535 but with a preface dated 1522. For a history of civil tolerance down to the sixteenth century see Vermeersch, *Tolérance*, pp. 122-200.

[41] "Dialogue Concerning Heresies," *Works*, pp. 214, 276-77, 279; "Supplication of Souls," *ibid.*, p. 290; "Debellacion of Salem and Bizance," *ibid.*, p. 938. For Fisher's description of the Church's different attitude toward simple and lapsed heretics see *Assertionis Lutheranae confutatio*, p. ccccxxxv. For formulas used in delivering the heretic to the civil power see Vermeersch, *Tolérance*, p. 146.

[42] Silvester, *Summa*, foll. 298ʳ-99ʳ; Fisher, *Assertionis Lutheranae confutatio*, p. ccccxxix.

[43] *Utopia*, p. 284. "For unless they by quick repentance approve the amendment of their lives to the priests, they be taken and punished of the council as wicked and irreligious" *(ibid.)*.

[44] Taft, *Apologye*, pp. 131-32, 313-15; "Dialogue Concerning Heresies," *Works*, p. 275; Aquinas, *Summa theologica*, II-II, q. 10, a. 3; Silvester, *Summa*, fol. 340ʳ. For a clear statement of the heinousness of the sin of heresy, without reference to ecclesiastical or civil punishment, see Alexander Anglus, *Summa que destructorium viciorum appellatur* (Nuremberge, 1496), Pars VI, Cap. xxxix (no pagination given).

[45] "Dialogue Concerning Heresies," *Works*, p. 275; Vermeersch, *Tolérance*, pp. 182-200, 300, 307, 371-72.

[46] Taft, *Apologye*, pp. 179-83; Fisher, *Defensio regie assertionis*, fol. 2ᵛ.

[47] Mansi, *Conciliorum collectio*, XXXII, 912-13; *Bullarium Romanum*, III, Pars III, 409-10; Hefele, *Conciles*, VIII, 472-73; Aubenas and Ricard, *L'église et Renaissance*, pp. 357-65; Vermeersch, *Tolérance*, pp. 177-78. On the great freedom and influence enjoyed by mystics in the Middle Ages, almost unbelievable since the Protestant Revolt, see Pierre Pourrat, *Christian Spirituality in the Middle Ages*, translated by S. P. Jacques (London, 1924), pp. 334-36.

[48] Roper, *Lyfe of Sir Thomas Moore*, edited by E. V. Hitchcock (London, 1935), p. 35. For Catholic theory see A. Michel, "Tolérance," *DTC*, XV, 1208-23.

[49] *Utopia*, p. 276; "Dialogue Concerning Heresies," *Works*, p. 155. For evidence by "doom of reason" for the mortality of a beast's soul and the immortality of man's soul see Pecock, *Folewer to Donet*, pp. 16-19. On Rorario see Vincentius Remer, *Summa philosophiae scholasticae*, fifth edition (Romae, 1925), II, Pars V *(Psychologia)*, p. 127, and *Enciclopedia Universal Ilustrada*, LII, 307-08. On Greek philosophers see Plutarch, "De placitis philosophorum," Lib. V, Cap. xx, *Opera omnia*, edited by Gulielmus Xylander (Frankfurt-am-Main, 1599), II, 908-09, and, for an account contemporary with More, see Gregorius Reisch, *Margarita philosophica* (Argentorati, 1504), Lib. XI, Cap. xxv, sig. lliiʳ.

Chapter IV

1 *Utopia*, pp. 276-77.

2 More, "Four Last Things," *Works*, pp. 78-79; *Dialogue of Comfort*, pp. 391-92; "Quod pro fide mors fugienda non est," *Omnia Latina opera*, fol. 132ʳ; "A Treatise of Dieying Well," in Gee, *Lupset*, pp. 272, 277; Ficino, "Theologia Platonica," *Opera*, I, 385; see Plato, *Republic*, I, 17.

3 More, "Passion," translated by Bassett, *Works*, p. 1355; Fisher, "Funeral Sermon of Henry VII," *English Works*, I, 276-77; Erasmus, "De praeparatione ad mortem," *Opera*, V, 1310; Antoninus, *Summa*, IV, 256; Silvester, *Summa*, fol. 474ʳ; Johannes Geiler, *Nauicula penitentie* (Argentorati, 1512), sig. Aavᵛ. On the Christian conception of death see A. Michel, "Mort," *DTC*, X, 2489-99.

4 *Utopia*, p. 277; Baptista Mantuanus, *De patientia libri tres, de vita beata dialogus, etc.* (Argentorati, 1510), fol. cxvʳ⁻ᵛ; Erasmus, "Declamatio de morte," *Opera*, IV, 618; "In Ps. XXXVIII," *ibid.*, V, 466; "The Religious Banquet," *Colloquies*, pp. 97-98; *Eras. Ep.*, IV, 510-11, translated by J. H. Lupton, *The Lives of Jehan Vitrier . . . and John Colet*, Written in Latin by Erasmus in a Letter to Justus Jonas (London, 1883), p. 9; *Adagia*, No. 1249 *(Optimum non nasci)*, col. 560, citing Quintilian, Pliny, Valerius Maximus, and Herodotus. See also Erasmus, "Similia (ex Seneca)," *Opera*, I, 591-92; *Adagia*, No. 1816 *(Senex bos non lugetur)*, col. 747; Fisher, "A Spirituall Consolation," *English Works*, I, 353.

5 "Four Last Things," *Works*, p. 77; Letter of Margaret Roper to More, *ibid.*, p. 1432; "Treatise on the Passion," *ibid.*, p. 1299; "Life of John Picus," *ibid.*, pp. 8-9; "Interpretation of Psalm XV," *ibid.*, pp. 18-19; "Mortem non esse metuendam cum sit finis malorum," *Omnia Latina opera*, fol. 23ʳ; *The Latin Epigrams of Thomas More*, edited by L. Bradner and C. A. Lynch (Chicago, 1953), p. 159; More to Roper, *Correspondence*, pp. 542-43; More to Bonvisi, *ibid.*, p. 563; Plato, *Euthyphro, Apology, Crito, Phaedo, Phaedrus*, translated by H. N. Fowler (London, 1926), pp. 280-82; Erasmus, *The Praise of Folly*, translated by H. H. Hudson (Princeton, 1941), p. 119. See also Antoninus, *Summa*, I, 122ᵛ; Ficino, "Theologia Platonica," *Opera*, I, 385; Plato, *Republic*, II, 9-11; Lupset, "A Treatise of Dieying Well," in Gee, *Lupset*, p. 271; Ellis Heywood, *Il Moro* (Fiorenza, 1556), pp. 179-80. On philosophy as "the meditation of death" see also Mantuanus, *De patientia*, fol. lxxxviiiʳ, and Erasmus, "In epitaphium Nepotiani scholia," *Hieronymi opera*, I, 14ᵛ, and "Ad Principiam Marcellae epitaphium scholia," *ibid.*, I, 53ʳ.

6 *Utopia*, pp. 277-78. "Mores actaque eius recensent, nec ulla uitae pars aut saepius aut libentius quam laetus tractatur interitus" *(ibid.)*.

7 Colet, *Super opera Dionysii*, pp. 137-38, 143; Vergil, *De inventoribus* (1644), p. 488, quoted *ibid.*, p. 138, n. 1. On early Christian burial see H. Leclercq, "Funérailles," *DACL*, V, 2705-15.

8 Erasmus, "The Funeral," *Colloquies*, pp. 296-97; More, "Four Last Things," *Works*, p. 79.

9 *Utopia*, p. 214; Vergil, *De inventoribus*, p. 180; Erasmus, translation of Lucian's "De luctu," *Opera*, I, 196; E. Valton, "Crémation," *DTC*, III, 2314. On Greek and Roman disposal of the dead see Mau, "Bestattung," *Pauly's Real-*

Encyclopädie der classischen Altertumswissenschaft (henceforth cited as *RE*), III, 331-59.

10 *Utopia*, pp. 278-79. In his scholia to "Epitaphium Nepotiani," *Hieronymi opera*, I, 11ᵛ, Erasmus observes that praise of the dead contributes to the consolation of the living.

11 Plato, *Republic*, I, 491; *Laws*, II, 435 (see II, 241); Antoninus, *Summa*, I, 144ʳ; Aquinas, *Summa theologica*, III, q. 10, a. 2; Joseph Hontheim, "Heaven," *CE*, VII, 173; J. M. Hervé, *Manuale theologiae dogmaticae*, eighteenth edition (Parisiis, 1939), IV, 678; Suárez, "De divina substantia," *Opera*, I, 170-74; "De angelis," *ibid.*, II, 649-55.

12 Erasmus, "Declamatio de morte," *Opera*, IV, 622; More, "Dialogue Concerning Heresies," *Works*, pp. 187-89.

13 *Utopia*, pp. 223-24; Erasmus, *Adagia*, No. 3464 *(Bibere mandragoram)*, col. 1189; Plutarch, "Lycurgus," *Lives*, translated by B. Perrin (London, 1914-1926), I, 295; Plato, *Laws*, II, 265-67. Plato orders the bodies of impious men to "be cast outside the borders without burial" *(Laws*, II, 383).

14 *Laws*, II, 265-67; *Republic*, I, 131; Diogenes Laertius, *Lives of Eminent Philosophers*, translated by R. D. Hicks (London, 1925), II, 235, 645; Seneca, Ep. LVIII, "On Being," *Ad Lucilium epistulae morales*, translated by R. M. Gummere (London, 1917-1920), I, 409 (see also Ep. LXX, "On the Proper Time to Slip the Cable," *ibid.*, II, 56-73).

15 See Thalheim, "Selbstmord," *RE*, IIA, 1134-35.

16 More, *Dialogue of Comfort*, pp. 252-88; Erasmus, "The Religious Banquet," *Colloquies*, p. 98; "The Lying-In Woman," *ibid.*, pp. 232-33. See Augustine, *De civitate Dei*, Lib. I, Cap. xx, *PL*, XLI, 34-35, and Aquinas, *Summa theologica*, II-II, q. 64, a. 5.

17 *Dialogue of Comfort*, pp. 259, 262, 264, 267-68, 273-74, 278, 286. See A. Michel, "Suicide," *DTC*, XIV, 2739-49.

Chapter V

1 *Utopia*, pp. 186, 279. On divination and vain observance see Thomas Slater, *A Manual of Moral Theology*, sixth edition (London, 1928), I, 141-45; H. Noldin and A. Schmitt, *Summa theologiae moralis*, twenty-seventh edition (Oeniponte, 1940), II, 151-65; and T. Ortolan, "Divination," *DTC*, IV, 1441-55. On astrology in particular see Edwin F. Healy, *Moral Guidance* (Chicago, 1942), pp. 79-82, and Max Jacobi, "Astrology," *CE*, II, 18-25. On the general problem of superstitious practices at this time see Aubenas and Ricard, *L'église et Renaissance*, pp. 380-82.

2 Augustine, *De civitate Dei*, Lib. VIII, Cap. xix, *PL*, XLI, 243-44; Pico, "Disputationum in astrologiam libri XII," *Opera*, I, 278-494; Erasmus, *Adagia*, No. 1278 *(Qui bene conjiciet hunc vatem)*, col. 573; No. 1620 *(Meliores nancisci aves)*, col. 691; "Antibarbari," *Opera*, X, 1731; Barclay, *The Ship of Fools*, edited by T. H. Jamieson (Edinburgh, 1874), II, 20; Sebastian Brant, *Stultifera nauis*, Latin translation by Jacobus Locher (Basileae, 1497), fol. lxxxvʳ⁻ᵛ; Kristeller, *Ficino*, p. 310; Lynn Thorndike, *A History of Magic and Experimental Science* (New York, 1923-1941), V, 279; Max Jacobi, "Astrology," *CE*, II, 18-25.

³ More, "Epigrammata," *Omnia Latina opera*, foll. 22ᵛ-23ʳ, 24ʳ⁻ᵛ, 27ᵛ; *Works*, Ciiiiᵛ, pp. 120-21; John Marsden, *Philomorus*, second edition (London, 1878), pp. 233-35. For More's epigrams on astrology see *Latin Epigrams*, pp. 156-59, 169, 174, 192, 197.

⁴ *Utopia*, p. 279; *Dialogue of Comfort*, p. 264; "Dialogue Concerning Heresies," *Works*, pp. 129, 131; Suárez, "De fide," *Opera*, XII, 123; Erasmus, "Ratio verae theologiae," *Opera*, V, 115.

⁵ *Utopia*, p. 279; Suárez, "De fide," *Opera*, XII, 221.

⁶ "Dialogue Concerning Heresies," *Works*, p. 201; "Confutation of Tyndale," *ibid.*, pp. 455, 458-59; see letter to Bugenhagen, *Correspondence*, p. 334. See the article by A. Michel, "Miracle," *DTC*, X, 1798-1859.

⁷ *Utopia*, p. 274; Smith, *Teaching of Church*, I, 13; Knox, *Miracles* (London, 1950), p. 9.

⁸ Aquinas, *De potentia*, q. 6, a. 5, ad 5 (see *Summa theologica*, II-II, q. 178, a. 2, ad 3) ; Sebastianus Tromp, *De revelatione Christiana*, fourth edition (Romae, 1937), pp. 121-22; Guilelmus Wilmers, *De religione revelata* (Ratisbonae, 1897), pp. 157-58. For an objective discussion of miracles among Jansenists see Knox, *Enthusiasm*, pp. 227-28, 372-88. See Mantuanus, *De patientia*, foll. lxxviʳ-lxxviiʳ, for the view that miracles, since capable of performance by angels and nature as well as by God, are not an infallible sign of revelation and therefore miracles come from faith rather than the reverse.

⁹ *Utopia*, pp. 279-80; Pico, "De dignitate hominis," *Opera*, I, 217; Ficino, Letter to Anthonius Ziliolus Sophronius Venetus, *Opera*, I, 853-54; Erasmus, *Colloquies*, p. 408; *Adagia*, Introduction, col. 10. See also Erasmus, "The Religious Feast," *Colloquies*, p. 83; *De conscribendis epistolis* (Amstelodami, 1670), p. 48; "De misericordia Domini," *Opera*, V, 561; "Concio de puero Iesu," *ibid.*, V, 602.

Chapter VI

¹ *Utopia*, pp. 143, 280-81. "Hii quo magis sese seruos exhibent, eo maiore apud omnes in honore sunt" (*ibid.*, p. 281).

² More to a Monk, *Correspondence*, p. 190; Telle, *Erasme de Rotterdam et le septième sacrement* (Genève, 1954), pp. 2, 5-6, 47-48. See the articles by E. Dublanchy, "Ascétisme," *DTC*, I, 2055-78, and H. Leclercq, "Cénobitisme," *DACL*, II, 3047-3248.

³ J. S. Brewer, *The Reign of Henry VIII* (London, 1884), I, 51; Stapleton, *More*, p. 10; *Eras. Ep.*, IV, 521, translated by Lupton, *Vitrier and Colet*, p. 34; Barclay, *Ship of Fools*, II, 322-28. For a general view of the state of the regular clergy see Aubenas and Ricard, *L'église et Renaissance*, pp. 275-80.

⁴ David Wilkins, editor, *Concilia Magnae Britanniae et Hiberniae* (London, 1737), III, 630-32; British Museum, Arundel MS. 68, fol. 69ʳ⁻ᵛ.

⁵ *Utopia*, pp. 74-75; Jerome, "Regula monachorum," *Opera*, II, 175ᵛ; Geiler, *Nauicula penitentie*, sig. Liiᵛ; Erasmus, *Adagia*, No. 633 *(Artem quaevis alit terra)*, col. 307; *Eras. Ep.*, IV, 103; Note to Luke 2:12, "Novum testamentum," *Opera*, VI, 231; "De pronunciatione," *ibid.*, I, 922; "Apologiae in Beddam," *ibid.*, IX, 647; G. Roger Huddleston, "Monasticism," *CE*, X, 462.

[6] *Utopia*, p. 145; "Answer to *Supper*," *Works*, p. 1048; *Constitutiones*, Ex., c. 4, n. 28; P. III, c. 1, n. 6; English translation, Rules 13, 44, *Summary of the Constitutions*, etc. (Roehampton, 1926), pp. 7, 21; Hefele, *Conciles*, VIII, 460.

[7] *Utopia*, pp. 279-80; Colet, "A Ryght Fruitfull Monicion Concernynge the Order of a Good Cristen Mannes Lyfe," quoted in Joseph H. Lupton, *A Life of John Colet* (London, 1887), p. 307. See A. Poulain, "Contemplation," and E. Gurdon, "Contemplative Life," *CE*, III, 324-30. For the difference and relationship between the active and the contemplative life as expressed by the fourteenth-century Walter Hilton, whom More recommends ("Confutation of Tyndale," *Works*, p. 356), see *The Scale of Perfection*, new edition, edited by John B. Dalgairns (London, 1901), pp. 315-37, and *Minor Works*, edited by Dorothy Jones (New York, 1929), pp. 3 ff. Consult also the anonymous *Cloud of Unknowing*, edited by P. Hodgson (London, 1944), pp. 31 ff., 57 ff.

[8] Erasmus, "Apologiae in Beddam," *Opera*, IX, 647; "Hieronymi vita," *Opuscula*, p. 145; *Of the Imitation of Christ*, I, 17, III, 12, revised translation (London, 1926), pp. 28, 122.

[9] "Consuetudines domus nostrae," *Jacobus Trajecti: Narratio de inchoatione domus clericorum in Zwollis*, edited by M. Schoengen (Amsterdam, 1908), pp. 244-45. For "The Original Constitution of the Brethren of the Common Life at Deventer" see Albert Hyma, *The Christian Renaissance* (New York, 1925), Appendix C, pp. 440-76. This book of Hyma's is a history of the *Devotio moderna*. Hughes, *History of Church*, III, 215-25, claims that the divorce of the *Devotio moderna* from theological learning was its great weakness and that "Erasmus is the greatest witness to what the *Devotio Moderna* lacked." In his *Geschichte des Konzils von Trient*, second edition (Freiburg, 1951—), I, 116, Hubert Jedin sees the new element in the *Devotio moderna* as being the earnest concentration on the old goal: the following of Christ; but he warns not to see a sign of exhaustion in its secluded piety nor to interpret its renunciation of scientific theology as undogmatic Christianity. See also Pourrat, *Christian Spirituality*, pp. 252-64, 291-308. For the history of the Brethren of the Common Life between 1380 and 1520 see Albert Hyma, *The Brethren of the Common Life* (Grand Rapids, 1950). This book contains a chapter entitled "The Original Version of the *Imitation of Christ*" (pp. 145-94), which credits the classic to Gerard Zerbolt.

[10] *Eras. Ep.*, IV, 521, translated by Lupton, *Vitrier and Colet*, p. 34; E. Gilliat-Smith, "Brethren of the Common Schools," *CE*, IV, 166-67. For the Congregation of Windesheim see R. Webster, "Windesheim," *CE*, XV, 651-52; Hyma, *Renaissance*, pp. 46-49, 82-89, 136-57; and Hyma, *Brethren of Common Life*, pp. 127-44. On the Congregation of Bursfeld see Aubenas and Ricard, *L'église et Renaissance*, pp. 280-81, and M. Ott, "Bursfeld," *CE*, III, 84-85. See especially the report based on contemporary accounts of monasteries and monastic reform by P. S. Allen, "Monasticism," *Age of Erasmus* (Oxford, 1914), pp. 66-101. On Erasmus' attitude toward the Brethren of the Common Life see Mestwerdt, *Anfänge*, pp. 182-95.

[11] Erasmus, "Moriae encomium," *Opera*, IV, 485-86, translated by Hudson, *Praise of Folly*, p. 102 (on the authorship of the scholia to the 1515 Froben edition

see *Eras. Ep.*, II, 407, Introduction) ; "The Soldier and the Carthusian," *Colloquies*, pp. 138-39; Pourrat, *Christian Spirituality*, pp. 309-18.

¹² *Utopia*, p. 269; *Latin Epigrams*, p. 242; More to Dorp, *Correspondence*, pp. 67-68; More to a Monk, *ibid.*, pp. 194-96, 204; More to Bugenhagen, *ibid.*, p. 343. Geldenhauer's *Satyrae octo ad verae religionis cultores* (Lovanii, 1515), is reprinted in his *Collectanea*, pp. 144-76. For his later vulgar satire against monks (1522) see "De origine monachorum" and "De origine Antichristi," *ibid.*, pp. 50-51. The narrowness of the rules of Dominic, Augustine, and Francis, designed for a few, is contrasted with the holy and "heavenly philosophy" of Christ, intended for all, in *Duae epistole Hērici Stromeri Auerbachij et Gregorij Coppi Calui* (Lipsiae, 1520), sigg. Aiv^v-Bi^r.

¹³ More, "Dialogue Concerning Heresies," *Works*, p. 121; "Confutation of Tyndale," *ibid.*, pp. 397, 430; [Cyprien Marie Boutrais], *History of the Great Chartreuse*, translated by E. Hassid (London, 1933), pp. 190, 207-08.

¹⁴ "Interpretation of Psalm XV," *Works*, p. 19; More to Bugenhagen (*c.* 1526), *Correspondence*, p. 343.

¹⁵ *Utopia*, pp. 193-94, 280-81; Erasmus, *Adagia*, No. 3001 *(Dulce bellum inexpertis)*, col. 1062; No. 69 *(Homo homini deus)*, No. 2001 *(Herculei labores)*, *Adagia*, 1526 edition, pp. 46-48, 583-91, cited in Theodore C. Appelt, *Studies in the Contents and Sources of Erasmus' "Adagia"* (Chicago, 1942), pp. 63, 65.

¹⁶ *Imitation of Christ*, II, 6, III, 47, revised translation, pp. 71, 190-92.

¹⁷ Dudley, *The Tree of Commonwealth*, edited by D. M. Brodie (Cambridge, 1948), pp. 71-77; Fisher, *Assertionis Lutheranae confutatio*, p. ccccli.

¹⁸ "Confutation of Tyndale," Preface, *Works*, p. 340; Stapleton, *More*, p. 133, quoting the letter to Bugenhagen (*Correspondence*, p. 353) ; Suárez, "De spe," *Opera*, XII, 616-18; E. Towers, "Sanctifying Grace," in Smith, *Teaching of Church*, I, 576-80.

¹⁹ More, "Confutation of Tyndale," *Works*, pp. 363-64, 529-31; Letter to Bugenhagen, *Correspondence*, pp. 342-44, 348, 352 (read the whole section, pp. 340-60) ; Erasmus, "De amabili ecclesiae concordia," *Opera*, V, 485; "Ecclesiastes," *ibid.*, V, 1080.

²⁰ *Dialogue of Comfort*, pp. 172-77. Early in the sixteenth century John Major was teaching at Paris that, although God does not do so by His ordinary power, nevertheless He could accept by His absolute power the natural acts of a rational creature, if He wished, as rewardable (III *Sent.*, dist. 18, q. 1, fol. 40^v, quoted in Ricardo Villoslada, *La Universidad de Paris durante los estudios de Francisco de Vitoria, O.P.: 1507-1522* [Roma, 1938], p. 154). Earlier, Ockham had held that man's naturally good acts acquire supernatural value and merit simply by God's acceptance (*ibid.*, p. 85).

²¹ *Utopia*, pp. 194, 274, 280.

²² *Utopia*, pp. 194, 210, 281.

²³ Jerome, "De abstinentia philosophorum antiquorum, sacerdotum, aliorumque sanctorum" and "De temperatis ieiuniis," chapters in "Regula monachorum," *Hieronymi opera*, II, 172^r-73^r; "Against Jovinian," *Nicene and Post-Nicene Fathers*, Second Series, VI, 391-98; Tertullian, "On Prescription," *Ante-Nicene Christian Library*, edited by A. Roberts and J. Donaldson (Edinburgh, 1882-1903), XV, 48-49 (*PL*, II, 54-55).

24 *Utopia*, pp. 281-82; Tunstall, *In laudem matrimonii oratio* (Londini, 1518), sig. A3^{r-v}.

25 *Utopia*, pp. 271, 282.

26 *Utopia*, pp. 77, 282; More to a Monk, *Correspondence*, pp. 195, 197; More to Erasmus, *Eras. Ep.*, IV, 224; Erasmus, *Adagia*, No. 1498 *(Esernius cum Pacidiano)*, cols. 648-51. On Gerard Groote's attitude toward the word *religio* see Hyma, *Renaissance*, pp. 25-26. For necessary and careful distinctions of *religio* consult Silvester, *Summa*, fol. 536^r. For Budé's definition and discussion see *Annotationes . . . in . . . Pandectarum libros* (Parisiis, 1542), pp. 335-37. For an example of how More used to bait supercilious clerics see Richard Pace's story of More and two Scotists who tried to explain why Arthur could make a cloak of giants' beards (*De fructu qui ex doctrina percipitur* [Basileae, 1517], pp. 83-84).

27 Erasmus, "Hieronymi vita," *Opuscula*, pp. 145-46; "In epistolam ad Rusticum monachum de forma vivendi scholia," *Hieronymi opera*, I, 20^r; Vergil, *De inventoribus*, p. 415; Hefele, *Conciles*, VIII, 311, 451-64, 517-24, 532-35.

28 *Utopia*, p. 190; *History of Great Chartreuse*, pp. 189, 228; Erasmus, "The Soldier and the Carthusian," *Colloquies*, pp. 137-38; R. Webster, "The Carthusian Order," *CE*, III, 390.

29 *Utopia*, p. 210; "Confutation of Tyndale," *Works*, p. 368; More to Bugenhagen, *Correspondence*, p. 360; Erasmus, "De interdicto esu carnium," *Opera*, IX, 1197. Silvester asserts that it is the natural law which prescribes fasting for mastery of the flesh and then cites Aquinas to the effect that the necessity of fasting for the correction of sins or for satisfaction by way of penance or for the elevation of the mind to spiritual values falls under the precept of the law of nature (*Summa*, fol. 321^{r-v}).

30 *Utopia*, pp. 210, 281.

31 *Utopia*, pp. 210, 281-82, 291; Erasmus, "In Ps. XXXIII," *Opera*, V, 388 (see "Ecclesiastes," *ibid.*, V, 875, on the advantages of fasting). See also Aquinas, *Quaestiones quodlibetales*, V, a. 18, on the purpose, extent, and so forth, of mortification, including fasting. He declares, for example, that the individual who so weakens his strength by fasting and other austerities as to be unable to carry out his life's duties indubitably commits a sin.

32 *Utopia*, p. 210; Erasmus, "Responsio ad Albertum Pium," *Opera*, IX, 1143 (see his whole defense, 1143-47); Preface, *Colloquies*, pp. x, xiii, xv; *Speculum sacerdotale*, edited by Edward H. Weatherly (London, 1936), pp. 55-56 (see also pp. 62-63). For the many reasons for dispensation and excuse from fasting see Silvester, *Summa*, fol. 323^{r-v}.

33 Bibliothèque Nationale, Lat. MS. 1523, foll. 236^r-38^v; Archivo general de Simancas, P.R., MSS. 21-26, fol. 2^r.

Chapter VII

1 "Oratio ad clerum in convocatione," in Samuel Knight, *Life of Dr. John Colet* (London, 1724), pp. 276, 293.

2 *Utopia*, pp. 281-82, 285. See B. Jarrett and others, "Third Orders," *CE*, XIV, 637-48.

3 More to Dorp, *Correspondence*, pp. 46-47; Archivo general de Simancas, P.R., MSS. 21-26, foll. 4ᵛ-5ʳ; *Bullarium Romanum*, III, Pars III, 399, 438-39; *Disciplinary Decrees of the General Councils*, translated by H. J. Schroeder (St. Louis, 1937), pp. 473, 496; Aubenas and Ricard, *L'église et Renaissance*, pp. 333-34.

4 *Utopia*, pp. 281-82, 285; "Dialogue Concerning Heresies," *Works*, pp. 231-33; "Confutation of Tyndale," *ibid.*, p. 485; Aeneas Silvius to Frunt, December 7, 1457, Ep. CCCVII, *Opera omnia* (Basileae, 1571), pp. 809-10; Hefele, *Conciles*, X, 515-23, 530, 537, 552-53.

5 *Summa contra gentiles*, III, 136-37 (see also *Summa theologica*, II-II, qq. 151-52, especially q. 152, a. 2, ad 1); Erasmus, "Exemplum epistolae suasoriae," *De conscribendis epistolis*, p. 250; *De duplici copia verborum ac rerum* (Lugduni, 1543), p. 208. On the date of *De conscribendis epistolis* see *Eras. Ep.*, I, 198, V, 63.

6 More, "Supplication of Souls," *Works*, pp. 295, 305-07; Starkey, *Dialogue*, pp. 148 ff. On the *Dialogue* W. Schenk, Pole's latest biographer, writes: "We cannot be quite certain that every one of Pole's alleged opinions were actually held by him at that time. In most cases, however, there seems to be no reason why Starkey should have distorted Pole's views. We can, at any rate, regard this work as evidence that questions of this kind were discussed in Pole's circle" (*Reginald Pole, Cardinal of England* [London, 1950], p. 26). For opinions on sacerdotal celibacy and marriage from 1484 to 1521 see Telle, *Erasme*, pp. 190-91, n. 1.

7 *Utopia*, pp. 281-82; "Exemplum epistolae suasoriae," *De conscribendis epistolis*, pp. 241-42, 245, 247-49.

8 *Utopia*, pp. 281-82; Harpsfield, *More*, pp. 13-14; Augustine, *De civitate Dei*, Lib. XIX, Cap. i, *PL*, XLI, 622.

9 "Exemplum epistolae suasoriae," *De conscribendis epistolis*, p. 252; Notes to 1 Corinthians 7 and 1 Timothy 3, "Novum testamentum," *Opera*, VI, 685, 934; "Ratio verae theologiae," *ibid.*, V, 87; "Apologiae in Beddam," *ibid.*, IX, 488.

10 *De inventoribus*, pp. 298-99.

Chapter VIII

1 *Utopia*, pp. 282-83; "Dialogue Concerning Heresies," *Works*, pp. 182-83; Plato, *Laws*, I, 420-21, n. 2.

2 *Sacri sacerdotii defensio*, edited by H. K. Schmeink (Münster, 1925), p. 22.

3 More, *Latin Epigrams*, p. 195; "Dialogue Concerning Heresies," *Works*, pp. 225-26; Starkey, *Dialogue*, p. 83; Henry O. Taylor, *Thought and Expression in the Sixteenth Century* (New York, 1920), II, 50; *Imitation of Christ*, IV, 5, revised translation, p. 249; Peter Cantor, *Verbum abbreviatum*, PL, CCV, 102-07, cited in Joseph Jungmann, *The Mass of the Roman Rite*, translated by F. A. Brunner (New York, 1951-1955), I, 131; Gilmore, *World of Humanism*, pp. 165-76. On the state of the secular clergy see Aubenas and Ricard, *L'église et Renaissance*, pp. 330-34.

4 *Konzil von Trient*, I, 121-22.

5 "Dialogue Concerning Heresies," *Works*, pp. 225, 227, 232; "Passion," translated by Bassett, *ibid.*, p. 1371. On the state of the episcopacy at this time see

Aubenas and Ricard, *L'église et Renaissance*, pp. 313-18, and Hughes, *History of Church*, III, 440-44.

[6] "Dialogue Concerning Heresies," *Works*, pp. 227-28; Silvester, *Summa*, fol. 209ᵛ.

[7] Colet, "Oratio," in Knight, *Colet*, pp. 274, 279-81; Wilkins, *Concilia*, III, 652.

[8] Mansi, *Conciliorum collectio*, XXXII, 675, 874 ff., 895-96, 999-1002. On Antonio Pucci see *Eras. Ep.*, III, 379-80, and Hefele, *Conciles*, VIII, 429-30.

[9] Colet, "Exposition of Epistle to Romans," *Opuscula quaedam theologica*, pp. 88-90, 129, 162-63; *Enarratio in epistolam ad Romanos*, p. 118; see Budé's attack "in indignos sacerdotio" (unworthy bishops) in France and other countries in *Annotationes in Pandectarum libros*, pp. 84-85.

[10] Vergil, *De inventoribus*, pp. 412-13; *The Life of Fisher*, transcribed from MS. Harleian 6382 by Ronald Bayne (London, 1921), pp. 34-35, 69-70; Erasmus, "In epistolam ad Paulinum scholia," *Hieronymi opera*, IV, 5ʳ. For Budé's adverse comments on the wealth and behavior of priests and bishops see *De asse et partibus eius* (Venetiis, 1522), foll. 225ᵛ-35ᵛ.

[11] Fisher, "Seven Penitential Psalms," *English Works*, I, 179-81; Dudley, *Commonwealth*, pp. 51-56.

[12] *Adagia*, No. 2201 *(Sileni Alcibiadis)*, cols. 866-73; Preface, *Colloquies*, pp. ix-xii, 121-22; "In epistolam ad Damasum scholia," *Hieronymi opera*, III, 60ʳ; Jerome to Demetrias, Ep. CXXX, *Nicene and Post-Nicene Fathers*, Second Series, VI, 260-72. Geiler attacks as evil, together with unworthy ecclesiastics, those who intrude others into the clerical state (*Nauicula siue speculū fatuorum* [Argentorati, 1511], sigg. giiᵛ-hiʳ).

[13] Barclay, *Ship of Fools*, I, 159; II, 57-63; Brant-Locher, *Stultifera nauis*, fol. lxxxiiiᵛ; John Skelton, *Complete Poems*, edited by P. Henderson (London, 1931), pp. 282-321.

[14] Aubenas and Ricard, *L'église et Renaissance*, pp. 171-81; Hughes, *History of Church*, III, 440-44, 446-50; Hefele, *Conciles*, VIII, 475-500, 548-58; Gilmore, *World of Humanism*, pp. 65-66, 262-63.

[15] Dudley, *Commonwealth*, pp. 25, 103; Archivo general de Simancas, P.R., MSS. 21-26, fol. 2ᵛ; Bibliothèque Nationale, Lat. MS. 1523, foll. 131ʳ-32ᵛ, 142ᵛ-44ʳ.

[16] *Utopia*, pp. 269-70, 283; Plato, *Laws*, I, 419-21; Fisher, *Defensio regie assertionis*, fol. 129ʳ; C. Cronin, "The Sacrament of Order," in Smith, *Teaching of Church*, II, 1030; Patres Societatis Iesu, *Theologia dogmatica, polemica, scholastica, et moralis, praelectionibus publicis in alma universitate Wirceburgensi accommodata* (Lutetiae Parisiorum, 1852-1854), V, Pars II, 394-401. Carthusians elect their priors by secret ballot (*History of Great Chartreuse*, p. 210).

[17] *Utopia*, pp. 7-8. "Quippe sanctum ducit ambitum, quem non honoris aut quaestus ratio, sed pietatis respectus pepererit" *(ibid.)*.

[18] Thomas Waldensis (Thomas Netter), *Antiquitatum fidei catholicae ecclesiae doctrinale*, edited by Bonaventura Blanciotti (Venetiis, 1757-1759), III, 382, 715; Denzinger, *Enchiridion*, Nos. 424, 608; *Theologia Wirceburgensis*, V, Pars II, 394; A. Michel, "Ordre-Ordination," *DTC*, XI, 1276. On the assumption of strictly sacerdotal functions by laymen among the Waldensians see Jacques Bénigne Bossuet, *Histoire des variations des églises protestantes* (Paris, 1688),

II, 171-72. On the role of the Waldensians in history at this time see Aubenas and Ricard, *L'église et Renaissance*, pp. 368-72.

19 Burnet, *History of Reformation*, IV, 475, 484-85, 487; Sturge, *Tunstal*, p. 223, and Appendix XXII, p. 383. For Book X, Chapters x-xi, see *Hystoria ecclesiastica* (Parisiis, [1505?]), foll. cixʳ-cxiʳ; Rufinus (I, ix-x), *PL*, XXI, 478-84; Socrates (I, xix-xx), *Patrologiae cursus completus: series Graeca* (henceforth cited as *PG*), LXVII, 125-34; and Theodoret (I, xxii-iii), *PG*, LXXXII, 970-74.

20 *Utopia*, p. 164; *Latin Epigrams*, pp. 195-96; *Eras. Ep.*, IV, 116; Erasmus, "Epistola in pseudevangelicos," *Opera*, X, 1586; Colet, *Super opera Dionysii*, p. 123; "Exposition of Epistle to Romans," *Opuscula*, p. 98; Hughes, *History of Church*, III, 439-50.

21 Fisher, *Sacerdotii defensio*, pp. 22, 82-83; "Seven Penitential Psalms," *English Works*, I, 77; Erasmus, "Ecclesiastes," *Opera*, V, 821-22, 830. On admonition of the laity see also *Cloud of Unknowing*, p. 65.

22 Dudley, *Commonwealth*, pp. 25, 32, 43; Alexander Anglus, *Destructorium viciorum*, Pars IV, Cap. xiv (no pagination given); *Life of Fisher*, edited by Bayne, pp. 34-35, 73.

23 *Utopia*, pp. 283-84.

24 Erasmus, "Ecclesiastes," *Opera*, V, 790.

25 Silvester, *Summa*, foll. 226ʳ-27ʳ (complete treatment of excommunication on foll. 218ᵛ-63ᵛ); Erasmus, *Praise of Folly*, p. 100; "Iulius exclusus," *Opuscula*, p. 107. Fisher, *Assertionis Lutheranae confutatio*, pp. ccxciii-ix, gives reasons for fearing excommunication in refutation of Luther's challenge: "Christians ought to be taught more to love than to fear excommunication." On excommunication at this time see Aubenas and Ricard, *L'église et Renaissance*, pp. 325-26.

26 More, "Dialogue Concerning Heresies," *Works*, pp. 214, 276-77.

27 *Eras. Ep.*, II, 154; *Adagia*, No. 161 *(Senis mutare linguam)*, col. 108; "De pueris statim ac liberaliter instituendis," *Opera*, I, 491; Wimpheling, *Adolescentia* (Argentinae, 1515), fol. viʳ; Colet, "Exposition of Epistle to Romans," *Opuscula*, p. 55. See also Erasmus, "Christiani matrimonii institutio," *Opera*, V, 710, and *Imitation of Christ*, I, 3, revised translation, p. 7.

28 *Utopia*, pp. 185, 284-85; Palsgrave to More, *Correspondence*, p. 404; *Latin Epigrams*, pp. 206, 227. The point of the latter epigram is clear from 2 Corinthians 3:6: "for the letter kills, but the spirit gives life." On the courses of study in English grammar schools and universities see Clara P. McMahon, *Education in Fifteenth-Century England* (Baltimore, 1947), pp. 69-83, 101-07. On lay control see *ibid.*, pp. 100-01, 108-14.

29 Schroeder, *Decrees of General Councils*, p. 495; *Bullarium Romanum*, III, Pars III, 398-99.

30 *Utopia*, p. 285.

31 More, "In Lutherum," *Omnia Latina opera*, foll. 70ᵛ, 74ʳ; Letter to Bugenhagen, *Correspondence*, p. 339; "Confutation of Tyndale," *Works*, pp. 428-29, 623; Fisher, *Assertionis Lutheranae confutatio*, p. cccxxvii; Augustine, *Liber de haeresibus*, Cap. xxvii, *PL*, XLII, 26-27. Augustine's statement is based on the work of St. Epiphanius, whose authority here is questioned: see E. Amann, "Quintilliens," *DTC*, XIII, 1598. Irenaeus reports that the Gnostic Marcus

gave women the power of consecrating the Eucharist (*Theologia Wirce-burgensis*, V, Pars II, 417). See Netter, *Doctrinale*, II, 70, Note d, and II, 71, Note a, for information on heretical priestesses; III, 371-72, on the charge against Wyclif that women might be ordained as priests and administer the sacraments; and III, 373, for a description of the Pepuzians.

32 *Utopia*, p. 164.

33 *Utopia*, pp. 145, 147-48; "Supplication of Souls," *Works*, pp. 303-04, 312; "Answer to *Supper*," *ibid.*, p. 1048.

34 *Utopia*, pp. 285-87.

35 Archivo general de Simancas, P.R., MSS. 21-26, fol. 7^r; Wilkins, *Concilia*, III, 614, 616-17, 651, 713; *Soul of Man*, quoted in Knight, *Colet*, p. 192, Note O; Fisher, *Sacerdotii defensio*, pp. 17, 75. On the parliament of 1515 see Robert Keilwey, *Relationes quorundam casuum* (Londini, 1602), foll. 180^v-85^v, and, as more reliable, *LP*, II, Part I, Nos. 1312-14, pp. 351-54. For a contemporary treatise of clerical immunity from taxes, exile, and so forth, to be dated 1491 according to the dedicatory letter, see Johannes Lupus (Juan López), *De libertate ecclesiastica, etc.* (Argentinae, 1511), foll. 2^r-35^r. Consult also E. Magnin, "Immunités ecclésiastiques," *DTC*, VII, 1218-62; Gairdner, *Lollardy*, I, 279-84; Brewer, *Henry VIII*, I, 250-54; Mackie, *Earlier Tudors*, pp. 291-95; Gasquet, *Reformation*, pp. 59-64. On the related topic of sanctuary see Wilkins, *Concilia*, III, 621-22, and Gasquet, *Reformation*, pp. 50-54.

36 More, *Apologye*, p. 54; "Regimini universalis ecclesiae," Mansi, *Conciliorum collectio*, XXXII, 907 ff.; Schroeder, *Decrees of General Councils*, pp. 500-03, 641-44.

37 More to Cromwell, *Correspondence*, p. 498; Fisher, *Assertionis Lutheranae confutatio*, pp. ccccxlvii-iii; Archivo general de Simancas, Legajo 806 años 1480-1549, frag., fol. ii^{r-v}; De Vocht, *Acta Mori*, pp. 14, 156-57; Jedin, *Konzil von Trient*, I, 122-23. More's *Works*, pp. 1424-28, and contemporary accounts give seven, not ten, as the number of years of study. Chambers, *More*, p. 195, explains that More first wrote "seven" and "then altered the word to 'ten' in his final copy."

38 *Utopia*, pp. 287-89; Erasmus, *Adagia*, No. 926 *(Ne ignifer quidem reliquus est factus)*, col. 418.

39 *Praise of Folly*, p. 101; Gasquet, *Reformation*, p. 87. For German and French warrior bishops of the time see Aubenas and Ricard, *L'église et Renaissance*, pp. 314-17.

40 Aquinas, *Summa theologica*, II-II, q. 40, a. 2; Antoninus, *Summa*, III, 63^v, 68^r; Erasmus, "Hieronymus Hedibiae: scholia," *Hieronymi opera*, IV, 70^r; Fisher, *Assertionis Lutheranae confutatio*, p. ccccxxxv; Suárez, "De caritate," *Opera*, XII, 741-42; Hughes, *History of Church*, III, 419-20; Mansi, *Conciliorum collectio*, XXXII, 557. For other contemporary documents on the relation of the clergy to war see Silvester, *Summa*, fol. 54^{r-v}, and Lupus, *De libertate ecclesiastica, etc.*, foll. 59^r-62^v. For satirical verse on Julius II, especially his resemblance to Julius Caesar, see Geldenhauer, *Collectanea*, pp. 18-19.

41 Mansi, *Conciliorum collectio*, XXXII, 843-45, 927; *Eras. Ep.*, I, 550; Harpsfield, *More*, p. 68; Ferdinand Geldner, *Die Staatsauffassung und Fürstenlehre des Erasmus* (Berlin, 1930), p. 166; Hefele, *Conciles*, VIII, 432.

42 *Eras. Ep.*, I, 553, translated by F. M. Nichols, *Epistles of Erasmus* (London, 1901-1918), II, 123; *Eras. Ep.*, III, 368; "Similia," *Opera*, I, 614.

43 "Novum testamentum," *Opera*, VI, 242, 320, 784; *Eras. Ep.*, I, 518; *Adagia*, No. 1401 *(Spartam nactus es, hanc orna)*, cols. 618-19.

44 "Ad Philippum panegyricus," *Opera*, IV, 535; "Modus orandi," *ibid.*, V, 1129; *Education of Christian Prince*, pp. 252-54.

45 Erasmus, *Adagia*, No. 3001 *(Dulce bellum inexpertis)*, cols. 1077, 1082; "Querela pacis," *Opera*, IV, 628, 634, 636, 638, translated by T. Paynell, *Complaint of Peace*, edited by W. J. Hirten (New York, 1946), pp. 12-13, 33-34, 39-40, 46; Clichtoveus, *De bello et pace* (Parisiis, 1523), foll. 24ᵛ-27ʳ; Colet, "On the Composition of Christ's Mystical Body, the Church," *Opuscula*, p. 35.

Chapter IX

1 Plato, *Republic*, I, 343-45; Vespucci, *The Four Voyages*, translated by M. E. Cosenza, in *The Cosmographiae Introductio of Martin Waldseemüller in Facsimile, Followed by the Four Voyages of Amerigo Vespucci, etc.*, edited by C. G. Herbermann (New York, 1907), p. 97; *Mundus novus*, translated by G. T. Northup (Princeton, 1916), p. 6.

2 Aquinas, *Summa theologica*, II-II, q. 81, a. 2, ad 3; Scotus, *Opus Oxoniense*, III, d. 9, q. un., n. 1 *(Opera*, XIV, 386)*; Ficino, "De Christiana religione," *Opera*, I, 2; Letter of Ficino to Benedictus Collucius, *ibid.*, I, 647; Colet, "Exposition of Epistle to Romans," *Opuscula*, p. 52; Erasmus, *De conscribendis epistolis*, pp. 197-98; "Explanatio symboli," *Opera*, V, 1150.

3 *Utopia*, p. 294; Aquinas, *Summa theologica*, II-II, q. 81, a. 7; II-II, q. 82, a. 1; *Contra gentiles*, III, 119; Antoninus, *Summa*, III, 176ᵛ; Colet, *Super opera Dionysii*, p. 52; Adolphe Tanquerey, *The Spiritual Life*, second edition, translated by H. Branderis (Tournai, 1930), pp. 153-56, 492-93; Knox, "The Charge of Religious Intolerance," in *Fame of Blessed Thomas More*, p. 36.

4 "Enarratio Ps. 'Quare fremuerunt,'" *Opera*, V, 210; "Enchiridion," *ibid.*, I, 65-66; *Eras. Ep.*, I, 405; *Colloquies*, pp. 99, 138; *Adagia*, No. 195 *(Barbae tenus sapientes)*, col. 120; No. 2201 *(Sileni Alcibiadis)*, col. 863.

5 "Ratio verae theologiae," *Opera*, V, 113; "Apologia adversus monachos quosdam Hispanos," *ibid.*, IX, 1070, 1088-89; "Declarationes ad censuras facultatis theologiae Parisiensis," *ibid.*, IX, 863.

6 J. Huizinga, *Erasmus*, translated by F. Hopman (New York, 1924), p. 128.

7 More, "Picus," *Works*, p. 8. "Verae pietatis non indiligens cultor est, etiamsi ab omni superstitione alienissimus" (*Eras. Ep.*, IV, 21).

8 *Assertionis Lutheranae confutatio*, p. ccclxx; *De ueritate corporis et sanguinis Christi*, foll. 35ᵛ-36ʳ, 39ᵛ, 123ʳ.

9 *Utopia*, pp. 143-45, 289, 291, 298; Vossius, *Opera* (Amstelodami, 1695-1701), IV, 340; Sandys, *A History of Classical Scholarship* (Cambridge, 1908), II, 307-09; Aquinas, *Summa theologica*, II-II, q. 147, a. 7.

10 Mansi, *Conciliorum collectio*, XX, 779-80; XXII, 1136; XXIII, 547-48, 764; XXVI, 1065, cited by A. Villien, "Fêtes," *DTC*, V, 2186.

11 Barclay, *Eclogues*, edited by B. White (London, 1928), pp. 209-10; *Ship of Fools*, II, 174-78.

[12] *Adagia*, No. 1512 *(Ignavis semper feriae sunt)*, cols. 655-56; No. 1828 *(Inertium chorus)*, col. 749; "De amabili ecclesiae concordia," *Opera*, V, 504; "Christiani matrimonii institutio," *ibid.*, V, 663; Note to Romans 14:5, "Novum testamentum," *ibid.*, VI, 640; *Eras. Ep.*, IV, 117; Archivo general de Simancas, P.R., MSS. 21-26, fol. 2ʳ; Wilkins, *Concilia*, III, 701-02. See Silvester, *Summa*, fol. 167ʳ⁻ᵛ, for the avoidance of pharisaical observance of Sundays and holy-days, for example, in regard to manual labor.

[13] "Answer to *Supper*," *Works*, pp. 1047-48.

Chapter X

[1] "Dialogue Concerning Heresies," *Works*, p. 122; "Confutation of Tyndale," *ibid.*, p. 413.

[2] "Ad Eustochium virginem epitaphium Paulae matris: scholia: antidotus," *Hieronymi opera*, I, 80ʳ⁻ᵛ.

[3] *Utopia*, pp. 289-90; *History of Great Chartreuse*, p. 164; Lawrence Hendriks, *The London Charterhouse* (London, 1889), pp. 88-89.

[4] *Utopia*, pp. 214, 290-91; Strabo, *Geography*, VII, 175; Vergil, *De inventoribus*, p. 136.

[5] Augustine, *De civitate Dei*, Lib. IV, Cap. xxxi, *PL*, XLI, 138; Vergil, *De inventoribus*, p. 136; Colet, "Exposition of Epistle to Romans," *Opuscula*, p. 66. On the absence of images in early Rome see especially Plutarch, "Numa," *Lives*, I, 333-35, and Vergil, *De inventoribus*, p. 136.

[6] "Moriae encomium," *Opera*, IV, 443-44, 454, and notes, translated by Hudson, *Praise of Folly*, pp. 56, 67.

[7] "De amabili ecclesiae concordia," *Opera*, V, 501; "In Ps. LXXXV," *ibid.*, V, 553; "Explanatio symboli," *ibid.*, V, 1187; "Ep. in pseudevangelicos," *ibid.*, X, 1586; "Ep. ad fratres Germaniae inferioris," *ibid.*, X, 1610; Allen, "Erasmus on Church Unity," *Erasmus: Lectures and Wayfaring Sketches* (Oxford, 1934), p. 90.

[8] "Dialogue Concerning Heresies," *Works*, p. 121.

[9] "Dialogue Concerning Heresies," *Works*, pp. 116-18, 121. For an English enumeration and refutation of arguments against images and pilgrimages in the fifteenth century see Pecock's *Repressor*, I, 136-75, 191 ff. For *Dives et Pauper* see Gasquet, *Reformation*, pp. 262-71. The *Speculum sacerdotale* begins with reasons for veneration of the saints and proper methods thereof (pp. 1-2). Vergil, *De inventoribus*, sketches the history of image veneration in the Christian Church (pp. 400-04) and enumerates contemporary abuses in regard to statues on the part of the ignorant (pp. 405-06). On the whole question of images and their veneration see V. Grumel, "Culte des images," *DTC*, VII, 766-844, and H. Leclercq, "Images," *DACL*, VII, 180-302.

Chapter XI

[1] *Utopia*, p. 291; *Apologye*, p. 119.

[2] *Utopia*, pp. 291-92: "odii iraeue in quenquam sibi conscii, . . . ad sacrificia non ingerunt sese, uindictae celeris magnaeque metu."

3 More, "Confutation of Tyndale," *Works*, p. 438; Letter of Margaret Roper to Alice Alington, *Works*, p. 1436 (*Correspondence*, p. 520); Erasmus, "Ad Oceanum epitaphium Fabiolae: scholia," *Hieronymi opera*, I, 89^v; Scotus, *Opus Oxoniense*, IV, d. 17, nn. 5, 7 (*Opera*, XVIII, 505, 507).

4 Bede, *Commentary on Epistle of St. James* (*PL*, XCIII, 39), Pseudo-Augustine, *De vera et falsa poenitentia* (*PL*, XL, 1113, 1122), Peter Lombard, *Sentences*, IV, d. 17, Albertus Magnus, *In IV*, d. 17, aa. 58-59, Aquinas, *In IV*, d. 17, q. 3, a. 2, ad 2; Scotus, *Opus Oxoniense*, IV, d. 14, q. 4 and d. 17, q. un.— all cited in A. Boudinhon, "Lay Confession," *CE*, IX, 94-95, E. Hanna, "Penance," *ibid.*, XI, 623-24, and A. Vacant, "Absolution: Sentiments des anciens scolastiques," *DTC*, I, 168-91; W. H. Kent, "Epistle of James," in Cuthbert Lattey and Joseph Keating, editors, *Westminster Version of the Sacred Scriptures* (London, 1913—), *New Testament*, IV, 103; Hyma, *Renaissance*, pp. 77-78, 373-74; Bossuet, *History of the Variations of the Protestant Churches*, anonymous English translation (New York, [1845]), II, 85.

5 *Utopia*, pp. 292-93.

6 Fisher, *Defensio regie assertionis*, fol. lxiii^r; Erasmus, *Adagia*, No. 3699 (*Orphica vita*), col. 1247, referring to Plato, *De legibus*, Lib. VI (English translation, I, 493); Ludwig Ziehen, "Opfer," *RE*, XXXV, 582.

7 *Utopia*, pp. 293-94; "Dialogue Concerning Heresies," *Works*, p. 118; Aquinas, *Contra gentiles*, III, 119; *Summa theologica*, II-II, q. 81, a. 7.

8 *Enarratio in epistolam ad Romanos*, pp. 60-61.

9 *Canons and Decrees of the Council of Trent*, translated by H. J. Schroeder (St. Louis, 1941), pp. 144-47; *A Relation of the Island of England*, translated by C. A. Sneyd (London, 1847), p. 23; Vergil, *Anglicae historiae libri vigintisex* (Gandavi, [1556-1557]), p. 31; Denys Hay, editor, *The Anglica Historia of Polydore Vergil* (London, 1950), Introduction, p. xii.

10 More, "Dialogue Concerning Heresies," *Works*, pp. 118-19; "Confutation of Tyndale," *ibid.*, p. 783; Erasmus, "Moriae encomium," *Opera*, IV, 453-54, translated by Hudson, *Praise of Folly*, p. 66; "Responsio ad Albertum Pium," *Opera*, IX, 1156; "In epistolam adversus Vigilantium scholia," *Hieronymi opera*, III, 58^r. See also Pecock, *Crysten Religioun*, pp. 244-46.

11 *The Priest's New Ritual* (New York, 1940), p. 27; Colet, "Exposition of Epistle to Romans," *Opuscula*, p. 116; Erasmus, "Enchiridion," *Opera*, V, 37; "The Soldier and the Carthusian," *Colloquies*, pp. 137-38; D'Anghiera, *De orbe novo*, I, 99; *History of Great Chartreuse*, pp. 204-05; Hendriks, *London Charterhouse*, p. 80.

12 *Utopia*, pp. 27-28, 294-95; Vespucci, *Mundus novus*, p. 8; *Four Voyages*, p. 98; Edward Arber, editor, *The First Three English Books on America* (Birmingham, 1885), p. xxvii; Plato, *Timaeus*, p. 251; *Republic*, II, 512-15. Baumstark, *Morus*, p. 99, exclaims at this point: "Papageno? O guter Morus!" perhaps a reference to the feather garment of Papageno in Mozart's *Die Zauberflöte*.

13 *Utopia*, p. 295; Caryl Coleman, "Birds (in Symbolism)," *CE*, II, 576-77; H. Leclercq, "Oiseau," *DACL*, XII, 2038-58.

14 *Imitation of Christ*, IV, 5, revised translation, p. 250; Erasmus, "Moriae encomium," *Opera*, IV, 481-82, translated by Hudson, *Praise of Folly*, pp. 97-98;

"Querela pacis," *Opera*, IV, 628, translated by Paynell, *Complaint of Peace*, p. 15.

15 *Utopia*, p. 295; Brant-Locher, *Stultifera nauis*, foll. liiii, ci; Barclay, *Ship of Fools*, I, 220-24, II, 153-57; British Museum, Arundel MS. 68, fol. 69ʳ. On those chattering in choir see Geiler, *Nauicula fatuorum*, sig. qiiiᵛ-ivʳ, and on those profaning sacred places, *ibid.*, sigg. Tivᵛ-Uiiʳ.

16 Erasmus, *Adagia*, 2665 (βωμολόχος, βωμολοχεύεσθαι), col. 1001; "In Ps. LXXXV," *Opera*, V, 533-34; Budé, *De asse*, fol. 234ʳ⁻ᵛ; More, *Utopia*, p. 295; *Imitation of Christ*, IV, 1, revised translation, pp. 235-36.

Chapter XII

1 *Utopia*, pp. 295-96.

2 Pope, *Essay on Criticism*, Part II, l. 365; Plato, *Republic*, I, 247, 255; "De modo cantandi," quoted in *History of Great Chartreuse*, pp. 165-66; Starkey, *Dialogue*, pp. 134, 137; Erasmus, "In Ps. LXXXV," *Opera*, V, 523. See the articles on chant by H. Leclercq and A. Gatard, *DACL*, III, 256-332.

3 Erasmus, Note to 1 Corinthians 14:19, "Novum testamentum," *Opera*, VI, 731-32; Aubenas and Ricard, *L'église et Renaissance*, p. 375. On song schools in England see McMahon, *Education in England*, pp. 118-22.

4 "Responsio ad Albertum Pium," *Opera*, IX, 1155; "Ep. in pseudevangelicos," *ibid.*, X, 1586.

5 "In Ps. IV," *Opera*, V, 243; "In Ps. XXII," *ibid.*, V, 333; "In Ps. XXXVIII," *ibid.*, V, 427; "In Ps. LXXXV," *ibid.*, V, 523; "De amabili ecclesiae concordia," *ibid.*, V, 503; "Christiani matrimonii institutio," *ibid.*, V, 718; "Ecclesiastes," *ibid.*, V, 942; "Modus orandi," *ibid.*, V, 1101.

6 *De inventoribus*, p. 353.

7 Wilkins, *Concilia*, III, 686.

8 *Correspondence*, p. 188.

9 Augustinus Theiner, editor, *Acta genuina concilii Tridentini* (Zagrabiae, n. d.), II, 122; Schroeder, *Council of Trent*, pp. 151, 424. On church music before and after the Council of Trent see Karl G. Fellerer, "Das Tridentinum und die Kirchenmusik," in Georg Schreiber, editor, *Das Weltkonzil von Trient: Sein Werden und Wirken* (Freiburg, 1951), I, 447-62.

10 *Utopia*, pp. 297-98.

11 More, "Confutation of Tyndale," *Works*, p. 581.

12 More to Margaret Roper, *Correspondence*, p. 543; Erasmus, "Apophth. Lib. III—Socratica," *Opera*, IV, 155; "Enchiridion," *ibid.*, V, 52; "In Ps. XXXIII," *ibid.*, V, 395; *Praise of Folly*, translated by Hudson, p. 56.

13 More to Holt, *Correspondence*, pp. 3-4; Barclay, *Ship of Fools*, I, 140; More, "Epigrammata," *Omnia Latina opera*, fol. 25; *Latin Epigrams*, p. 179; Erasmus, Note to Matthew 6:7, "Novum testamentum," *Opera*, VI, 35; "Modus orandi," *ibid.*, V, 1121-22 (see pp. 1122-23 for a brief development of the seven petitions of the Paternoster); More, *Utopia*, p. 298 ("difficillima morte obita ad deum peruadere, quam ab eo diutius prosperrimo uitae cursu distineri").

14 *Utopia*, p. 307.

Chapter XIII

[1] Wimpheling, *Adolescentia*, fol. vi^r (italics added) ; Auḃenas and Ricard, *L'église et Renaissance*, pp. 19, 387; Dermenghem, *Morus*, p. 179. For movements of reform in European countries before 1517 see Jedin, *Konzil von Trient*, I, 111-32.

[2] Colet, "Oratio ad clerum in convocatione, 1511," in Knight, *Colet*, pp. 273-85, 289-308; Burnet, "Reflections," p. 5, quoted in *The Phoenix* (1708), II, iv, Preface, and cited in Lupton, *Colet*, p. 179, n. 1, but see *History of Reformation*, edited by Pocock, III, 89; *LP*, II, Part II, No. 2046.

[3] *Utopia*, p. 102; Budé, *De asse*, fol. 233^v. For a reference to, and explanation of, "Lesbia structura" and "plumbea norma" see Budé, *Annotationes*, p. 2.

[4] "Seven Penitential Psalms," *English Works*, I, 170.

[5] Pace, *De fructu*, pp. 32-33; Sermon of Aegidius Viterbiensis, Conc. Lat. V, Mansi, *Conciliorum collectio*, XXXII, 675; Sermon of Bernardus Zane, Conc. Lat. V, *ibid.*, XXXII, 703. On Egidio see Aubenas and Ricard, *L'église et Renaissance*, p. 223; and on Zane see Hefele, *Conciles*, VIII, 350-53.

[6] *Calendar of Letters . . . between England and Spain* (London, 1862-1954), II, Nos. 82, 89, 93, 96, pp. 90, 100-03, 108-09; *LP*, II, Part II, No. 2864, p. 920.

[7] *Fastorum libri duodecim* (Argentorati, 1518), sig. aii^v-v^v.

[8] *Assertionis Lutheranae confutatio*, p. dxiii; *Convulsio calumniarum Ulrichi*, sig. Niii^v.

[9] Gilson, *Reason and Revelation*, p. 70; Monceau, *Histoire littéraire de l'Afrique chrétienne*, p. 133, quoted in Knox, *Enthusiasm*, p. 60; Erasmus, "Ep. in pseudevangelicos," *Opera*, X, 1585.

Chapter XIV

[1] *Utopia*, p. 102; Erasmus, "Methodus," *Novum instrumentum omne* (Basileae, 1516), sig. bbb4r^r; "In epistolam ad Nepotianum de vita clericorum et sacerdotum scholia: antidotus," *Hieronymi opera*, I, 6^v.

[2] Colet, *Enarratio in primam epistolam S. Pauli ad Corinthios*, edited by J. H. Lupton (London, 1874), pp. 89-95; "A Ryght Fruitfull Monicion," in Lupton, *Colet*, p. 308.

[3] "In epistolam ad Gerontiam viduam de monogamia scholia: antidotus," *Hieronymi opera*, I, 62^r; "In primum librum adversus Iovinianum scholia," *ibid.*, III, 24^v-25^r, 30^v; "In librum secundum adversus Iovinianum scholia," *ibid.*, III, 46^r.

[4] *Annotationũ libri duo, alter in annotatiões prioris aeditionis noui testamenti Desiderij Erasmi, alter in annotatiões posterioris aeditiõis eiusdẽ* (Parisiis, [1519-1520?]), foll. xiii^v-iiii^r.

[5] *Utopia*, pp. 135-37, 257; Plato, *Republic*, I, xxxiv, 331, 453-55, 475; Campbell, *More's Utopia and Social Teaching*, p. 133; Dermenghem, *Morus*, pp. 159-66; *Eras. Ep.*, IV, 21; Erasmus, "De amabili ecclesiae concordia," *Opera*, V, 475; Pecock, *Repressor*, II, 497; Augustine, *Liber de haeresibus*, Cap. ii. For the kind of reason which could dissuade More from having a community of wives and children in his *Utopia* see Aquinas, *In VIII Libros Politicorum Aristotelis*

Expositio, Lib. II, Lect. 2-3. On differences in regard to marriage and family in More, Erasmus, Bacon, and Campanella consult Dermenghem, *Morus,* pp. 159-66. On all aspects of marriage see the exhaustive article by several hands, "Mariage," *DTC,* IX, 2044-2331.

[6] *Utopia,* pp. 153-54; Plato, *Laws,* I, 177-79; *Relation of Island of England,* pp. 24-27, 75-77.

[7] *Utopia,* pp. 156, 230; *Latin Epigrams,* p. 231; *Life of Fisher,* edited by Bayne, p. 19; Vitoria, "De potestate civili," in Scott, *Spanish Origin,* pp. xci-ii; Erasmus, "Christiani matrimonii institutio," *Opera,* V, 650, 697; *Eras. Ep.,* IV, 19.

[8] More, *Utopia,* pp. 140, 226-27; "Dialogue Concerning Heresies," *Works,* p. 233; "Treatise on the Passion," *ibid.,* p. 1275; *Latin Epigrams,* p. 226; Erasmus, *Adagia,* No. 3097 *(Mulierem ornat silentium),* col. 1105; "The Uneasy Wife," *Colloquies,* p. 127; "Enchiridion," *Opera,* V, 20; *Eras. Ep.,* X, 139.

[9] *Utopia,* pp. 137, 139-40, 145, 168, 228, 257; Plato, *Republic,* I, 449-53, 483; *Laws,* II, 57 ff., 87 ff.; Erasmus, "Christiani matrimonii institutio," *Opera,* V, 694; "In epistolam ad Paulinum de institutione monachi scholia," *Hieronymi opera,* I, 45ᵛ-46ʳ. On pilgrimages at this time, especially to Jerusalem, see Allen, *Age of Erasmus,* pp. 225-51.

[10] *Utopia,* pp. 162-63; Plato, *Republic,* I, 463-65; Mau, "Ammen," *RE,* I, 1844; Erasmus, "The Lying-In Woman," *Colloquies,* pp. 228-29, 236-38; A. Benoist, *Quid de puerorum institutione senserit Erasmus* (Parisiis, 1876), pp. 3-4. See also Wilson, *Arte of Rhetorique,* p. 111, quoted in Thomas Elyot, *The Gouernour,* edited by H. H. S. Croft (London, 1880), I, 29, Note B.

[11] *Utopia,* Introduction, pp. xxxiii-iv, 224; Erasmus, "Christiani matrimonii institutio," *Opera,* V, 650, 665-66; "The Old Men's Dialogue," *Colloquies,* p. 177; Plato, *Republic,* I, 465; *Laws,* I, 311, 461, 501, II, 143, 427-29; Aristotle, *Politics,* translated by H. Rackham (Cambridge, 1950), p. 621; Silvester, *Summa,* fol. 210ʳ; Schroeder, *Council of Trent,* pp. 183-85; Antonius Arregui, *Summarium theologiae moralis,* thirteenth edition (Romae, 1937), p. 522, n. 1; Hefele, *Conciles,* XI, 511-13, 525-29, 538, 541-46, 554-58. According to English law "full age in male or female is twenty one years" (William Blackstone, *Commentaries,* fifth edition [Oxford, 1773], I, 463). On the relation of guardian to ward assailed by Erasmus, Blackstone writes: ". . . while the infant was in ward, the guardian had the power of tendering him or her a suitable match, . . . which if the infants refused, they forfeited the value of the marriage . . . to their guardian; that is, so much as a jury would assess, or any one would *bona fide* give to the guardian for such an alliance: and, if the infants married themselves without the guardian's consent, they forfeited double the value. . . . This seems to have been one of the greatest hardships of our antient tenures" (II, 70).

[12] Erasmus, Note to 1 Corinthians 7:39, "Novum testamentum," *Opera,* VI, 703; "Ad annotationes Lei," *ibid.,* IX, 249; "Christiani matrimonii institutio," *ibid.,* V, 626, 641-42, 654, 665, 667-68; "The Unequal Marriage," *Colloquies,* pp. 316-23; *Adagia,* No. 2031 *(Non licet bis in bello peccare),* col. 812.

[13] More, "Dialogue Concerning Heresies," *Works,* p. 165; Plutarch, *Lives,* I, 247-49, 391-93; Plato, *Republic,* I, 435-37; *Laws,* I, 459, II, 427-29; Ioannes

Iovianus Pontanus, *Opera omnia soluta oratione composita* (Venetiis, 1518-1519), I, xlix^r.

¹⁴ More, *Latin Epigrams*, pp. 181-83; Colet, "A Ryght Fruitfull Monicion," in Lupton, *Colet*, pp. 307-08.

¹⁵ *Utopia*, pp. 225-27.

Chapter XV

¹ *Utopia*, pp. 227-29.

² Plato, *Laws*, II, 445; Vergil, *De inventoribus*, p. 17; Tunstall, *In laudem matrimonii*, sig. A7^{r-v}.

³ *Opus Oxoniense*, IV, d. 26, q. un., n. 9 (*Opera*, XIX, 160-61), quoted and explained in Minges, *Scoti doctrina*, I, 523-24, II, 686-87.

⁴ Stapleton, *More*, p. 97; *Biblia Latina cum postillis Nicolai de Lyra* (Venetiis, 1489), IV, C9^r, P3^v.

⁵ On divorce and the dissolubility of marriage see Aquinas, *Contra gentiles*, III, 122-23; *In IV Libros Sententiarum*, d. 33, q. 2, a. 1; *Supplementum*, q. 67, a. 1; Scotus, *Opus Oxoniense*, IV, d. 26, q. 1, nn. 9-10 (*Opera*, XIX, 160-61) and d. 33, q. 3, nn. 4-6 (*ibid.*, XIX, 386-88).

⁶ Erasmus, Notes to Matthew 19:3 and 1 Corinthians 7:39, "Novum testamentum," *Opera*, VI, 97-98, 692, 694-95, 698, 701-02; "Ad annotationes Lei," *ibid.*, IX, 262-70; More, Letter to a Monk, *Correspondence*, p. 171. On the views of the fathers and ecclesiastical writers mentioned by Erasmus see *Theologia Wirceburgensis*, V, Pars II, 547-51, and Dominicus Palmieri, *Tractatus de matrimonio Christiano* (Romae, 1880), pp. 149-67. See also the treatment by A. Villien, "Divorce," *DTC*, IV, 1455-78.

⁷ Erasmus, "Novum testamentum," *Opera*, VI, 692, 702; "Responsio ad notationes novas Ed. Lei," *ibid.*, IX, 262; "Apologiae in Beddam," *ibid.*, IX, 572-75; Lee, *Annotationes*, foll. viii^v, lxvii^v-lxxiv^v, xcvii^v-xcviii^v, cxiii^v-cxx^v; Silvester, *Summa*, fol. 158^r.

⁸ Erasmus, "Christiani matrimonii institutio," *Opera*, V, 617-55.

⁹ For a brief and accurate treatment see Chambers, *More*, pp. 223-30.

¹⁰ *Utopia*, p. 229.

¹¹ Otto Cartellieri, *Am Hofe . . .* , p. 58, cited in Geldner, *Staatsauffassung des Erasmus*, p. 111, n. 2 (see English translation by Malcolm Letts, *The Court of Burgundy* [London, 1929], pp. 55, 252); Aubenas and Ricard, *L'église et Renaissance*, pp. 127, 324-25, 327-28; Brant-Locher, *Stultifera nauis*, fol. xliiii; Barclay, *Ship of Fools*, I, 174; Max Cary, *History of Rome Down to the Reign of Constantine*, revised edition, edited by Russell Meiggs (London, 1951), p. 489. See R. Parayre and others, "Adultère," *DTC*, I, 463-511.

¹² *Utopia*, pp. 60-63; Erasmus, *Education of Christian Prince*, p. 228; "Ad Innocentium de muliere septies icta scholia," *Hieronymi opera*, I, 106^r; "Christiani matrimonii institutio," *Opera*, V, 648, 700; "Exomologesis," *ibid.*, V, 153; see also "De amabili ecclesiae concordia," *ibid.*, V, 499.

¹³ Erasmus, *Colloquies*, p. 191; *Adagia*, No. 829 *(Tenedia bipennis)*, p. 261 (1526 edition); No. 3010 *(Placiadae)*, col. 1085; No. 3525 *(Onobatis)*, col. 1205; Vergil, *De inventoribus*, pp. 201-02.

[14] *Utopia*, pp. 224-25; Hefele, *Conciles*, VIII, 311; B. Dolhagaray, "Fornication," *DTC*, VI, 600-11.

[15] *Latin Epigrams*, pp. 107-08, 229-30; Stapleton, *More*, pp. 95-96; Allen, *Age of Erasmus*, p. 205. Erasmus' original statement reads: "Cum aetas ferret, non abhorruit a puellarum amoribus, sed citra infamiam, et sic vt oblatis magis frueretur quam captatis, et animo mutuo caperetur potius quam coitu" (*Eras. Ep.*, IV, 17).

[16] *Utopia*, p. 231; "Debellacion of Salem and Bizance," *Works*, pp. 959, 1019; Alexander Anglus, *Destructorium viciorum*, Pars II, Cap. iv (no pagination given); Silvester, *Summa*, fol. 419^v; Hadrianus VI, *Questiones quodlibetice*, fol. xciii^r.

Chapter XVI

[1] *Utopia*, p. 229.

[2] *Utopia*, pp. 221-22, 263.

[3] *Utopia*, pp. 158, 161, 176, 200, 208. See Erasmus, *Adagia*, No. 3001 *(Dulce bellum inexpertis)*, col. 1066.

[4] *Utopia*, pp. 64-71, 221-22.

[5] Michels and Ziegler, editors, *Utopia*, Einleitung, p. xxxi; Oncken, in Ritter, translator, *Utopia*, Einleitung, p. 30*; Bendemann, *Staats- und Sozialauffassung des Morus*, pp. 50-53; Dietzel, "Beiträge zur Geschichte des Sozialismus und Kommunismus," *Vierteljahrsschrift für Staats- und Volkswirtschaft*, V, 394, cited by Bendemann, pp. 52-53, n. 25.

[6] *Utopia*, p. 121; Chambers, *More*, p. 144; Donner, *Utopia*, p. 31. See Dermenghem, *Morus*, p. 144.

[7] Augustine, *De civitate Dei*, Lib. XIX, Cap. xv, *PL*, XLI, 643; Erasmus, "Christiani matrimonii institutio," *Opera*, V, 670. On views of slavery in the ancient world see W. L. Newman, editor, *The Politics of Aristotle* (Oxford, 1887), I, 138-58.

[8] *Utopia*, p. 231; Scotus, *Opus Oxoniense*, IV, d. 36, q. 1, n. 2 *(Opera*, XIX, 446)*; Aureolus, *In IV librum sententiarum*, d. 36, q. un., a. un., cited in Allard, *Dictionnaire apologétique de la foi catholique* (Paris, 1925-1928) (henceforth cited as *DAFC*), I, 1497-98; Antoninus, *Summa*, III, 60^v; Silvester, *Summa*, fol. 423^r. Silvester, *ibid.*, fol. 588^r, classifies Scotus' three ways of becoming a (true) slave under law *(ex iure)* and adds two: birth *(ex nativitate)* and purchase *(ex emptione)*. Angelus de Clavasio, *Summa angelica*, fol. cccxviii^{r-v}, adds the way of servile birth to the three ways of Scotus. In "The Inquisition of 1517, Inclosures and Evictions, Edited from the Lansdowne MS. I. 153," *Transactions of the Royal Historical Society*, New Series, VI, 193, I. S. Leadam writes of England: "The latter [villeins in gross] were described as mere slaves or serfs, chattels who could be sold or transferred from one lord to another. According to Fitzherbert [*Surueyenge*, Chap. xiii, p. 31, edition of 1539] 'bondmen' existed in his day, early in the sixteenth century, and in 1521 there were 'a good number' . . . on the Duke of Buckingham's lands."

[9] Vespucci, *Four Voyages*, pp. 117-18; Pontanus, "De obedientia," *Opera*, I, 24^{r-v}; Allard, "Slavery," *CE*, XIV, 39; J. K. Ingram, "Modern Slave Trade,"

Encyclopaedia Britannica, XX, 779; Hughes, *History of Church,* III, 452. On the recrudescence of slavery in the modern world see J. Dutilleul, "Esclavage," *DTC,* V, 486-503.

10 Vicente Beltrán de Heredia, "El padre Matías de Paz, O.P., y su tratado 'De dominio regum Hispaniae super Indos,' " *La Ciencia Tomista,* XL (1929), 185.

11 Matías de Paz, "De dominio regum Hispaniae super Indos," edited by Vicente Beltrán de Heredia, *Archivum Fratrum Praedicatorum,* III (1933), 142-43; Silvester, *Summa,* fol. 588ʳ.

12 Paz, "De dominio," *Archivum Fratrum Praedicatorum,* III, 142-46. The precise translation of the Aristotelian terms given in Latin by Paz as *principatus despoticus, imperium politicum,* and *imperium regale* varies with the context. The first has been translated as "mastership," "mastership of slaves," "the rule of a master," "the authority of the master," "the authority of a master over slaves," or "the control of slaves"; the second, as "statesmanship," "the authority of the statesman," "the authority of a magistrate in a republic," "republican government," "political rule," or "constitutional rule"; the third, as "monarchy," "the rule of the monarch," "royal rule," or "monarchical" or "royal government." See Aristotle, *Politics,* translated by Rackham, pp. 14-15, 28-29, 58-59; *Politica,* translated by B. Jowett, in Vol. X, *The Works of Aristotle,* edited by W. D. Ross (Oxford, 1908-1952), 1253 b 18-20, 1255 b 16-20, 1259 b 1-5; *The Politics of Aristotle,* translated by E. Barker, revised edition (Oxford, 1948), pp. 1, 9, 17, 32, 104-05, 111-12.

13 Vitoria, "De jure gentium et naturali" and "De bello," in Scott, *Spanish Origin,* pp. cxiii-iv, cxxiv.

14 Carlyle, *Past and Present* (New York, n. d.), pp. 204-05.

Chapter XVII

1 Cicero, *De officiis* I. xi, translated by W. Miller (London, 1921), p. 37; Vincent of Beauvais, *Speculum doctrinale* (Strasbourg, 1473), Lib. XI, Cap. xxvi, cited in Ortolan, "Guerre," *DTC,* IV, 1901; Erasmus, *Adagia,* No. 3001 *(Dulce bellum inexpertis),* col. 1063; "Querela pacis," *Opera,* IV, 640.

2 Clichtoveus, *De bello et pace,* fol. 19ᵛ; Antoninus, *Summa,* III, 65ʳ; Sermons of Egidio of Viterbo and Antonio Pucci, Mansi, *Conciliorum collectio,* XXXII, 672, 892-93.

3 Ryan, *Modern War and Basic Ethics* (Washington, 1933), pp. 39-40; Yves de La Brière, "Paix et Guerre," *DAFC,* III, 1261; Augustine, *De civitate Dei,* Lib. XIX, Cap. vii, xii-iii, xv, *PL,* XLI, especially 634, 637-42, 643-44 (see also Lib. IV, Cap. iv-vi, *ibid.,* 115-17). For traditional views of contemporary moralists on war see Silvester, *Summa,* foll. 48ᵛ-49ʳ, and Angelus de Clavasio, *Summa angelica,* foll. xxiᵛ-iiiʳ.

4 Clichtoveus, *De bello et pace,* foll. 29ʳ-39ᵛ; Erasmus to Jodocus Jonas, *Eras. Ep.,* IV, 525, translated by Lupton, *Vitrier and Colet,* pp. 43-44; Marquardus de Hatstein to John Colet, *Epistolae aliquot eruditorum uirorum,* p. 119.

5 Erasmus, *Education of Christian Prince,* pp. 249-55; "In epistolam ad Gerontiam viduam de monogamia scholia," *Hieronymi opera,* I, 41ʳ; "Moriae encomium," *Opera,* IV, 493; "Consultatio de bello Turcico," *ibid.,* V, 354; Notes to

Matthew 26:52, Luke 3:14, 22:36, "Novum testamentum," *ibid.*, VI, 137, 241-42, 317-21. See the letters to Antony of Bergen (1514) and to John Fisher (1516), *Eras. Ep.*, I, 554, II, 245-46.

6 Erasmus, *Adagia*, No. 3001 *(Dulce bellum inexpertis)*, cols. 1061, 1066, 1071-72, 1074-76, 1080; No. 3454 *(Inscitia confidentiam parit)*, col. 1187; "Querela pacis," *Opera*, IV, 628, 638-39, translated by Paynell, *Complaint of Peace*, pp. 12-13, 46, 49-50; *Praise of Folly*, translated by Hudson, pp. 30-31; Lee, *Exhibita quaedam . . . in consilio caesareo ante belli indictionem; responsio cordatissima nomine caesareae maiestatis ad eadem* ([Antwerp], 1528), sig. C2^v.

7 Erasmus, "Responsio ad Albertum Pium," *Opera*, IX, 1141, 1192-93; "Explanatio symboli," *ibid.*, V, 1193; see also "Institutio principis Christiani," IV, 607; "In evangelium Lucae paraphrasis," VII, 312.

8 Suárez, "De caritate," *Opera*, XII, 737-38, 752.

9 *Utopia*, p. 81; Aquinas, *Summa theologica*, II-II, q. 40, a. 1, c.; Silvester, *Summa*, fol. 52; Vitoria, "De jure belli," translated in Scott, *Spanish Origin*, pp. lviii, lxi.

10 *Utopia*, p. 243; *Dialogue of Comfort*, p. 341.

11 Vitoria, "De jure belli," translated in Scott, *Spanish Origin*, p. liv; Suárez, "De caritate," *Opera*, XII, 743; Erasmus to Antony of Bergen, *Eras. Ep.*, I, 553; "Querela pacis," *Opera*, IV, 633; *Adagia*, No. 201 *(Aut regem aut fatuum nasci oportet)*, col. 124; No. 1401 *(Spartam nactus es, hanc orna)*, cols. 616-17, 619; *Education of Christian Prince*, p. 240. For a brief and excellent summary of the Italian wars, 1494-1517, see Gilmore, *World of Humanism*, pp. 156-60.

12 *Utopia*, pp. 81-97; Letters to Stephen Poncher and Francis I, *Eras. Ep.*, II, 454-55, 476-77; Vitoria, "De jure belli," translated in Scott, *Spanish Origin*, p. liii; Chambers, *More*, p. 102; A. F. Pollard, *Henry VIII* (London, 1930), pp. 67-68. For a good account of the background for the counsel to the king of France see Brewer, *Henry VIII*, I, 96 ff.

13 *Utopia*, pp. 243-44; Sermon of Bernardus Zane, Conc. Lat. V, Sess. 1, Mansi, *Conciliorum collectio*, XXXII, 705-06; Barclay, *Ship of Fools*, II, 192-209; Chambers, *More*, p. 388, citing Chapuys, *Spanish Calendar*, IV, ii, 114; Aubenas and Ricard, *L'église et Renaissance*, p. 190; Hefele, *Conciles*, VIII, 502-03, 598-606; Fisher, *Assertionis Lutheranae confutatio*, pp. ccccxxxvi-xlviii; Ianus Damianus, *De expeditione in Turcas elegeia* (Basileae, 1515), sigg. Aii^r-Bi^r; Mantuanus, "Obiurgatio cum exhortatione ad capienda arma contra infideles ad potentatus Christianos," in *Vita Dionysij Areopagitae* (Mediolani, 1521), sigg. GGi^r-HHv^v.

14 *Utopia*, p. 244; Plutarch, "Lycurgus," *Lives*, I, 297; Vitoria, "De bello," translated in Scott, *Spanish Origin*, pp. cxvii-iii (see "De Indis," p. xliv).

15 Vitoria, "De Indis," and "De jure belli," translated in Scott, *Spanish Origin*, pp. xlv, l-li; Suárez, "De caritate," *Opera*, XII, 744.

16 *Utopia*, pp. 244-45; *LP*, II, No. 204, p. 68. See the present writer's "St. Thomas More and His Utopian Embassy of 1515," *Catholic Historical Review*, XXXIX (1953), 272-97.

17 *Utopia*, pp. 245-46.

[18] *Utopia*, pp. 154-55; John P. Noonan, *General and Special Ethics* (Chicago, 1947), p. 294. On the morality behind colonization see T. Ortolan, "Guerre," *DTC*, VI, 1924-26.

[19] More, "Confutation of Tyndale," *Works*, p. 428; Plato, *Republic*, I, 163-65; D'Anghiera, *De orbe novo*, I, 257; Vitoria, "De Indis," translated in Scott, *Spanish Origin*, pp. xiv, xxxvi-xl; Dublanchy, "Morale," *DTC*, X, 2449. For the interpretations by sixteenth-century theologians of Alexander VI's bull on the division of the New World see J. Dutilleul, "Esclavage," *DTC*, V, 487-88.

[20] Vitoria, "De Indis," translated in Scott, *Spanish Origin*, pp. xliv-vi.

Chapter XVIII

[1] *Utopia*, pp. 247-48; Erasmus, "Ad Philippum panegyricus," *Opera*, IV, 535; Robert Fabyan, *The New Chronicles of England and France*, edited by H. Ellis (London, 1811), p. 678.

[2] Περὶ ἱερωσύνης *(De sacerdotio) of St. John Chrysostom*, edited by J. Arbuthnot Nairn (Cambridge, 1906), pp. 19-20. For early editions see Introduction, pp. xxxvi, lvi. For this reference I am indebted to a member of the faculty of theology at West Baden College who prefers to remain anonymous.

[3] *Utopia*, pp. 252, 258-62; Erasmus, "Querela pacis," *Opera*, IV, 634; Aquinas, *Summa theologica*, II-II, q. 40, a. 3; Antoninus, *Summa*, III, 68^v; Silvester, *Summa*, fol. 50^v.

[4] *Utopia*, pp. 248-51; T. Ortolan, "Guerre," *DTC*, VI, 1929.

[5] *Utopia*, pp. 248-50; Erasmus, *Adagia*, No. 1643 *(Argenteis hastis pugnare)*, col. 697.

[6] Erasmus, *Education of Christian Prince*, p. 153; Tacitus, *Histories and Annals*, translated by C. H. Moore and J. Jackson (London, 1925-1937), II, 519.

[7] C. R. Thompson, *The Translations of Lucian by Erasmus and St. Thomas More* (Ithaca, 1940), pp. 29-44; Mansi, *Conciliorum collectio*, XXVII, 765-66. On the history of tyrannicide see A. Bride, "Tyrannicide," *DTC*, XV, 1988-2015.

[8] *Utopia*, pp. 84, 250-51; Brewer, editor, *LP*, II, Part I, Introduction, p. cclxix, and No. 1973, p. 573. For the De la Poles see Genealogical Table I and key, Mackie, *Earlier Tudors*, pp. 655-56.

[9] *Utopia*, pp. 83-84, 251; *LP*, II, Part I, No. 1973, p. 573; Erasmus, "Iulius exclusus," *Opuscula*, p. 108-14.

[10] *Utopia*, p. 251; Roper, *More*, pp. 20-21.

[11] *Utopia*, pp. 252-55.

[12] Letter to Ammonius, *Eras. Ep.*, II, 149; *Epistolae obscurorum virorum*, translated by F. G. Stokes (London, 1909), I, 358; Brewer, *Henry VIII*, I, 101-09.

[13] *Utopia*, pp. 48-51; *LP*, II, Part I, No. 1067, p. 282, No. 1991, p. 580; *Calendar of Letters . . . between England and Spain*, II, Nos. 68, 86, pp. 68-69, 94; Machiavelli, *The Prince and Other Works*, translated by A. H. Gilbert (Chicago, [1941]), pp. 131-38, 236-39.

[14] Ernest Gilliat-Smith, *The Story of Bruges* (London, 1901), pp. 256-305; Adolphus W. Ward and others, editors, *The Cambridge Modern History* (New York, 1902-1912), I, 453; Allen, *Age of Erasmus*, pp. 169-75.

[15] Erasmus, *Adagia*, No. 514 *(In Care periculum)*, col. 253; No. 1523 *(Bellum haudquaquam lachrymosum)*, cols. 660-61; No. 3001 *(Dulce bellum inexpertis)*, col. 1073; No. 3225 *(Mores hominum regioni respondent)*, col. 1128; "Querela pacis," *Opera*, IV, 641, translated by Paynell, *Complaint of Peace*, p. 52. For a plea (April 4, 1516) of the Swiss captains in the emperor's service to those in the service of the French "to abandon their enterprise and return, otherwise they will have to fight their own countrymen," see *LP*, II, Part I, No. 1737, pp. 490-91.

[16] Erasmus, *Colloquies*, p. 139; Vitoria, "De bello," translated in Scott, *Spanish Origin*, p. cxix.

[17] Suárez, "De caritate," *Opera*, XII, 750-51; Silvester, *Summa*, fol. 51ᵛ.

[18] *Utopia*, pp. 243, 257-58 (note); "Passion," translated by Bassett, *Works*, p. 1356; Plato, *Republic*, I, 165-67, 485; Plutarch, "Lycurgus," *Lives*, I, 215-17; *LP*, II, Part I, No. 482, p. 138.

[19] *Utopia*, pp. 238-42, 263.

[20] Skelton, "Speak, Parrot," *Complete Poems*, pp. 279-80; Elyot, *Gouernour*, II, 251, 260-61; Dudley, *Commonwealth*, pp. 26-27.

[21] *Utopia*, pp. 238-39; Erasmus, *Education of Christian Prince*, pp. 238-39; Machiavelli, *Prince*, p. 149. For a more or less contemporary treatment, an edition of which was printed in 1511, of the liceity, circumstances, and so forth, of alliances, see Joannes Lupus, "Tractatus dialogicus de confederatione principum et potestatum," in *De libertate ecclesiastica, etc.*, foll. 36ʳ-70ʳ.

[22] *Utopia*, p. 259; Plutarch, "Lycurgus," *Lives*, I, 277.

[23] *Utopia*, p. 263; Plato, *Republic*, I, 499-501; Clichtoveus, *De bello et pace*, fol. 20ᵛ. According to Deuteronomy, Chapters 20-21, if a city surrenders peacefully, its inhabitants are to be left unharmed and are merely to pay tribute; if the city is taken by assault, all males are to be put to the sword, presumably as combatants, and all women and children to be made captives. See Paterson, "War," Hastings' *Encyclopedia of Religion and Ethics*, XII, 684.

[24] More to Wolsey, *Correspondence*, p. 294; Silvester, *Summa*, fol. 51ᵛ; Vitoria, "De bello," translated in Scott, *Spanish Origin*, pp. lxii-iv, lxx, cxx, cxxiv; Suárez, "De caritate," *Opera*, XII, 753; Ortolan, "Guerre," *DTC*, VI, 1929.

[25] *Utopia*, pp. 263-64.

[26] Vitoria, "De jure belli," translated in Scott, *Spanish Origin*, pp. lv-vi, lxv-vii, lxix, cxiii; Suárez, "De caritate," *Opera*, XII, 745, 753-54, 757.

Chapter XIX

[1] *Utopia*, pp. 307-08.

LIST OF PRINCIPAL ABBREVIATIONS AND SHORT TITLES

CE: The Catholic Encyclopedia: An International Work of Reference
on the Constitution, Doctrine, Discipline, and History of the Catholic Church, edited by Charles G. Herbermann and others.

DACL: Dictionnaire d'archéologie chrétienne et de liturgie, edited by
Fernand C. Cabrol and others.

DAFC: Dictionnaire apologétique de la foi catholique, edited by
Adhémar D'Alès and others.

DTC: Dictionnaire de théologie catholique, contenant l'exposé des
doctrines de la théologie catholique, leurs preuves, et leur histoire,
edited by Alfred Vacant and others.

Eras. Ep.: Opus epistolarum Des. Erasmi Roterodami, edited by Percy
S. Allen and others.

LP: Letters and Papers, Foreign and Domestic, of the Reign of Henry
VIII, edited by John S. Brewer and others.

PG: Patrologiae cursus completus: series Graeca, edited by Jacques P.
Migne.

PL: Patrologiae cursus completus: series Latina, edited by Jacques P.
Migne.

RE: Pauly's Real-Encyclopädie der classischen Altertumswissenschaft,
edited by August F. von Pauly and others. A-P.

REA: Continuation of the above. R-Z.

Utopia: The "Utopia" of Sir Thomas More, in Latin from the Edition
of March 1518, and in English from the First Edition of Ralph
Robynson's Translation in 1551, edited by Joseph H. Lupton.

Works: The Workes of Sir Thomas More Knyght . . . Wrytten by Him
in the Englysh Tonge, edited by William Rastell.

1. Works before A.D. 1600

Aeneas Silvius or Sylvius [Piccolomini]. *See* Pius II, Pope.

Agrippa, Henricus Cornelius, von Nettesheim. *De occulta philosophia libri tres.* Coloniae, 1533.

Alexander Anglus. *Summa que destructorium viciorum appellatur.* Nuremberge, 1496.

Allen, Percy S., and others, editors. *Opus epistolarum Des. Erasmi Roterodami.* 11 vols. Oxford, 1906-1947. Cited as *Eras. Ep.*

Angelus Carletus de Clavasio. *Summa angelica de casibus conscientiae.* Lugduni, 1512.

Anghiera, Pietro Martire d'. *De orbe novo: The Eight Decades of Peter Martyr D'Anghera* [*sic*], translated by Francis A. MacNutt. 2 vols. New York, 1912.

Ante-Nicene Christian Library. See Roberts, Alexander, and James Donaldson, editors.

Antoninus, St. *Summa sacrae theologiae, iuris pontificii et caesarei.* 4 vols. Venetiis, 1581-1582.

Arber, Edward, editor. *The First Three English Books on America,* [*?1511*]-*1555 A.D., Being Chiefly Translations, Compilations, &c., of Pietro Martire of Anghiera, . . . Sebastian Münster, the Cosmographer, . . . Sebastian Cabot, of Bristol.* Birmingham, England, 1885.

Archivo general de Simancas. Legajo 806, años 1480-1549.

———— P.R., MSS. 21-26.

Aristotle. *Politics,* translated by Harris Rackham. Cambridge, Massachusetts, 1950.

———— *The Politics of Aristotle,* revised edition, translated by Ernest Barker. Oxford, 1948.

Aristotle. *The Politics of Aristotle,* edited by William L. Newman. 4 vols. Oxford, 1887.

———— *The Works of Aristotle Translated into English,* edited by William D. Ross. 12 vols. Oxford, 1908-1952.

Auerbach, Heinrich Stromer. *See* Stromer, Heinrich.

Barclay, Alexander. *The Eclogues,* edited by Beatrice White. London, 1928.

————, translator. *The Ship of Fools,* edited by T. H. Jamieson. 2 vols. Edinburgh, 1874.

Bayne, Ronald, editor. *See Life of Fisher, The.*

Beatus Rhenanus [= Beat Bild of Rheinau]. *Veterum aliquot de arte rhetorica traditiones.* Basileae, 1521.

Bergenroth, Gustav A., and others, editors. *Calendar of Letters, Despatches, and State Papers, Relating to the Negotiations between England and Spain, Preserved in the Archives at Simancas and Elsewhere [1485-1553].* 13 vols. London, 1862-1954.

Bibliothèque Nationale. Lat. MS. 1523.

Brant, Sebastian. *Stultifera nauis . . . per Iacobum Locher . . . in Latinū traducta eloquiū . . .* Basileae, 1497.

———— *See* Barclay, Alexander, translator.

Brewer, John S., and others, editors. *Letters and Papers, Foreign and Domestic, of the Reign of Henry VIII.* 21 vols. London, 1862-1932. Cited as *LP.*

British Museum. Arundel MS. 68. Contains "Articuli defectuum detectorum in visitacione facta nono die Septembris anno [1511], per . . . Warham archiepiscopum" (fol. 69) and "Reformationes facte tempore eiusdem visitationis" (fol. 70).

Budé, Guillaume. *Annotationes . . . in quatuor et viginti Pandectarum libros.* Parisiis, 1542.

———— *Libri V de asse et partibus eius.* Venetiis, 1522.

Bullarum, privilegiorum, ac diplomatum Romanorum pontificum amplissima collectio. 14 vols. Romae, 1733-1762. Cited as *Bullarium Romanum.*

Calendar of Letters, Despatches, and State Papers . . . between England and Spain. See Bergenroth, Gustav A., and others, editors.

Chrysostom, John, St. Περὶ ἱερωσύνης *(De sacerdotio),* edited by J. Arbuthnot Nairn. Cambridge, England, 1906.

Cicero, Marcus Tullius. *De officiis,* translated by Walter Miller. London, 1921.

Clichtoveus, Jodocus. *De bello et pace opusculum, Christianos principes ad sedandos bellorum tumultus et pacem componendam exhortans.* Parisiis, 1523.

Cloud of Unknowing, The. See Hodgson, Phyllis, editor.

Colet, John. *Enarratio in epistolam S. Pauli ad Romanos: An Exposition of St. Paul's Epistle to the Romans,* edited by Joseph H. Lupton. London, 1873.

———— *Enarratio in primam epistolam S. Pauli ad Corinthios: An Exposition of St. Paul's First Epistle to the Corinthians,* edited by Joseph H. Lupton. London, 1874.

———— *Opuscula quaedam theologica: Letters to Radulphus on the Mosaic Account of the Creation, Together with Other Treatises,* edited by Joseph H. Lupton. London, 1876.

———— *Super opera Dionysii: Two Treatises on the Hierarchies of Dionysius,* edited by Joseph H. Lupton. London, 1869.

Coppus, Gregorius, Calvus. *See* Stromer, Heinrich.

Damianus, Ianus. *De expeditione in Turcas elegeia, etc.* Basileae, 1515.

De Vocht, Henry, editor. *Acta Thomae Mori: History of the Reports of His Trial and Death from an Unedited Contemporary Narrative.* Louvain, 1947.

Denzinger, Henricus. *Enchiridion symbolorum, definitionum, et declarationum de rebus fidei et morum,* twenty-third edition, edited by Clemens Bannwart and Ioannes Bapt. Umberg. Friburgi Brisgoviae, 1937.

Diogenes Laertius. *Lives of Eminent Philosophers,* translated by Robert D. Hicks. 2 vols. London, 1925.

Dominici, Johannes. *Lucula noctis,* edited by Edmund Hunt. Notre Dame, Indiana, 1940.

Donaldson, James, and Alexander Roberts, editors. *Ante-Nicene Christian Library: Translations of the Writings of the Fathers Down to A.D. 325.* 25 vols. Edinburgh, 1882-1903.

Dudley, Edmund. *The Tree of Commonwealth,* edited by Dorothy M. Brodie. Cambridge, England, 1948.

Duns Scotus, Joannes. *Opera omnia.* 26 vols. Parisiis, 1891-1895.

Elyot, Thomas. *The Boke Named the Gouernour*, edited by Henry H. S. Croft. 2 vols. London, 1880.

Epistolae aliquot eruditorum uirorum, ex quibus perspicuum quãta sit Eduardi Lei uirulentia. Basileae, 1520.

Epistolae obscurorum virorum. See Stokes, Francis G., translator.

Erasmus, Desiderius. *Adagiorum opus.* Lugduni, 1541.

—————— *The Complaint of Peace*, translated by Thomas Paynell and edited by W. J. Hirten. New York, 1946.

—————— *De duplici copia verborum ac rerum commentarii duo.* Lugduni, 1543.

—————— *The Education of a Christian Prince*, translated by Lester K. Born. New York, 1936.

—————— *The Epistles of Erasmus from His Earliest Letters to His Fifty-First Year Arranged in Order of Time*, translated by Francis M. Nichols. 3 vols. London, 1901-1918.

—————— *Inquisitio de fide: A Colloquy by Desiderius Erasmus Roterodamus, 1524*, edited by Craig R. Thompson. New Haven, 1950.

—————— *Liber utilissimus de conscribendis epistolis.* Amstelodami, 1670.

—————— *The Lives of Jehan Vitrier, Warden of the Franciscan Convent at St. Omer, and John Colet, Dean of St. Paul's, London*, translated by Joseph H. Lupton. London, 1883.

—————— *Novum instrumentum omne.* Basileae, 1516.

—————— *Opera omnia . . . studio et opera Joannis Clerici.* 10 vols. Lugduni Batavorum, 1703-1706.

—————— *Opus epistolarum.* See Allen, Percy S., and others, editors.

—————— *Opuscula: A Supplement to the Opera Omnia*, edited by Wallace K. Ferguson. The Hague, 1933.

—————— *The Praise of Folly*, translated by Hoyt H. Hudson. Princeton, 1941.

—————— *The Whole Familiar Colloquies*, translated by Nathan Bailey. London, 1877.

—————— , editor. *See* Jerome, St.

Eusebius Pamphili Caesariensis. *Hystoria ecclesiastica.* Parisiis, [1505?].

Fabyan, Robert. *The New Chronicles of England and France*, edited by Henry Ellis. London, 1811.

Ficino, Marsilio. *Opera . . . omnia.* 2 vols. Basileae, 1576.

Ficino, Marsilio. *Supplementum Ficinianum: opuscula inedita et dispersa*, edited by Paul O. Kristeller. 2 vols. Florentiae, 1937.

Fisher, John, St. *Assertionis Lutheranae confutatio*. Coloniae, 1525.

────── *Confutatio secundae disceptationis per Jacobum Fabrum Stapulensem habite*. Parisiis, 1519.

────── *Convvlsio* [*sic*] *calvmniarum Vlrichi Veleni Minhoniensis quibus Petrum nunquam Romae fuisse cauillatur . . . Petrus fuit Romae*. Parisiis, [1522?].

────── *De ueritate corporis et sanguinis Christi in eucharistia*. [Coloniae], 1527.

────── *Defensio regie assertionis contra Babylonicam captiuitatem.* Coloniae, 1525.

────── *The English Works of John Fisher, Bishop of Rochester*, edited by John E. B. Mayor. Part I. London, 1876.

────── *Sacri sacerdotii defensio contra Lutherum (1525)*, edited by Hermann K. Schmeink. Münster, 1925.

Geiler, Johannes, von Kaisersberg. *Nauicula penitentie*. Argentorati, 1512.

────── *Nauicula siue speculū fatuorum*. Argentorati, 1511.

Geldenhauer, Gerardus, Noviomagus. *Collectanea*, edited by Jacob Prinsen. Amsterdam, 1901.

Hadrian VI, Pope [= Hadrianus Florentinus de Traiecto]. *Questiones quotlibetice*. Lovanii, 1515.

Harpsfield, Nicholas. *The Life and Death of Sr Thomas Moore, Knight*, edited by Elsie V. Hitchcock. London, 1932.

Heywood, Ellis. *Il Moro, d'Heliseo Heivodo Inglese*. Fiorenza, 1556.

Hilton, Walter. *Minor Works*, edited by Dorothy Jones. New York, 1929.

────── *The Scale (or Ladder) of Perfection*, new edition, edited by John B. Dalgairns. London, 1901.

Hodgson, Phyllis, editor. *The Cloud of Unknowing, and the Book of Privy Counselling*. London, 1944.

Holinshed, Raphael. *The Chronicles of England, Scotland, and Ireland*. 3 vols. in 2. London, 1587.

Horace [Quintus Horatius Flaccus]. *Horace's Art of Poetry*, made English by the Right Honorable Earl of Roscommon [Wentworth Dillon, Fourth Earl]. London, 1680.

Imitation of Christ. See Thomas Kempis (reputed author).

Jerome, St. *Opera omnia . . . cum argumentis et scholiis Des. Erasmi.* 9 vols. Basileae, 1516.

Keating, Joseph, and Cuthbert Lattey, editors. *Westminster Version of the Sacred Scriptures.* London, 1913—.

Keilwey, Robert. *Relationes quorundam casuum selectorum ex libris Roberti Keilvvey.* Londini, 1602.

Lattey, Cuthbert, and Joseph Keating, editors. *Westminster Version of the Sacred Scriptures.* London, 1913—.

Lee, Edward. *Exhibita quaedam . . . in consilio caesareo ante belli indictionem; responsio cordatissima nomine caesareae maiestatis ad eadem.* [Antwerp], 1528.

——— *Sunt in hoc volumine: Apologia . . . contra quorundam calumnias. . . . Annotationū libri duo, alter in annotatiões prioris aeditionis noui testamenti Desiderij Erasmi, alter in annotatiões posterioris aeditiõis eiusdē. Epistola apologetica . . . qua respondet duabus Desiderij Erasmi epistolis.* Parisiis, [1519-1520?].

Letters and Papers . . . of the Reign of Henry VIII. See Brewer, John S., and others, editors.

Life of Fisher, The. Transcribed from MS. Harleian 6382 by Ronald Bayne. London, 1921.

Locher, Iacobus, translator. *See* Brant, Sebastian, *Stultifera nauis.*

Lucretius Carus, Titus. *De rerum natura,* translated by William H. D. Rouse. London, 1931.

Lupset, Thomas. *See* Gee, John A., *The Life and Works of Thomas Lupset,* in Part 2 below.

Lupton, Joseph H., editor. *The "Utopia" of Sir Thomas More, in Latin from the Edition of March 1518, and in English from the First Edition of Ralph Robynson's Translation in 1551.* Oxford, 1895. Cited as *Utopia.*

———, translator. *See* Erasmus, Desiderius, *The Lives of Jehan Vitrier . . . and John Colet.*

Lupus, Johannes [= Juan López]. *De libertate ecclesiastica tractatus . . . Tractatus dialogicus de confederatione principum et potentatum.* Argentinae, 1511.

Machiavelli, Niccolò. *The Prince and Other Works,* translated by Allan H. Gilbert. Chicago, [1941].

Mansi, Joannes Dominicus, and others, editors. *Sacrorum conciliorum nova et amplissima collectio,* second edition. 60 vols. Paris, 1899-1927.

Mantuanus, Baptista [= Joannes Baptista Spagnola or Spagnuoli]. *De patientia libri tres, de vita beata dialogus, etc.* Argentorati, 1510.

—— *Fastorum libri duodecim.* Argentorati, 1518.

—— *Vita Dionysij Areopagitae libri tres. Obiurgatio cum exhortatione cõtra ĩfideles ad potentatus Christianos liber unus.* Mediolani, 1521. Contains other works.

Migne, Jacques P., editor. *Patrologiae cursus completus: series Graeca.* 104 vols. Paris, 1857-1860. Cited as *PG*.

——, editor. *Patrologiae cursus completus: series Latina.* 221 vols. Paris, 1844-1880. Cited as *PL*.

More, Thomas, St. *The Apologye of Syr Thomas More, Knyght,* edited by Arthur I. Taft. London, 1930.

—— *The Correspondence of Sir Thomas More,* edited by Elizabeth Frances Rogers. Princeton, 1947.

—— *A Dialogue of Comfort.* In *Utopia and A Dialogue of Comfort,* revised edition. London, 1951.

—— *The Latin Epigrams of Thomas More,* edited by Leicester Bradner and Charles A. Lynch. Chicago, 1953.

—— *Omnia quae hucusque ad manus nostras peruenerunt Latina opera.* Lovanii, 1565.

—— *Thomas Morus: Utopia,* edited by Victor Michels and Theobald Ziegler. Berlin, 1895.

—— *Utopia. See* Lupton, Joseph H., editor.

—— *Utopia,* translated by Gerhard Ritter, with an introduction by Hermann Oncken. Berlin, 1922.

—— *Works. See* Rastell, William, editor.

Netter, Thomas. *Antiquitatum fidei catholicae ecclesiae doctrinale,* edited by Bonaventura Blanciotti. 3 vols. Venetiis, 1757-1759.

Nicholas of Lyra. *Biblia Latina cum postillis Nicolai de Lyra.* 4 vols. Venetiis, 1489.

Nichols, Francis M., translator. *See* Erasmus, Desiderius, *The Epistles.*

Noviomagus, Gerardus. *See* Geldenhauer, Gerardus, Noviomagus.

Pace, Richard. *De fructu qui ex doctrina percipitur liber*. Basileae, 1517.

Paynell, Thomas, translator. *See* Erasmus, Desiderius, *The Complaint of Peace*.

Paz, Matías de. "De dominio regum Hispaniae super Indos," edited by Vicente Beltrán de Heredia, *Archivum Fratrum Praedicatorum*, III (1933), 133-81.

Pecock, Reginald. *Book of Faith*, edited by J. L. Morison. Glasgow, 1909.

———— *The Donet*, edited by Elsie V. Hitchcock. London, 1921.

———— *The Folewer to the Donet*, edited by Elsie V. Hitchcock. London, 1924.

———— *The Repressor of Over Much Blaming of the Clergy*, edited by Churchill Babington. 2 vols. London, 1860.

———— *The Reule of Crysten Religioun*, edited by William C. Greet. London, 1927.

Peter Martyr. *See* Anghiera, Pietro Martire d'.

Piccolomini, Enea Silvio de. *See* Pius II, Pope.

Pico della Mirandola, Giovanni. *Ioannis Pici . . . [et] Ioannis Francisci Pici . . . Opera quae extant omnia*. 2 vols. Basileae, [1601].

Pius II, Pope. *Aeneas Sylvius Piccolominei Senensis . . . opera quae extant omnia*. Basileae, 1571.

Plato. *Euthyphro, Apology, Crito, Phaedo, Phaedrus*, translated by Harold N. Fowler. London, 1926.

———— *Laws*, translated by Robert G. Bury. 2 vols. London, 1926.

———— *The Republic*, translated by Paul Shorey. 2 vols. London, 1930-1935.

———— *The Statesman and Philebus*, translated by Harold N. Fowler; *Ion*, translated by Walter R. M. Lamb. London, 1925.

———— *Timaeus, Critias, Cleitophon, Menexenus, Epistles*, translated by Robert G. Bury. London, 1929.

Plutarch. *Lives*, translated by Bernadotte Perrin. 11 vols. London, 1914-1926.

———— *Opera omnia*, edited by Gulielmus Xylander. 2 vols. Frankfurt-am-Main, 1599.

Pontanus, Ioannes Iovianus. *Opera omnia soluta oratione composita*. 3 vols. Venetiis, 1518-1519.

Rastell, William, editor. *The Workes of Sir Thomas More Knyght . . . Wrytten by Him in the Englysh Tonge.* London, 1557. Cited as *Works.*

Reisch, Gregorius. *Margarita philosophica.* Argentorati, 1504.

Relation of the Island of England about 1500, A. See Sneyd, Charlotte A., translator.

Roberts, Alexander, and James Donaldson, editors. *Ante-Nicene Christian Library: Translations of the Writings of the Fathers Down to A.D. 325.* 25 vols. Edinburgh, 1882-1903.

Roper, William. *The Lyfe of Sir Thomas Moore, Knighte,* edited by Elsie V. Hitchcock. London, 1935.

Sabunde, Raymond of. *Theologia naturalis sive liber creaturarum.* Lugduni, 1541.

———— *Viola anime per modum dyalogi inter Raymundum Sebundium . . . et dominum Dominicum seminiuerbium.* Coloniae, 1501.

Schaff, Philip, and Henry Wace, editors. *A Select Library of the Nicene and Post-Nicene Fathers of the Christian Church,* second series. 14 vols. New York, 1890-1900.

Schroeder, Henry J., translator. *Canons and Decrees of the Council of Trent.* St. Louis, 1941.

————, translator. *Disciplinary Decrees of the General Councils.* St. Louis, 1937.

Seneca, Lucius Annaeus. *Ad Lucilium epistulae morales,* translated by Richard M. Gummere. 3 vols. London, 1917-1920.

Sidney, Philip. *The Defense of Poesy,* edited by Albert S. Cook. Boston, 1890.

Silvester de Prierio [= Silvestro Mazzolini]. *Summa summarū que Siluestrina dicitur.* Bononie, 1514.

Skelton, John. *The Complete Poems of John Skelton, Laureate,* edited by Philip Henderson. London, 1931.

Sneyd, Charlotte A., translator. *A Relation, or Rather a True Account, of the Island of England . . . about the Year 1500.* London, 1847.

Society of Jesus. *Summary of the Constitutions, Common Rules, Rules of Modesty, and an Epistle on Obedience.* Roehampton, 1926.

Soto, Dominicus. *In quartum sententiarum commentarii.* Venetiis, 1569.

Speculum sacerdotale, edited from British Museum MS. Additional 36791 by Edward H. Weatherly. London, 1936.

Stapleton, Thomas. *The Life and Illustrious Martyrdom of Sir Thomas More (Part III of "Tres Thomae," Printed at Douai, 1588.)*, translated by Philip E. Hallett. London, 1928.

Starkey, Thomas. *A Dialogue between Cardinal Pole and Thomas Lupset*, edited by Joseph M. Cowper. London, 1871.

Stokes, Francis G., translator. *Epistolae obscurorum virorum: The Latin Text with an English Rendering*. 2 vols. London, 1909.

Strabo. *Geography*, translated by Horace L. Jones. 8 vols. London, 1917-1932.

Stromer, Heinrich. *Duae epistole Hērici Stromeri Auerbachij et Gregorij Coppi Calui medicorū que statū reipublicae Christianae hoc seculo degenerātis attigūt*. Lipsiae, 1520. Epigrams against Edward Lee at end of book.

Suárez, Franciscus. *Opera omnia*. 28 vols. Parisiis, 1856-1878.

Tacitus, Cornelius. *Histories and Annals*, translated by Clifford H. Moore and John Jackson. 4 vols. London, 1925-1937.

Theiner, Augustinus, editor. *Acta genuina concilii Tridentini*. 2 vols. Zagrabiae, n. d.

Thomas Kempis (reputed author). *Of the Imitation of Christ Four Books*, revised translation. London, 1926.

Trovamala, Baptista. *Liber qui rosella casuum appellatur*. Venetiis, 1495.

Tunstall, Cuthbert. *In laudem matrimonii oratio*. Londini, 1518.

Vergilius, Polydorus. *The Anglica Historia of Polydore Vergil, A.D. 1485-1537*, edited by Denys Hay. London, 1950.

——— *Anglicae historiae libri vigintisex*. Gandavi, [1556-1557].

——— *De rerum inventoribus libri octo*. Argentorati, 1606.

Vespucci, Amerigo. *The Four Voyages*, translated by Mario E. Cosenza. In *The Cosmographiae Introductio of Martin Waldseemüller in Facsimile, Followed by the Four Voyages of Amerigo Vespucci, with Their Translation into English*, edited by Charles G. Herbermann. New York, 1907.

——— *Mundus novus: Letter to Lorenzo Pietro di Medici*, translated by George T. Northup. Princeton, 1916.

Vitoria, Francisco de. For translations of "De Indis" and other works, see the Appendices in Scott, James B., *Spanish Origin*, in Part 2 below.

Voecht, Jacobus Traiecti, known as de. *Narratio de inchoatione domus clericorum in Zwollis*, edited by M. Schoengen. Amsterdam, 1908.

Wace, Henry, and Philip Schaff, editors. *A Select Library of the Nicene and Post-Nicene Fathers of the Christian Church*, second series. 14 vols. New York, 1890-1900.

Waldensis, Thomas. *See* Netter, Thomas.

Westminster Version of the Sacred Scriptures. See Lattey, Cuthbert, and Joseph Keating, editors.

Wilkins, David, editor. *Concilia Magnae Britanniae et Hiberniae.* 4 vols. London, 1737.

Wimpheling, Jakob. *Adolescentia.* Argentinae, 1515.

2. Works since A.D. 1600

Adams, Robert P. *The Philosophic Unity of More's "Utopia."* Chapel Hill, 1941. Reprinted from *Studies in Philology*, XXXVIII (1941), 45-65.

Allen, Percy S. *The Age of Erasmus.* Oxford, 1914.

——— *Erasmus: Lectures and Wayfaring Sketches.* Oxford, 1934.

Ames, Russell A. *Citizen Thomas More and His Utopia.* Princeton, 1949.

Andreae, Johann Valentin. *Christianopolis: An Ideal State of the Seventeenth Century*, translated by Felix Emil Held. New York, 1916.

Appelt, Theodore C. *Studies in the Contents and Sources of Erasmus' "Adagia."* Chicago, 1942.

Arregui, Antonius M. *Summarium theologiae moralis*, thirteenth edition. Romae, 1937.

Aubenas, Roger, and Robert Ricard. *L'église et la Renaissance (1449-1517).* Paris, 1951. Vol. XV in Augustin Fliche and Victor Martin, editors, *Histoire de l'église* (Paris, 1934—).

Baron, Hans. "Der Humanismus und die thomistische Lehre von den gentiles salvati," *Archiv für Reformationsgeschichte*, XLIII (1952), 254-63.

Baumstark, Reinhold. *Thomas Morus.* Freiburg im Breisgau, 1879.

Bendemann, Oswald. *Studie zur Staats- und Sozialauffassung des Thomas Morus.* Charlottenburg, 1928.

Benoist, A. *Quid de puerorum institutione senserit Erasmus.* Parisiis, 1876.

Blackstone, William. *Commentaries on the Laws of England*, fifth edition. 4 vols. Oxford, 1773.

Bossuet, Jacques Bénigne. *Histoire des variations des églises protestantes*. 2 vols. Paris, 1688.

———— *History of the Variations of the Protestant Churches*, translated anonymously. 2 vols. New York, [1845].

[Boutrais, Cyprien Marie]. *The History of the Great Chartreuse*, by a Carthusian Monk, translated by E. Hassid. London, 1933.

Bremond, Henri. *Sir Thomas More (The Blessed Thomas More)*, translated by Harold Child. London, 1904.

Brewer, John S. *The Reign of Henry VIII from His Accession to the Death of Wolsey*. 2 vols. London, 1884.

Burnet, Gilbert. *The History of the Reformation of the Church of England*, edited by Nicholas Pocock. 4 vols. Oxford, 1865.

Cabrol, Fernand C., and others, editors. *Dictionnaire d'archéologie chrétienne et de liturgie*. 15 vols. Paris, 1907-1953. Cited as *DACL*.

Campbell, William E. *More's Utopia and His Social Teaching*. London, 1930.

Canonizationis beatorum martyrum Iohannis Card. Fisher . . . et Thomae Mori . . . informatio. Typis Vaticanis, 1944.

Capéran, Louis. *Le problème du salut des infidèles*. 2 vols. Toulouse, 1934.

Cartellieri, Otto. *The Court of Burgundy*, translated by Malcolm Letts. London, 1929.

Cary, Max. *History of Rome Down to the Reign of Constantine*, revised edition, edited by Russell Meiggs. London, 1951.

Chambers, Raymond W. *Thomas More*. London, 1935.

Constant, Gustave L. J. *The Reformation in England. I. The English Schism, Henry VIII (1509-1547)*, translated by R. E. Scantlebury. New York, 1934.

Copleston, Frederick. *A History of Philosophy*. 3 vols. to date. London, 1946—.

D'Alès, Adhémar, and others, editors. *Dictionnaire apologétique de la foi catholique*. 4 vols. Paris, 1925-1928. Cited as *DAFC*.

Dávila, Iulius. *Introductio ad philosophiam, et logica*. Mexici, 1945.

De Raeymaeker, Louis. *Introduction to Philosophy*, translated by Harry McNeill. New York, 1948.

Dermenghem, Emile. *Thomas Morus et les utopistes de la Renaissance.* Paris, 1927.

Dieckmann, Hermannus. *De revelatione Christiana.* Friburgi Brisgoviae, 1930.

Donner, Henry W. *Introduction to Utopia.* London, 1945.

Fame of Blessed Thomas More, The, Being Addresses Delivered in His Honour at Chelsea, July 1929. Introductory essay by Raymond W. Chambers. London, 1929.

Fliche, Augustin, and Victor Martin, editors. *Histoire de l'église.* 21 vols. to date. Paris, 1934—.

Gairdner, James. *Lollardy and the Reformation in England: An Historical Survey.* 4 vols. London, 1908.

Gasquet, Francis Aidan. *Cardinal Pole and His Early Friends.* London, 1927.

—————— *The Eve of the Reformation: Studies in the Religious Life and Thought of the English People in the Period Preceding the Rejection of the Roman Jurisdiction by Henry VIII.* London, 1913.

Gee, John A. *The Life and Works of Thomas Lupset, with a Critical Text of the Original Treatises and the Letters.* New Haven, 1928.

Geldner, Ferdinand. *Die Staatsauffassung und Fürstenlehre des Erasmus von Rotterdam.* Berlin, 1930.

Gilliat-Smith, Ernest. *The Story of Bruges.* London, 1901.

Gilmore, Myron P. *The World of Humanism: 1453-1517.* New York, 1952.

Gilson, Etienne. *La philosophie au moyen âge des origines patristiques à la fin du quatorzième siècle,* second edition. Paris, 1947.

—————— *Reason and Revelation in the Middle Ages.* New York, 1938.

Harris, Charles R. S. *Duns Scotus.* 2 vols. Oxford, 1927.

Healy, Edwin F. *Moral Guidance.* Chicago, 1942.

Hefele, Charles-Joseph [= Karl Joseph von], and others. *Histoire des conciles d'après les documents originaux,* translated and edited by H. Leclercq. 11 vols. Paris, 1907-1952.

Hendriks, Lawrence. *The London Charterhouse: Its Monks and Its Martyrs.* London, 1889.

Herbermann, Charles G., and others, editors. *The Catholic Encyclopedia: An International Work of Reference on the Constitution, Doctrine, Discipline, and History of the Catholic Church.* 17 vols. New York, 1907-1922. Cited as *CE.*

Heredia, Vicente Beltrán de. "El padre Matías de Paz, O.P., y su tratado 'De dominio regum Hispaniae super Indos,'" *La Ciencia Tomista*, XL (1929), 173-90.

Hervé, Jean M. *Manuale theologiae dogmaticae*, eighteenth edition. 4 vols. Parisiis, 1939.

Hexter, Jack H. *More's "Utopia": The Biography of an Idea*. Princeton, 1952.

History of the Great Chartreuse, The. See [Boutrais, Cyprien Marie].

Hollis, Christopher. *Thomas More*. Milwaukee, 1934.

Hughes, Philip. *A History of the Church: An Introductory Study*. 3 vols. New York, 1934-1947.

Huizinga, Johan. *Erasmus*, translated by Frederick Hopman. New York, 1924.

Hyma, Albert. *The Brethren of the Common Life*. Grand Rapids, 1950.

——— *The Christian Renaissance: A History of the "Devotio Moderna."* New York, 1925.

Janet, Paul. *Histoire de la science politique dans ses rapports avec la morale*, fourth edition. 2 vols. Paris, 1913.

Jedin, Hubert. *Geschichte des Konzils von Trient*, second edition. 4 vols. to date. Freiburg, 1951—.

Jungmann, Joseph A. *The Mass of the Roman Rite: Its Origins and Development (Missarum sollemnia)*, translated by Francis A. Brunner. 2 vols. New York, 1951-1955.

Kautsky, Karl. *Thomas More and His Utopia*, translated by Henry J. Stenning. London, 1927.

Knight, Samuel. *The Life of Dr. John Colet . . . with an Appendix Containing . . . Several Original Papers Relating to the Said Life*. London, 1724.

Knox, Ronald A. *Enthusiasm: A Chapter in the History of Religion*. New York, 1950.

——— *Miracles*. London, 1950.

Kristeller, Paul O. *The Philosophy of Marsilio Ficino*, translated by Virginia Conant. New York, 1943.

Leadam, Isaac S. "The Inquisition of 1517, Inclosures and Evictions, Edited from the Lansdowne MS. I. 153," *Transactions of the Royal Historical Society*, New Series, VI (1892), 167-314; VII (1893), 127-292; VIII (1894), 251-331; XIV (1900), 267-86.

Lovejoy, Arthur O. *The Great Chain of Being.* Cambridge, Massachusetts, 1936.

Lupton, Joseph H. *A Life of John Colet . . . with an Appendix of Some of His English Writings.* London, 1887.

Mackie, John D. *The Earlier Tudors: 1485-1558.* Oxford, 1952.

Mackintosh, James. *Miscellaneous Works,* new edition. 3 vols. London, 1854.

McMahon, Clara P. *Education in Fifteenth-Century England.* Baltimore, 1947.

Marsden, John H. *Philomorus: Notes on the Latin Poems of Sir Thomas More,* second edition. London, 1878.

Martin, Victor, and Augustin Fliche, editors. *Histoire de l'église.* 21 vols. to date. Paris, 1934—.

Mestwerdt, Paul. *Die Anfänge des Erasmus: Humanismus und "Devotio Moderna."* Leipzig, 1917.

Michelet, Jules. *Histoire de France jusqu'au seizième siècle.* 17 vols. Paris, 1852-1867.

Minges, Parthenius. *Das Verhältnis zwischen Glauben und Wissen, Theologie und Philosophie nach Duns Scotus.* Paderborn, 1908.

———— *Ioannis Duns Scoti doctrina philosophica et theologica.* 2 vols. Ad Claras Aquas, 1930.

Morgan, Arthur E. *Nowhere Was Somewhere: How History Makes Utopias and How Utopias Make History.* Chapel Hill, 1946.

Noldin, Hieronymus, and Albertus Schmitt. *Summa theologiae moralis,* twenty-seventh edition. 3 vols. Oeniponte, 1940.

Noonan, John P. *General and Special Ethics.* Chicago, 1947.

Palmieri, Dominicus. *Tractatus de matrimonio Christiano.* Romae, 1880.

Pauly, August F. von, and others, editors. *Pauly's Real-Encyclopädie der classischen Altertumswissenschaft,* neue Bearbeitung, begonnen von Georg Wissowa, . . . herausgegeben von Wilhelm Kroll. 22 vols. [A-P]. Stuttgart, 1894—. Cited as *RE.*

———— *Pauly's Real-Encyclopädie der classischen Altertumswissenschaft,* zweite Reihe. 8 vols. [R-Z]. Stuttgart, 1914—. Cited as *REA.*

Pegis, Anton C. *St. Thomas and the Greeks.* Milwaukee, 1939.

Pineau, J.-B. *Erasme: sa pensée religieuse.* Paris, 1924.

Pollard, Alfred F. *Henry VIII.* London, 1930.

Pourrat, Pierre. *Christian Spirituality in the Middle Ages*, translated by S. P. Jacques. London, 1924.

Remer, Vincentius. *Summa philosophiae scholasticae*, fifth edition. 3 vols. Romae, 1925.

Renaudet, Augustin. *Erasme et l'Italie*. Genève, 1954.

Ricard, Robert, and Roger Aubenas. *L'église et la Renaissance (1449-1517)*. Paris, 1951. Vol. XV in Augustin Fliche and Victor Martin, editors, *Histoire de l'église* (Paris, 1934—).

Rickaby, Joseph. *St. Augustine's City of God: A View of Its Contents*. London, 1925.

Ryan, John K. *Modern War and Basic Ethics*. Washington, 1933.

Sandys, John E. *A History of Classical Scholarship*. 3 vols. Cambridge, England, 1908.

Schenk, Wilhelm. *Reginald Pole, Cardinal of England*. London, 1950.

Schmitt, Albertus, and Hieronymus Noldin. *Summa theologiae moralis*, twenty-seventh edition. 3 vols. Oeniponte, 1940.

Schreiber, Georg, editor. *Das Weltkonzil von Trient: Sein Werden und Wirken*. 2 vols. Freiburg, 1951.

Scott, James B. *The Spanish Origin of International Law: Francisco de Vitoria and His Law of Nations*. Oxford, 1934. Appendices contain translations of Vitoria's works by various hands.

Slater, Thomas. *A Manual of Moral Theology*, sixth edition. 2 vols. London, 1928.

Smith, George D., editor. *The Teaching of the Catholic Church: A Summary of Catholic Doctrine*. 2 vols. New York, 1949.

Smith, Preserved. *Erasmus: A Study of His Life, Ideals, and Place in History*. New York, 1923.

Sturge, Charles. *Cuthbert Tunstal: Churchman, Scholar, Statesman, Administrator*. London, 1938.

Sullivan, Frank, and Majie Padberg Sullivan. *Moreana, 1478-1945: A Preliminary Check List of Material By and About Saint Thomas More*. Kansas City, 1946.

Tanquerey, Adolphe. *The Spiritual Life: A Treatise on Ascetical and Mystical Theology*, second edition, translated by Herman Branderis. Tournai, 1930.

Taylor, Henry O. *Thought and Expression in the Sixteenth Century*. 2 vols. New York, 1920.

Telle, Emile V. *Erasme de Rotterdam et le septième sacrement.* Genève, 1954.

Theologia Wirceburgensis. See Wirceburgenses.

Thompson, Craig R. *The Translations of Lucian by Erasmus and St. Thomas More.* Ithaca, 1940.

Thorndike, Lynn. *A History of Magic and Experimental Science.* 6 vols. New York, 1923-1941.

Tromp, Sebastianus. *De revelatione Christiana,* fourth edition. Romae, 1937.

Vacant, Alfred, and others, editors. *Dictionnaire de théologie catholique, contenant l'exposé des doctrines de la théologie catholique, leurs preuves, et leur histoire.* 15 vols. Paris, 1908-1950. Cited as *DTC.*

Vermeersch, Arthur. *La tolérance.* Louvain, n. d.

Villoslada, Ricardo G. *La Universidad de Paris durante los estudios de Francisco de Vitoria, O.P.: 1507-1522.* Roma, 1938.

Vossius, Gerardus Joannes. *Opera.* 6 vols. Amstelodami, 1695-1701.

Ward, Adolphus W., and others, editors. *The Cambridge Modern History.* 13 vols. New York, 1902-1912.

Wilmers, Guilelmus. *De religione revelata.* Ratisbonae, 1897.

Wirceburgenses. *RR. Patrum Societatis Jesu theologia dogmatica, polemica, scholastica, et moralis, praelectionibus publicis in alma universitate Wirceburgensi accommodata,* editio altera. 6 vols. Lutetiae Parisiorum, 1852-1854.

Zigliara, Thomas Maria. *Summa philosophica,* sixteenth edition. 3 vols. Paris, 1919.

INDEX

367